Praise for *Building Applications and Components with Visual Basic .NET*

"Ted shows a great depth of knowledge all the way down to the underlying mechanics of .NET. The author's depth in certain areas, like Events and Delegates, makes this a very useful book."

—*Gregory A. Beamer, Microsoft MVP*

"The content in *Building Applications and Components with Visual Basic .NET* is quite unique; I don't think any other book covers the OOP features in the detail as this book does. This book is a definitive guide for all VB developers looking to master OOP skills."

—*Darshan Singh, Managing Editor, PerfectXML.com*

"As a whole, the book is excellent—clear, and concise enough while still giving all the necessary details."

—*Gerard Frantz, Consultant*

"Ted does a good job explaining the various OOP concepts and the high-level view of the CLR and related concepts. I definitely learned some things about the CLR that I didn't know, and I found it a good read."

—*Paul Vick, Technical Lead, Visual Basic .NET, Microsoft Corp.*

"When Ted's first book came out in 1998 I dashed to the bookstore in a Harry-Potter-esque frenzy. That book taught me everything I needed to know about VB6, COM, MTS, etc. Now five years later, I have the privilege of reviewing his new VB.NET book (and also counting Ted as a good friend). Ted has done it again: combining the deep experience he's gained in his years working with DevelopMentor with his strong grasp of all things .NET, Ted has given us a book that's as easy to read as it is deep, informative, and accurate. This is THE book you need if you want to go long with Visual Basic .NET. To quote my Amazon review of his first book: 'Thank you Ted, you've done us all a service by writing this great new volume on Visual Basic .NET and the .NET Framework.'"

—*George Bullock, MSDN*

"As you move forward into the .NET Framework with Visual Basic .NET, you'll find the material in this book to be valuable."

—*From the Foreword by Rocky Lhotka*

Building Applications
and Components
with Visual Basic .NET

Microsoft .NET Development Series

John Montgomery, *Series Advisor*
Don Box, *Series Advisor*
Martin Heller, *Series Editor*

The **Microsoft .NET Development Series** is supported and developed by the leaders and experts of Microsoft development technologies including Microsoft architects and DevelopMentor instructors. The books in this series provide a core resource of information and understanding every developer needs in order to write effective applications and managed code. Learn from the leaders how to maximize your use of the .NET Framework and its programming languages.

Titles in the Series

Keith Ballinger, *.NET Web Services: Architecture and Implementation*, 0-321-11359-4

Don Box with Chris Sells, *Essential .NET Volume 1: The Common Language Runtime*, 0-201-73411-7

Mahesh Chand, *Graphics Programming with GDI+*, 0-321-16077-0

Anders Hejlsberg, Scott Wiltamuth, Peter Golde, *C# Language Specification*, 0-321-15491-6

Alex Homer, Dave Sussman, Mark Fussell, *A First Look at ADO.NET and System.Xml v. 2.0*, 0-321-22839-1

Alex Homer, Dave Sussman, Rob Howard, *A First Look at ASP.NET v. 2.0*, 0-321-22896-0

Microsoft Common Language Runtime Team, *The Common Language Runtime Annotated Reference and Specification*, 0-321-15493-2

Microsoft .NET Framework Class Libraries Team, *The .NET Framework CLI Standard Class Library Annotated Reference*, 0-321-15489-4

Microsoft Visual C# Development Team, *The C# Annotated Reference and Specification*, 0-321-15491-6

James S. Miller and Susann Ragsdale, *The Common Language Infrastructure Annotated Standard*, 0-321-15493-2

Fritz Onion, *Essential ASP.NET with Examples in C#*, 0-201-76040-1

Fritz Onion, *Essential ASP.NET with Examples in Visual Basic .NET*, 0-201-76039-8

Ted Pattison and Dr. Joe Hummel, *Building Applications and Components with Visual Basic .NET*, 0-201-73495-8

Chris Sells and Justin Gehtland, *Windows Forms Programming in Visual Basic .NET*, 0-321-12519-3

Chris Sells, *Windows Forms Programming in C#*, 0-321-11620-8

Damien Watkins, Mark Hammond, Brad Abrams, *Programming in the .NET Environment*, 0-201-77018-0

Shawn Wildermuth, *Pragmatic ADO.NET: Data Access for the Internet World*, 0-201-74568-2

Building Applications and Components with Visual Basic .NET

■ **Ted Pattison**

with Dr. Joe Hummel

♦♦Addison-Wesley

Boston • San Francisco • New York • Toronto • Montreal
London • Munich • Paris • Madrid
Capetown • Sydney • Tokyo • Singapore • Mexico City

The publisher offers discounts on this book when ordered in quantity for bulk purchases and special sales. For more information, please contact:

U.S. Corporate and Government Sales
(800) 382-3419
corpsales@pearsontechgroup.com

For sales outside of the U.S., please contact:

International Sales
(317) 581-3793
international@pearsontechgroup.com

Visit Addison-Wesley on the Web:
www.awprofessional.com

ISBN: 0-201-73495-8
Text printed on recycled paper
1 2 3 4 5 6 7 8 9 10—CRS—0706050403
First printing, October 2003

Library of Congress Cataloging-in-Publication Data

Pattison, Ted, 1962-
   Building applications and components with
Visual Basic .NET / Ted Pattison, with Dr. Joe
Hummel.
      p. cm.
   ISBN 0-201-73495-8 (alk. paper)
   1. Microsoft Visual BASIC. 2. BASIC (Computer
program language) 3. Microsoft .NET. I. Hummel,
Joe. II. Title.

QA76.73.B3P257 2003
005.2'68--dc22

                              2003016759

To my loving wife, Amy, and my beautiful daughters, Sophie and Daisy. You are the only components my application will ever need.
—Ted

To my wife, Beth, who makes this possible and worthwhile.
—Joe

Contents

4 Classes 155

5 Inheritance 205

Foreword by Francesco Balena

If Ted Pattison were a product, it would be a dream for any advertising agency. I mean, one of those products that sell by themselves: you don't really need to *promote* them, just let folks out there know that they're available. From this perspective, if the main goal for a foreword was to convince potential buyers to become actual readers, I'd say that my job is quite limited and that can be summarized in a sentence: *Want to learn Visual Basic .NET? Buy this book.* Period.

Still reading? Not convinced yet? Good, I have an excuse to talk a bit more about the book and its author, and throw in some personal memories.

I first met Ted at VBITS conferences, near the end of last millennium (not many years ago, but it sounds more impressive…), where both of us were delivering sessions and full-day seminars. As I've told him countless times, having to cope with his machine-gun-speed speech was just a bit too hard for my non–U.S. ears. However, I made a point not to miss his sessions, even if he talked on topics I was already familiar with. The reason was simple: Ted is a natural born teacher and he complements his natural talent with a rigorous approach to the material, right-on-focus code samples, and thorough explanations. Thus I always find it interesting *how* he delivers his material as much as *what* his talks are all about.

When I read *Programming Distributed Applications with COM and Visual Basic 6.0,* and its second edition that covers COM+ as well, I wasn't surprised to see that his teaching talent can fit the written page so nicely. That book found a place on the desk of many VB6 developers willing to leave the safe harbors of RAD programming to face the challenges of enterprise-level applications.

All Ted's talks and books, including the one you're reading now, have one thing in common: he isn't really interested in covering every single keyword or secondary detail about a language, a product, or a technology. Rather, he is more concerned in providing solid foundations about the basic concepts. This attitude is even more valuable now that Visual Basic has so many new features—inheritance, constructors, attributes, delegates, just to name a few—and most programmers are puzzled about when each one should be used, and how.

You didn't have to be familiar with object-oriented programming under previous versions of the language. In fact, you could create moderately large business applications without even coding a single class. In practice, VB6 classes were only a means to create COM components, but the language didn't really promote object-oriented design or programming. The rules have now changed, and you simply can't ignore the ins and outs of objects if you want to build robust, efficient, and scalable applications.

I am sure that this book will work wonderfully in helping developers in moving to the new world of Visual Basic .NET and the Microsoft .NET Framework. VB has become more powerful than ever, and you need the experience of a guy such as Ted Pattison to tame the new power and find your way in this object-oriented maze.

—Francesco Balena
Microsoft MSDN Regional Director for Italy
Author of *Programming Microsoft Visual Basic .NET*
Founder of VB-2-The-Max, www.vb2themax.com

Foreword by Rocky Lhotka

The computer industry is cyclical. We oscillate between loving thin client terminal or browser-based interfaces and thick client interfaces. We've gone from procedural or modular designs to object-oriented designs and now we're returning to procedural designs in the form of Web services.

In the background, however, there's been a trend that doesn't seem so cyclical: component-based design. Whether we're doing a thin or intelligent client, we build our applications with components. Components are used when building procedural, object-oriented or Web service based applications.

Components are the common coin of the industry. Visual Basic and the venerable VBX components popularized the concept in the early '90s. The subsequent switch to COM and ActiveX components broadened the use of components from UI widgets to a wide variety of pre-built libraries.

Perhaps more importantly, Visual Basic 4 enabled us to build our own components. That was seven years ago, and since that time components have become pervasive. Not only in Visual Basic programming, but also in C++ and Java.

Today, virtually all applications are a composition of various components, working in concert to provide the desired functionality. We use components to create both Windows and web UI's, to manage middle-tier code and to access data. How do you create code to run in MTS or COM+? You create a component. How do you create a Web service? You create a component.

Microsoft's Component Object Model (COM) technology has been the most popular component-based technology over the past several years. COM, especially when programmed from Visual Basic, made component-based programming relatively easy. Not only could most developers use components, most developers could create them.

More recently, Microsoft has developed the .NET Framework. The .NET Framework is a powerful development platform. It incorporates the component-based features of COM, while overcoming COM's limitations, especially around deployment and versioning.

Perhaps more importantly, the .NET Framework merges component-based and object-oriented concepts into a seamless whole. In COM it was not possible to use inheritance between components, but in .NET it is common practice for us to inherit from a class in a different component. This is true even if that other component was written in a different programming language. So now, not only is Visual Basic .NET fully object-oriented, but the underlying development platform itself is object-oriented.

Of course with great power comes some complexity. That's where this book comes into play.

The key to successfully using the new capabilities of the .NET Framework and of Visual Basic .NET is in understanding what the capabilities are and how to implement them. In this book Ted has done an excellent job of walking through the features of Visual Basic .NET in a clear and methodical manner.

In going through the book, I learned a number of things, and had other key features reinforced. This book provides the foundational information that is required to successfully use Visual Basic .NET and the .NET Framework for application and component development.

As you move forward into the .NET Framework with Visual Basic .NET, you'll find the material in this book to be valuable. This is true for both Windows and Web developers, and for both data-centric and object-oriented developers. Whether you are using or creating components, you will find Visual Basic .NET to be a powerful and fun tool, and I think that this book will help you make the most of it.

—Rocky Lhotka
Magenic Technologies

Preface

The .NET Framework is a development platform that was released by Microsoft in the beginning of 2002. Using the .NET Framework is strategic because it allows companies to develop software that leverages Microsoft's most recent innovations for building distributed applications. This platform also provides features that make it easier, less costly, and more secure to deploy applications in a network environment.

Visual Basic .NET is a new programming language that has been designed especially for the .NET Framework. Once you learn how to write and test code with Visual Basic .NET, you will be able to take advantage of the .NET Framework's many new features. This, in turn, will allow you to build networked applications and reusable component libraries that make the most of what Microsoft has to offer.

For developers with experience using earlier versions of Visual Basic, some parts of the Visual Basic .NET language will seem very familiar. For example, Visual Basic .NET uses the same syntax for declaring variables and for controlling the flow of execution using constructs such as `If` statements and `While` loops. The fact that Visual Basic .NET feels like earlier versions of Visual Basic means that Visual Basic developers can continue to program using the same style as in the past. The similarities between versions also make it easier to port Visual Basic 6 code to Visual Basic .NET.

While Visual Basic .NET is in many ways similar to earlier versions of Visual Basic .NET, it is definitely not the same. Visual Basic .NET is far more powerful than—and therefore very different from—any previous version of Visual Basic. You should expect a significant learning curve if you are migrating from Visual Basic 6 to Visual Basic .NET, because the new language introduces many programming features that have never been part of Visual Basic. If you're migrating from an object-oriented programming language such as C++ or Java, your transition to Visual Basic .NET will likely be a bit easier, but there are still plenty of details you must learn. It is our intention to provide you with those details.

Who Should Read This Book?

Building Applications and Components with Visual Basic .NET is meant for developers who want to write applications and component libraries for the .NET Framework using Visual Basic .NET. This book has been written for developers who have previous experience with an earlier version of Visual Basic or VBA. It has also been written for developers who are migrating to Visual Basic .NET from C++ and Java.

What Experience Do You Need?

The typical reader is assumed to be an intermediate to advanced developer who has experience with Visual Basic, C++, or Java. You should already know how to create a simple class definition that contains fields and methods. You should know why it's important to use encapsulation and how to define certain class members as private. Finally, you should understand the difference between a class, an object, and an object reference.

It's helpful (but not essential) that you know the basics of computer science. It would be impossible to conduct an in-depth discussion of developing software for the .NET Framework without talking about issues such as scope, lifetime, the call stack, the heap, and threads. If you lack this kind of background, I ask you to ponder how things work at a lower level.

It's also helpful (but not essential) that you know how the Component Object Model (COM) works. COM supplies the underlying plumbing that allows Visual Basic 6 developers to build applications using component DLLs. Understanding COM has made developers much more adept at using Visual Basic 6. While the .NET Framework replaces COM with a newer, more flexible infrastructure, many of the underlying principles remain the same. Some principles, however, have changed to make development easier. You must also know about COM to understand how interoperability works between Visual Basic .NET and Visual Basic 6.

What Will You Learn?

For the average developer who's become comfortable and productive with Visual Basic 6, making the transition to Visual Basic .NET will require a nontrivial effort. You must learn an entirely new platform and become familiar with a new set of development tools. You must also learn the Visual Basic .NET programming language. This endeavor poses many challenges, because Visual Basic .NET is much different and far more powerful than any previous version of Visual Basic. Along the way, you must learn new concepts, new keywords, and new syntax.

The goal of this book is to help you make the transition to Visual Basic .NET as smoothly and quickly as possible. It first introduces the essential architectural pieces of the .NET Framework. It then explores the new programming features that have been added to the latest version of Visual Basic. Here's a high-level list of topics covered in the book:

- The .NET Framework and the Common Language Runtime (CLR)
- Building applications and component libraries for the CLR
- The Framework Class Library (FCL)
- The Common Type System (CTS)
- New object-oriented programming (OOP) features
- New Visual Basic keywords and syntax required to support new OOP features
- Programming with delegates and events
- Using structured exception handling
- Managing memory using values and objects
- Naming, building, deploying, and revising assembly DLLs
- Interoperating with COM and Visual Basic 6

What's Not in This Book?

Building Applications and Components with Visual Basic .NET does not contain many step-by-step instructions. Therefore, this book won't appeal to those readers who just want to know how to perform a specific task but don't care why. While the authors sympathize with the need for "how," the goal here is longer-term—to build your understanding of the "why" behind .NET and Visual Basic .NET.

While this book focuses on object-oriented programming with Visual Basic .NET, it does not provide an in-depth discussion of issues relevant to object-oriented design (OOD). You will be introduced to many new OOP features and the syntax required to use them. In its coverage of these topics, however, the book focuses on the syntax and the effect that the syntax has on the behavior of your code. You will need to consult different resources if you want to learn about advanced high-level OOD topics such as design patterns or modeling with UML.

This book also does not cover topics related to creating distributed applications. In particular, it will not teach you how to use ASP.NET or .NET Remoting. While the book does cover details that are important to developers who are creating client and server applications alike, you will have to consult additional resources to learn how to make your applications communicate across the network.

If you're looking for a book with a great big example application that you can use as a starting point, *Building Applications and Components with Visual Basic .NET* isn't the right book for you, either. Most of the code listings are short, between 5 and 20 lines. When a code listing is provided, the authors always try to use as few lines as possible to focus your attention on a particular point. In particular, the code fragments often omit extraneous things such as error handling. For this reason, the book's style doesn't lend itself to readers who are looking for designs or code to simply copy-and-paste into production applications. When it comes to presenting concepts, the goal here is to teach you how to fish, as opposed to simply giving you fish.

Online Support for This Book

I maintain a support site for this book at http://Barracuda.net/Publications/ VBNET. At this URL, you can download example code that appears this book. Using the downloads, you can easily run, test, and debug Visual Basic .NET code that illustrates the key points and syntax discussed in each chapter. I also plan to use this site to pre-release new chapters that I am writing for the next edition of this book.

As a mortal, I am far from perfect. The book's support site will therefore maintain a list of errata—that is, typos and technical inaccuracies in the book. If you find an error within this book and you'd like to tell me about it, please forward it in an e-mail message to VBErrata@Barracuda.net.

Acknowledgments

A useful book is rarely the product of a single person. This certainly was not the case as I worked on the manuscript for *Building Applications and Components with Visual Basic .NET* over the last two years. Many folks made incredibly valuable contributions along the way.

I would first like to thank Dr. Joe Hummel for joining me on this project and helping me finish the book months (and possibly years) before I would have completed the work on my own. I thank Joe for his corrections of my technical inaccuracies, for his rewriting of my damaged prose, and for his overall contribution to helping me shape the story in this book. I hope to work with Dr. Joe on many more projects in the future.

I would like to thank Francesco Balena and Rocky Lhotka for contributing the forewords for this book. I feel fortunate to have such good friends whom I consider to be living legends. The Visual Basic community has certainly benefited from their published works, and we all look forward to more books from them in the future. You should also look for any opportunity to hear Francesco play the saxophone or hear Rocky tell a joke. You will not be disappointed.

I also appreciate the candid honesty of my incredible team of energetic reviewers. My thanks go out to Greg Beamer, George Bullock, James W. Cooper, Gerard Frantz, Martin Heller, Rocky Lhotka, Jason Masterman,

Fritz Onion, Ethan Roberts, Darshan Singh, Doug Turnure, Jason Whittington, Jim Wilson, Mike Woodring, and Paul Vick. I firmly believe that a hard-core critical review is a technical author's best friend. My philosophy is that if a reviewer has nothing bad to say, he shouldn't say anything at all. These guys certainly didn't let me down in this respect. Thanks again.

I would like to thank all the technical people in the industry who have helped to shape the way I think about software development and the .NET Framework. I will always be grateful to Don Box, who helped me so much early in my career. I would also like to say thanks to Craig Andera, Bob Beauchemin, Niels Berglund, Scott Bloom, Keith Brown, Calvin Caldwell, Henk de Koning, Peter Drayton, Tim Ewald, Jon Flanders, Andrew Gayter, Justin Gehtland, Ken Getz, Ian Griffiths, Martin Gudgin, Stu Halloway, Simon Horrell, Paul Kirby, John Lam, Jose Mojica, Ted Neward, Jeff Prosise, Brian A. Randell, Brent Rector, Jeffrey Richter, Steve Rodgers, Dave Schmitt, Chris Sells, George Shepherd, Dan Sinclair, and Aaron Skonnard. There are doubtlessly many other talented people who deserve my thanks from companies such as DevelopMentor, Microsoft, and QuickStart. My ability to solicit feedback and to exchange ideas with all these people throughout the last decade has been priceless.

Last but not least, I'd like to thank the tireless staff at Addison-Wesley, who make publishing a reality. A warm and heartfelt thanks goes out to my acquisitions editor, Stephane Thomas, for contributing so much energy and enthusiasm throughout the project and for constantly lying to her boss that I was still on schedule. I would like to thank several other editors for their assistance during the production phase, including Amy Fleischer, Jill Hobbs, and Michael Mullen. Finally, I would like to thank John Montgomery, Martin Heller, Stacey Giard, and all the other people at Microsoft who worked so hard to put together the Microsoft .NET Development Series with Addison-Wesley. I feel fortunate to be in such good company.

—Ted Pattison
Manhattan Beach, CA
September 2003

About the Authors

Ted Pattison graduated from Vanderbilt University with a degree in physics in 1985. After working for four years as a professional sound engineer in Los Angeles, he enrolled in the graduate program at the University of California at Irvine where he received an M.B.A. degree in 1990.

Ted embarked on his career as a software developer and educator when he joined QuickStart Technologies in 1990. In his time at QuickStart, Ted wrote several LAN-based business solutions using Visual Basic and SQL Server. He also authored and taught developer-oriented training courses. Ted wrote his first training course on Microsoft Access in 1991 while the original product was still in beta. Since that time Ted has written over a dozen training courses targeting professional software developers.

In 1994, Ted left QuickStart to join DevelopMentor. At DevelopMentor, Ted was responsible for writing curriculum and delivering training courses. Ted was fortunate to work under the guidance of Don Box and along side a very talented group of content authors including Bob Beauchemin, Keith Brown, Tim Ewald, Fritz Onion, Jason Masterman Chris Sells and Mike Woodring. Ted can be credited with pioneering DevelopMentor's Visual Basic curriculum as well as authoring their first Java training course.

In the summer of 2003, Ted partnered with Jason Masterman to form *Barracuda.NET*, a company dedicated to helping developers and companies become successful in building networked applications. Go to http://Barracuda.NET to find out more about the services that Barracuda.NET can provide to your company.

As an author, Ted wrote the best-selling title *Programming Distributed Applications with COM+ and VB 6.0* and is a regular contributor to *MSDN* magazine, where he writes the "Basic Instincts" column. Ted also plays in the notorious Band on the Runtime, a musical group dedicated to instilling a sense of humor in the software industry. Ted's band mates include David Chappell, Don Box, George Bullock, George Shepherd, Sarah Shor and Francesco Balena.

Dr. Joe Hummel is an assistant professor of Computer Science at Lake Forest College and a .NET trainer for DevelopMentor. He has a PhD in Computer Science from the University of California, Irvine, and has been working with DevelopMentor and Visual Basic since 1993.

1

The .NET Framework

L ET'S START BY asking an obvious question: What is .NET? That's not such an easy question to answer because the term ".NET" can mean many different things. The problem arises because so many of the product teams within Microsoft are using .NET as an all-encompassing marketing stamp to brand their new products. As a consequence, the term ".NET" is too generic by itself to have much meaning. If you're an experienced Windows developer, you should consider .NET to be a catch-all marketing slogan following in the grand tradition of OLE, ActiveX, and Windows DNA.

Now let's ask a more specific question: What is the .NET Framework? The .NET Framework is a development platform that provides companies with the tools for building applications and component libraries. These development tools include things like programming languages, compilers, and debuggers. The .NET Framework also provides a rich set of classes that make it especially attractive to companies that are building distributed applications for today's larger network environments such as the Internet. The built-in classes that are distributed as part of the .NET Framework are collectively known as the *Framework Class Library (FCL)*.

The architecture of the .NET Framework is based on a standard execution engine called the Common Language Runtime (CLR). The CLR is meant to provide a universal runtime environment for applications and component libraries. Microsoft specifically developed the architecture of the .NET Framework so that different implementations of the CLR could be created for different hardware platforms and operating systems. Of course, the company has invested a great deal of time and money to create an implementation of the .NET Framework targeted specifically for the Windows operating system.

This chapter begins by examining the architecture of both the .NET Framework and the CLR. The goal is to examine all of the pieces of this development platform and explain how they fit together. First, the chapter considers how the code for an application or a component library is compiled. Next, it describes how this code is loaded and run by the CLR. Finally, it explores how developers can leverage the classes of the FCL to build various kinds of applications. The chapter concludes by discussing the different motivations for migrating to the .NET Framework and the challenges you'll face when you do so.

The Road to the .NET Framework

The .NET Framework marks a monumental shift for Windows developers. It is the result of billions of dollars being spent in research and development. Before discussing the .NET Framework, however, let's take a rapid-fire tour through some of the events that led up to it. By looking at the history of Microsoft's development platforms, you can gain an appreciation for many of the important factors that have influenced the architecture and design of the .NET Framework.

In the beginning, there was *DOS*. Microsoft's very first desktop operating system was specifically designed to run on the Intel x86 architecture. DOS was a very successful product that gained industry-wide acceptance largely because it enabled software developers to create applications that supplied users with simple input screens and commands that could be run to automate business processes. While you might be hard-pressed to refer to DOS as a modern development platform, it does represent the humble roots for everything else that followed.

Microsoft followed up on DOS by introducing a desktop operating system named Windows. The initial release of *Windows* was a 16-bit extension to DOS. Windows provided a much richer development platform than DOS through its inclusion of a set of libraries known as the *Windows API* for building applications with a graphical user interface (GUI). Like DOS, Windows enjoyed industry-wide acceptance as a development platform for building desktop applications.

After Microsoft had achieved success with Windows as a desktop operating system, the company decided to enter the marketplace for server-side operating systems. Recognizing that the 16-bit version of Windows that sat on top of DOS would not make a very good server foundation, the engineers at Microsoft created a completely new 32-bit operating system named Windows NT. *Windows NT* was a great advancement for Microsoft's development platform because it offered much higher levels of performance, reliability, and security than the 16-bit version of Windows.

In building Windows NT, Microsoft replaced the original Windows API with a more extensive set of native libraries known as the *Win32 API*. By replacing this part of the underlying platform, Microsoft forced software developers and their companies to spend a good deal of time and money porting their existing Windows applications to Windows NT and the Win32 API. Despite the high expense, these companies' efforts to port code to Windows NT were worthwhile because their software would now run on Microsoft's new, strategic platform. As a consequence, the software could execute faster, more reliably, and more securely, and these companies could reach a larger number of customers.

When you consider the factors that influenced the architecture of the .NET Framework, it is important to acknowledge the role played by the *Component Object Model (COM)*. COM is a Microsoft technology that makes it possible to distribute and reuse code in terms of component DLLs. Code reuse in COM is based on a simple object-oriented programming (OOP) model. COM also supports the interoperability of code written in different languages. For example, it's very common to write applications in Visual Basic 6 (VB6) that leverage COM-based DLLs written in C++.

One more important event had a noticeable impact on the design and architecture of the .NET Framework. In the late 1990s, it was hard for anyone in the software industry (including people at Microsoft) to ignore the hoopla surrounding the release of the Java platform from Sun Microsystems. Java is like COM in the sense that it promotes the ideas of component-based development. At the same time, programming on the Java platform has several obvious advantages over programming with COM and the Win32 API. A few examples will illustrate this superiority.

Java's programming model includes support for many modern features, such as static methods, method overloading, parameterized constructors, inheritance, structured exception handling, and garbage collection. These features were sorely missing from COM. The Java platform also provides a rich set of class libraries that are consistently accessible through an object-oriented API. Furthermore, Java code is compiled into a platform-independent form, which provides Java developers with the opportunity to run their compiled code on many different operating systems and hardware platforms. As a result of all these features, the Java platform began to win a good deal of mindshare in the software industry. Microsoft knew that a competitive response was in order.

This concludes our whirlwind tour through the events that led up to the .NET Framework and set the stage for what was to occur next. As far back as 1997, many people at Microsoft recognized that the time was right to create a new development platform from the ground up. It was time to make another big shift, akin to the shift from DOS and 16-bit Windows to Windows NT. Over time, this project to reinvent Microsoft's development platform came to be known as the .NET Framework.

The first thing that Microsoft engineers concluded about their new platform was that the Win32 API had to be replaced. After all, the Win32 API is quite primitive in the sense that it was designed for developers who were programming in C. Consequently, the Win32 API does not reflect any of the modern object-oriented design principles. Furthermore, the C-based nature of the Win32 API made it impossible to access some of its functionality from higher-level languages such as Visual Basic.

Microsoft engineers also knew that the new platform would have to address some of the most common complaints about COM. First, the OOP support in COM was noticeably less elegant than the OOP support in Java. Second, customers often complained that COM was difficult to master because it required developers to learn too many low-level details. Third, companies complained that COM had numerous deployment issues that made it tricky to distribute and revise component DLLs.

Microsoft engineers came to one more important conclusion: They acknowledged that there were significant benefits to a development platform that was not tightly coupled to a particular operating system or hardware architecture. They knew it would be valuable if software written to target the .NET Framework could run on high-end server computers and handheld devices as well as traditional PCs. Therefore, they decided to design the architecture of the .NET Framework to be platform independent.

The Architecture of the .NET Framework

To continue our discussion of the .NET Framework, let's consider the basics of how it works. The .NET Framework provides a standard runtime environment based on an execution engine known as the Common Language Runtime (CLR). The CLR is responsible for loading code as well as managing the execution of that code. Software written to target the .NET Framework's CLR is known as *managed code*.

The high-level architecture of the .NET Framework decouples managed code from both the underlying operating system and the underlying hardware platform. When you create a DLL or an EXE that targets the .NET Framework, you are not restricted to running your code on an Intel x86 architecture or a 32-bit version of Windows. As shown in Figure 1.1, a single binary image of your code has the potential to be downloaded and run on several target platforms.

The .NET Framework currently runs on the most recent 32-bit versions of Windows: Windows 98, Windows ME, Windows NT, Windows 2000, and Windows XP. It is typically installed on top of these operating systems by running a setup program such as the *Microsoft .NET Framework Redistributable*.

The version of the .NET Framework for lightweight devices is called the .NET *Compact Framework* (CF). The CF has been designed with a much smaller footprint, which makes it possible to run managed code on handheld devices that cannot provide the memory resources or processing power of a standard desktop PC. For example, the CF allows you to target mobile users by creating a new generation of applications designed to run on Pocket PCs, Windows CE devices, and cell phones.

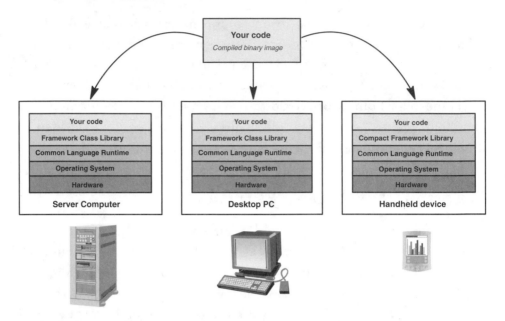

FIGURE 1.1: The architecture of the .NET Framework was created with cross-platform capabilities in mind.

Microsoft Windows Server 2003 is Microsoft's first operating system that includes the .NET Framework as part of its native installation. Microsoft Windows Server 2003 is available in a 32-bit version for standard server machines as well as a 64-bit version for high-end server machines. In general, you can expect Microsoft to include a version of the .NET Framework as a native part of all future operating system releases.

Take a moment and consider the implications of this architecture. What if you wanted to produce a component DLL that calculated tax payments? You would be able to create and distribute a single component DLL that could run on a desktop PC, a handheld device, or a high-end multiprocessor server computer running a 64-bit version of Windows Server 2003. As you can see, removing a component's dependencies on 32-bit Windows and Intel's x86 architecture represents a great advance for Microsoft's development platform.

In the future, other implementations of the .NET Framework will likely emerge apart from those shown in Figure 1.1. Microsoft has drafted a specification known as the *Common Language Infrastructure (CLI)* that provides the blueprints for creating implementations of the .NET Framework on other operating systems such as UNIX and Apple's OS X. In fact, at the time of this writing, significant portions of the .NET Framework exist on both FreeBSD (via Microsoft's *Rotor* or SSCLI project) and Linux (via the open-source *Mono* project).

Managed Code and Assemblies

Managed code must be written in a programming language that was specifically designed to target the .NET Framework. Today, Microsoft's two most popular languages for writing managed code are Visual Basic .NET and C#. Of course, programmers can choose from plenty of other managed languages. There is even a managed version of COBOL.

Every managed language requires a special compiler that can compile source code into a special form that is compatible with the CLR. In particular, managed code must be compiled into an *assembly*, as shown in Figure 1.2.

Assemblies play a critical role in the .NET Framework. An assembly is the primary mechanism used to package managed code for distribution and deployment. As such, it is the fundamental unit in which code is designed, distributed, reused, deployed, and versioned. Assemblies are the building blocks with which you create .NET applications.

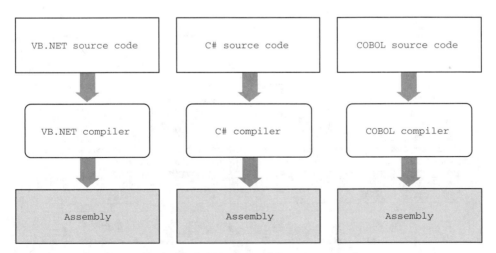

FIGURE 1.2: Managed code is compiled into assemblies.

An assembly is a logical unit that is physically composed of one or more files. The vast majority of the assemblies that you will use and produce, however, will consist of a single file. While an assembly can be made up of multiple files, the discussion in this chapter will focus on single-file assemblies.

In many cases, an assembly will have a file extension that is already familiar to Windows developers. For example, the assembly for a desktop application could have the file name MyApp.exe. The assembly for a component library might have the file name MyLibrary.dll. While the file extensions of most assemblies will seem familiar, what's inside an assembly is not.

The contents of an assembly differ dramatically from the contents of any EXE or DLL that was produced for the Windows platform throughout the 1990s. Each assembly must be generated in such a way as to meet the strict requirements of the CLR. Figure 1.3 shows the internal view of two simple assemblies, one for a desktop application and the other for a component DLL.

Managed compilers are designed to build assemblies that adhere to the standard format expected by the CLR. You should be able to see that an assembly contains component metadata and executable instructions. The component metadata describe the assembly and the types it contains. The executable instructions represent a compiled form of your programming logic.

From the developer's perspective, an assembly is simply a collection of one or more managed types that are packaged together and shipped as a

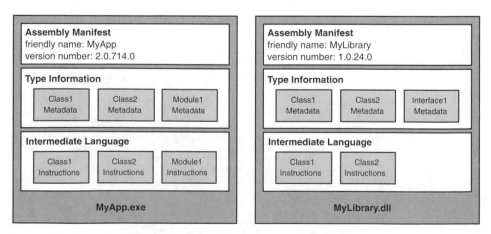

FIGURE 1.3: An assembly is a container of types.

unit. When you are designing a component library, it's important to see an assembly as an encapsulation boundary. As the producer of an assembly, you can decide which types are publicly exposed to the consumers of your assembly. You can also decide which types will be hidden from your consumers.

From the perspective of the CLR, an assembly is a loadable unit of code. The CLR is always in charge of loading assemblies and overseeing the execution of the managed code inside. Let's take another look at Figure 1.3 and discuss why the contents of an assembly are laid out in this specific manner.

The first thing you should observe about an assembly is that it contains an extensive set of component metadata. As you can see, some metadata describe each and every type defined within the assembly. In addition, one section of metadata contains a high-level description of the assembly itself called the *assembly manifest*.

The assembly manifest contains the assembly's friendly name and version number. The friendly name consists of the assembly's file name without the file extension. For example, the friendly name of the assembly file `MyLibrary.dll` is simply `MyLibrary`. The assembly manifest may also contain a culture setting, a public key, and a digital signature. The culture setting is used for assemblies that have been localized for different languages. The public key and digital signature can be used to identify and authenticate the developer or company that produced the assembly, as well as to verify that the assembly has not been tampered with.

In addition to providing tracking information about the assembly, the assembly manifest contains a list of dependent assemblies. A *dependent assembly* is an assembly on which the current assembly depends. For example, if `MyApp.exe` creates objects from classes defined in `MyLibrary.dll`, then `MyLibrary.dll` is a dependent assembly of `MyApp.exe`. When you build `MyApp.exe`, the compiler is required to add information to the assembly manifest to document that the application relies on `MyLibrary.dll`.

An assembly's collection of dependent assemblies is often called a list of *references*. Each reference tracks details about a specific dependent assembly, including its friendly name, version number, culture setting, and public key. The reference list within an assembly is critical because the CLR uses it to locate and load dependent assemblies at runtime. Chapter 11 goes into much greater detail about assembly naming, deployment, and configuration.

The second thing you should observe about the assemblies in Figure 1.3 is that their executable instructions are compiled into and distributed in a generic form of assembly code known as *intermediate language (IL)*. This approach is very different from that taken in previous versions of Visual Basic. For example, when you compile an application you've written in Visual Basic 6.0, the compiler produces machine-level assembly code specific to the Intel x86 architecture and 32-bit Windows operating system. When you compile the code you've written in Visual Basic .NET, the compiler generates executable instructions that do not have those same dependencies. Instead, your compiled code is platform independent.

It's important to acknowledge the role played by IL in the .NET Framework. IL is a compiled format that is similar to—yet very different from—traditional assembly code. IL is similar to assembly code in that it contains low-level instructions for loading operands, performing arithmetic, and branching. It is very different from traditional assembly code in that it contains no dependencies on a particular processor architecture or specific operating system. Microsoft's decision to use IL means that your code can be deployed on any operating system and hardware platform supported by the .NET Framework.

Attributes

The origin of one aspect of the .NET Framework programming model can be traced back to Microsoft Transaction Server (MTS) and COM+. The programming model of the .NET Framework embraces the notion of declarative or *attribute-based* programming. In this style of development, the behavior of entities such as classes and methods can be extended using attributes. The idea is that developers can declare their need for services through the application of attributes, instead of implementing those services themselves. The good news is that the .NET Framework takes the notion of attribute-based programming much further than either MTS or COM+.

In the MTS and COM+ programming models, only a handful of system-defined attributes exist that could be applied to applications, classes, and methods. In contrast, the use of attributes is much more common and far more flexible in the .NET Framework. Any developer or development team now has the ability to create a custom attribute, and then respond appropriately to the presence of that attribute using *reflection*.

Many development teams within Microsoft that are producing libraries for the .NET Framework have created their own custom attributes. You will likely apply these attributes to your code on a regular basis. The support for attributes is especially elegant in the .NET Framework because you apply attributes directly in your source code. Here's a simple example of applying attributes to an assembly and class definition in Visual Basic .NET:

```
'*** assembly-level attribute
<Assembly: AssemblyVersion("1.0.24.0")>

'*** class-level attribute
<Serializable()> Class Customer
   Public Name As String
   Public Phone As String
End Class
```

As you can see, it's fairly easy to apply an attribute. You simply supply the name of the attribute, surrounded by the < and > characters, immediately before the definition of the entity to which you'd like to apply it. Note that you must prefix the attribute name with the `Assembly` keyword and a colon when you target an attribute at the assembly level. When you compile your code, the attributes you've applied and their parameterized settings are recorded within the component metadata of your assembly. The CLR, as well as other tools and developers, can then inspect your code, determine how you've applied their attributes, and respond accordingly.

Custom attributes add a new and powerful dimension to component-based development. Web services are a great example of an attribute-driven mechanism. Designs that involve custom attributes will be particularly useful to companies building custom frameworks that sit on top of the .NET Framework. For example, a company could define custom attributes to provide services to customers using its framework.

Choosing a Managed Language

Many developers aren't sure which managed language to choose when initially migrating to the .NET Framework. After all, they have quite a few good choices when it comes to picking a managed language. Developers often ask the question, "Should I use Visual Basic .NET or C#?" The authors of this book respond by saying "yes."

Visual Basic .NET is the newest version of the Visual Basic language. It has been redesigned to accommodate the new programming model defined by the .NET Framework. One design goal of Visual Basic .NET was to make the language as compatible as possible with older versions of Visual Basic, for two reasons. First, it makes it possible to leverage the skills and intuition of millions of developers who already know how to program in Visual Basic. Second, it makes it easier to port existing code written in previous versions of Visual Basic.

C# is another productivity-oriented language designed for the .NET Framework, but it has a somewhat different intended audience than that targeted by Visual Basic .NET. C# is specifically designed for developers who already have experience with C, C++, or Java. In other words, it is designed for developers who are accustomed to programming in a language with semicolons, curly braces, and case-sensitivity.

How does a developer or a company choose between Visual Basic .NET and C#? Anyone who knows both languages will tell you that the functional differences between them are quite minor. Each language has a handful of features that the other doesn't support, but the differences in productivity, flexibility, and performance are ultimately quite small. Many of the issues that companies considered when deciding between Visual Basic 6.0 and C++ are no longer relevant when trying to decide between Visual Basic .NET and C#.

Ideally, you should choose between Visual Basic .NET and C# based on your previous experience with other languages and your stylistic preferences when writing code. Stay out of the religious wars when it comes to arguing which language is better. Neither Visual Basic .NET nor C# is a hands-down winner over the other. After all, your code will be compiled into IL no matter which language you choose.

Furthermore, there's nothing to say you cannot learn more than one managed language. Once you have mastered writing managed code with Visual Basic .NET, you will find it much easier to read and write C#. The .NET Framework gives you the flexibility to choose between Visual Basic .NET and any other managed language on a project-by-project, or even component-by-component, basis. The level of language interoperability across managed languages is far improved over what was available in the days of COM. For example, it is possible (and quite common) to create classes in Visual Basic .NET that inherit from classes defined using C#, and vice versa. In fact, many of the classes in the FCL are written in C#, yet you'll work with them seamlessly as if they were written in Visual Basic .NET.

The Common Language Runtime Environment

The CLR is an execution engine for running managed code. You should think of it as a controlled runtime environment. The CLR manages just about every aspect of how your managed code is loaded and run. A few examples will demonstrate its pervasiveness.

The CLR is responsible for loading your assemblies and allocating the memory required for your classes and objects. After your code has been loaded and execution begins, it continues to monitor the execution of all managed code so as to provide services and ensure that nothing out of the ordinary occurs. For example, when an application has finished using an object, the CLR is responsible for reclaiming the object's memory through an internal mechanism known as garbage collection. Before the CLR can carry out any of its responsibilities, it must somehow load itself into the hosting Windows process. Let's take a moment to discuss how this is accomplished.

Managed compilers such as the Visual Basic .NET compiler add a special file header whenever they generate a managed assembly file. This special file header causes the Windows operating system to automatically load a DLL named MSCOREE.DLL and initialize a session of the CLR. A quick example will give you an idea of how this process works.

Suppose you launch a managed .NET application named MyApp.exe from Windows Explorer. After Windows creates a new process for this application, it then loads MSCOREE.DLL. Once the DLL has been loaded, Windows calls a special initialization function using a standard entry point in MSCOREE.DLL that allows the CLR to initialize a session of its managed runtime environment.

It turns out that MSCOREE.DLL doesn't contain much code. Rather, this DLL simply provides an entry point for the CLR to bootstrap another DLL that contains the actual implementation. In the case where you launch a desktop application via Windows Explorer, MSCOREE.DLL initializes the CLR session by loading the DLL named MSCORWKS.DLL, as shown in Figure 1.4.

The implementation of the CLR in MSCORWKS.DLL is optimized for applications that run on a computer with a single processor. Note that an alternate implementation of the CLR exists in a DLL named MSCORSVR.DLL. MSCORSVR.DLL differs from MSCORWKS.DLL in that it contains an implementation of the CLR optimized to increase throughput for server-side applications running on computers with multiple processors.

An advanced server-side application that's been designed to host managed code can be written to initialize a session of the CLR with MSCORSVR.DLL instead of MSCORWKS.DLL. This strategy effectively increases the scalability of the application as a whole. For example, the ASP.NET runtime environment will initialize a session of the CLR with MSCORSVR.DLL instead of MSCORWKS.DLL when you run an ASP.NET application on a computer with more than one processor.

The managed code within MyApp.exe can be neither loaded nor run until a session of the CLR has been initialized. Once the CLR session has

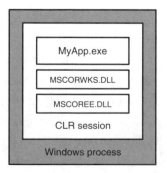

FIGURE 1.4: System-supplied DLLs are used to load and initialize a session of the CLR.

been initialized, the CLR can turn its attention to the code inside the assembly. The CLR inspects the component metadata in `MyApp.exe` to ensure that it meets the necessary requirements for the managed runtime. Because the assembly represents an EXE, the CLR must also locate an entry point method in the application so that it can pass control to the managed code now compiled into `MyApp.exe`. Keep in mind that the code inside `MyApp.exe` is still in the form of IL, so it is not yet in a form where it can be executed by the underlying hardware.

Before the code from an assembly is executed, it undergoes a final round of *just-in-time (JIT) compilation*. The CLR supplies a JIT compiler that is responsible for translating the IL within assemblies into native machine code that can be directly executed on the underlying processor chip architecture. Figure 1.5 illustrates how all of these pieces fit together.

When the CLR loads an assembly, it is not required to conduct a full JIT compilation of the assembly's entire IL. That would make load times unacceptably long for large assemblies. Instead, the CLR employs a more granular scheme where the IL from an assembly is JIT compiled gradually over the lifetime of an application, one method at a time. In particular, a method is JIT compiled the first time it is called in a session of the CLR. Once the

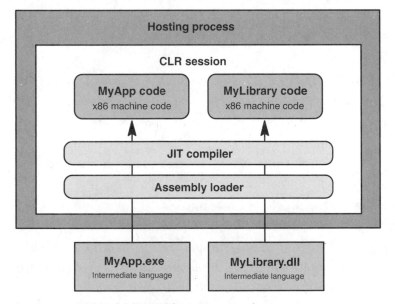

FIGURE 1.5: Within the CLR, JIT happens at runtime.

CLR has JIT compiled the code behind the entry point method of `MyApp.exe`, the CLR calls this method to pass control over to the application's code. The application can then go about its business, doing whatever it needs to do.

Next, let's consider how the CLR loads a component DLL. For example, what would happen if `MyApp.exe` were programmed against `MyLibrary.dll`? When does the CLR load the code from `MyLibrary.dll`? The CLR typically loads a component DLL the first time it is accessed by the application `MyApp.exe`.

The first time the code in `MyApp.exe` calls into the code of `MyLibrary.dll`, the CLR knows that it must locate the assembly file and load it into memory. Recall that the CLR gathers information about this dependent assembly from the reference list of `MyApp.exe`'s assembly manifest. It is able to obtain information such as the DLL's name and version number. The CLR then uses this information to locate the assembly file to be loaded.

For now, let's skip the details of how the CLR locates the appropriate assembly file; this process, known as *assembly resolution*, is discussed in depth in Chapter 11. Let's assume that the CLR has located the dependent assembly in the same directory as `MyApp.exe`, and that it begins to load the DLL into memory. As with `MyApp.exe`, the CLR doesn't have to JIT compile all the IL within `MyLibrary.dll` during the initial loading. Instead, it performs JIT compilation on a method-by-method basis, as calls come into `MyLibrary.dll`.

This example assumes that the assembly `MyLibrary.dll` is already installed on the same machine as `MyApp.exe`. Alternatively, the client application `MyApp.exe` could be configured to download the correct version of `MyLibrary.dll` on demand and across the Internet. Clearly, the CLR provides several different options with respect to deploying and configuring the assemblies for your component DLLs.

This example has illustrated the simplest deployment scenario in which the dependent assembly is deployed in the same directory as the hosting application. In .NET terminology, this directory is known as the *AppBase* directory; a dependent assembly deployed within it is known as a *private assembly*. We'll defer the discussion of more complicated assembly deployment options until Chapter 11.

AppDomains

Now that you've seen the basics of how managed code is loaded into a Windows process, it's time to present a new concept: an *AppDomain*. The programming model of the .NET Framework defines an AppDomain as a scope of execution. For example, when managed code is executing, it must always be executing within the scope of a specific AppDomain. Whenever you create an object from a managed class, that object must always be created within the confines of a specific AppDomain.

An AppDomain is similar to a Windows process in several ways. Both provide an application with a scope of execution and a private set of environment variables. Also, both can be used to isolate one piece of code from another; this isolation is valuable because it effectively strengthens the fault tolerance and security of an application. Finally, both an AppDomain and a Windows process can be independently shut down, restarted, and debugged.

While an AppDomain and a Windows process share some similarities, they also have some important differences. In particular, AppDomains are recognized by the programming model of the .NET Framework but processes are not. This makes sense because the .NET Framework has been designed to run on smaller operating systems that might not embrace the notion of a process. For example, the manufacturers of handheld devices might face an undue burden if they were required to provide process-oriented operating systems similar to Windows. The AppDomain concept provides many of the same benefits as a Windows process, yet can be implemented on lightweight devices with a much smaller footprint.

An AppDomain is a programmable entity. For example, a developer can use one to access environment variables via the FCL. Consequently, you can program an application against the current AppDomain to retrieve information such as the physical path to the AppBase directory. Each AppDomain also provides an extensible collection of name/value pairs that developers can use to store and retrieve application-specific data.

How do AppDomains fit into the framework of the CLR? The Windows platform is a process-oriented operating system. When managed code runs on this platform, it must always run inside a process. Several processes on a single machine might all be simultaneously running independent ses-

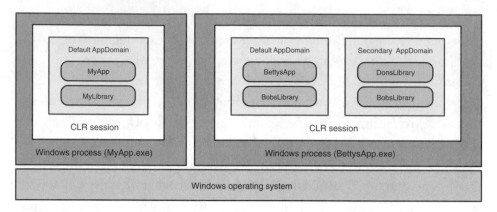

FIGURE 1.6: An AppDomain is an execution scope within a Windows process.

sions of the CLR. The CLR must initialize its execution environment on a process-by-process basis, as shown in Figure 1.6.

When you are writing managed code for the CLR, you should understand the relationship between Windows processes and AppDomains as depicted in Figure 1.6. Each AppDomain is restricted to a single process, but multiple AppDomains might be running inside a single process. As a result, it's possible to isolate the code in one assembly from the code in another without occurring the overhead of running them in separate processes.

AppDomains allow the CLR to provide a valuable optimization to Windows developers. It's far less expensive to spawn multiple AppDomains in a single process than to launch multiple processes. It's also far less expensive to execute method calls across AppDomain boundaries as opposed to process boundaries.

When the CLR initializes a session of the managed execution environment for a specific Windows process, it always creates a default AppDomain as shown in Figure 1.6. Note that the application on the left has only the default AppDomain, while the application on the right has a secondary AppDomain in addition to its default AppDomain. For simple applications, no secondary AppDomain is necessary. In contrast, a more sophisticated application can be written to spawn one or more secondary AppDomains so as to run code from certain assemblies in isolation.

Take another look at the application on the right of Figure 1.6. As you can see, `BettysApp.exe` spawns a secondary AppDomain to run the code from `DonsLibrary.dll` in isolation. In this example, both `BettysApp.exe` and `DonsLibrary.dll` use a third assembly named `BobsLibrary.dll`. That is, the code from `BobsLibrary.dll` is loaded separately into each of the two AppDomains. The assemblies you will write will typically be loaded on an AppDomain-by-AppDomain basis, too.

Most developers who use the .NET Framework will never write code to spawn and manage secondary AppDomains. However, many will need to write code that targets hosting environments such as ASP.NET that can spawn multiple AppDomains inside a single Windows process. Therefore, having a basic understanding of AppDomains is important to becoming proficient with the programming model of the .NET Framework.

Managed Execution

Now that you have been introduced to the basics of the CLR environment, let's discuss a few important advantages of managed execution. Think back to the days of software development before the .NET Framework. When developers write code in languages like C and C++, they are typically required to allocate their own memory and to access this memory through the use of pointers. The programming model of the CLR strongly discourages developers from writing managed code that interacts with memory in this fashion. Instead, the CLR automatically manages memory behind the scenes. This required shift in programming style represents one of the more significant changes for developers who are migrating from C++ to Visual Basic .NET or C#.

As a case in point, consider that managed code in the CLR runs under normal conditions in what is called *safe mode*. Code running in safe mode is prohibited from directly allocating memory as well as from using pointers to access memory. By removing low-level memory-management responsibilities from programmers, the managed execution environment makes programmers more productive. By prohibiting programmers from directly touching memory, it eliminates a large category of bugs that have been notorious for crashing Windows applications written in C and C++.

The fact that managed code cannot directly manage or access memory should not have equally dramatic effects on the typical Visual Basic developer. After all, the original version of Visual Basic was successful largely because of its underlying premise that low-level memory management should never be the responsibility of programmers. From the beginning, Visual Basic developers have relied on a runtime environment that conducts memory management behind the scenes. In this sense, the runtime environment of the CLR is similar to the runtime environment used by earlier versions of Visual Basic.

The introduction of the .NET Framework makes it necessary to have a term for describing code that is not explicitly written to target the managed execution environment—namely, unmanaged code. Earlier versions of Visual Basic can produce only *unmanaged code*, whereas Visual Basic .NET can produce only managed code. Herein lies a fundamental difference between the old and the new.

In rare scenarios, it's necessary for managed code to use pointers and to access memory directly—for example, when managed code is written to interoperate with older unmanaged code written in C or C++. This kind of unmanaged code exists within the libraries of the Win32 API, for instance. Many functions within the Win32 API require programmers to work in terms of pointers and preallocated memory buffers. Such functions can be difficult or impossible to call from managed code that is running in safe mode.

It is possible to relax the rules enforced by the CLR by declaring a unit of code as *unsafe*. Code that runs in unsafe mode is permitted to do many things that are otherwise impossible. C# and a few other managed languages support writing unsafe code; Visual Basic .NET does not.

On the one hand, the lack of support for writing unsafe code in Visual Basic .NET limits the degree to which you can interoperate with older legacy code written in C and C++. On the other hand, it does not limit your ability to write general application code. General application code should be written to run in safe mode no matter which language is used. Remember—just one line of unsafe code that misuses a pointer can crash an application. Running as much code as possible in safe mode makes your applications and component libraries more robust.

Safe mode does more than just protect against poorly written code. It also defends against attacks such as those involving viruses and worms. The extra level of security afforded by safe mode is particularly important in today's world in which users download both applications and component libraries across the Internet. By removing an attacker's ability to access memory directly, the managed execution environment can provide an extra layer of protection.

To see why this protection is important, consider this question: Over the last few years, how much have you heard about the viruses and worms that plague the software industry? Most likely, you have heard quite a bit. In particular, you may have either experienced or heard about the Nimda virus and other viruses like it. Devastating attacks on the Windows platform such as these have come from malicious code that plays tricks with pointers using a *buffer overflow attack*. An important design goal of the .NET Framework was to defend against such threats.

Earlier, you saw that IL and JIT compilation gives an assembly cross-platform capabilities. This approach offers a second important benefit: The act of JIT compiling code at runtime allows the CLR to run verification checks. As a consequence, the CLR can ensure that the IL instructions in an assembly conform to the rules of managed execution in safe mode.

If a user inadvertently downloads managed code that breaks the rules of safe mode, the CLR will catch this problem in its verification checks and prevent the code from running. Using this scheme, a computer that downloads verifiably safe code from an untrusted source across the Internet gains the ability to protect itself in a way that isn't possible when downloading unmanaged code, or when downloading a managed assembly that contains unsafe code.

Managed execution provides a few security-related features in addition to safe mode. For example, a company can distribute its assemblies with a digital signature. This strategy provides a layer of protection against tampering, because the CLR performs an authentication check whenever it loads an assembly with a digital signature. In this way, the CLR can discern whether anyone has altered the contents of the assembly since the time it was digitally signed and distributed by its producer. If the CLR detects any trace of tampering, it will not load the assembly or execute any code contained within it.

The .NET Framework supplies another important security feature, *Code Access Security (CAS)*. CAS is a security layer provided by the CLR that sits on top of the underlying security provided by the operating system. Its real value comes from its recognition that today's applications are assembled using components and that certain components can be more trusted than others.

Consider a simple example. When you launch an application from an EXE file on the local hard disk, the CLR runs the application by granting full permissions to its code. Therefore, CAS does not impose any security restrictions on top of the security restrictions that are already imposed by the operating system. But what happens if the application needs to download some mobile code from the Internet in the form of a DLL? You might not want that mobile code to run with the same permissions as the application itself. Instead, you might want to run this mobile code in a sandbox with a more restrictive set of security permissions.

In traditional Windows security, permissions are configured in terms of users. However, this kind of security does not recognize the need to configure permissions in terms of code. As a result, Windows security always runs an application and the DLLs it loaded with the same set of permissions.

CAS provides a valuable complement to Windows security. It lets you configure permissions differently for each assembly used by an application. Thus you can run mobile code with a different set of permissions than the permissions assigned to the hosting application. For example, you might configure CAS so that a DLL downloaded from a partially trusted source cannot access the local file system.

As you see, the managed execution environment of the CLR provides many valuable features and services. All in all, the CLR provides a value-added layer on top of the underlying platform that makes applications more robust and more secure. It also makes applications easier to write, test, debug, and deploy.

The Framework Class Library

Every implementation of the .NET Framework ships with a set of built-in classes: the *Framework Class Library (FCL)*. The classes of the FCL vary widely in scope. Some provide useful APIs for performing common tasks, such as formatting text, maintaining collections, and retrieving environment variables. Others provide support for more exotic operations, such as managing a GUI, accessing a database management system (DBMS), serializing objects, evaluating regular expressions, and programming security.

Of course, not all classes of the FCL are supported in every implementation of the .NET Framework. For example, a good deal of functionality is available through the Windows Forms-based classes of the FCL that do not exist in the .NET Compact Framework. Therefore, code that uses these Windows-specific classes of the FCL will not run on lightweight devices that support only the CF.

An important caveat applies to developers who are participating in cross-platform development: You must restrict your usage of class libraries to those that are supported on all the target platforms. It is not the .NET Framework's use of IL alone that allows you to write applications and component libraries that work across platforms. Rather, it is the use of IL combined with your knowledge of which class libraries exist on specific implementations of the .NET Framework that make writing cross-platform code possible.

The CLI specification defines a core set of classes that are required to exist in every implementation of the .NET Framework, known as the *Base Class Library (BCL)*. If you restrict your class usage to the BCL, your code will run on any .NET Framework implementation. When you use a class that isn't part of the BCL, you must ensure that the corresponding class library exists on all .NET Framework implementations you plan to target.

Of course, not every project built on the .NET Framework has the requirement of running across platforms. In fact, you will probably create many projects that target only the Windows platform. In this case, you should feel free to leverage the class libraries that are distributed along with the CLR on the Windows platform. Be aware, however, that the classes of the FCL can even vary across versions of the Windows operating system. For example, ASP.NET is available on Windows Server 2003, Windows XP, and Windows 2000, but not on Windows NT or Windows 98.

System-Supplied Class Libraries

Let's explore some of the more common assemblies of the FCL included on the Windows platform. To begin this discussion, we revisit the earlier example involving MyApp.exe and MyLibrary.dll. This example was somewhat of an oversimplification because it did not use any of the system-provided assemblies of the FCL. Now it's time to go into more detail.

Every managed application depends on one or more assemblies from the FCL, so it's essential to understand which FCL assemblies are used most frequently. Figure 1.7 provides a more realistic view of the actual assemblies used by a typical Visual Basic .NET application.

First, notice the assembly named mscorlib. This assembly is critical in the development of managed code because it contains core system-supplied types. It would be impossible to write code without using these core types. Therefore, every assembly you create will have a dependency on mscorlib and will have mscorlib in its list of references.

A second assembly named System holds other important system-defined types that are specific to the Windows version of the .NET Frame-

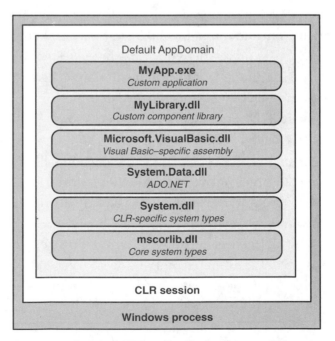

FIGURE 1.7: A typical .NET application loads many different assemblies.

work. You will often reference this assembly when you build projects that target the Windows platform. Keep in mind that classes within the System assembly do not necessarily exist in other implementations of the .NET Framework, such as the Compact Framework.

In addition to mscorlib and System, many other system-supplied assemblies are part of the FCL on the Windows platform. Table 1.1 lists some of the more commonly used assemblies distributed in the Windows version of the FCL.

The assemblies supplied by the FCL cover a very large surface area, and Table 1.1 is not an exhaustive list of the assemblies available to Windows developers who are targeting the CLR. Indeed, there are quite a few other FCL assemblies that are not listed here. Furthermore, you can expect the functionality of the FCL to expand in the years ahead.

Like the Win32 API before it, the FCL on the Windows platform is simply too large to be mastered by a single developer. Some developers will acquire expertise in ADO.NET and ASP.NET, whereas others will acquire expertise in areas such as XML processing or security programming. The important thing to remember is that all of these libraries are accessible through a consistent programming model as well as from different managed languages such as Visual Basic .NET and C#.

The Microsoft.VisualBasic Assembly

Table 1.1 also includes an assembly named Microsoft.VisualBasic, which was designed by the Visual Basic .NET team. The target audience for this assembly consists of all developers who are using the Visual Basic .NET programming language. The Microsoft.VisualBasic assembly is considered a standard part of the .NET Framework and the Compact Framework.

The Microsoft.VisualBasic assembly serves two primary purposes. First, it supplies a set of helper methods to the Visual Basic .NET compiler. When this compiler transforms source code into IL, it often generates extra code behind the scenes to call these helper methods in the Microsoft.VisualBasic assembly. For this reason, every assembly built using the Visual Basic .NET language has a dependency on the Microsoft.VisualBasic assembly.

Second, the Microsoft.VisualBasic assembly supplies a set of methods and constants that are directly accessible to developers who are programming

TABLE 1.1: Commonly Used Assemblies of the FCL

Assembly Name	Assembly File	Purpose
mscorlib	mscorlib.dll	Core system types
System	System.dll	CLR-specific system types
System.Data	System.Data.dll	ADO.NET
System.DirectoryServices	System.DirectoryServices.dll	Active Directory
System.Drawing	System.Drawing.dll	Windows graphics functionality
System.EnterpriseServices	System.EnterpriseServices.dll	Services formerly known as COM+ 1.0
System.Management	System.Management.dll	Windows computer management
System.Messaging	System.Messaging.dll	MSMQ messaging services
System.Security	System.Security.dll	Programmatic security
System.Web	System.Web.dll	ASP.NET
System.Web.Services	System.Web.Services.dll	Additional Web service support for ASP.NET
System.Windows.Forms	System.Windows.Forms.dll	Windows Forms framework
System.XML	System.XML.dll	Support for programming in Extensible Markup Language (XML)
Microsoft.VisualBasic	Microsoft.VisualBasic.dll	Visual Basic methods, constants, and attributes

in Visual Basic .NET. These methods and constants will be familiar to developers who used earlier versions of Visual Basic. For example, if you inspect the public members available inside the `Microsoft.VisualBasic` assembly, you will find many methods that have the same names and the same parameter lists as those that are available in Visual Basic 6.

Let's look at an example. Many developers with experience in Visual Basic have become accustomed to processing text by calling functions from the VBA runtime such as `UCase`, `InStr`, and `StrComp`. A corresponding set of wrapper methods exists in the `Microsoft.VisualBasic` assembly that make methods of the same name available for programming in Visual Basic .NET. For example, you can convert a text value to uppercase using the wrapper version of `UCase`:

```
Dim s1, s2 As String
s1 = "Wrapsody in Blue"
s2 = Microsoft.VisualBasic.UCase(s1)
```

Alternatively, you can use a shortened syntax that makes calling `UCase` in Visual Basic .NET exactly the same as calling it in Visual Basic 6:

```
Dim s1, s2 As String
s1 = "Wrapsody in Blue"
s2 = UCase(s1)
```

Thus you can program in Visual Basic .NET as if you were still writing code in Visual Basic 6. The fact that the `Microsoft.VisualBasic` assembly contains methods and constants that are familiar makes it easier to port existing code to Visual Basic .NET. It can also make it easier for developers to migrate to Visual Basic .NET, because they can use the same function names that they used in the past. However, it's important to understand that many methods in the `Microsoft.VisualBasic` assembly, such as `UCase`, `InStr`, and `StrComp`, do not actually perform the work you ask them to do. Instead, they are merely wrapper methods that call other methods in `mscorlib`, which then perform the actual work.

Whether you decide to leverage the set of wrapper methods built into the `Microsoft.VisualBasic` assembly or choose to avoid them is a matter of programming style. Using these wrapper functions offers two immediate advantages: It's easier to port code, and you can continue to write new code just as you have in the past. The disadvantages of calling wrapper functions like UCase, InStr, and StrComp are also twofold: The use of wrapper functions can degrade performance, and it can lead to inconsistencies that make your code more challenging to maintain.

Let's discuss the performance issue first. As mentioned earlier, many methods in Microsoft.VisualBasic are simply wrappers around other methods from mscorlib. In many cases, you can streamline performance by seeking out these other methods in mscorlib and calling them directly. For example, you can convert a text value to uppercase by calling the method named ToUpper defined for the String type in mscorlib:

```
Dim s1, s2 As String
s1 = "Eliminating the middle man"
s2 = s1.ToUpper()
```

The second problem with using Microsoft.VisualBasic wrapper methods is that this practice can lead to inconsistent programming styles. For example, imagine a Visual Basic .NET project that involves several developers. What would happen if some developers used wrapper methods such as UCase while other developers used native mscorlib methods such as ToUpper? In other words, does it create problems if some developers write code *the VB6 way* while other developers write code *the .NET way*?

This issue becomes even more complicated when you consider that some methods in Microsoft.VisualBasic are more than just wrapper methods. That is, some methods supplied by the Microsoft.VisualBasic assembly add extra validation checks and functionality beyond that available in the other assemblies of the FCL. For example, the Microsoft.VisualBasic assembly contains financial functions such as DDB, IRR, PPmt, and SLN that you may have used in earlier versions of Visual Basic. These functions are not simply wrapper methods around other methods in mscorlib, but rather represent value-added functionality supplied by the Microsoft.VisualBasic assembly.

In addition to the familiar methods, the Microsoft.VisualBasic assembly exposes a familiar set of constants such as vbCrLf and vbTab. Use of such constants doesn't involve the same performance tradeoffs as the use of wrapper methods, due to the manner in which constants are handled during compilation. When you use a constant from Microsoft.VisualBasic (or any other assembly), the Visual Basic .NET compiler takes the literal value of the constant and embeds it directly into the IL. As a result, the use of constants never involves extra calls to `Microsoft.VisualBasic` at runtime. Chapter 4 explores constants in more detail.

After this discussion of the purpose of the `Microsoft.VisualBasic` assembly, you should be able to make two observations:

* All Visual Basic .NET developers must rely on this assembly to some degree.
* Some developers and companies will heavily leverage what's inside this assembly, while other developers and companies will try to minimize their reliance on VB6-style wrapper methods.

In deciding how to approach programming with the .NET Framework, you should think through the tradeoffs involved with respect to productivity, performance, and maintainability. It might even be a good idea to establish guidelines as to what developers should use and what they should avoid from the `Microsoft.VisualBasic` assembly. Such guidelines can help to promote higher levels of consistency across projects and programming teams.

Application Frameworks of the FCL

When you want to develop a .NET application, you can choose between several kinds of applications, including both desktop and server-side applications. Let's take a moment to discuss some of the more common kinds of applications that you can build using Visual Basic .NET.

Console Applications

A *console application* is the simplest kind of application. You can think of a console application as a managed batch file that gives you the ability to perform batch-oriented tasks and to display messages to the user through the console window. When you write a console application, it's a simple matter to display messages to the console window by calling methods from a system-provided class named `Console`. Once you compile a console application into an assembly, you can run it from either Windows Explorer or a DOS-style command prompt.

What if you want to create an application that's more sophisticated than a console application? Fortunately, the FCL assists you by providing valuable application frameworks:

- It provides the *Windows Forms* application framework for creating Windows forms-based desktop applications with a GUI.
- It provides the *ASP.NET* application framework for creating server-side applications that communicate with client applications across the network using Hypertext Transfer Protocol (HTTP).

Windows Forms Applications

Windows Forms applications typically involve a rich user interface with forms that contain controls such as text boxes, list boxes, data grids, command buttons, and drop-down menus. The Windows Forms framework effectively replaces all preexisting forms packages from earlier versions of Visual Basic.

If you've created form-based applications with a previous version of Visual Basic, you'll be right at home designing Windows Forms applications in .NET. That's because Visual Studio .NET complements the Windows Forms framework with a productivity-enhancing form designer. This new form designer is very similar to what Visual Basic developers have used in the past, so experienced developers can get up to speed quickly when they need to create their first Windows Forms applications.

The core implementation for the Windows Forms framework is distributed in an assembly named `System.Windows.Forms`. Note that the Windows Forms framework depends on the graphics rendering capabilities of another assembly of the FCL named `System.Drawing`. Figure 1.8 shows the assemblies loaded by a typical Windows Forms application created with Visual Basic .NET.

While this book uses the Windows Forms framework as an example many times, you should not expect it to include in-depth details on the intricacies of working with forms, modal dialogs, and controls. Instead, it is recommended that you read *Windows Forms Programming in Visual Basic .NET* by Chris Sells and Justin Gehtland. This book explains how things work "under the hood" in the Windows Forms framework and covers advanced topics such as how to localize your applications for users who

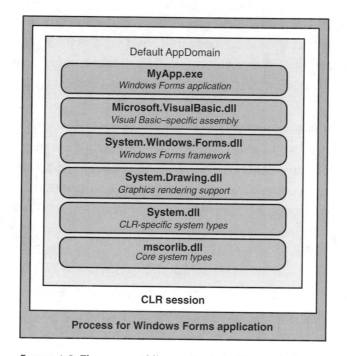

FIGURE 1.8: These assemblies are loaded with a typical Windows Forms application.

speak different languages and how to use background threading in a safe and responsible manner.

ASP.NET Applications

ASP.NET is a server-side hosting environment that has been integrated with Microsoft's *Internet Information Services (IIS)* Web server technology to respond to client requests sent across the network using HTTP. It replaces the original ASP framework. Additional .NET frameworks then sit atop ASP.NET—most importantly, *Web Forms* (the Web-based equivalent of Windows Forms) and *Web Services* (Web-callable objects).

When you want to create a server-side application using the ASP.NET framework, you are not required to supply an assembly in the form of an EXE file. Instead, ASP.NET provides a hosting environment with its own server-side worker process. Your code is typically deployed in ASP.NET pages and component DLLs. The ASP.NET runtime automatically loads your code when clients begin to submit requests to your application.

The implementation of the ASP.NET application framework is spread across many different files. Some of these files are managed assemblies; others are unmanaged executables and DLLs. The core FCL assembly for ASP.NET is `System.Web`. Figure 1.9 shows a potential layout for applications, assemblies, and Windows processes when you deploy several ASP.NET applications in Windows Server 2003.

The ASP.NET runtime runs each ASP.NET application in its own private AppDomain. Windows Server 2003 and IIS6 provide even more options with respect to application pooling. For example, these features allow you to configure each ASP.NET application to run in a private worker IIS6 worker process or in a shared IIS6 worker process along with other ASP.NET applications.

The ASP.NET application framework allows you to build two styles of server-side applications: Web applications and Web services. A *Web application* is a server-side application that responds to HTTP requests by returning a Hypertext Markup Language (HTML)–based user interface to a client browser. A *Web service* is a server-side application that responds to nonvisual HTTP requests based on Simple Object Access Protocol (SOAP) and XML.

Nothing in the ASP.NET application framework requires client-side machines to run the .NET Framework or the Windows operating system. For example, you can create a Web application with ASP.NET that caters to clients running a browser such as Netscape or Mosaic on an operating system such as Apple's OS X.

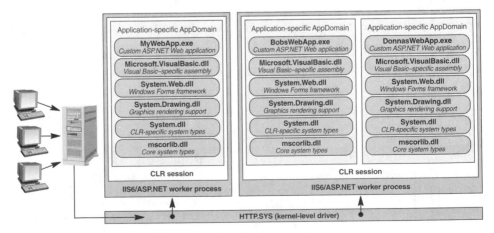

FIGURE 1.9: ASP.NET is a server-side application framework.

It is not the intention of this book to provide you with all the details required to develop applications with ASP.NET. While ASP.NET will be cited as an example .NET application, you should seek out other resources if you want to get up to speed on developing applications with this framework. In particular, *Essential ASP.NET* by Fritz Onion, which is available in both Visual Basic .NET and C# editions, is highly recommended. This book provides a thorough description of the ASP.NET architecture as well as the critical details you need for developing and deploying Web applications with ASP.NET.

Migration to .NET

Motivation for Migration

You have just seen an architectural overview of the .NET Framework, including both the CLR and the FCL. If you're an experienced Windows developer, you can see that the .NET Framework will change almost every aspect of how you develop applications. No doubt about it—migrating to the .NET Framework will have significant impact on you and your company. Therefore, you should carefully consider your motivations for making such a big move.

The first motivation for migrating is that the .NET Framework has become a critical part of Microsoft's development strategy. Over the last few years, Microsoft has redirected an overwhelming percentage of its energy and its investment in research and development in an effort to improve the .NET Framework and related technologies. The .NET Framework is unquestionably the future of Microsoft's development platform.

Microsoft's intention in the not-too-distant future is to move all application and component programming away from the Win32 API and older COM-based APIs and over to the .NET Framework. While this transition may take years to complete, it has already begun and poses a serious dilemma for companies that have already started—or that are planning to start—software projects based on older Windows technologies. The reality is that if you don't migrate soon, you're going to be left behind.

The second motivation for migrating is one that developers will find highly appealing: The .NET Framework provides a much better environment for designing, writing, and debugging software. When you choose to move to the .NET Framework, you benefit from decades of lessons learned from OOP and component-based technologies. Like COM, the .NET Framework provides a foundation for component-based programming with language neutrality. Like Java, it provides rich support for OOP and a platform-neutral format for shipping code. Once you get used to writing code in a managed language like Visual Basic .NET, you'll never want to write in an unmanaged language again.

A third motivation for migrating to the .NET Framework is to take advantage of the FCL. The sheer surface area covered by the classes of the FCL is impressive. The FCL provides much more functionality than the libraries Microsoft created for Visual Basic 6, including advanced support for evaluating regular expressions, processing XML, and running XSL transforms.

A fourth motivation is to take advantage of Microsoft's latest innovations in code distribution and deployment. The CLR provides solutions for many of the problems that have plagued application and DLL deployment in COM. For example, you can deploy an ASP.NET application by simply copying its ASP.NET pages and DLLs to a production Web server using XCOPY or File Transfer Protocol (FTP). This style of deployment marks a significant improvement over COM because it is no longer necessary to register DLLs or to add any type of configuration information to the Windows Registry. As a result, migrating to the .NET Framework can significantly lower the cost of maintaining and administering server-side applications in a production environment.

The .NET Framework offers several other advancements in the area of code deployment and distribution. For example, the CLR provides an innovative scheme for deploying multiple versions of a component DLL on the same computer in a side-by-side fashion. It also provides new mechanisms for downloading code on demand and across the Internet in a safe and reliable fashion.

A fifth motivation for migrating to the .NET Framework has to do with improved levels of security. We live in an age of interconnected computers where attacks from viruses and other types of malicious software are commonplace. The .NET Framework adds several new layers of defense on top of the security provided by the underlying operating system. The security layers discussed earlier include assembly signing, safe mode, verification checks during JIT compilation, and CAS.

A sixth motivation for migrating is to leverage the capabilities of Windows Server 2003, IIS6, and ASP.NET so as to build better and faster Web applications. While the original ASP framework has been used extensively throughout the software industry, companies are finding many tangible benefits by converting to ASP.NET, including improvements in performance, developer productivity, and code maintainability. ASP.NET and IIS6 also provide features for caching and state management that can further improve an application's performance and ability to scale in a Web farm environment.

A seventh motivation for migrating is to build distributed applications that work in larger networked environments such as the Internet. Before the introduction of the .NET Framework, much of Microsoft's strategy for building distributed applications was based on a remote communications protocol known as *Distributed COM (DCOM)*. Many companies found that DCOM provided an effective means for building distributed applications for a LAN environment. Unfortunately, they also found it difficult to use DCOM across larger networks due to problems related to scalability, security, configuration, and firewalls.

The .NET Framework provides a foundation for developing networked applications through distributed services such as ASP.NET and *.NET Remoting*. These services make it possible for applications to communicate across firewalls and to embrace Internet-style security standards. Therefore, the .NET Framework makes it possible to create distributed applications where users can communicate with server computers located at the opposite end of the planet. This scheme represents quite an improvement over the days when Microsoft's strategy for building distributed applications was based on DCOM.

An eighth motivation for migrating to the .NET Framework relates to the integration of applications across vendor and platform boundaries. Suppose you need to integrate a Windows application with an application that runs on an IBM mainframe computer. In the past, developers were forced to rely on expensive bridging technologies from third-party vendors. To combat this problem, the software industry has recently pushed for the adoption of open standards for Web services. Web services promote an easier and less costly approach toward cross-vendor and cross-platform integration.

Today's open standards for Web services include XML, XSD (XML Schema), SOAP, and WSDL (Web Service Description Language). The .NET Framework has been designed and implemented from the ground up to support these new open standards. This foundation sets the .NET Framework apart from other development platforms in which support for these open standards has simply been bolted on top.

A ninth motivation for migrating to the .NET Framework is the ability to leverage the CF so as to write applications that target lightweight devices such as Pocket PCs, Windows CE devices, and cell phones. The .NET Framework provides you with a unique opportunity to move beyond software development for traditional PCs and create a new generation of applications for mobile users. This expansion certainly opens up a world of possibilities for companies and developers who have previously worked on applications intended solely for the Windows platform.

The tenth and final motivation for migrating to the .NET Framework could be the one that offers the greatest justification for actually starting the transition: Migration doesn't have to be an "all or nothing" proposition. In other words, you don't have to migrate all your code at once. The .NET Framework provides excellent levels of interoperability between your new managed code and existing code written in unmanaged languages such as Visual Basic 6 and C++. This flexibility makes it possible to migrate using an incremental approach. The key point is that you can begin to take advantage of the .NET Framework without having to throw away the code that represents one of your company's most tangible assets.

Challenges in Migration

Of course, migration to the .NET Framework also carries some costs. For example, experienced Windows developers have a great deal to learn if they are to use the .NET Framework effectively. The same thing can be said for system administrators who will be responsible for deploying and maintaining applications written to target the .NET Framework. This chapter concludes by discussing the challenges and the learning curves that lie ahead when you decide to migrate from a previous version of Visual Basic to Visual Basic .NET.

Your first challenge is to become familiar with a new suite of development tools. Your initial goal should be to acquire a solid understanding of how the Visual Basic .NET compiler works. You must also learn how to use the new integrated development environment (IDE) supplied by Visual Studio .NET. Many aspects of managing projects as well as writing and debugging code will differ from what you have experienced in the past. Furthermore, you can't be satisfied with learning how to use just one tool, Visual Studio .NET. In reality, a handful of essential developer utilities have not been integrated with Visual Studio .NET. Learning how to use these tools is critical if you plan to take full advantage of the features offered by the .NET Framework.

Your second challenge is to master the Visual Basic .NET language. This task will be a nontrivial undertaking, because the language introduces many new OOP concepts and lots of new syntax that did not exist in previous versions of Visual Basic. As a Visual Basic .NET developer, you must become comfortable with features such as strict type checking, shared methods, method overloading, parameterized constructors, inheritance, interfaces, delegates, and structured exception handling.

Your third challenge is to gain an understanding of the inner workings of the CLR. If you had enough time to learn the inner workings of COM, you'll immediately appreciate how a knowledge of the underlying platform makes you a better developer. Once again you'll need to devote some time to becoming familiar with the new development platform, because the CLR differs significantly from COM. If you are new to both COM and the CLR, recognize this fact: Learning the inner details of the new platform pays big dividends in the long run.

Your fourth challenge is to become familiar with the classes of the FCL. It's time to leave behind older, COM-based class libraries such as ADO and MSXML. When you migrate to the .NET Framework, seek out and use the equivalent managed libraries, such as ADO.NET (`System.Data`) and the .NET Framework's XML parser (`System.XML`).

Your fifth challenge centers on learning how to distribute, deploy, and revise assemblies. While the .NET Framework introduces many advances with respect to deployment and versioning, some of the new disciplines you need to learn are not necessarily intuitive. And knowing how DLLs are deployed and revised in COM is not enough. You must learn a whole new set of rules and best practices for the .NET Framework.

Your sixth and final challenge is to decide what to do with projects written in earlier versions of Visual Basic. For example, what should you do with that DLL project developed last year in Visual Basic 6? Perhaps it has taken your company a few years to evolve this DLL's business logic and to remove all its bugs. Should you port the project to Visual Basic .NET or should you leave it in its current state? If you decide to leave the project in Visual Basic 6, you'll need to learn about the .NET Framework's interoperability layer so that you can integrate this unmanaged DLL with new projects written in Visual Basic .NET or C#.

SUMMARY

The .NET Framework is a development platform based on a standard execution engine called the CLR and a new set of classes called the FCL. It provides an environment for writing software that is much better than—and quite different from—anything that Microsoft has produced in the past. The .NET Framework represents a monumental shift for Microsoft—the company has completely reinvented its development platform and rebuilt it from the ground up.

The CLR is a managed execution environment. Developing software for the CLR involves using a managed compiler to build assemblies. Assemblies are important because they are the containers for distributing your code. This chapter introduced some of the features of the CLR's managed environment that will help to improve the overall quality and maintainability of your code.

There are several possible motivations for migrating to the .NET Framework. Migration offers many advantages and new capabilities. Furthermore, you can decide to migrate to the .NET Framework all at once or by taking an incremental approach.

Of course, migration also carries some tangible costs. Developers and system administrators face an intimidating learning curve to take full advantage of the .NET Framework. It will be quite a journey to migrate from Visual Basic 6 to both the .NET Framework and Visual Basic .NET. The remainder of this book focuses on helping you make this transition.

2

Developing with Visual Basic .NET

I N CHAPTER 1, you saw how the pieces of the .NET Framework fit together. Now it's time to take your knowledge of this architecture and apply it in a practical manner. This chapter will give you a head start in developing applications and component libraries using Visual Basic .NET. Your goal is to become comfortable with writing, compiling, testing and debugging managed code.

To develop software using the Visual Basic .NET language, you must learn how to use the Visual Basic .NET compiler and Visual Studio .NET. In addition, several important development tools are available. This chapter discusses how to manage projects and how to compile code into an assembly. You will also learn how to inspect, test, and debug code within an assembly once you have compiled it. By the time you reach the end of this chapter, you will possess the basic skills needed to develop simple desktop applications and component libraries for the CLR using Visual Studio .NET.

If you plan to write managed code, you should obtain and install a copy of *Visual Studio .NET*. Visual Studio .NET provides an integrated development environment (IDE) that is considered indispensable by many developers. It provides support for project management, color-coding of code, IntelliSense, and visual debugging. The Visual Studio .NET IDE also provides wizards that offer a handy starting point for projects based on various .NET frameworks, such as Windows Forms and ASP.NET.

Another option for the .NET developer is the *.NET Framework SDK* (software developer's kit), a free download that includes the CLR, the FCL, and command-line tools for VB.NET and C# development (as well as development in other languages). The .NET Framework SDK does not include any form of IDE.

If you simply want to run (but not develop) .NET assemblies, then you only need to install the .NET Framework. It is available via Windows Update or as a separate download known as the *Redistributable .NET Framework*. Both methods install the necessary runtime files for the CLR and FCL if they are not present already; the .NET Framework requires Windows 98 or later.

Getting Started

As a .NET developer, you must run a server-like operating system: Windows NT (sp6a), 2000, XP, or another operating system. If you plan to develop Web-based applications, you should also ensure that IIS is installed. When you run the setup program to install Visual Studio .NET, the installation process first checks whether it needs to install any of the necessary runtime files for the .NET Framework. If you are running Windows Server 2003, the correct files may already be present on your development workstation. By contrast, operating systems such as Windows XP and Windows 2000 do not natively support .NET. Therefore, the Visual Studio .NET setup program will install any needed runtime files that are not already present on your development workstation.

Next, the Visual Studio .NET setup program installs the .NET Framework SDK. This important collection of software includes documentation and developer utilities that will be very helpful in your .NET development efforts. Keep in mind that the .NET Framework SDK and Visual Studio .NET are two separate products. While there is a high degree of integration between the two, they were created by different teams at Microsoft.

After completing the tasks outlined above, the setup program installs the Visual Studio .NET IDE. When it has finished, you are ready to start developing with Visual Studio .NET. From this point forward, this book will assume that you have a development workstation running a Windows operating system such as Windows Server 2003, Windows XP, or Windows 2000, and that you have already installed Visual Studio .NET.

One primary goal of this book is to elucidate the theory behind the programming model of the .NET Framework so that you can effectively write, test, and deploy software with Visual Basic .NET. Therefore, the book will supply important information about the Visual Basic .NET compiler and various utilities of .NET Framework SDK. In doing so, it will provide many details about what the Visual Studio .NET IDE is doing behind the scenes on your behalf. This information will prove invaluable at times when the Visual Studio .NET IDE isn't able to do exactly what you want it to do.

By the time this book is published, Visual Studio .NET (VS.NET) 2003 will have been officially released. While VS.NET 2002 is based on version 1.0 of the .NET Framework, VS.NET 2003 is based on version 1.1. Given the side-by-side versioning support in .NET, you can safely install both versions of the .NET Framework on your client machines, and both versions of Visual Studio .NET on your development machine. As a developer, it's your responsibility to recognize which set of tools you are using so that you can understand which version of the .NET Framework your code is built against. If you work at the command-line level, the command path will dictate which version of the tools you are using; if you are in doubt about the version, execute "`vbc.exe /version`" to find out. When working with Visual Studio, remember that assemblies built with VS.NET 2002 target version 1.0 of the .NET Framework, whereas assemblies built with VS.NET 2003 target version 1.1. See Chapter 11 for a discussion of issues related to deployment and versioning.

The Visual Basic .NET Compiler

For your Visual Basic .NET code to be transformed into an EXE or a DLL, it must be compiled by the Visual Basic .NET compiler. The Visual Basic .NET compiler is built into the .NET Framework and can be accessed using several different techniques. One approach is to use the command-line compiler utility named `VBC.EXE`. Interestingly, this utility ships with the

.NET Framework itself—neither Visual Studio .NET nor the .NET Framework SDK is needed to compile and run managed code written in Visual Basic .NET.

Unlike in earlier versions of Visual Basic, the compiler for Visual Basic .NET is not attached to any particular development tool, such as Visual Studio .NET. As a consequence, you can write code for applications and component libraries in the Visual Basic .NET language using any source code editor. For example, you can create a Visual Basic .NET source file using a simple editor such as NOTEPAD.EXE, then compile this source file into an EXE or a DLL by calling VBC.EXE from the Windows shell CMD.EXE, a makefile, or a DOS-style batch file.

While you probably won't write much code outside the Visual Studio .NET environment, let's begin our discussion of compiling and testing code without the use of Visual Studio .NET. There is a good reason for taking this approach. Once you understand the fundamentals of how the Visual Basic .NET compiler works without Visual Studio .NET, you will find it much easier to understand the many extra things that Visual Studio .NET is doing for you behind the scenes. Without an understanding of how things work at the compiler level, it is difficult to fully appreciate what Visual Studio .NET adds to the big picture.

Writing a Simple Console-Based Application

It's time to write and test your first application. Let's start by writing and compiling a very simple console-based application named MyApp.exe. Study the source code depicted in Listing 2.1, which has been defined in the source file MyApp.vb. This application defines two classes: MyApp and Human. Both classes exist in a single file, whose name ends by convention with the .vb extension.

LISTING 2.1: A console application

```
Class MyApp
  Shared Sub Main()
    Dim human1 As Human = New Human()
    human1.Name = "Bob"
    System.Console.WriteLine( human1.Speak() )
  End Sub
End Class
```

```
Class Human
  Public Name As String

  Public Function Speak() As String
    Return "I am a human named " & Me.Name
  End Function
End Class
```

Unlike in earlier versions of Visual Basic, you do not have to define each class in a separate source file in Visual Basic .NET. You have the flexibility to maintain the code for a single project in as many .vb files as you'd like, and to compile them into a single assembly for distribution. This and many other options are made possible through Visual Studio .NET and by various switches of the command-line compiler utility VBC.EXE.

Listing 2.1 also contains some examples of new features that have recently been added to the Visual Basic language. First, the Main method is defined as a shared method using the Shared keyword. The concept of shared methods is discussed in more detail in Chapter 3. For now, suffice it to think of "shared" as being similar to "global." Thus MyApp.exe provides a shared method named Main so that the CLR can find an entry point into the application.

Also notice that the method definition of Main includes a variable named human1 that is initialized on the same line on which it is declared. This convenient new syntax isn't supported in earlier versions of Visual Basic. Along the same lines, the Speak method returns a value to the caller using a Return statement. More details about these handy features and a few others are provided at the end of this chapter.

When you'd like to compile this simple application into an executable assembly, you can call on the services of VBC.EXE. For example, you can compile the source code from MyApp.vb into an EXE by running VBC.EXE from the command line as follows:

```
vbc /t:exe MyApp.vb
```

The switch /t:exe informs the Visual Basic .NET compiler utility that the target of the build process is a console-based application.

If you bring up a command shell using `CMD.EXE`, you may not be able to run `VBC.EXE` because this utility is not located within a directory specified along the `SYSTEM` path. However, the installation of Visual Studio .NET provides a way to bring up a command-line shell that's initialized with the proper `SYSTEM` path information. The `Windows Start` menu located within the Microsoft Visual Studio .NET project group contains a shortcut with the caption "`Visual Studio .NET Command Prompt`." You should be able to find this shortcut under the subgroup named `Visual Studio .NET Tools`. If you bring up a command-line shell using this shortcut, you should be able to run `VBC.EXE` without any problems.

In this example, the Visual Basic .NET compiler automatically names the output assembly file `MyApp.exe` because the name of the source file is `MyApp.vb`. You could choose a different name for the output assembly file by passing the switch `/out` to `VBC.EXE`. Once you have built the assembly file `MyApp.exe`, you can run this application from the command line by issuing the following command:

```
MyApp.exe
```

Figure 2.1 provides a demonstration.

When you run this application, it prints the message "I am a human named Bob" to the console window. While this output might seem trivial, you should think through the complexity of what is actually occurring. As

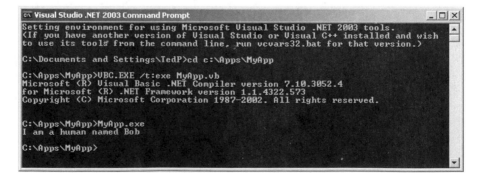

FIGURE 2.1: Compiling and running a console-based application

you saw in Chapter 1, running `MyApp.exe` spawns a new process that initializes a session of the CLR. The CLR then determines the location of the `Main` method that serves as the entry point into your application, and calls this method. The code in `Main` is then transformed from IL into platform-specific machine code by the JIT compiler supplied as part of the CLR. Finally, the CLR executes `Main`, thereby passing control to your code. When the `Main` method completes its work, the application is done and the process is unloaded.

Writing and Using a Component Library

Now that you've seen how to create a simple .NET application, it's time to take the next step and compile a class definition into a component DLL. In this case, we'll compile our definition for `Human` into a separate assembly named `MyLibrary.dll`. After that, we'll modify `MyApp.exe` to use the `Human` class definition from this external assembly.

Let's start by creating a separate source file named `MyLibrary.vb` that will contain the code for the component DLL. Inside this source file, we will add a definition for the `Human` class that is very similar to the definition in Listing 2.1. Here's the code for the source file named `MyLibrary.vb`:

```
Public Class Human
  Public Name As String

  Public Function Speak() As String
    Return "I am a human named " & Me.Name
  End Function
End Class
```

Note the minor change made to the definition of `Human`: This class is now declared with the `Public` access modifier. Types such as classes that are defined inside an assembly are not accessible to other assemblies unless they are explicitly defined using the `Public` keyword.

When you want the compiler to build a component DLL instead of an EXE, you pass `VBC.EXE` the switch `/t:library`. For example, you can compile `MyLibrary.vb` into an assembly named `MyLibrary.dll` by issuing the following command:

```
vbc /t:library MyLibrary.vb
```

Next, let's modify the application `MyApp.exe` so that we can use it. We start by removing the definition of the `Human` class from `MyApp.vb`:

```
Class MyApp
  Shared Sub Main()
    Dim human1 As Human = New Human()
    human1.Name = "Bob"
    System.Console.WriteLine( human1.Speak() )
  End Sub
End Class
```

While the definition of the `Human` class has disappeared from `MyApp.vb`, the definition of the `MyApp` class remains unchanged. It still uses the class definition of `Human` to create an object and call the `Speak` method. You should observe that programming against the `Human` class is the same regardless of whether the definition for `Human` exists in the current assembly or in a dependent assembly.

You can't program against a public class defined inside `MyLibrary.dll` unless your development workstation has a copy of this assembly. This point illustrates a very important aspect of software development in the .NET Framework: The component-based programming model of the .NET Framework is based on the notion of binary reuse. To reuse a component library, you must have a copy in its compiled form before you can compile other assemblies against it. This approach differs from other styles of development, where reuse is achieved by compiling your project along with the source code from other projects.

> In a *monolithic* application, there are no separate components; all source code files are compiled into a single application assembly. In this case, the application `MyApp.exe` is built as follows: `vbc /t:exe MyApp.vb MyLibrary.vb`. Contrast this approach with how component-based applications are built...

To build this new version of the application `MyApp.exe`, you must point the Visual Basic .NET compiler to the dependent assembly `MyLibrary.dll`. You accomplish this goal by running `VBC.EXE` and referencing the assembly using the `/r` switch:

```
vbc /t:exe MyApp.vb /r:MyLibrary.dll
```

The /r switch tells VBC.EXE that the code inside MyApp.vb uses public types defined in MyLibrary.dll. During compilation, VBC.EXE must locate MyLibrary.dll, inspect the Human class definition within the DLL, and ensure that the code in MyApp.vb is using the Human class in a legal manner. VBC.EXE also embeds into the assembly manifest of MyApp.exe a reference to the assembly MyLibrary.dll, including its *friendly name* and version number. This reference is very important because the CLR uses it to load the proper version of MyLibrary.dll at runtime.

Once you've compiled MyApp.vb into an executable assembly with a reference to MyLibrary.dll, you should be able to run the application. As in the previous example, running the application first spawns a new process that initializes a session of the CLR. The CLR then calls the main entry point for the application, triggering a JIT compilation of Main from MyApp.exe. This time, however, the CLR must also load MyLibrary.dll before it can create a Human object.

In this example, MyApp.exe was compiled with a single reference to MyLibrary.dll. In reality, MyApp.exe contains references to two other dependent assemblies. MyApp.exe picks up these two additional references because the Visual Basic .NET compiler always implicitly references mscorlib.dll and Microsoft.VisualBasic.dll during every build.

Apart from mscorlib.dll and Microsoft.VisualBasic.dll, the Visual Basic .NET compiler requires that you explicitly reference any assembly whose public types you program against. For example, if you write code in MyLibrary.dll against public types from both the System assembly and the assembly for ADO.NET, you would have to build your component DLL as follows:

```
vbc /t:library MyLibrary.vb /r:System.dll /r:System.Data.dll
```

As you might expect in a component-based model, building the application MyApp.exe still requires only a single reference to MyLibrary.dll.

At this point, you may be wondering: How does the VB.NET compiler find a referenced assembly? Likewise, how does the CLR find assemblies at runtime? For now, it suffices to say that the current directory is searched, as well as a global repository. We'll save the real discussion of this issue until Chapter 11.

Inspecting an Assembly with the `ILDASM.EXE` Utility

The .NET Framework SDK ships with a handy utility named `ILDASM.EXE` that allows you to look inside an assembly and inspect its contents. Once you've launched this utility from the command line, you can use the `Open` command from the `File` menu to open any valid assembly. If you followed along with the previous example and created the assemblies `MyApp.exe` and `MyLibrary.dll`, try inspecting them with `ILDASM.EXE` to see how this important utility works.

Once you've opened an assembly with `ILDASM.EXE`, the utility supplies a tree view control that allows you to inspect the types and members defined inside the assembly. Figure 2.2 shows the internal view of `MyLibrary.dll` when you inspect it using `ILDASM.EXE`.

As you can see, `ILDASM.EXE` enables you to inspect a compiled build of `MyLibrary.dll` and determine that this assembly contains a single public class named `Human`. Inside the definition of the `Human` class, you can see the definitions for the `Name` field, the `Speak` method, and another method named `.ctor`. The `.ctor` member is a *constructor*, a special method used to initialize new `Human` objects. (Constructors are discussed in depth in Chapter 4.)

You can find a great deal of information about an assembly (and about .NET) by using `ILDASM.EXE`. For example, double-clicking `MANIFEST` opens a window that displays assembly-level metadata, including the assembly's version number and reference list of dependent assemblies.

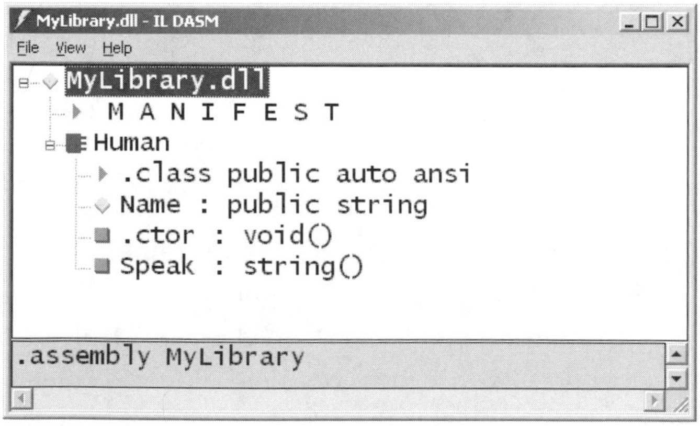

FIGURE 2.2: The `ILDASM.EXE` utility

`ILDASM.EXE` also allows you to see private types and private members as well as their public counterparts. `ILDASM.EXE` even goes so far as to show the IL generated by the compiler for any method definition. Simply double-click a method name in the tree view, and `ILDASM.EXE` will open a window showing the method's implementation in IL.

It can be a valuable learning experience to inspect the assemblies you produce with `ILDASM.EXE`. By seeing how the Visual Basic .NET compiler translates your source code into the required language-neutral format (i.e., IL), you can observe many important aspects of how the Visual Basic .NET language maps to the programming model of the .NET Framework.

Of course, `ILDASM.EXE` can be used to inspect assemblies other than your own. When you begin to work with an assembly from another company, it can be insightful to inspect its contents. If you have a curious nature, you can also use `ILDASM.EXE` to inspect Microsoft's system-supplied assembly files, such as `mscorlib.dll`, `Microsoft.VisualBasic.dll`, and `System.Data.dll`. Open a command shell and drill down into the directories below `C:\Windows\Assembly\GAC`.

> Worried about protecting your intellectual property from the prying eyes of ILDASM.EXE? To be honest, there's only so much you can do to protect yourself. If you release an assembly to the outside world, it can be reverse-engineered to not only IL, but also C#. Anakrino is one such tool for turning an assembly into C# (free; see http://www.saurik.com/net/exemplar/). One effective protection scheme uses obfuscators; Visual Studio .NET 2003 ships with a trial-version obfuscator. You can check out an obfuscator that the authors use named Demeanor at http://wiseowl.com.

Understanding Namespaces

The concept of *namespaces* is very important to the programming model of the .NET Framework and to Visual Basic .NET. Namespaces organize types in an effort to prevent naming conflicts. The full name of a type includes the name of its enclosing namespace. Therefore, two classes defined with the same name will not conflict with one another as long as they are defined in different namespaces.

Let's look at a simple example to illustrate the importance of name-spaces. Imagine you are writing an application in which you reference two other assemblies. What would happen if both of these assemblies contained a public type named Human? How would you write code to differentiate one definition of Human from the other? The answer: It would be impossible to differentiate between these two definitions of Human unless one or both were defined in a unique namespace.

A namespace is a user-defined scope for defining managed types. Visual Basic .NET provides the Namespace keyword that enables you to create your own namespaces. For example, you can define Human inside a name-space named AcmeCorp with the following code:

```
Namespace AcmeCorp

   Public Class Human
     '*** class definition
   End Class

End Namespace
```

The most important thing to understand about this example is that there is no longer a type named Human. Instead, the name of the type is now AcmeCorp.Human; this name is referred to as the type's *fully qualified* name. By default, a program that uses this type must now refer to it by its fully qualified name, as in the following example:

```
Class MyApp
   Shared Sub Main()
     Dim obj As New AcmeCorp.Human

     '*** additional code omitted for clarity
   End Sub
End Class
```

As you can see, namespaces help you avoid naming conflicts. They pro-vide unique prefixes for type names, thereby giving all developers the abil-ity to make their type names unique. Any type that is not defined within a specific namespace exists in a top-level namespace that has no name. This top-level namespace is referred to as the *default namespace* or the *global namespace*.

The explicit use of namespaces might be unnecessary when you are creating classes that are used only inside the current assembly. After all, it's not too difficult to avoid naming conflicts within a single project. However, the use of namespaces is critical when you are developing component libraries that will be used by other programmers and other companies. Defining your public types in a unique namespace is the only way to guarantee that your type names will not conflict with type names from other assemblies.

The architects of the .NET Framework reserved a namespace named `System` for the .NET Framework's core types and for types defined within the FCL. The `System` namespace provides a fairly predictable set of built-in primitives types for dealing with things like Boolean values, integers, and floating-point numbers. The FCL also provides standard classes for other common types, such as strings and arrays. You can program against these system-supplied types by using their fully qualified names, as in the following example:

```
Dim var1 As System.Int32
Dim var2 As System.String
Dim var3 As System.Object
```

In contrast, managed languages like Visual Basic .NET and C# provide native keywords that map directly to commonly used system types. For example, Visual Basic .NET provides the `Integer` keyword, which can be substituted for `System.Int32`. C# provides the `int` keyword, which maps to the same type. Here's an example of rewriting the previous code using language-specific keywords provided by the Visual Basic .NET language:

```
Dim var1 As Integer
Dim var2 As String
Dim var3 As Object
```

It doesn't really matter whether you use the actual type names or the language-specific keywords. Once you've compiled your code, there is absolutely no difference. The choice is simply a matter of preference. Many developers, however, feel that using the native keywords is better programming style because it's a more natural approach.

Another important aspect of namespaces is their ability to be nested. For example, many types defined by ADO.NET exist in a namespace named

Data that is nested inside the System namespace. The fully qualified name for this namespace is System.Data. Types defined inside this namespace have names such as System.Data.Dataset. In fact, some types in the FCL exist in namespaces that are nested five or six levels deep.

Namespace declarations in Visual Basic .NET provide an easy way for you to create your own nested namespaces. Here's a code sample that illustrates two different ways to nest namespaces:

```
Namespace AcmeCorp
   Namespace HumanResources
     Public Class Human
       '*** class definition
     End Class
   End Namespace
End Namespace

Namespace MegaCorp.Personnel
   Public Class Human
     '*** class definition
   End Class
End Namespace
```

Two types are defined in this example: AcmeCorp.HumanResources.Human and MegaCorp.Personnel.Human. As you can see, one Namespace declaration can be nested inside another such declaration. You can also define a type inside a nested namespace by using a single Namespace declaration and separating the name of each namespace with a "." (period) character. Namespace declarations may span source code files as well as assemblies.

Importing Namespaces

When you write client-side code against a type that is defined inside a namespace, you must give the Visual Basic .NET compiler enough information so that it can determine which type you are using. For example, if you are programming against a type named Human that is defined inside a namespace named AcmeCorp.HumanResources, you can simply use the fully qualified name: AcmeCorp.HumanResources.Human.

Another, more convenient option is based on the Imports statement provided by Visual Basic .NET. The Imports statement makes the name(s) of one or more namespaces implicit throughout a source file. For example, you can program against the type AcmeCorp.HumanResources.Human by using its short name `Human` once you have imported the `AcmeCorp.Human-Resources` namespace at the top of your source file:

```
Imports AcmeCorp.HumanResources

Class MyApp
  Shared Sub Main()
    Dim obj As New Human

    '*** additional code omitted for clarity
  End Sub
End Class
```

Importing a namespace makes it unnecessary to use full qualification when programming against a type. That is, you are afforded the syntactic convenience of typing `Human` instead of `AcmeCorp.HumanResources.Human`. You can add as many `Imports` statements to the top of a source file as you like.

While importing namespaces is often convenient, it can sometimes result in ambiguities that yield compile-time errors. Imagine you import two namespaces named `AcmeCorp.HumanResources` and `MegaCorp.Personnel`, both of which contain a class named `Human`. When you refer to the type `Human` in your code without full qualification, the Visual Basic .NET compiler raises an error because it cannot determine which of the two `Human` definitions you want to use:

```
Imports AcmeCorp.HumanResources
Imports MegaCorp.Personnel

Class MyApp
  Shared Sub Main()
    Dim obj As New Human '*** compile time error

    '*** additional code omitted for clarity
  End Sub
End Class
```

One solution to this problem is to use the appropriate fully qualified name. A nice alternative is to use an `Imports` *alias*. The `Imports` statement supports the ability to "alias" a namespace to a shorter, more convenient name. The following example defines two such aliases, `ACHR` and `MCP`, and resolves the earlier ambiguity by applying an alias:

```
Imports ACHR = AcmeCorp.HumanResources
Imports MCP = MegaCorp.Personnel

Class MyApp
  Shared Sub Main()
    Dim obj As New ACHR.Human '*** no compiler error

    '*** additional code omitted for clarity
  End Sub
End Class
```

In this case, the abbreviated name ACHR is used as an alias for the AcmeCorp.HumanResources namespace. Aliasing a namespace in this fashion helps to avoid ambiguities in general, and it is especially convenient when you are working with namespaces that are nested several levels deep and need to resolve ambiguities between them.

In summary, you can either use fully qualified type names or import namespaces and use shorter type names. You can also alias a namespace to another name. In any case, the technique you use has no effect on your code after it has been compiled.

All issues related to importing and aliasing namespaces are resolved at compile time. As a consequence, no runtime cost is imposed for importing or aliasing namespaces. When some question related to the importing or aliasing of a namespace cannot be resolved at compile time, the Visual Basic .NET compiler will issue an error message.

One final point about namespaces: It is very easy for a new programmer to blur the distinction between a namespace and an assembly. In fact, namespaces and assemblies are very different from one another. They have no formal association in the programming model of the .NET Framework.

For example, the types defined within a single namespace can be spread across several different assemblies. Similarly, a single assembly can contain types defined within several different namespaces. Thus namespaces and assemblies can have a many-to-many relationship.

While no formal association exists between assemblies and namespaces, developers who design component libraries often prefer to create a unique namespace for each assembly project so as to uniquely identify all its types. For example, all the public types defined within an assembly named AcmeCorp.HumanResources.dll could be defined in a namespace named

`AcmeCorp.HumanResources`. While this approach is commonly used to organize the types defined within component libraries, you should understand that it is nothing more than a convention

The important thing to remember is that you reference assemblies and you import namespaces. Let's repeat that point: You reference assemblies and you import namespaces. Some programmers are fooled into thinking that they don't need to reference an assembly because they have used the `Imports` statement to import its primary namespace. In fact, `Imports` does not affect which assemblies are referenced.

You must reference an assembly if you plan to program against the public types defined inside it. In contrast, importing a namespace is always optional. Importing namespaces simply makes it more convenient for you to type your code. And here's one more interesting thing to note concerning namespaces and assemblies: The Visual Basic .NET compiler will generate an error message during a build if you attempt to import a namespace that isn't defined in either the assembly under construction or one of the assemblies being referenced. This error typically indicates that you are missing an assembly reference.

The FCL consists of many thousands of items: namespaces, classes, enumerations, and so on. Navigating through the FCL is a challenge, so here are some tools to help:

- Visual Studio's *Object Browser* (View menu, Other Windows) will help you browse any referenced assemblies.

- Visual Studio's *Help* feature has the FCL indexed, or you can browse the FCL by drilling-down on the namespaces (`Help`, `Contents`, `MSDN library`, `.NET Development`, `.NET Framework SDK`, `.NET Framework`, `Reference`, `Class Library`).

- *wincv* is a Windows-based class viewer that ships as part of the .NET Framework SDK. Open a command window, type "`wincv`", and you should see the following:

This tool searches the FCL as you type; unfortunately the output display is limited to C#.

Developing with Visual Studio .NET

We apologize for making you suffer through learning how to compile and test Visual Basic .NET code without the assistance of the Visual Studio .NET IDE. But there's a good reason for approaching things from this perspective first. Now that you've seen the fundamentals of how the Visual Basic .NET compiler works, you will better appreciate how Visual Studio .NET adds another layer of value on top of it.

Development with Visual Studio .NET is based on the notion of projects and solutions. A *Visual Studio .NET project* represents a single build target such as an EXE or a DLL. For example, Visual Studio .NET allows you to create *console application projects*. Whenever you build such a project, the Visual Studio .NET IDE runs the Visual Basic .NET compiler in the same manner as when you ran VBC.EXE passing the /t:exe switch to compile your code. Visual Studio .NET provides a Project Properties dialog that allows you to adjust project-wide settings that have the same effect as passing various switches to VBC.EXE.

Interestingly, Visual Studio .NET doesn't rely on the command-line compiler utility VBC.EXE. Instead, it accesses the Visual Basic .NET compiler through a COM-based component library named MSVB7.DLL. The Visual Studio .NET team created MSVB7.DLL to supply extra functionality for special features in the Visual Studio .NET IDE such as background compilation and IntelliSense.

When you attempt to build a project using Visual Basic .NET, the IDE feeds your source code files to the Visual Basic .NET compiler. If your code contains one or more compile-time errors, the Visual Basic .NET compiler will not be able to build the project and the Visual Studio .NET IDE will display the corresponding error messages. If your code is free of compile-time errors, the Visual Basic .NET compiler will build an assembly and the Visual Studio .NET IDE will provide a message that the build was successful.

A *Visual Studio .NET solution* is a collection of one or more projects (see Figure 2.3). Creating a solution that contains multiple projects has some obvious benefits. You can write, test, and debug the source code for several assembly projects inside a single session of the Visual Studio .NET IDE. Likewise, you can work with multiple languages, as a single solution can, for example, have one project based on Visual Basic .NET and another project based on C#. If you need to debug a solution that involves multiple languages, you will find that it's a fairly easy matter to single-step from code written in one managed language into code written in another managed language.

FIGURE 2.3: Each project in Visual Studio .NET contains a list of references.

In addition to console application projects, Visual Studio .NET provides *class library projects* for producing component DLLs. When you compile a class library project, the Visual Studio .NET IDE runs the Visual Basic .NET compiler in the same manner as when you ran `VBC.EXE` and passed the `/t:library` switch to compile your code. A class library project allows you to package a set of classes as a single assembly that you can reuse across several different applications.

References and Namespaces Revisited

Recall that the Visual Basic .NET compiler must be given a list of references to dependent assemblies whenever it builds an assembly. References are required whenever you want to write code in one assembly that uses the public types from other assemblies. Visual Studio .NET makes this process very simple because it tracks a list of references on a per-project basis. Figure 2.3 shows a reference list for a project created in Visual Studio .NET. You can easily add references to a project via the `Project` menu.

Whenever you build a project, Visual Studio .NET runs the Visual Basic .NET compiler in the same fashion as when you ran `VBC.EXE` and passed a `/r` switch for each reference. Recall that the Visual Basic .NET compiler automatically references the two assemblies `mscorlib` and `Microsoft.Visual-Basic`; you will not see either of these assemblies within a project-specific reference list.

When you create a new project in Visual Studio .NET, the IDE automatically adds a few references to the list—namely, references to commonly used assemblies such as `System.dll`, `System.Data.dll`, and `System.XML.dll`. For some kinds of projects, the Visual Studio .NET IDE may add even more references. In addition to references that are added automatically, you are often required to manually add certain references. For example, in Figure 2.3, the reference to `MyLibrary` was added to the reference list for project `MyApp` by right-clicking on `References`.

The IntelliSense feature of Visual Studio .NET has been integrated to inspect a project's list of references. In particular, the public types of a dependent assembly become available through IntelliSense once you have added a reference to the assembly in your project.

Visual Studio .NET supports *project references* as well as standard assembly file references. A project reference allows one project to reference another project inside the same solution. In Figure 2.3, the console application project `MyApp` has a project reference to the class library project `MyLibrary`. An important benefit to using project references is that when you build a solution, Visual Studio .NET knows to compile a dependent assembly such as `MyLibrary` before it compiles an assembly that relies on it such as `MyApp`. Project references also make it easier to single-step between projects when you need to debug your code.

Now that we have seen how Visual Studio .NET assists you in managing references, let's turn our attention to how Visual Studio .NET assists you with managing namespaces. This area can be a little confusing at first, but it's important to understand just how Visual Studio .NET is trying to help you.

Visual Studio .NET provides a technique that allows you to define all the types for a project inside a single project-wide namespace. This technique does not require an explicit namespace declaration using the `Namespace` keyword as shown earlier. Instead, Visual Studio .NET includes a project-wide setting for the *root namespace*. You can see and modify the setting for the root namespace by accessing the `Project Properties` dialog, as shown in Figure 2.4.

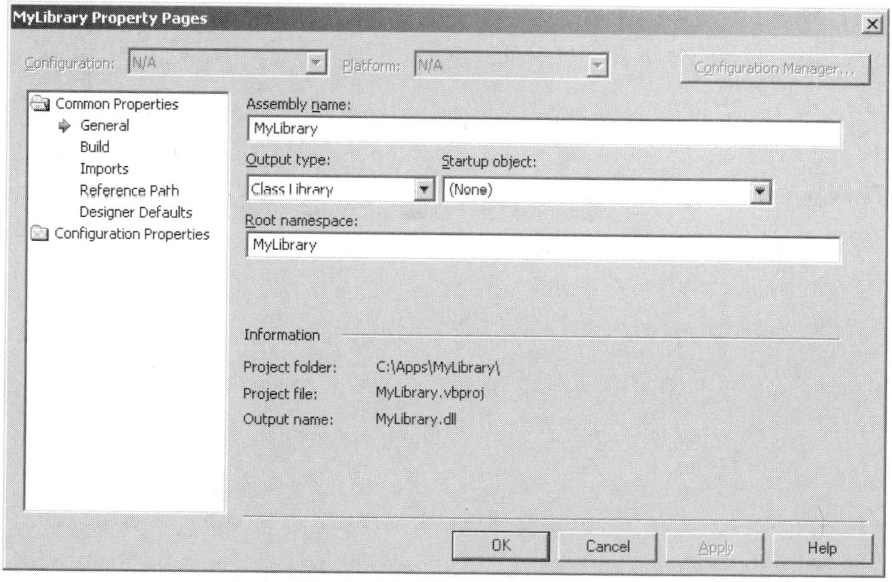

FIGURE 2.4: Each Visual Basic .NET project contains a setting for the root namespace.

When Visual Studio .NET compiles your code, every type that is built into the resulting assembly is defined within the scope of a namespace specified by the project's root namespace setting. This relationship can catch programmers off guard if they expect types defined outside the scope of an explicit `Namespace` declaration to be defined at the top-level default namespace.

When you create a new Visual Basic .NET project, the IDE automatically assigns it a default setting for the root namespace that has the same name as the project itself. If you want to define types in the default namespace or if you only want to scope your types using explicit `Namespace` declarations, then you must clear the root namespace setting for your project before compiling your code.

In addition to supporting the definition of types within a project-wide namespace, Visual Studio .NET provides a means for importing namespaces on a project-wide basis. As noted earlier, a namespace can be imported on a per-file basis using the `Imports` statement. Visual Studio .NET also allows you to import namespaces on a project-wide basis by using a list of imported namespaces accessible through the `Project Properties` dialog, as shown in Figure 2.5.

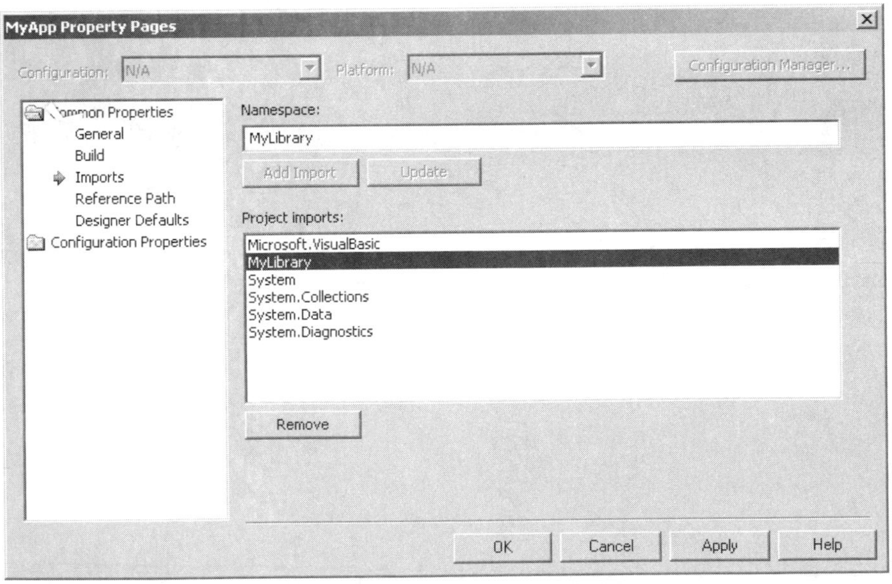

FIGURE 2.5: You can import namespaces on a project-wide basis.

The project wizards for Visual Studio .NET automatically add a few commonly used namespaces to this list when you create a new project. You can manually add other namespaces to this list as well. Whether you use the `Imports` statement in your code or add your imported namespaces to the project-wide list in Visual Studio .NET is a matter of programming style. Both techniques have the same effect, and importing the same namespace using both techniques won't create any problems.

Some programmers prefer to import namespaces on a project-wide basis because this technique eliminates the need to include redundant `Imports` statements across multiple source files in a project. Other programmers prefer the explicit use of the `Imports` statements because it documents what's going on inside every particular source file within a project. Choose whichever technique you like best. One consideration in your decision-making process might be that the `Imports` statement allows you to alias a namespace to a different name, whereas the Visual Studio .NET feature for importing namespaces on a project-wide basis does not.

Creating Form-Based Applications

Over the last decade, Visual Basic has gained a reputation as one of the fastest and easiest tools for building Windows desktop applications. One major reason that Visual Basic has emerged as an industry-leading development tool is the fact that a developer can create a GUI application in a fraction of the time that it takes to complete the same job using C or C++. When many people think of Visual Basic, they often envision it as a rapid application development (RAD) tool for building desktop applications with a rich user interface.

If you have experience with a previous version of Visual Basic, you probably know how to build a form-based application. If so, you are accustomed to using a form designer that allows you to create a friendly user interface by dragging and dropping controls onto a form design surface. You are also familiar with the use of a property sheet associated with a form or control in the Visual Basic IDE. Property sheets allow you to configure the appearance and behavior of forms and controls without writing code. In this way, they help speed up application development.

Developing applications with Visual Basic is such a quick process in part because of the manner in which you write the code to define an application's behavior. Form-based development with Visual Basic relies on an event-driven model. This event-driven paradigm has allowed the Visual Basic IDE to make it extremely easy for you to add code to the event handlers associated with forms and controls. You simply double-click a command button in design view, the Visual Basic IDE takes you to the event handler for that button's `Click` event, and you write your code.

While writing the event handlers for a Visual Basic application, you have always been able to run and test your code by pressing the friendly F5 key. Many developers fondly remember their first day using Visual Basic when they created and tested their first Windows application within minutes of launching the IDE.

There's good news on that front with the new development tools: Visual Studio .NET provides the same type of RAD environment that Visual Basic developers used for building GUI applications. The people who designed the Visual Studio .NET IDE put a great deal of effort into making the new environment similar to what came before. Many of the skills and intuitions you acquired while working with earlier versions of the Visual Basic form designer will make you instantly productive in building form-based applications for the .NET Framework.

With Visual Studio .NET, you create a form-based application by creating a *Windows application project*. A Windows application project represents a productivity layer on top of the Windows Forms framework. While the new form designer might seem similar to the one in Visual Basic 6, in reality the underlying architecture for hosting Windows applications is radically different.

Some of the code behind a form in a Windows application project will seem foreign because the Windows Forms framework is based on two new libraries, `System.Windows.Forms` and `System.Drawing`. While you can get up and running quickly with Windows application projects, you should expect to spend some time to fully master programming these new class libraries.

Walkthrough of Creating a Windows Application

While this book will not spend much time discussing user interface design, you should know how to create and debug a simple Windows application.

After all, most Visual Basic developers pride themselves on their ability to create a simple GUI application in a matter of minutes. If you don't know how to use the forms designer in Visual Studio .NET, you must learn the basics to be considered a true VB programmer.

Once you can create and test a simple Windows application, you have the skills needed to write simple programs and thereby familiarize yourself with the syntax used throughout this book. Creating a simple Windows application as a test client can also prove helpful when you need to test and debug the code from a class library project.

If you haven't created a Windows application before, it's time to create your first one. This task won't take very long. If you already have experience creating and debugging Windows applications with Visual Studio .NET, feel free to skim through this section.

First, create a new Windows application project and name it `MyApp`. Once you have created this new project, you should be able to navigate to the point where you are looking at the form in design view (see Figure 2.6).

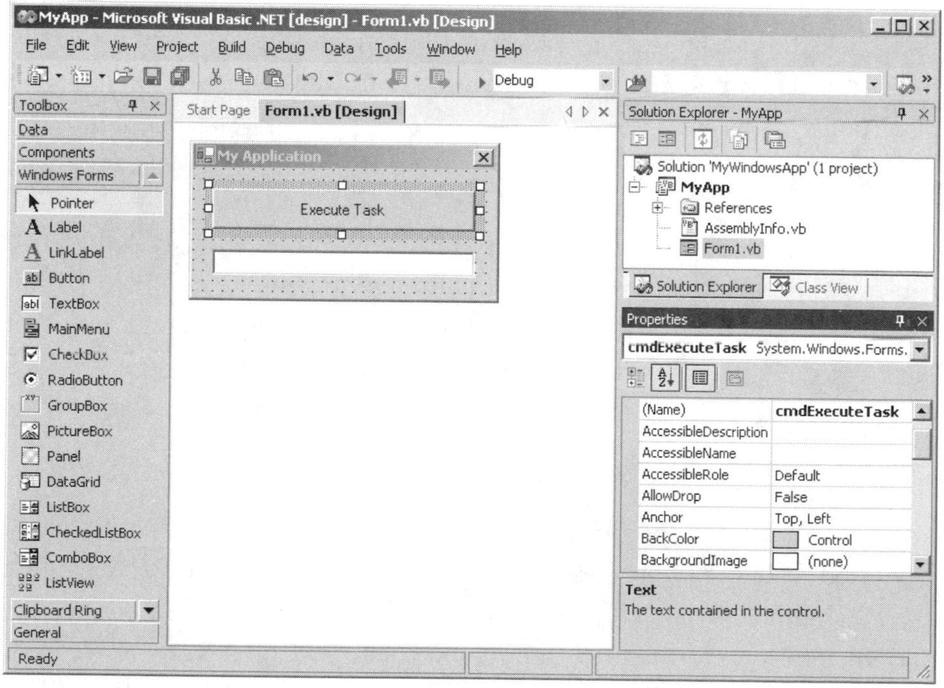

FIGURE 2.6: The start of a Windows application

Locate the property sheet for the form and change the form's caption by modifying its Text property to have a string value of "My Application" (or choose a more creative caption if you'd like).

Next, add a command button by dragging and dropping one from the toolbox. Click the button in design view, navigate to the property sheet for the new command button, and rename the button—change its (Name) property—to cmdExecuteTask. Also, change the Text property of the command button to "Execute Task" so that users of this application will see an appropriate caption that tells them what the button is supposed to do.

While you are still in form design view, double-click the command button. The Visual Basic .NET IDE will take you to the form's *code-behind* window and place you inside an event handler named cmdExecuteTask_Click. Inside this handler, write a simple line of code to pop up a dialog on the screen. You can accomplish this task by calling the Show method on a class named MessageBox that is defined within the System.Windows.Forms namespace. In other words:

```
System.Windows.Forms.MessageBox.Show("Hello, World!")
```

Because the System.Windows.Forms namespace is automatically imported when you create a new Windows application project, you may also type the following:

```
MessageBox.Show("Hello, World!")
```

If you're an old-time Visual Basic programmer who's feeling nostalgic, you can accomplish the same task by using the MsgBox method defined within the Microsoft.VisualBasic assembly. MsgBox is a wrapper method that has been designed to mimic the MsgBox statement from previous versions of Visual Basic:

```
MsgBox("Hello, World!")
```

You can call this method directly because the namespace is automatically imported whenever you create a new Visual Basic .NET project. Note that the MsgBox method is defined within the Microsoft.VisualBasic namespace and, therefore, is more than just a simple wrapper around MessageBox.Show.

At this point you should be able to run and test your application. Press the F5 key. The title bar of Visual Studio .NET will change to contain "[run]", and the form will appear on the Windows desktop. When you click the command button, a message box should appear on the screen with your message. Note that the Visual Studio .NET title bar will display "[run]" whenever your application is running. This fact is important to remember if you are unable to edit your code for some reason; the application is probably still running.

Next, stop the application and go back to form design view. View the form itself so that you can extend the GUI. Add an input control to your form by dragging and dropping a text box onto the form; rename this text box to txtMessage. Next, modify the code in cmdExecuteTask_Click to take the input value from the text box and display it in a message box. You can accomplish this with the following code:

```
MessageBox.Show(txtMessage.Text)
```

You have now created an application that accepts input from the user. Test your application to confirm that it works properly. Run the application, type a message into the text box, and then press the command button. Your message should appear within the message box that is displayed to the user.

Note that when you program against the Windows Forms framework, you cannot use the default property of a control in the same manner as in previous versions of Visual Basic. In other words, you cannot write code that looks like this:

```
'*** this code does not compile
txtMessage = "Hello, World!"
```

Instead, you must explicitly indicate which property you are programming against. The following line of code will fix the problem:

```
txtMessage.Text = "Hello, World!"
```

One more thing before we move on to the next topic: When testing your code, it's often quite convenient to use more sophisticated controls, such as list boxes or combo boxes, to maintain a visual collection of string values. Using the toolbox of the forms designer, add a list box control to your form and rename it to lstMessages. Next, modify the code behind the command button to add the input value from txtMessage into the control lstMessages. You can accomplish this with the following code:

```
lstMessages.Items.Add(txtMessage.Text)
```

Now test the application. When you run it, you should be able to interactively add new string values to the list box.

As a final step, add one more command button that allows you to clear out the contents of a list box. You can accomplish this goal by adding a second command button to the form that has a handler for the Click event with the following code:

```
lstMessages.Items.Clear()
```

If you were able to follow along with these instructions, you now have the skills required to create and test simple Windows applications with user-friendly controls such as command buttons, text boxes, and list boxes. Your ability to create simple Windows applications will enable you to write and test code quickly using the syntax and programming techniques introduced throughout this book. Now let's move forward and discuss how to debug code using the visual debugger supplied by Visual Studio .NET.

Debugging Projects

The .NET Framework and Visual Studio .NET provides excellent support for debugging application code. Most programmers who have used Visual Studio .NET agree that the new debugging support is richer and more reliable than that available in any previous version of Visual Studio.

Debugging support starts at the project level. When you create a new project in Visual Studio .NET, the project has two configurations: a *Debug configuration* and a *Release configuration*. A new project is created with the Debug configuration as the active configuration, with the idea being that you should write and test your projects using the Debug configuration. You would then switch over to the Release configuration, via the Build menu, whenever you need to produce a build version of an assembly for distribution.

The process of debugging code requires that the Visual Basic .NET compiler create a file containing symbolic debug logic in addition to the assembly. For example, if you want to debug code in the application MyApp.exe, the compiler must generate a file named MyApp.pdb that contains symbolic debugging information needed by the Visual Studio .NET debugger to allow you to work in debug mode. Fortunately, Visual Studio .NET automatically informs the Visual Basic .NET compiler that it should create .pdb files as needed when you build projects using the Debug configuration.

When your project is in the Debug configuration and you want to test your application in debug mode, you simply press the F5 key. Your application will begin to run and you can interact with it as if you were a typical user. When running and testing an application in debug mode, you can readily trace the flow of execution through the program. You also have the ability to inspect the values of variables and the states of various objects at any point using the Debug menu's Windows command.

Testing an application in debug mode makes it much easier to find and fix errors in your code. For example, if your code experiences an unexpected runtime exception while running in debug mode, the Visual Studio .NET debugger will bring up a dialog that asks whether you want to go into break mode. If you choose to enter break mode, the debugger will take you to the line of code that experienced the exception. You can then inspect the value of local variables as well as other objects and values that are in scope at this point in your program. Whenever your application is in break mode, the Visual Studio .NET title bar will display "[break]".

What if you prefer to single-step your way through the code? Single stepping shows how the execution of code flows at runtime. You can also inspect the state of any variable and any object immediately before or after any particular line of code executes. Using the debugger in this fashion enables you to find insidious errors that don't trigger runtime exceptions but still make the application logic incorrect. It's also a great way to become familiar with code that has been written by someone else.

The quickest way to perform single stepping is by setting breakpoints. When your code is executing in debug mode and it reaches a breakpoint, the Visual Studio .NET debugger pauses execution on the line of code containing the breakpoint. You can then single-step to execute that line of code, as well as the lines that follow. The Visual Studio .NET debugger also provides menu commands and keyboard shortcuts for stepping into, stepping over, and stepping out of the code for methods.

Table 2.1 lists the new debugging keyboard shortcuts for Visual Studio .NET. Ideally, you should commit these default keyboard shortcuts to memory, as they can greatly increase your speed and proficiency at debugging.

TABLE 2.1: Debugging Keystrokes

Keystroke	Command	Purpose
F5	Start (with debugging)	Run the application and allow single stepping
Shift+ F5	Stop debugging	Shut down the application running in debug mode
Ctrl+ F5	Start without debugging	Run the application without single-stepping support
Shift+B or F9	Set breakpoint	Set a point where execution breaks
Ctrl+Shift+F9	Clear all breakpoints	Remove all breakpoints from code
F10	Step over	Execute the code for the method call in one step
F11	Step into	Step into the code of the method being called
Shift+F11	Step out	Complete execution of the current method in one step

Note that Visual Studio .NET also provides the option of remapping the keyboard to support the same debugging keystrokes that were used in Visual Basic 6.0 (see `Tools`, `Options`, `Environment`, `Keyboard`, `Keyboard mapping scheme`).

Clearly, Visual Studio .NET offers a very powerful debugger, and it's critical that you learn how to use it effectively. In addition, the `System.Diagnostics` namespace contains some handy classes that have been designed to further assist you in debugging your code.

Let's look at an example of using the `Debug` class from the `System.Diagnostics` namespace. You can use the `Debug` class to write messages to the Debug window of Visual Studio .NET. You might find it useful to sprinkle calls to `Debug.WriteLine` throughout the source code for an application, like this:

```
'*** debug message 1
Debug.WriteLine("Application main form now loading")
```

```
'*** debug message 2
Debug.WriteLine("Database connection established successfully")

'*** debug message 3
Debug.WriteLine("Application now unloading")
```

These calls to `Debug.WriteLine` allow you to trace the code's flow of execution while the application is initializing and running in debug mode.

The `Debug` class provides even more debugging power, however. For instance, it allows you to programmatically interact with the debugger by calling methods that make assertions about the state of your program. Many programming languages support assertions, which allow developers to document their assumptions about the design of their code. For example, at a certain point you might make an assumption that an object reference is valid (i.e., not `Nothing`) or that a string value is not the empty string. You can document these kinds of assumptions by using calls to `Debug.Assert`, as shown in the following method:

```
Imports System.Diagnostics

Public Class HumanManager
  Public Sub ProcessHuman(ByVal target As Human)

    '*** assert specific conditions are true
    Debug.Assert(Not target Is Nothing, "Expecting target object")
    Debug.Assert(target.Name <> "")

    '*** perform work only if assertions are true

  End Sub
End Class
```

When you test your application and an expression passed to `Debug.Assert` evaluates to `False`, the application will stop running and a modal dialog will indicate that an assertion has failed. As shown in Figure 2.7, this dialog displays the names of methods that were chained together when the assertion failed. If you click the `Retry` button on this dialog, your code will go into break mode. You can then make a closer inspection and determine why your assumptions were deemed incorrect.

Why should you use assertions? Assertions make it easier to track down and fix bugs in your software, especially in a team-based development environment where assumptions may not be communicated clearly. Many

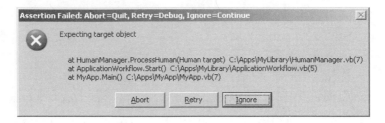

FIGURE 2.7: Dialog box resulting from a failed assertion

developers find that the investment required to add assertions has a significant payback—it shortens the debugging cycle.

One final note about the `Debug` class: The functionality of this class is available to you only when you compile and test your code using the Debug configuration. When you compile your code using the Release configuration, the Visual Basic .NET compiler is smart enough to ignore any calls made to the methods of the `Debug` class. In other words, calls to methods in the `Debug` class are never compiled into the IL of a release build. It is as if you had never written these calls at all, which means that it is safe to leave these calls in your source code base.

Fundamental Changes to Visual Basic

The Visual Basic .NET language isn't a simple upgrade from previous versions of the Visual Basic language. Rather, it's an entirely new language that's been designed from the ground up to accommodate the new programming model and the new type system of the .NET Framework. While the creators of Visual Basic .NET did their best to make this new language as familiar as possible to experienced Visual Basic developers, you should expect many things to be different.

The fact that Visual Basic .NET is so different presents you with an obvious challenge. It will definitely take time to master all of the language's new features. In fact, it will take the next seven chapters of this book just to cover the advancements in object-oriented programming. But there is a bright side to this picture: The changes make Visual Basic .NET a much better language than any previous version of Visual Basic.

The final part of this chapter focuses on a few of these fundamental changes to the language. The goal here is to provide a solid foundation for the chapters that follow, which cover these and other topics in much greater detail. Let's begin by discussing a few new conveniences offered by Visual Basic .NET, then examine some other new features designed to improve the quality and maintainability of your code.

New Conveniences

Visual Basic .NET provides some valuable new conveniences compared with earlier versions of Visual Basic. For example, it's now possible to define multiple variables on the same line using a single As clause. For example, it's possible to define three Integer variables with the following code:

```
Dim x, y, z As Integer
```

In Visual Basic .NET, this line of code results in three Integer variables. In earlier versions of Visual Basic, you would have to supply the variables x and y with their own As clauses if you wanted all three variables to be of type Integer.

Visual Basic .NET also introduces new syntax for declaring and initializing a variable with a single line of code. While many new programmers will probably take this syntax for granted, those of us who are accustomed to using two lines to declare and initialize our variables since the days of Visual Basic 1 will be very thankful for this convenience. Here are three ways to take advantage of this new initialization syntax in Visual Basic .NET:

```
Dim x As Integer = 10
Dim human1 As Human = New Human()
Dim human2 As New Human()
```

The third line in this example uses the As New syntax, which is treated differently in Visual Basic .NET than it was in its predecessor languages. With earlier versions of Visual Basic, many experienced developers frowned upon the As New syntax because it resulted in "lazy initialization." That is, the object was not actually created until the first access to a member such as a method or property occurred. Lazy initialization negatively affected performance and made it more difficult to debug an application.

With Visual Basic .NET, the `As New` syntax doesn't result in lazy initialization, so this syntax doesn't suffer the same problems as in the earlier versions of Visual Basic. In the previous example, the third line with the `As New` syntax is effectively the same as the second line. When you use the `As New` syntax in this fashion, the object being created is initialized and assigned to the reference variable before the next line of code begins to execute.

The convenient new in-line initialization syntax can also be used for fields inside the definition of a class or a structure. Here's an example in which three field values are initialized using the new syntax features:

```
Public Class Human
  Public CreationDate As Date = Date.Now
  Public Pet1 As Dog = New Dog()
  Public Pet2 As New Dog()
End Class
```

The Visual Basic .NET language introduces new operators such as `+=` and `-=`. These operators, which have always been part of the C programming language, can be make your code a little more concise. Let's consider a simple example that demonstrates how to use one of these operators. Look at the following line of code:

```
x = x + 1
```

It can now be rewritten with the `+=` operator:

```
x += 1
```

The `+=` operator allows you to add the value of x to the value on the right-hand side of the operator and assign the resulting sum back to x itself. This syntax is more concise because you type the variable x only once.

Here are a few more examples of the use of these new C-style operators:

```
'*** using += and -= with the Integer type
Dim i As Integer    '*** i = 0
i += 5              '*** i = 5
i -= 3              '*** i = 2

'*** using &= with the String type
Dim s As String
s &= "Hello "       '*** s = "Hello "
s &= " world"       '*** s = "Hello world"
```

Another nice syntactic addition to Visual Basic .NET is the fact that methods can now use `Return` statements. As is the case with many other languages, a `Return` statement halts method execution and returns control to the caller. When a method is defined as a function, a `Return` statement can also be used to pass a return value back to the caller. For example:

```
Public Function Add(ByVal x As Double, ByVal y As Double) As Double
  Return x + y
End Function
```

Removal of Inconsistencies and Idiosyncrasies

When the Visual Basic .NET team at Microsoft created their new language, they did not have a design goal of being backward compatible with any previous version of Visual Basic. This fact is noteworthy because Visual Basic .NET is the first version of the Visual Basic language that was not designed to support all forms of syntax from previous versions.

Given the many new features that were added to Visual Basic .NET, it was impossible to ensure complete backward compatibility. Unfortunately, these discrepancies can make it nontrivial to migrate software projects written in early versions of Visual Basic to Visual Basic .NET. On the other hand, the designers of Visual Basic .NET saw the loss of backward compatibility as an opportunity—that is, as the first chance in a decade to "clean house" by removing the many unfortunate syntax features that had been added to the language since the time of Visual Basic 1.0.

One obvious example of idiosyncratic syntax in earlier versions of Visual Basic is the use of the `Set` statement during assignment. The `Set` statement is no longer required (or allowed) when assigning an object to a reference variable. As a consequence, the code for assigning an object reference to a variable now looks just like the code for assigning an `Integer` value or a `Double` value to a variable. You no longer have to differentiate between objects and primitive types during assignment.

The new syntax for assigning objects to reference variables also invalidates code written in any previous version of Visual Basic. The following example illustrates the fundamental difference between all previous versions of Visual Basic and Visual Basic .NET:

```
'*** compiles in VB6 but not in Visual Basic .NET
Dim human1 As Human
Set human1 = New Human

'*** compiles in Visual Basic .NET but not in VB6
Dim human2 As Human
human2 = New Human()
```

The Visual Studio .NET IDE strips the Set keyword out of your code whenever it sees that you have used this syntax in an assignment. Thus, even when your brain tells you to type something the old Visual Basic 6 way, Visual Studio .NET automatically updates your code to make it syntactically correct for Visual Basic .NET.

Another important syntactic change introduced in Visual Basic .NET involves the rules for passing parameters. This change is a very welcome one, because the syntax for when a parameter value must be passed using parentheses has always been confusing. In earlier versions of Visual Basic, parameter values were typically surrounded with parentheses when a function was called, but not surrounded with parentheses when a sub was called. In some situations, however, these rules were reversed. It's fair to say that the idiosyncratic syntax for parameter passing found in earlier versions of Visual Basic made the language more difficult to learn and use.

In Visual Basic .NET, the rules for using parentheses in parameter passing are much simpler. You must always pass parameter values using parentheses when calling either a function or a sub, but parentheses are optional when calling a function or sub that takes no parameters. Clearly, these new rules are much more consistent and far easier to learn. As in the case of using the Set keyword during assignment, Visual Studio .NET detects when you have used the older syntax for passing parameters and attempts to correct your code.

Improved Scoping Rules

Visual Basic .NET introduces several improvements with respect to scoping local variables. For example, you can now define two variables having the same name within a single method definition as long as they are defined within different blocks that do not overlap in scope. As a result, the following code is legal in Visual Basic .NET (it was illegal in previous versions of Visual Basic):

```
Public Sub Method1(ByVal x As Boolean, ByVal y As Boolean)

  If x Then
    Dim i As Integer
    i = 10
    '*** do something with i
  End If

  If y Then
    Dim i As Integer     '*** this is a different i!
    i = 20
      '*** do something with i
  End If

End Sub
```

This code contains two If statements, each of which is a statement block that defines its own unique scope. The scopes defined by these two statement blocks do not overlap. Unlike in earlier versions of Visual Basic, you can declare variables to have the same name in these two scopes and they will not conflict with each other. This represents a nice improvement over earlier versions of Visual Basic, in which the compiler recognized only a single level of scoping for an entire method definition.

Visual Basic .NET is also stricter in its enforcement of scoping rules. For example, you cannot access a variable from outside the scope in which it is defined. As a result, the following code compiles in earlier versions of Visual Basic but is now illegal in Visual Basic .NET:

```
If x Then
  Dim i As Integer
  i = 10  '*** this compiles correctly
End If

i = 20     '*** compile-time error in VB.NET
```

You can see that Visual Basic .NET tightens up the rules by prohibiting a sloppy style of coding. Also, Visual Basic .NET does not allow you to use the same variable name in blocks that overlap in scope. For example, the following code will result in a compile-time error:

```
Dim i As Integer

If x Then
  Dim i As Integer  '*** compile-time error (redeclaration)
  i = 20
End If
```

This kind of code is illegal in Visual Basic .NET because it creates the potential for a programmer to accidentally hide a variable defined at an outer scope with a variable declared in an inner scope. In effect, Visual Basic .NET adds a safeguard to protect you from writing dangerous code that leads to subtle problems with readability and correctness. Its scoping behavior is now consistent with that of other modern languages such as C# and Java.

Structured Exception Handling

While some aspects of programming with Visual Basic .NET are similar to programming with earlier versions of Visual Basic, other aspects are very different. One area where things have changed significantly involves the way in which developers handle error conditions. The .NET Framework supports the reporting and handling of error conditions through a feature known as *structured exception handling*.

Chapter 9 is devoted to the topic of structured exception handling. Here, we will simply introduce the basic concepts related to how exceptions work to facilitate their discussion in the chapters that lead up to Chapter 9.

The main idea underlying structured exception handling is relatively simple: An exception is an object that is used to signal that something has gone wrong during program execution. This idea is quite unlike the concept used in earlier versions of Visual Basic, in which error conditions were denoted by integer error codes. More specifically, in Visual Basic .NET either a method or the CLR can *throw* an exception to signal that an error condition has occurred. When an exception is thrown, other methods have an opportunity to *catch* the exception and branch off into contingency code designed to handle various kinds of error conditions.

To see how this process works, let's look at a simple example. Suppose that you are writing a method definition and decide that you need to report an error condition back to your caller. Although you could use the `Err.Raise` syntax offered by previous versions of Visual Basic, you are strongly encouraged to embrace the structured .NET approach. In Visual Basic .NET, you report an error condition by explicitly creating an exception object and using a `Throw` statement:

```
Public Class Class1
  Public Shared Sub Method1()
    '*** report error to caller
    Throw New Exception("Oh no! An error has occurred!")
  End Sub
End Class
```

In the preceding code, an exception is an object created using the New operator. The Throw statement terminates execution of the current method and throws the exception object back to the method's caller. When an exception is thrown, it acts as a signal to inform the caller that something went wrong that prevented the method from completing successfully. The exception object also contains information about a particular error condition, which it makes available to exception-handling code.

The way in which you handle error conditions also differs from the approach taken in previous versions of Visual Basic. That is, you no longer structure your code in terms of On Error GoTo statements, but instead trap error conditions by structuring your code within a Try statement. A Try statement catches and handles an exception with a Catch block. For example, you can catch and handle the exception thrown by Method1 with the following code:

```
Class MyApp
  Shared Sub Main()

    Try
      Class1.Method1()

    Catch ex As Exception
      '*** handle exception thrown by Method1
      MsgBox("There's been a problem: " & ex.Message)

    End Try

  End Sub
End Class
```

This brief introduction to throwing and catching exceptions has barely scratched the surface of what you need to know to write code using structured exception handling. Chapter 9 will cover these concepts in much greater detail, in recognition of the fact that structured exception handling is a way of life in the .NET Framework. The CLR and classes of the FCL throw exceptions whenever they need to report an error condition. There-fore, it's an absolute necessity that you become comfortable writing `Try` statements that contain `Catch` blocks. It's inevitable that exceptions will occur, and your code must be prepared to handle them.

Finally, structured exception handling makes Visual Basic .NET a much better language. The `On Error GoTo` syntax used in previous versions of Visual Basic has gained a reputation for yielding "spaghetti" code, because the flow of execution through the error-handling code could become very convoluted. Structured exception handling greatly improves this situation by forcing you to write error-handling code in a more constrained way. The resulting code is easier to read and easier to maintain.

Strict Type Checking

The Visual Basic .NET compiler provides two important compile-time options known as `Option Explicit` and `Option Strict`. Each option can be enabled or disabled in Visual Studio .NET on a project-by-project basis using the `Project Properties` dialog, as shown in Figure 2.8.

In addition to configuring `Option Explicit` and `Option Strict` at the project level, you can configure these settings at the file level. For example,

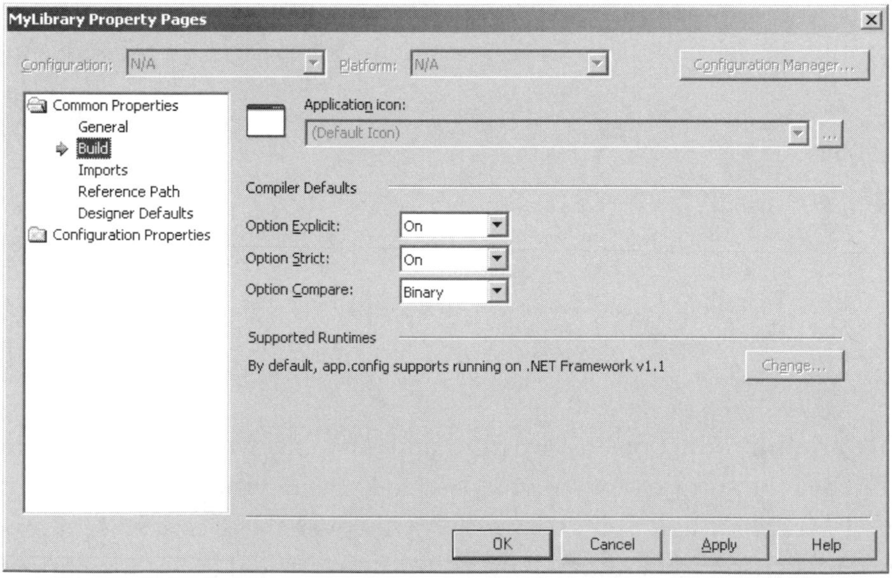

FIGURE 2.8: `Option Strict` and `Option Explicit` are configurable at the project level.

you can enable these options by placing the following statements at the top of a source file:

```
Option Explicit On
Option Strict On
```

You can also disable these options by using the same code but replacing On with Off.

Placing these statements at the top of a source files overrides the project-wide setting for Visual Studio .NET for that source file. It is only source files that don't include these settings that are compiled with the project-wide settings. Also keep in mind that each of these compile-time options has a default setting if you don't explicit set your preferences. By default, Visual Studio .NET and VBC.EXE enable Option Explicit and disable Option Strict.

When Option Explicit is enabled, you are required to explicitly declare any variable before using it. This option, which works the same way as in previous versions of Visual Basic, is important because it allows you to discover simple errors at compile time, such as misspelled variable names. You should always compile your code using Option Explicit.

When Option Strict is enabled, the compiler uses a feature known as *strict type checking*. With strict type checking, the compiler generates errors when it thinks that your code contains bugs. In other words, the compiler becomes more restrictive about what forms of syntax it will allow. The motivation for this approach is simple: A bug is much easier to locate and fix when it is detected at compile time. Once a bug sneaks by the compiler and into your compiled code, it becomes much more evasive. Therefore, a bug that isn't caught by the compiler is more expensive to locate and fix.

Strict type checking is one of the best new features of Visual Basic .NET. You should make it a point to always compile your code using Option Strict. Always remember that this feature is disabled by default; you have to make a conscious effort to turn it on. You are encouraged to get into the habit of enabling Option Strict whenever you create a new project.

The first thing you will notice about strict type checking is that it forces you to be explicit about the types you are using throughout your code. That is, you must declare each local variable, parameter, field, and property with an As clause using an explicit type. If you forget to include an As clause, the compiler will generate an error and refuse to compile your code until you correct the problem. The error generated by the compiler points you to the line of code that requires the As clause. This rapid identification makes it easier to write code that is more disciplined and more likely to be correct.

When strict type checking is disabled, Visual Basic .NET doesn't require the use of As clauses. When you define a variable, parameter, or field without an As clause, the Visual Basic .NET compiler implicitly uses the type Object. However, using the Object type by mistake can yield inefficient and buggy code. Thus working without strict type checking allows for a sloppy, error-prone coding style.

The second thing you will notice about strict type checking is that it changes the rules for programming against variables of type Object. When strict type checking is disabled, Visual Basic .NET supports *late binding*. Late binding is a feature based on the notion that a caller can invoke a method without requiring the compiler to see the method definition at compile time. You might say that a method call using late binding is like a shot in the dark, because the compiler doesn't get a chance to verify that you've called the method using the proper syntax. The compiler cannot determine whether the target object (or class) even supports the method at all. Instead, it generates code that allows the caller to discover the method definition and bind to its implementation at runtime. While late binding is a feature you generally want to avoid, its discussion here will be presented at a high level so you can see how it affects the way you write code.

Visual Basic .NET supports late binding when two conditions are met. First, you must turn off strict type checking by disabling Option Strict. Second, you must attempt to call a method or property through an Object reference. Here's a simple example:

```
Dim human1 As Object = New Human()
human1.Juggle()
```

In this example, a Human object is created and assigned to the Object variable named human1. Next, a call to the Juggle method is made through the variable human1. Now let's ask an important question: What would happen if the Human class did not support a method named Juggle? In this case, the compiler does *not* catch the problem; rather, it happily compiles the code into an assembly. However, the method call will certainly fail at runtime because the Juggle method doesn't exist. You now have a bug that will reveal itself *only* if you manage to execute the call during testing.

Late binding causes problems because the compiler never checks whether the class member being referenced actually exists. Furthermore, if you are calling a method, the compiler never confirms that your parameter list has the correct number and type of parameters. In other words, late binding eliminates the benefits of compile-time type checking. Conversely, when you enable Option Strict, the compiler performs compile-time type checking at full strength. There is no middle ground.

The third thing you will notice about strict type checking is that it affects conversions between different types. This relationship is especially obvious to developers who are migrating from an earlier version of Visual Basic. Let's look at a simple example in which an Integer variable is converted to a variable of type Byte:

```
Dim x As Integer = 1000
Dim y As Byte = x
```

An Integer variable can hold a wide range of numbers that are too large to fit inside a Byte value. For this reason, converting from an Integer variable to a Byte variable is known as a *narrowing conversion*. The conversion from an Integer to a Byte is not guaranteed to succeed because it has the potential to experience an *overflow error*. The question in this situation becomes whether the compiler should allow you to perform a narrowing conversion implicitly. Is the potential failure that could result from this narrowing conversion something that the programmer has taken into account, or is it a potential bug in the code?

Strict type checking makes it illegal to perform a narrowing conversion implicitly. Instead, a compile-time error will result if you try to perform an implicit conversion from Integer to Byte as shown in the last example. If you want to perform the narrowing conversion, you must perform the conversion explicitly:

```
Dim x As Integer = 1000
Dim y As Byte = CByte(x)
```

The motivation behind this approach is to make potential failure points more obvious in the code. Now that you have made your intentions clear, the Visual Basic .NET compiler will generate the code needed to convert an Integer value to a Byte value. At this point, the compiler assumes that your code has been written to deal with any potential exceptions that may result from the conversion.

Let's look at another example of what can go wrong during a narrowing conversion. Sometimes a narrowing conversion may succeed but still result in unwanted side effects. Consider the following code, in which a Double value is assigned to an Integer variable:

```
Dim x As Double = 3.141592
Dim y As Integer = x
```

The Double type and the Integer type were designed to hold different kinds of data. A Double variable can contain significant digits after the decimal point, whereas an Integer variable cannot. As a consequence, the floating-point number 3.141592 is truncated to a value of 3 when it is converted to an integer. Once again, the Visual Basic .NET compiler will not allow you to perform this kind of narrowing conversion implicitly. If you want to perform this narrowing conversion, you must make your intentions clear to the compiler with an explicit conversion:

```
Dim x As Double = 3.141592
Dim y As Integer = CInt(x)
```

As you see, strict type checking prohibits implicit conversions that have the potential to result in overflow errors or a loss of precision. One more example of an implicit narrowing conversion will demonstrate another key point. Look at following code and guess whether it will compile when strict type checking is enabled:

```
Dim x As Double = 3
Dim y As Integer = x
```

Your intuition might tell you that this code will compile. After all, a numeric value of 3 can be successfully converted to an Integer variable without an overflow error or a loss of precision. In fact, this code will not compile when strict type checking is enabled. The compiler never inspects the actual data inside the variables—it just considers the fact that one type is a Double and the other type is an Integer. From the compiler's perspective, any conversion from `Double` to `Integer` has the potential to experience overflow or precision loss and, therefore, cannot be performed implicitly.

Let's end this section by examining one final example. What happens when you attempt to convert an `Integer` to a `Double` without using an explicit conversion?

```
Dim x As Integer = 3
Dim y As Double = x
```

In this example, an implicit conversion is legal even with strict type checking in effect. That's because the conversion from an `Integer` to a `Double` is a *widening conversion*. Any numeric value that can be expressed as an `Integer` can be converted to a `Double` without any risk of an overflow error or loss of precision. When a conversion is guaranteed to succeed without any side effects, the compiler will always allow you to perform it implicitly. Such is always the case with a widening conversion.

To summarize, three things about strict type checking will affect the way you write code:

- You must explicitly define the type of each variable, parameter, field, property, and function with an `As` clause.
- You get higher levels of compile-time type checking because late binding is prohibited.
- Implicit narrowing conversions are not allowed. If you want to perform a narrowing conversion, you must do so explicitly.

You have probably realized that you will use more explicit conversions in Visual Basic .NET than you did in earlier versions of Visual Basic. To help with this requirement, the language provides several conversion operators to explicitly convert values from one type to another: `CBool`, `CByte`, `CChar`, `CDate`, `CDbl`, `CDec`, `CInt`, `CLng`, `CObj`, `CShort`, `CSng`, and `CStr`. In addition, a generic conversion operator named `CType` allows you to explicitly convert from any type to any other type. Using the `CType` operator has the same effect as using one of the type-specific conversion operators (when one exists). For example:

```
Dim x As Integer = 3
Dim y As Short = CShort(x)      '*** this line
Dim z As Short = CType(x, Short) '*** is the same as this line
```

The Visual Basic .NET conversion operators provide the calling syntax of a standard function, but are built into the language itself. Because they result in conversions that are not guaranteed to succeed, it is common practice to perform explicit narrowing conversions inside a `Try` statement so you can add a `Catch` block to deal with any failed conversions.

Programming with Boolean Values under Option Strict

Use of the `Boolean` type with strict type checking enabled is something that requires a little extra attention, especially from developers who are migrating to Visual Basic .NET from other languages. Programmers who used C, C++, and previous versions of Visual Basic were often overly casual about converting between `Boolean` values and values of various integer types. The implicit assumption was that an integer variable with a value of 0 translates to a `Boolean` value of `False` and a nonzero integer value translates to a `Boolean` value of `True`. You should avoid this assumption when programming in Visual Basic .NET, because it can lead to code that's hard to read and maintain.

Let's look at an example of this style of code. In previous versions of Visual Basic, you could write the following `If` statement:

```
Public Sub Method1(ByVal param1 As Integer)
  If param1 Then
    '*** this code executes if param1 <> 0
  End If
End Sub
```

When `Option Strict` is enabled, you cannot implicitly convert between a numeric type and the `Boolean` type. Therefore, the preceding code will not compile in Visual Basic .NET. Although Visual Basic .NET does allow you to explicitly convert back and forth between numeric types and the `Boolean` type, this approach is considered bad style and should be avoided. In a situation in which a `Boolean` type is expected, you should always provide an expression that evaluates to a value of either `True` or `False`, like this:

```
Public Sub Method1(ByVal param1 As Integer)
   If param1 <> 0 Then
     '*** this code executes if param1 <> 0
   End If
End Sub
```

Logical Comparisons versus Bitwise Operations

Now that we have discussed evaluating Boolean expressions, it makes
sense to talk about how the behavior of operators such as And, Or, XOr, and
Not has changed from previous versions of Visual Basic. These operators
can still be used to perform either logical comparisons or bitwise operations. For example, you can perform a logical comparison between two
Boolean values using the Or operator in the following manner:

```
Dim x, y, z As Boolean
x = True
y = False
z = x Or y   '*** (z = True)
```

The Or operator has always been somewhat confusing in Visual Basic,
because you can also use it to conduct a bitwise operation. For example,
suppose you want to calculate the union of bits between two Integer values. You can use the Or operator in the following manner:

```
Dim x, y, z As Integer
x = 3         '*** 1 bit and 2 bit on
y = 5         '*** 1 bit and 4 bit on
z = x Or y   '*** 1 bit, 2 bit and 4 bit on (z = 7)
```

While Visual Basic .NET continues to permit you to use And, Or, XOr,
and Not to perform either logical comparisons or bitwise operations, you
should note that strict type checking requires you to work exclusively in
terms of either Boolean values or integral values. Therefore, the following
code will not compile with Option Strict enabled:

```
Dim x As Boolean = True
Dim y As Integer = 3
Dim z As Integer = x Or y   '*** compile error
```

As you can see, strict type checking prohibits sloppy code in which a programmer has not distinguished between a logical comparison and a bitwise

operation. This change represents another improvement over previous versions of Visual Basic.

Visual Basic .NET provides improved support for making logical comparisons by introducing the `AndAlso` and `OrElse` operators. These new operators are like the `And` and `Or` operators in the sense that they perform logical comparisons. However, `AndAlso` and `OrElse` work only with `Boolean` values, so they effectively enforce higher levels of type safety than do the `And` and `Or` operators.

The `AndAlso` and `OrElse` operators provide one additional benefit. Unlike the `And` and `Or` operators, they perform *short-circuiting*, which means they do not evaluate the expression on the right-hand side of the operator if they can determine the outcome from the expression on the left-hand side.

A quick example will illustrate how short-circuiting works. Suppose you write a class with two functions named `Method1` and `Method2`, both of which return `Boolean` values. If you use these two functions as input to the `And` operator, both functions will be called in all cases:

```
'*** Method2 is always called
If Method1() And Method2() Then
  '*** statement block
End If
```

If the call to `Method1` returns a value of `False`, the `And` operator will yield `False` regardless of what `Method2` returns. In this situation, there is no need for the `And` operator to call and evaluate the return value of `Method2`. However, because the `And` operator does not perform short-circuiting, `Method2` will be called in all cases.

In Visual Basic .NET, if you write the same code but replace the `And` operator with the `AndAlso` operator, short-circuiting will occur:

```
'*** Method2 is called only if Method1 returns True
If Method1() AndAlso Method2() Then
  '*** statement block
End If
```

In this way, short-circuiting can improve performance by eliminating unneeded calls. Of course, the introduction of short-circuiting doesn't just improve performance; it also facilitates writing more concise code. Consider the following code, which uses the `And` operator instead of the `AndAlso` operator:

```
Public Sub ProcessHuman(ByVal target As Human)
  If (Not target Is Nothing) And (target.Name <> "") Then  '*** danger!
    '*** statement block
  End If
End Sub
```

Given this method implementation, what will happen if the caller passes the `target` parameter a value of `Nothing`? This code will experience a runtime exception because it attempts to access the instance property `Name` using a parameter value that doesn't point to a valid `Human` object. To write the correct code using the `And` operator, you would have to structure your code using an `If` statement nested inside another `If` statement. Alternatively, you could employ a more concise style of syntax by using the `AndAlso` operator:

```
Public Sub ProcessHuman(ByVal target As Human)
  If (Not target Is Nothing) AndAlso (target.Name <> "") Then
    '*** statement block
  End If
End Sub
```

The short-circuiting behavior of the `AndAlso` operator handles this type of situation in a more elegant fashion. If the expression on the left-hand side of the `AndAlso` operator determines that `target` contains a value of `Nothing`, the code that attempts to access the `Name` property will never execute.

Let's summarize the reasons why you should prefer the `AndAlso` and `OrElse` operators over the `And` and `Or` operators when you need to conduct a logical comparison:

- They produce compile-time errors when you mistakenly use something other than a `Boolean` value as input.
- They are guaranteed to produce a `Boolean` value as output.
- They provide short-circuiting, which has the potential to make your code faster and more concise.

SUMMARY

A variety of tools are available for building applications and components with Visual Basic .NET—most importantly, the Visual Basic .NET compiler and the Visual Studio .NET IDE. The more you learn about these two tools, the more adept you will become at writing and compiling applications and component DLLs.

It is important that you learn to distinguish between assemblies and namespaces. An assembly represents the fundamental unit of compiled, distributable code. A namespacc is a user-defined scope for defining types. Namespaces are used to prevent naming conflicts across assemblies. Some aspects of dealing with assembly references and namespaces are addressed at the compiler level, whereas others are handled automatically by Visual Studio .NET.

This chapter has given you a head start in building and debugging form-based applications within the Visual Studio .NET IDE. As indicated here, several of its new features make Visual Basic .NET different from— and better than—any previous version of Visual Basic. Chapter 3 will build on the lessons learned here by introducing a fundamental piece of the .NET Framework: the Common Type System.

■3■

The Common Type System

W HAT IS A *TYPE*? This might seem like a simple question, but it's not. Furthermore, this question has a different answer depending on whether you are working with Visual Basic 6, C++, Java, or the .NET Framework. This chapter explains what it means to be a type that is defined within the programming model of the .NET Framework. This special sort of type is known as a *managed type*.

At the end of the day, a .NET application is nothing more than a set of managed types that have been compiled into one or more assemblies. The CLR has the responsibility of loading the assemblies as well as the managed types within them. However, the CLR can load and execute the code within a type only if that type conforms to a set of rules defined by a core piece of the .NET Framework architecture—the *Common Type System (CTS)*.

The CTS recognizes several kinds of managed types, including classes, interfaces, enumerations, and structures. While different kinds of managed types exist, the CTS requires all managed types to share certain traits and characteristics. Note, however, that many aspects of managed types differ from the types in unmanaged languages such as Visual Basic 6.

This chapter will teach you the fundamentals of the CTS. It begins by presenting some background information and a few key concepts that are critical to your understanding of how managed types work. Next, it discusses some of the more frequently used system types within the CTS. By the end of this chapter you will understand what it means to be a managed type, and you will be better prepared to move ahead to a more advanced discussion of how the CTS and Visual Basic .NET support object-oriented programming (OOP).

Motivation for the Common Type System

Unlike Sun's single-language development strategy, which utilizes the Java platform, Microsoft's development strategy hinges on the ability to mix and match programming languages. That is, a component library written in one language can be used by an application or component library written in another language. This flexibility allows a company to choose any of several languages on a project-by-project basis.

Long before Microsoft began to design the architecture of the .NET Framework, the company had a good deal of experience with cross-language interoperability. This experience came from Microsoft's creation and evolution of the Component Object Model (COM). Microsoft created the COM technology more than a decade ago to promote the idea of component-based development with language independence. While COM has been widely adopted within the software industry, its foundation contained a number of flaws that taught Microsoft some important lessons.

To see how the introduction of CTS has made things better, let's first describe some of the problematic issues with COM. C++ developers often produce COM-based DLLs that are unusable from Visual Basic or COM-enabled scripting languages such as JavaScript and VBScript. This inaccessibility usually results from the fact that many of C++'s built-in types for dealing with data items such as strings, arrays, and pointers are either impossible or impractical to program against from other high-level languages.

This problem is actually a symptom of a bigger problem. The architects of COM were overly constrained when they designed the COM type system, because they had to create a type system that accommodated several other preexisting type systems. These systems had been created by the designers of programming languages such as C, C++, Visual Basic, JavaScript, and VBScript—all of which had type systems designed with absolutely no regard for any other language's type system.

The architects of COM were further constrained because they wanted to integrate languages such as Visual Basic 3, VBScript, and JavaScript, which offered relatively limited support for OOP. As a result of these limitations, Microsoft was unable to integrate many of the important OOP features into COM's programming model. This omission certainly put COM at a disadvantage as compared with the Java platform.

In their work, the architects of the .NET Framework had the benefit of reflecting on the strengths and weaknesses of COM. They realized that allowing every language to define its own unique type system created compatibility problems. They knew they could improve language interoperability by creating a single underlying type system for every managed language. They also realized that all managed languages would have to support the same rich set of OOP features if the .NET Framework was to compete effectively with the Java platform. These realizations led Microsoft to create the CTS.

The CTS provides the backbone for the programming model of the .NET Framework. It defines a core set of system-defined types, the rules for creating user-defined types, and a standard set of OOP features. In short, the CTS makes it possible for the .NET Framework to offer language interoperability that is more reliable and more efficient than the language interoperability afforded through COM. This flexibility derives from the fact that every managed language is designed to sit on top of the same underlying programming model and type system.

The Common Language Specification

Of course, not every aspect of the CTS is universally supported by all managed languages. For example, some system-defined types and programming features are supported by certain managed languages but not by others. Microsoft's quest to achieve language interoperability is further complicated by the fact that some managed languages such as C# are case sensitive whereas other managed languages such as Visual Basic .NET are case insensitive.

Designing all managed languages to sit on top of the CTS is not enough to provide the highest levels of language interoperability. For this reason, Microsoft has drafted an additional document known as the *Common Language Specification (CLS)*. The CLS defines a subset of CTS types and programming features that must be supported across all managed languages.

When a company wants to produce a component DLL that will be equally accessible from every managed language, the component library should be written to be CLS-compliant.

Let's look at two problems that illustrate how the CLS promotes language interoperability. The first problem is that the CTS includes several system-defined types based on unsigned integers. There are three unsigned integer types that are supported by the C# language but not supported by the syntax of Visual Basic .NET. While a developer might write a component DLL in C# that exposes public methods with parameters based on unsigned integers, such a library would be inconvenient (although not impossible) to program against from Visual Basic .NET. Therefore, C# developers should avoid creating component DLLs that force users to program in terms of unsigned integers.

The second language interoperability issue is even worse. What would happen if a C# developer created a component DLL containing two public methods whose names differ only by case? For example, imagine you wanted to program against a public class written in C# that contains one public method named `getCustomer` and another public method named `GetCustomer`. The names of these two methods differ only by the case of their first character. In a case-insensitive language like Visual Basic .NET, how would you differentiate between calls to these two methods? You cannot. The Visual Basic .NET compiler would generate a compile-time error because you might be referring to either of two candidate methods. In this situation, the problem arises due to the ambiguity caused by mixing a case-sensitive language with a case-insensitive language. The bottom line is that the C# class in this example exposes functionality that is inaccessible from Visual Basic .NET.

The CLS is intended to prevent these kinds of problems with language interoperability. For example, the CLS prohibits the use of public methods that contain parameters based on unsigned integers. It also prohibits component DLLs that contain functionality accessible only to languages that support case sensitivity. (The CLS imposes many more restrictions in addition to the two mentioned here.) The key point is that the CLS can be used to guarantee that a component DLL will be equally accessible from any managed language. This guarantee is valuable to companies that produce and sell component DLLs because it enables them to reach many more potential customers.

When you are creating a component DLL, remember that only the calling signatures of the public members, exposed by public types, must meet the rules of CLS compliance. You are still free to use types and features that are not CLS-compliant when writing the private implementation details of a component library. This flexibility allows you to take full advantage of whatever managed language you are using.

The accessibility afforded by the CLS should prove particularly attractive to Visual Basic developers, because an overwhelming majority of the class libraries provided by the FCL are CLS-compliant. In the past, Visual Basic programmers have been frustrated to find that many parts of the Win32 API and COM-based APIs were inaccessible from their language of choice. Today, Visual Basic is no longer a second-class citizen when it comes to accessing the APIs of the underlying platform. This factor really levels the playing field when comparing Visual Basic to other semicolon-based languages.

Even as the CLS levels the playing field, it also raises the bar in terms of prerequisite programming skills required of Visual Basic developers. To make their language CLS-compliant, the designers of Visual Basic .NET had to add support for many OOP features not found in early versions of Visual Basic. Mastering the concepts and syntax associated with all of these new OOP features is an essential part of becoming an effective user of Visual Basic .NET.

Fundamental CTS Concepts

A managed type is the smallest unit of code that can be independently compiled, and it contains members such as fields, methods, and properties. As a Visual Basic .NET developer, you will be both a consumer and a producer of managed types. You will be consuming managed types from the assemblies referenced by your project. You will be producing a managed type each time you create a class, module, interface, enumeration, structure, or delegate.

Visual Basic .NET differs from earlier versions of Visual Basic in that all code must reside within the scope of a type definition. In previous versions of Visual Basic, you could write code at the global level using .bas modules. In Visual Basic .NET, attempting to declare a variable or function outside the scope of a type definition will produce a compile-time error.

Let's begin our discussion of the CTS by considering a few important programming concepts: inheritance, shared members, the call stack, and the difference between value types and reference types. While we will revisit many of these topics later in greater detail, it's important to introduce them now because these topics are critical to forming a basic understanding of the CTS and managed types.

Inheritance

Inheritance is an OOP feature that allows you to derive a new type from an existing type. Suppose type C inherits from type B. Then type C is known as the *derived type*, and type B is known as the *base type*. A derived type C inherits all members defined by its base type B, as well as all members defined by B's base type, and so on.

Inheritance is particularly important in the .NET Framework because the vast majority of system-defined and user-defined types have a base type. When a set of types are related through inheritance, they form a structure known as an *inheritance hierarchy*. The architects of the .NET Frame-

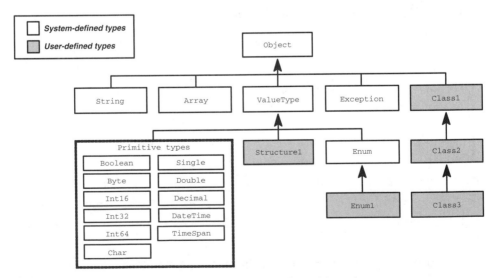

FIGURE 3.1: The CTS is based on a singly rooted inheritance hierarchy.

work designed the CTS around the inheritance hierarchy shown in Figure 3.1. Note that the system-defined types shown in this figure are all defined within the System namespace.

Figure 3.1 follows a standard OOP notation in which a derived type has an arrow that points up to its base type. For example, String inherits from Object. As shown in Figure 3.1, the CTS inheritance hierarchy consists of many levels, which means that some types inherit from a base type, which in turn inherits from another base type, and so on. For example, Boolean inherits from ValueType, which itself inherits from Object.

In Visual Basic .NET, user-defined types specify inheritance via the Inherits keyword. As an example, consider the code in Listing 3.1 where class Customer inherits from class Human. The result is that a customer has three fields (Name, Email, ID) and one method (SendEmail).

LISTING 3.1: Using inheritance to define a class

```
Public Class Human
  Public Name As String
  Public Email As String

  Public Sub SendEmail()
    '*** some implementation
  End Sub
End Class

Public Class Customer
  Inherits Human

  Public ID As Integer
End Class
```

The CTS defines an important rule: Every type must inherit either directly or indirectly from the Object type. This rule has only two exceptions. The first exception is fairly obvious: The Object type does not inherit from itself. The second exception is that interface types do not inherit from Object. With these two exceptions, every other managed type must inherit from Object. Because all the arrows in the CTS inheritance hierarchy eventually point back to the Object type, it is a *singly rooted* inheritance hierarchy.

The Visual Basic .NET compiler has been designed to generate type definitions that comply with the rules of the CTS. As a consequence, the compiler must often add extra information to your type definitions. For example, what happens when you compile a class definition that does not specify a base class? The Visual Basic .NET compiler does the right thing; it recognizes that your class definition has no base class and automatically generates a class definition that inherits from `Object`. Thus, in Listing 3.1, class `Human` inherits from `Object`.

Shared Members versus Instance Members

Members of a type can be defined to behave in one of two ways:

- A member defined in Visual Basic .NET using the `Shared` keyword is a *shared member* and is accessible directly through the type name.
- A member defined without the `Shared` keyword is an *instance member* and is accessed through an instance of that type.

Let's look at a simple example. The `String` class is a managed type that exposes both shared members and instance members. You can access a shared member directly using the class name. To access an instance member of the `String` class, however, you must first have a variable that references a `String` instance. Examine the following code:

```
Dim var1, var2, var3 As String
var1 = "Rose"
var2 = "bud"

'*** call shared method of String class
var3 = System.String.Concat(var1, var2)

'*** call instance method of String class
Dim index As Integer = var3.IndexOf("b")
```

The `Concat` method is a shared member of the `String` class, so it can be called using the name of the class. In contrast, the `IndexOf` method is an instance member of the `String` class, so it must be accessed through an instance of the `String` class. From the perspective of a programmer using a class, this example demonstrates the fundamental difference between shared members and instance members.

Instance members will be familiar to developers who are migrating from older versions of Visual Basic. Shared members will be a new concept, however, because they have never truly been supported in previous versions of Visual Basic. It's not that shared members are hard or tricky to use; it's just that your intuition needs to change a bit so you begin to notice them.

When you start using the core system types of the CTS, you will see that many types contain both instance members and shared members. Pay extra attention to them at first so that you will learn to differentiate between the two. You will be using classes such as the `String` class, which expose much of their functionality through shared public members. This approach is quite different from the programming undertaken in earlier versions of Visual Basic, in which the equivalent functionality was often exposed as a set of global functions in the VBA runtime library. As mentioned earlier, your intuition will need to change before you feel comfortable with this aspect of Visual Basic .NET.

Threads, Method Execution, and the Call Stack

Now let's consider how the CLR manages the execution of methods within a running .NET application. It's essential that you understand the basic concepts associated with managed execution and the call stack so that you can fully appreciate how managed types behave within the .NET Framework.

Let's start with the concept of a thread. A *thread* is an agent within a running application that executes code. Threads are not unique to the .NET Framework, of course. They are essential to all applications that run on 32-bit Windows as well as applications written for many other operating systems, such as UNIX. For example, Web servers use threads to efficiently handle hundreds of simultaneous requests from users. For our purposes here, we will limit the discussion to threads that are managed by the CLR, known as *managed threads*.

Whenever any method executes, it runs on a specific thread. Each thread maintains a private *call stack* so that methods may call other methods. The call stack serves a variety of purposes, including parameter passing, storing local variables, and keeping track of where a given method should return once its call is complete. When method A calls method B, for example, information is *pushed* on top of the call stack and the thread continues execution at method B. When method B eventually returns, information is *popped* from the call stack and execution resumes in method A.

In general, a method may call a second method, which may in turn call a third method, and so on. These method calls are said to form a *call chain*. Each call in the chain is the result of a method call that has not yet completed. The call stack, which is the physical representation of the call chain, is partitioned into divisions known as *stack frames*. There is one stack frame for each method call in the call chain, and this stack frame maintains the information relevant to that method call—parameters, local variables, and so on.

Let's look at a simple example to put things in perspective. The code in Listing 3.2 forms a call chain of three methods. The `Main` method represents the application's entry point. When you run the application, the CLR initializes the application's primary thread, including creating the thread's call stack. The CLR then initializes the thread to call `Main` and lets the thread run. The call to `Main` triggers the creation of a stack frame on the call stack and the start of program execution. As `Main` begins to execute, it maintains control over the thread until the call to `Method1` occurs. This call causes a new stack frame to be allocated on top of the call stack and execution to be subsequently transferred to `Method1`. As `Method1` executes, it calls `Method2`, which creates another stack frame on top of the stack and leads to another transfer of control. At this point the thread is now executing `Method2`, and the call stack is as shown in Figure 3.2.

LISTING 3.2: Three methods for forming a call chain

```
Class MyApp
   Shared Sub Main()
     BobsCode.Method1()
   End Sub
End Class

Class BobsCode
   Public Shared Sub Method1()
     BettysCode.Method2()
   End Sub
End Class

Class BettysCode
   Public Shared Sub Method2()
     '*** implementation
   End Sub
End Class
```

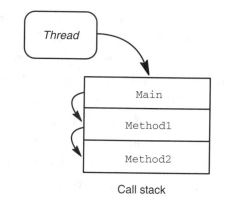

FIGURE 3.2: Threads use a call stack for execution of method calls.

Now you can make an important observation about the behavior of methods in a call chain. When one method calls another method, it is dependent upon the second method completing and returning control before the first method can continue execution. For example, once Method1 calls Method2, Method1 loses control over the thread and essentially waits in a suspended state until the call to Method2 completes. Similarly, Main waits in a suspended state until Method1 completes.

Each stack frame exists only for the length of time that its associated method is executing. When a method call completes execution and returns to its caller, the memory associated with the method's stack frame is released. For example, the stack frame for Method2 is cleaned up as the thread returns control to Method1. Likewise, the stack frame for Method1 is cleaned up as the thread returns control to Main.

Value Types and Reference Types

The CTS supports two fundamentally different kinds of types: *value types* and *reference types*. In .NET terminology, a *value* is an instance created from a value type, and an *object* is an instance created from a reference type. It's important to distinguish between value types and reference types because the CLR treats values and objects in a very different manner.

Looking back at Figure 3.1, notice the core system type named Value-Type. The CTS defines a value type as any type that inherits directly or indirectly from ValueType. Examples of values types include the built-in primitive types Boolean, Integer, Double, and Decimal; structures and enumerations are also value types. Any type that does not inherit from Val-ueType is considered to be a reference type. Examples of reference types include system-defined classes such as String and user-defined classes.

The primary difference between value types and reference types relates to how the CLR manages their memory. Let's look first at the declaration of a local variable as a value type and then compare it with the declaration of a local variable as a reference type. This example will give you the general idea of how the CLR differentiates between values and objects.

A local variable declaration based on a value type is a value. A value represents an allocation of memory such that the variable itself holds the associated data. Suppose you declare and initialize a local variable based on a value type such as Integer:

```
Class MyApp
   Shared Sub Main()
     Dim val1 As Integer = 10
     Dim val2 As Integer
   End Sub
End Class
```

As shown in Figure 3.3, the CLR allocates memory for the local variables val1 and val2 directly on the call stack within the stack frame for Main. The way things work with val1 is pretty simple because this variable holds a value containing the number 10. The programmer has not explicitly initialized the local variable val2 in this example, so it is auto-initialized with

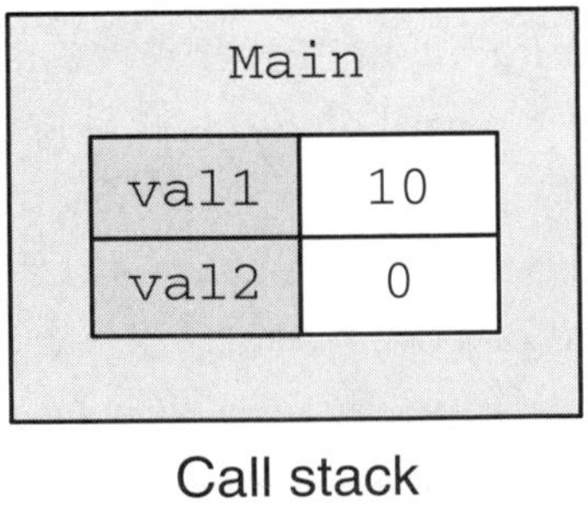

Call stack

FIGURE 3.3: A value type variable contains the value itself.

a default value of 0. The key observation here is that a variable based on a value type always holds an instance of a value type—that is, a value.

A variable declaration based on a reference type is more complex, because a reference type variable never holds the instance itself. Instead, the memory allocated for a reference type variable holds a *reference* to the instance (i.e., the object). A reference is a logical pointer that is capable of pointing to an object. You must go through a reference whenever you want to access an object's instance members. To see how this approach works, take a peek at the variable ref1 in Figure 3.4.

Let's extend the preceding code example to include a reference type in addition to a value type. Suppose you are writing code using a reference type such as the user-defined Human class shown in Listing 3.1. Examine the following:

```
Class MyApp
  Shared Sub Main()
    Dim val1 As Integer = 10
    Dim val2 As Integer
    Dim ref1 As Human = New Human()
    Dim ref2 As Human
  End Sub
End Class
```

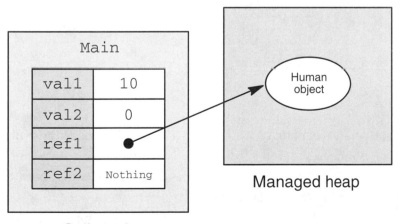

FIGURE 3.4: Reference variables refer to objects on the managed heap or to Nothing.

Figure 3.4 shows the resulting memory allocation. As you can see, the CLR treats the local variables `ref1` and `ref2` very differently from `val1` and `val2`. While the CLR allocates memory on the call stack for `ref1` and `ref2`, these local variables will never hold an actual object. Instead, the CLR allocates memory for `ref1` and `ref2` to hold references to objects, or a reference to `Nothing`.

In this code example, the `New` operator was used to create a `Human` object. The CLR never creates objects on the call stack, but rather allocates memory for objects in a different region of memory known as the *managed heap*. After the `New` operator creates a `Human` object, it returns a reference that is assigned to the local reference type variable `ref1`. Note that the local variable `ref2` is not explicitly initialized. Instead, it is auto-initialized to a value of `Nothing`, signifying that it doesn't refer to any object on the managed heap.

Comparing References with the `Is` Operator

A reference is just a logical pointer that either points to an object or has a value of `Nothing`. An application can have multiple references that point to the same object. In fact, sometimes you need to compare two references to see whether they point to the same object. Visual Basic .NET provides the `Is` operator for this purpose. Here's an example of the use of the `Is` operator to compare references:

```
Dim ref1 As Human = New Human()
Dim ref2 As Human = New Human()
Dim ref3 As Human = ref2

Dim test1, test2 As Boolean

test1 = ref1 Is ref2   '*** test1 = False
test2 = ref2 Is ref3   '*** test2 = True
```

The first two lines of code create distinct `Human` objects. The reference variable `ref1` points to the first `Human` object, and the reference variable `ref2` points to the second object. However, the third line of code doesn't create a new object. Instead, the assignment copies the reference to the second `Human` object into the reference variable `ref3`. As a result, both `ref2` and `ref3` point to the second `Human` object.

When you compare `ref1` and `ref2` with the `Is` operator, the expression evaluates to `False` because the two references do not point to the same object. In contrast, comparing `ref2` and `ref3` with the `Is` operator yields a result of `True` because both reference variables point to the same object.

Thus the `Is` operator returns a value of `True` when two reference variables point to the same object. This operator will also return a value of `True` if both references being compared have a value of `Nothing`. For example:

```
Dim ref1, ref2 As Human

'*** both references have an auto-initialized value of Nothing

Dim test1 As Boolean
test1 = ref1 Is ref2   '*** test1 = True
```

Finally, the `Is` operator is commonly used to test whether a reference variable points to a valid object. For example, you can use the `Is` operator to compare a reference variable to the literal value `Nothing`. If the comparison yields a value of `True`, then you know the reference variable doesn't point to a valid object. The following method definition demonstrates a common technique for checking a reference passed as an input parameter to ensure that it points to a valid object:

```
Sub ProcessHuman(ByVal target As Human)
  '*** check that caller passed a valid object
  If (Not target Is Nothing) Then
    '*** access Human object
  End If
End Sub
```

The `Is` operator is used for comparing references only; it cannot be used to compare values. For example, a compile-time error will result if you try to compare two `Integer` values with the `Is` operator.

Let's summarize this brief introduction to value types and reference types. An instance created from a value type is a value. A value is a formatted chunk of memory that can be allocated directly on the call stack. An instance created from a reference type is an object. Objects are never created on the call stack, but rather are always created on the managed heap. Furthermore, accessing an object requires that you first obtain a reference that points to it.

Core CTS Types

Now that you have a good understanding of the fundamental concepts associated with the CTS, let's take a quick tour through the system-supplied CTS types you will use most frequently. We'll start with the primitive types, and then discuss programming with the `Object`, `String`, and `Array` class types.

Primitive Types

It's difficult to imagine writing software without access to a rich set of built-in primitive types. Fortunately, the CTS supplies a set of CLS-compliant (i.e., language-neutral) primitive types for general application programming. These primitive types are listed in Figure 3.5, along with the Visual Basic .NET language keywords that map to these types.

Primitive types are value types, so you can use them to create values directly on the call stack. Thanks to this characteristic, using primitive types is very efficient. If you don't explicitly initialize a value type variable to a specific value, it will be auto-initialized to a default value, as shown in Figure 3.5.

You do not have to use the `New` operator when initializing a variable of a primitive type. As a result, primitive types are easier to work with than reference types. The following code initializes a few variables based on the four integer types and the two floating-point types:

```
'*** initialize integral types to their maximum values
Dim i1 As Byte = 255
Dim i2 As Short = 32767
Dim i3 As Integer = 2147483647
Dim i4 As Long = 9223372036854775807

'*** initialize floating-point types with maximum precision
Dim f1 As Single = 1.2345678
Dim f2 As Double = 1.23456789012345
```

You can also initialize a numeric variable with a hexadecimal number by employing the same formatting style from earlier versions of Visual Basic. You do so by using a hexadecimal number as a literal value with the `&H` prefix. Here's a simple example:

```
Dim i1 As Integer = &H100    '*** (i1 = 256)
Dim i2 As Integer = &H1FF    '*** (i2 = 511)
Dim i3 As Integer = &HFFFF   '*** (i3 = 65535)
```

CTS Type	VB keyword	Default value	Tag	Description
System.Boolean	Boolean	False	(none)	32-bit true/false value
System.Byte	Byte	0	(none)	8-bit unsigned integer value
System.Int16	Short	0	S	16-bit signed integer value
System.Int32	Integer	0	I	32-bit signed integer value
System.Int64	Long	0	L	64-bit signed integer value
System.Char	Char	ChrW(0)	c	16-bit UNICODE character value (0-65535)
System.Single	Single	0.0	F	32-bit floating-point number (7-8 points of precision)
System.Double	Double	0.0	R	64-bit floating-point number (15-16 points of precision)
System.Decimal	Decimal	0.0	D	96-bit fixed-point number (28 points of precision)
System.DateTime	Date	#01/01/0001#	#	64-bit long integer in IEEE date format
System.TimeSpan	(none)	00:00:00	(none)	64-bit long integer in IEEE time span format

FIGURE 3.5: CLS-compliant primitive types of the CTS

Keep in mind that the primitive types of the CTS are based on underlying classes, which conveniently expose many useful shared methods and properties (something that your intuition might not tell you if you are migrating from an earlier version of Visual Basic). For example, each numeric type exposes shared properties that return its minimum and maximum values, as in the following code:

```
Dim i1 As Integer = Integer.MinValue
Dim i2 As Integer = Integer.MaxValue
```

Each of the primitive numeric types also exposes a shared method named Parse. The Parse method accepts a string parameter and attempts to convert this string into the corresponding numeric value. The following example uses the Parse method with both the Integer type and the Double type to convert strings into numeric values:

```
Dim s1 As String = "44"
Dim i As Integer = Integer.Parse(s1)

Dim s2 As String = "1.2345678E4"
Dim d As Double = Double.Parse(s2)
```

The first call to Parse converts the string "44" into the Integer value 44. The second call to Parse involves a string value that is formatted using scientific notation. In this case, the string "1.2345678E4" is converted to the Double value 12345.678 (i.e., 1.2345678×10^4). Note that a call to Parse will throw an exception if you pass a string that cannot be converted to the specified numeric type.

> Suppose you need to convert a string like "1,000" to an integer value. Should you use Visual Basic .NET's `CInt()` operator, `Integer.Parse()`, or perhaps the typical C# approach with `System.Convert.ToInt32()`? As you'll see in the next section, `CInt()` is a value-added proposition that handles non-numeric characters like "," and "$", which the other methods do not.

If you are migrating from an earlier version of Visual Basic, note that the `Currency` type is not supported in either the CTS or Visual Basic .NET. The `Decimal` type is the closest match; it should be used with monetary values or when extra digits of precision are needed. The `Decimal` type supports 28 decimal digits of precision, while `Single` typically offers 7 digits and `Double` offers 15. On the other hand, `Single` and `Double` can represent a larger range of numbers, albeit with less precision:

```
Dim d   As Decimal = 1.12345678901234567890012345678D
Dim fps As Single  = 3.4028235E+38
Dim fpd As Double  = 1.79769313486231570E+308
```

The literal used to initialize the `Decimal` variable in this code has a D character appended to the end. The D character is a *type tag* that informs the Visual Basic .NET compiler that this literal value should be interpreted as a `Decimal`. In this case the type tag is important. If you omit the type tag, the compiler assumes that the literal type is a `Double` and you will lose about 12 digits of precision. Figure 3.5 shows the type tags supported by Visual Basic .NET for the primitive types.

Earlier versions of Visual Basic did not support the `Char` type, which is new to Visual Basic .NET. A variable of type `Char` is capable of holding a single Unicode character. You can initialize a `Char` variable with a single literal character in one of two ways: via the `CChar` conversion operator or with the c type tag. For example:

```
Dim c1 As Char = CChar("A")
Dim c2 As Char = "A"c
```

If you want to initialize a `Char` variable with the ASCII or Unicode character code itself, use the shared `ChrW` method from the `Strings` class as supplied by the `Microsoft.VisualBasic` assembly:

```
Dim tab As Char = Microsoft.VisualBasic.Strings.ChrW(9)
```

The `Microsoft.VisualBasic` assembly also provides several convenient constants that define commonly needed `Char` (and `String`) values:

```
Dim quote As Char = Microsoft.VisualBasic.ControlChars.Quote
Dim tab As Char   = Microsoft.VisualBasic.ControlChars.Tab
Dim eol As String = Microsoft.VisualBasic.ControlChars.CrLf
```

Finally, the CTS provides a very useful primitive type named `System.DateTime` that maps to the `Date` keyword in Visual Basic .NET. The `Date` type provides a large number of both shared and instance members. A variable of type `Date` can be initialized by using a string-based literal or by using a literal in the format `month/day/year` and surrounded by `#` characters. Here are some examples:

```
Dim d1 As Date = Date.Now
Dim d2 As Date = Date.Today
Dim d3 As Date = d2.AddDays(14)
Dim d4 As Date = #6/4/1962#
Dim d5 As Date = "June 28, 1962"
```

The CTS also provides the `System.DateTime` type with a complementary type named `System.TimeSpan`. Whereas a value based on the type `DateTime` represents a moment in time, a value of type `TimeSpan` represents a duration in time. Unfortunately, Visual Basic .NET does not map a friendly keyword to `TimeSpan` as it does to `DateTime`. As a result, you must program against this type using its CTS-supplied name. For example, the following code properly computes the number of days between today and January 1, 2005, taking leap years into account:

```
Dim d1 As Date = Date.Today
Dim d2 As Date = #1/1/2005#
Dim ts1 As System.TimeSpan = d2.Subtract(d1)
Dim days As Double = ts1.TotalDays
```

As you see, the `DateTime` and `TimeSpan` types are designed to complement each other. For example, many of the methods and properties exposed by the

`DateTime` type have parameters and return values based on the `TimeSpan` type. Likewise, many of the methods and properties exposed by the `TimeSpan` type have parameters and return values based on the `DateTime` type. Together, these two types make it easy to accurately perform all kinds of date arithmetic.

Converting between Primitive Types

Chapter 2 introduced the concept of strict type checking. Recall that strict type checking is a valuable compile-time feature that helps you write better code by prohibiting many forms of error-prone syntax. As noted in the earlier discussion of this feature, you should get in the habit of enabling strict type checking whenever you create a new project.

Strict type checking significantly affects how you write code because it outlaws most narrowing type conversions that occurred automatically in previous versions of Visual Basic. Figure 3.6 presents a matrix that defines which conversions between built-in primitive types in Visual Basic .NET can be performed implicitly, and which conversions must be performed explicitly.

As shown in Figure 3.6, a large percentage of the conversions between primitive types cannot be performed implicitly. As a consequence, programming in Visual Basic .NET is much different from programming in earlier versions of Visual Basic. In Visual Basic .NET, most narrowing conversions must be performed explicitly. For example, you must use an

		Converting to										
		Boolean	Byte	Short	Integer	Long	Char	Single	Double	Decimal	Date	String	Object
Converting from	Boolean	N/A	no	no	no	no	no	no	no	no	no	no	yes
	Byte	no	N/A	yes	yes	yes	no	yes	yes	yes	no	no	yes
	Short	no	no	N/A	yes	yes	no	yes	yes	yes	no	no	yes
	Integer	no	no	no	N/A	yes	no	yes	yes	yes	no	no	yes
	Long	no	no	no	no	N/A	no	yes	yes	yes	no	no	yes
	Char	no	no	no	no	no	N/A	no	no	no	no	yes	yes
	Single	no	no	no	no	no	no	N/A	yes	no	no	no	yes
	Double	no	no	no	no	no	no	no	N/A	no	no	no	yes
	Decimal	no	no	no	no	no	no	yes	yes	N/A	no	no	yes
	Date	no	no	no	no	no	no	no	no	no	N/A	no	yes
	String	no	no	no	no	no	no	no	no	no	no	N/A	yes
	Object	no	no	no	no	no	no	no	no	no	no	no	N/A

FIGURE 3.6: Implicit type conversions allowed in Visual Basic .NET

explicit conversion when converting from a floating-point type to an integer one, such as from a `Double` to an `Integer`:

```
Dim d As Double  = 3.14159
Dim i As Integer = CInt(d)   '*** i = 3
```

You must also use an explicit conversion to convert from a larger integer type to a smaller integer type.

Although Visual Basic .NET prohibits most implicit narrowing conversions, it does not prohibit all of them. For instance, you can implicitly convert from `Decimal` to either `Single` or `Double`, even with strict type checking enabled:

```
Dim x As Decimal = 1.2345678901234567890123456789D
Dim y As Single  = x    '*** y = 1.2345678
Dim z As Double  = x    '*** z = 1.23456789012346
```

The conversion from type `Decimal` to either `Single` or `Double` is a narrowing conversion because it has the potential to lose precision. Nevertheless, the Visual Basic .NET compiler allows you to perform this conversion implicitly without issuing an error message. In this case, it is possible to lose a small amount of precision.

The point being made here is that language designers have a degree of discretion regarding which kinds of implicit conversions are permitted. Ultimately, the rules for converting between primitive types are hard-coded into the logic of the Visual Basic .NET compiler. You will find that different managed languages demonstrate some minor differences with respect to the kinds of type conversions they allow implicitly.

Let's end this section by drilling down into the behavior of conversion operators such as `CInt`, `CDbl`, and `CType`. When you use one of these conversion operators to convert to a primitive type, the Visual Basic .NET compiler often generates extra value-added code to improve the conversion's chance of success. For example, what do you think happens when you write code to perform the following conversions from `Double` to `Integer`?

```
Dim d1 As Double = 7.5
Dim i1 As Integer = CInt(d1)

Dim d2 As Double = 8.5
Dim i2 As Integer = CInt(d2)
```

In this case, the Visual Basic .NET compiler doesn't just generate simple IL to perform a conversion from `Double` to `Integer`. Before it performs the conversion, the compiler creates extra code to call the `Round` method of the `System.Math` class. This extra call ensures that all conversions from floating-point numbers to integer types result in *banker's rounding*.

What is banker's rounding? It's a kind of rounding that usually results in greater accuracy than standard rounding. Consider floating-point numbers that lie exactly halfway between two `Integer` values, such as `7.5` and `8.5`. When these floating-point numbers are converted to `Integer` values, should they be rounded up or rounded down? The choice is not obvious.

The CLR uses a standard rounding scheme in which floating-point numbers that end with `.5` are always rounded up. Therefore, `7.5` would be rounded up to an `Integer` value of `8` and `8.5` would be rounded up to an `Integer` value of `9`. Of course, when many floating-point numbers end in `.5`, standard rounding becomes less accurate because every number is rounded up.

Banker's rounding works somewhat differently. The idea is to round down as often as one rounds up. With banker's rounding, if the value to the left of the decimal point is odd, the `.5` is rounded up; thus `7.5` is rounded up to the integer value `8`. Correspondingly, even numbers are rounded down; thus `8.5` is rounded down to the integer value `8`. On average, then, there should be an equal number of times when numbers are rounded down as when they are rounded up. As a result, banker's rounding is potentially more accurate than standard rounding.

As demonstrated by the rounding example, the Visual Basic .NET compiler often performs extra work behind the scenes on your behalf when you use the language's built-in conversion operators. This is one area where Visual Basic .NET adds value over other managed languages such as C#. For example, the C# compiler does not perform banker's rounding when you convert from a `Double` to an `Integer`. Instead, it carries out the conversion using standard rounding. If you wanted to use banker's rounding in C#, you would have to call the `System.Math.Round` method explicitly.

Another area in which the Visual Basic .NET compiler adds extra value is in the conversion from a string value to a numeric value. Examine the following code:

```
Dim s  As String  = "$1,000.99"
Dim d1 As Decimal = CDec(s)           '*** conversion succeeds
Dim d2 As Decimal = Decimal.Parse(s)  '*** conversion fails
```

When you perform a conversion such as that using `CDec`, the Visual Basic .NET compiler adds a call to a special helper method in the `Microsoft.VisualBasic` assembly. In this particular case, the compiler generates a call to a method named `FromString` that is provided by class `DecimalType` in the `Microsoft.VisualBasic.CompilerServices` namespace. This helper method performs a good deal of extra work to ensure that the conversion can be completed successfully, even in the presence of non-numeric characters such as "$" and ",". The standard .NET approach of calling `Decimal.Parse` fails with a runtime exception in this case.

Interestingly, the `FromString` method typically calls the `Parse` method of the underlying type to convert the string into a numeric value. As we saw earlier, the `FromString` method can do a few things that the `Parse` method cannot. Also note that the `FromString` method can convert strings that use the Visual Basic formatting style for hexadecimal numbers; the `Parse` method cannot. The `CDbl` operator is therefore successful in cases where the `Parse` method throws an exception:

```
Dim s  As String = "&HF00"
Dim d1 As Double = CDbl(s)           '*** conversion succeeds
Dim d2 As Double = Double.Parse(s)   '*** conversion fails
```

Of course, sometimes the `FromString` method will be unable to successfully convert a string value to a numeric value. Therefore, it may be necessary to catch an exception when you attempt to convert a string value. `FromString` throws an exception with a very specific error message when it fails. Consider the following code:

```
Dim s  As String = "junk"
Dim d1 As Double = CDbl(s)           '*** exception occurs
Dim d2 As Double = Double.Parse(s)   '*** exception occurs
```

When you attempt to convert a string value such as `"junk"` to a numeric value with the `CDbl` operator, an exception of type `InvalidCastException` is thrown with a friendly error message such as *Cast from string "junk" to type 'Double' is not valid*. When you attempt the same conversion using the

Parse method, an exception of type FormatException is thrown with a less-useful error message such as *Input string was not in a correct format.*

These examples demonstrate briefly how the Visual Basic .NET compiler adds an extra layer of value when you use the conversion operators that are built into the Visual Basic .NET language. Clearly, Visual Basic .NET adds a degree of productivity over other managed languages in this area. The idea is that the Visual Basic .NET compiler deals with many tedious details of type conversion so you don't have to. The intention is to make you more productive as a developer.

The Object Class

The Visual Basic .NET language supplies the Object keyword, which maps directly to the System.Object class. As shown in Figure 3.1, the Object class lies at the root of the CTS inheritance hierarchy. A key motivation for designing the CTS with a singly rooted inheritance hierarchy is that any type can be successfully converted to the Object class. Therefore, implicit conversions to the Object class are always legal. Here's an example of implicitly converting two values and one reference to variables of type Object:

```
'*** initialize instances of various types
Dim i As Integer = 10
Dim d As Double = 20.1
Dim human1 As Human = New Human()

'*** assign instances to Object variables
Dim obj1 As Object = i
Dim obj2 As Object = d
Dim obj3 As Object = human1
```

As shown in this code, you can always implicitly convert a value or a reference to the type Object. However, the reverse is never true when strict type checking is enabled. That is, under strict type checking, you cannot implicitly convert an Object value to any other type. This restriction makes sense because in general the compiler cannot determine what is stored in an Object variable. After all, an Object variable can store any type of value, or a reference to any type of object. The compiler sees that a conversion from Object to any other type has the potential to fail at runtime.

With strict type checking enabled, you must always perform an explicit conversion when assigning an `Object` variable to another type. The following code shows some examples of explicitly converting `Object` variables to more specific types:

```
'*** initialize Object variables to various values
Dim obj1 As Object = CInt(10)
Dim obj2 As Object = CDbl(20.1)
Dim obj3 As Object = New Human()

'*** explicitly convert Object variables back to specific types
Dim i2 As Integer = CInt(obj1)
Dim d2 As String = CDbl(obj2)
Dim human2 As Human = CType(obj3, Human)
```

It is very important for you to recognize that the `Object` class is a reference type. Therefore, when you create a local variable based on the `Object` class, you are really creating a reference. The following code illustrates a key point:

```
'*** create three Object variables
Dim ref1 As Object = New Human()
Dim ref2 As Object = ref1
Dim ref3 As Object
```

Figure 3.7 shows what happens when this code runs as part of some larger program. Three references are created on the call stack. The references `ref1` and `ref2` are initialized to point to the same `Human` object on the managed

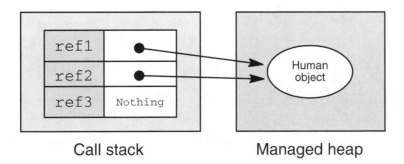

Call stack   Managed heap

FIGURE 3.7: Variables of type `Object` are references.

heap. The reference `ref3` is never explicitly initialized, so it is auto-initialized to a value of `Nothing`.

Here is the important point: Because the `Object` class is a reference type, an `Object` variable is always in one of two possible states—it either points to an object on the managed heap, or it has a value of `Nothing`. This idea isn't difficult to understand when you are working with references to obvious objects like strings and humans, but things become more interesting when you assign a *value* on the call stack to an `Object` variable. This type of assignment results in a phenomenon known as *boxing,* which is discussed next.

Boxing

In certain situations, the CLR must promote a value to an object so as to give it object-like characteristics—a process called boxing. To box a value, the CLR silently copies the memory for the value into a newly created wrapper object on the managed heap. The idea is that a boxed value can be treated like any other object, because it *is* an object.

A common situation in which boxing occurs is when you assign a value type to the `Object` type. Recall that an `Object` reference either is `Nothing` or points to an object on the managed heap. Therefore, assigning a value to an `Object` reference triggers the CLR to box the value. Here's a simple example:

```
'*** create value on the stack
Dim val1 As Integer = 42

'*** assign value to Object variable
Dim ref1 As Object = var1
```

Here `val1` is a value type variable created on the call stack. When you assign this value to the `Object` variable `ref1`, the CLR boxes the value by copying it into a newly created wrapper object on the managed heap, as shown in Figure 3.8. A reference to this wrapper object is then assigned to the `Object` variable `ref1`. In the end, two distinct instances of the value `42` exist.

Programmers do not have to write code to explicitly perform a boxing operation. Instead, the Visual Basic .NET compiler automatically determines when a boxing operation is required and generates the appropriate

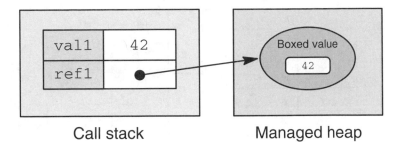

FIGURE 3.8: The CLR boxes a value type when you assign it to an Object reference.

IL. From the perspective of the programmer, boxing occurs transparently behind the scenes.

If you are curious as to whether boxing is being performed in a particular situation, you can use the ILDASM.EXE utility to inspect the IL within your assembly. By examining the IL for your methods, you can determine whether the Visual Basic .NET compiler added boxing instructions to your code.

The next question you might ask is this: Should you be concerned about boxing? The answer is: It depends. On the one hand, boxing slows things down because the CLR has to create, manage, and clean up after a heap-based object. On the other hand, the performance overhead of boxing a single value is usually insignificant. Nevertheless, you'll want to avoid the overhead associated with boxing on some occasions.

As an example, suppose you need to store 10,000 integer values in memory. To do so, you can use an Integer array or an Object array. The former is an array of values; the latter is an array of references. If you use the array based on the Object type, then every Integer value must be boxed. Obviously, forcing the CLR to create and manage 10,000 heap-based objects unnecessarily is something to avoid.

Apart from its effects on performance, boxing requires your attention because occasionally you'll need to *unbox* a value that has been boxed. That is, you may need to explicitly convert a boxed object back into a value type to retrieve its value. Carefully step through the following code:

```
Dim val1 As Integer = 42
Dim ref1 As Object = val1        '*** boxing
Dim val2 As Integer = CInt(ref1) '*** unboxing
```

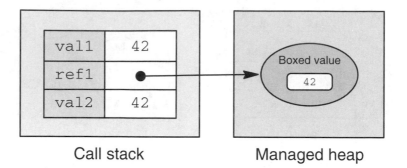

Call stack   Managed heap

FIGURE 3.9: Unboxing involves extracting the value from a heap-based wrapper object.

In this example, three different places in memory contain the integer value 42 (see Figure 3.9). In the last step, when the Object reference ref1 is converted and stored into the Integer variable val2, unboxing occurs. That is, the CLR copies the memory inside the heap-based wrapper object into a standard value type.

Unboxing always requires an explicit conversion when strict type checking is enabled. The previous code fragment performed an explicit unboxing operation using the CInt conversion operator. When you unbox a value using a conversion operator such as CInt, CDbl, or CType, the Visual Basic .NET compiler adds a call to a helper method named FromObject in the Microsoft.VisualBasic assembly. For example, in the case of CInt, the compiler adds a call to the FromObject method provided by the IntegerType class in the Microsoft.VisualBasic.CompilerServices namespace.

The FromObject method is similar to the FromString method that was described earlier in this chapter. Both methods perform extra work to ensure that the conversion has a greater chance of success. However, the FromObject method must work even harder than FromString because the source of the conversion could be a boxed numeric value, a string, or any other type of object or value.

Visual Basic .NET also provides the DirectCast operator, which offers an alternative technique for unboxing a value. This operator seeks to optimize conversions that involve unboxing values from Object references.

Examine the following code, which shows two alternative techniques for unboxing an `Integer` value:

```
Dim val1 As Integer = 42
Dim ref1 As Object = val1                       '*** box Integer value
Dim val2 As Integer = CType(ref1, Integer)      '*** unbox safely
Dim val3 As Integer = DirectCast(ref1, Integer) '*** unbox quickly
```

As shown here, you can unbox an `Integer` value by using either the `CType` operator or the `DirectCast` operator. In fact, the calling syntax is the same for both operators. The difference is that the `DirectCast` operator works more quickly, because it does not call helper methods in `Microsoft.Visu-alBasic`. When you use the `DirectCast` operator, the compiler simply adds an `unbox` instruction into the IL of the resulting assembly.

As you might expect, the `DirectCast` operator requires less overhead than operators such as `CInt`, `CDbl`, and `CType`, so the CLR unboxes a value in the most efficient way possible. The drawback to using `DirectCast` is that it is far more prone to failure. This operator succeeds only when the type of value you are unboxing is an exact match for the type to which you are converting.

An example will help illustrate this point. Consider the following code, in which an `Integer` is boxed and then unboxed in various ways:

```
'*** box an Integer value
Dim val1 As Integer = 42
Dim ref1 As Object = val1

'*** unbox the value
Dim s As Short = DirectCast(ref1, Short)        '*** fails
Dim i As Integer = DirectCast(ref1, Integer)    '*** succeeds
Dim l As Long = DirectCast(ref1, Long)          '*** fails
```

The `DirectCast` operator succeeds only if you unbox this value as an `Integer`. If you attempt to unbox an `Integer` value with `DirectCast` into some other type such as `Short` or `Long`, the operator fails at runtime and throws an exception. What should strike you as strange is that you cannot even perform a widening conversion from `Integer` to `Long`—the source type and the target type must match exactly.

While operators such as `CShort`, `CInt`, `CLng`, and `CType` result in more overhead, they succeed in many cases where `DirectCast` fails. If you opt for the more efficient approach and unbox using the DirectCast operator, you must ensure that the source type and the target conversion type are exact matches.

The DirectCast operator has another important restriction. Unlike the other conversion operators, it cannot be used when the source of the conversion is itself a value. As noted earlier, DirectCast can be used only when the source of the conversion is a reference type. For example, the following use of DirectCast yields a compile-time error because val1 is of type Integer:

```
Dim val1 As Integer = 42
Dim val2 As Short = DirectCast(val1, Short)   '*** compile-time error

Dim val1 As Integer = 42
Dim val2 As Short = CType(val1, Short)   '*** works correctly
```

Once again, the conversion operators such as CInt and CType are more flexible because they support the conversion of both values and references.

Let's summarize this discussion of the DirectCast operator. When you are unboxing a reference and you know that the boxed value and the target type are exact matches, the DirectCast operator is the fastest way to get the job done. When you are converting between primitive types, the other conversion operators such as CInt and CType are more flexible and safer to use. Finally, when you are converting between two reference types, the DirectCast and CType operators perform identically.

In general, it is recommended that you use the CType operator instead of the DirectCast operator. You should restrict your usage of DirectCast to situations where you are unboxing reference variables and can match the boxed value to the target conversion type.

What Happened to the Variant Type from Visual Basic 6?

Remember the Variant type from earlier versions of Visual Basic? When you migrate to Visual Basic .NET, you should consider this type to be a thing of the past. That's because Variant has not been included in the mainstream programming model of either the .NET Framework or the CTS.

The Visual Studio .NET IDE makes this point abundantly clear by detecting whenever you type the `Variant` keyword into a Visual Basic .NET source file and automatically replacing it with the `Object` keyword.

The `Object` class of the CTS is similar to the old `Variant` type from Visual Basic 6 in one sense: It is compatible with all other types. At the same time, another aspect of the `Object` class makes it very different from the old `Variant` type: The `Object` class always acts as a reference type. A major reason that the `Variant` type could not be migrated to the CTS was that its behavior switched between that of a value type and that of a reference type. Such behavior is illegal for a managed type in the .NET Framework. In the CTS, every type must behave as either a value type or a reference type.

You might notice that the libraries of the FCL do contain a type named `Variant`. This type is only intended for interoperability with unmanaged COM code written in languages such as Visual Basic 6. Even when you are writing such code, you probably won't need the `Variant` type because the interoperability layer between managed code and COM code is able to automatically convert these types behind the scenes.

Designing with the `Object` Class

Designing variables, parameters, and fields in terms of the `Object` class can provide a great deal of flexibility. For example, you can design a method with a parameter based on the `Object` class, as shown in Listing 3.3. One caller could invoke this method and pass an `Integer` value to it. Another caller could invoke this method and pass a `String` to it. When a caller's code is compiled against your method definition, the compiler will accept any type of parameter. Also remember that it's perfectly legal to call a method with an `Object` parameter by passing a value of `Nothing`.

You should make an important observation about method parameters defined in terms of the `Object` class: They do not allow for any kind of compile-time type checking. When a programmer calls a method with an `Object` parameter, the Visual Basic .NET compiler cannot make any assumptions about the type of the parameter that must be passed at run

LISTING 3.3: A method with increased flexibility due to the `Object` parameter

```
'*** param1 expects either an Integer or a String
Public Sub DoTask(ByVal param1 As Object)
  If param1 Is Nothing Then
    '*** throw ArgumentNullException to caller
  ElseIf TypeOf param1 Is Integer Then
    '*** process parameter as an Integer
  ElseIf TypeOf param1 Is String Then
    '*** process parameter as a string
  Else '*** handle all other cases
    '*** throw ArgumentException to caller
  End If
End Sub
```

time. As a consequence, the compiler cannot catch the mistake if the client-side programmer passes the wrong type of data. Thus any situation in which a caller passes an invalid parameter value becomes a runtime problem that must be addressed via defensive code practices.

Let's look more closely at Listing 3.3, which includes a method with an `Object` parameter. In particular, note that the code has been written in a defensive fashion to handle parameter values not of the expected type. When you write the implementation for a method that accepts an `Object` parameter, you must assume that the caller could pass any kind of parameter. In Listing 3.3, the `DoTask` method first checks whether the incoming parameter value is set to `Nothing`. If the parameter is not `Nothing`, `DoTask` then examines the type of the instance passed in `param1` as follows:

```
If TypeOf param1 Is Integer Then
```

Using similar syntax you can inspect the parameter to see whether it is of another type, such as `Double`, `String`, `Date`, or `Human`. Finally, the implementation of `DoTask` provides an `Else` clause to handle the situation when the caller passes a parameter of an unexpected type.

It is not recommended that you write code in this fashion. Quite the opposite—in most situations, you should avoid writing this kind of code. The need to program in this defensive style is one of the primary disadvantages to defining methods with parameters of type `Object`. When you define variables, parameters, and fields using more specific types, you eliminate the need for custom code that handles cases where you encounter inappropriate types, because the compiler ensures that only values of the proper type(s) are involved.

Programming with Strings

The CTS provides the `System.String` class to assist developers in working with strings of character-based data. The `String` class manages data internally using a private array of `Char` values, which means that strings are always stored using Unicode characters. The `String` class also provides a variety of public members to assist you with string-related tasks such as comparing, searching, parsing, and formatting. In Visual Basic .NET, the `String` keyword maps to the `System.String` class.

Note that the `String` class is a reference type and not a value type. As a consequence, strings are represented as first-class objects in the CTS. Also, when you declare a local variable using the `String` class, you are merely creating a reference on the call stack:

```
Dim s As String  '*** a reference variable, not the string itself!
```

When you assign a string to a `String` variable, you are actually setting the reference so that it points to a `String` object on the managed heap (much like in Figure 3.7).

The architects of the CTS chose to make the `String` class be a reference type to increase the efficiency of working with string data. Strings can become very large; it isn't uncommon for a string to consist of hundreds—or even thousands—of characters. In such cases it's impractical to allocate memory for strings on the call stack. Furthermore, it's expensive to make multiple copies of a large string when passing it from one method to another. It's much more efficient to pass the string by simply copying the reference to the `String` object.

While the `String` class is a reference type, you are not required to program against it in the same way that you do with other reference types. Instead, the `String` class receives special treatment from the Visual Basic .NET compiler. For example, when you want to create an object from other reference types, you must use the `New` operator. This step isn't necessary when you want to create a `String` object; you can simply assign a string literal:

```
Dim s1 As String = "Rosebud"
```

This technique allows you to write code in the same way as if you were initializing a value type variable. When you compile this code, the Visual Basic .NET compiler generates the IL required to create a `String` object on the managed heap and to initialize the reference variable `s1` so that it points to that object.

Remember that a `String` object is really just an array of `Char` values. If you want to inspect individual characters within a `String` object, use the instance property named `Chars`. The `Chars` property provides access to the individual `Char` values using a zero-based indexing scheme:

```
Dim s As String = "Rosebud"
Dim char1, char4, charN As Char
char1 = s.Chars(0)              '*** get first Char
char4 = s.Chars(3)              '*** get fourth Char
charN = s.Chars(s.Length - 1)   '*** get last Char
```

If you need to walk through a string and inspect each `Char` value individually, you can do so by using a simple `For Each` loop:

```
Dim s As String = "Rosebud"

Dim c As Char
For Each c In s   '*** loop executes once for each Char c in String s
  System.Console.WriteLine(c)
Next
```

Now let's look at an example that demonstrates how the `String` type differs from primitive types. Always remember that you are dealing with `String` references as well as `String` objects. Consider the following code, which creates three `String` references but only one `String` object:

```
Dim s1 As String = "Rosebud"
Dim s2 As String = s1
Dim s3 As String
```

Figure 3.10 shows the memory layout produced by this code. The first line of code creates a new `String` object and assigns the reference to variable `s1`. The next line copies the reference from `s1` into a second `String` variable `s2`. The result is two references that point to the same `String` object on the managed heap. The last line declares but never initializes the variable `s3`, so it is auto-initialized to the value `Nothing`.

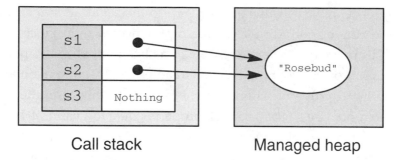

FIGURE 3:10: Strings are represented as objects on the managed heap.

Because the `String` class is a reference type, you occasionally have to differentiate between a `String` variable with a value of `Nothing` and a `String` variable that points to an empty `String` object. Consider the following code:

```
Dim s1 As String
Dim s2 As String = ""
Dim s3 As String = String.Empty
```

How do these three lines of code differ? The first line of code declares a reference variable s1. Because s1 is not explicitly initialized, it is auto-initialized with a value of `Nothing`. This result is very different from the effects of the next two lines of code. The second line explicitly initializes the reference s2 to point to a `String` object that represents an empty string. The third line of code has the same effect as the second in that s3 points to a `String` object that represents an empty string.

Now let's take this example one step further, discovering why a `String` variable pointing to an empty `String` object is often preferred over a `String` variable with a value of `Nothing`. Imagine a situation in which you want to access an instance member of the `String` class through a `String` reference. For example:

```
Dim s1 As String
Dim length1 As Integer = s1.Length '*** runtime exception

Dim s2 As String = String.Empty
Dim length2 As Integer = s2.Length '*** works without any problem
```

The reference s1 has a value of Nothing, so the application will throw a NullReferenceException if you attempt to access an instance member through it. In contrast, the reference s2 has been initialized to point to a valid String object, so it can be used to access an instance member such as the Length property without any problem. In this case, the String object referenced by s2 has a Length property equal to a value of 0. Clearly, a String reference pointing to an empty String object is safer to use.

You should consider initializing String references to a value of String.Empty instead of allowing them to auto-initialize to a value of Nothing. This approach is especially recommended when you are passing String references to other methods written by other developers. When you are writing methods that accept String parameters, also consider conducting tests to determine whether String references have a value of Nothing before using them to access instance members.

Concatenating Strings

In general programming, you are often required to build strings by concatenating other strings. Visual Basic .NET offers a variety of concatenation techniques. For example, you can concatenate strings with an explicit call to a shared method of the String class named Concat.

```
'*** create a new string object
Dim s1 As String = "Rose"
Dim s2 As String = "bud"

'*** call String.Concat explicitly
Dim s3 As String = String.Concat(s1, s2)
```

Alternatively, you can concatenate strings using the & operator. When you use this operator, the Visual Basic .NET compiler will typically call the Concat method for you behind the scenes:

```
'*** call String.Concat implicitly
Dim s4 As String = s1 & s2
```

In some cases, the Visual Basic .NET compiler will optimize the code by concatenating strings together at compile time. This technique speeds things up because an application doesn't have to perform the work at runtime. For example, if you concatenate two string literals such as "Rose" and "bud" within the same line of code, the compiler will concatenate them into a single string literal at compile time:

```
Dim s As String = "Rose" & "bud"    '*** optimized to s = "Rosebud"
```

Now that you have seen some simple examples of concatenating strings, it's time to take note of a very important characteristic of String objects: Once a String object has been initialized, its string data is *immutable*. As a consequence, you cannot, for example, change the length of the string held by a String object. Nor can you change any of the string's characters. From your perspective, a String object becomes a read-only entity once it has been created.

The fact that String objects are immutable makes their use more predictable. A simple example will illustrate this point. Imagine an application in which five different objects all hold references that point to a single String object. In this scenario, all five objects are looking at the same string data. What is the benefit of a String object being immutable in this situation? It's important to see no object can change the actual string from the perspective of the other four.

While String objects are immutable, this read-only behavior can be deceptive when you are writing code with Visual Basic .NET. You can write code that appears to modify a String object but actually doesn't, as in the following two lines of code:

```
Dim s1 As String = "Rose"   '*** create string object
s1 &= "bud"                 '*** create an entirely new string object
```

Here the first line of code loads a String object containing the string "Rose" and assigns a reference to the variable s1. What happens when the second line of code executes? It does not modify the first String object held by the reference s1. Instead, this line of code yields a new String object containing the string "Rosebud" and sets s1 to refer to this new object.

While the syntax of Visual Basic .NET provides the illusion that you can modify String objects, that's not the reality. In fact, the Visual Basic .NET compiler really generates extra code to create new String objects behind the scenes. While this can make things convenient, you have to be careful, because naive usage of the String class can result in inefficient code.

An example will demonstrate how performance trouble can result from misuse of this class. Imagine you are creating a server-side application in which you need to concatenate many different text elements to create an HTML page string. Listing 3.4 shows the typical approach. If you stop and think about this code, you should easily recognize that it will result in excessive overhead—the code will create and ultimately force the clean up of more than 100 String objects each time it executes. Obviously, this style of coding can adversely affect performance, especially if the server-side code is servicing many client requests.

LISTING 3.4: The **wrong** way to dynamically build a string

```
Dim WebPage As String = String.Empty
WebPage &= "<html>"        '*** create 1st String object
WebPage &= "<body>"        '*** create 2nd String object

For i = 1 To 100
   '*** use &= operator 100 times to generate HTML page content...
Next

WebPage &= "</body>"        '*** create 103rd String object
WebPage &= "</html>"        '*** create 104th String object
```

To concatenate large strings, you should use the StringBuilder class. As its name implies, the StringBuilder class allows you to build strings using a preallocated memory buffer. This approach enables you to avoid the overhead of creating many temporary String objects when you are dynamically constructing large, complicated strings.

The StringBuilder class is defined in the System.Text namespace. When you create a StringBuilder object, you can specify the initial number of characters that the buffer should hold; the buffer will grow as the amount of string data exceeds this initial amount. Once you have created the String-Builder object, you build the desired string by calling instance methods such as Append, Insert, Remove, and Replace. You then convert the contents of the buffer into a String object by calling its ToString method.

Listing 3.5 demonstrates the proper use of the StringBuilder class to efficiently build the same HTML page string shown in Listing 3.4.

Listing 3.5 The correct way to dynamically build a string

```
'*** create StringBuilder object with initial size of 1024 characters
Dim sb As New System.Text.StringBuilder(1024)

'*** append string data to buffer
sb.Append("<html>")
sb.Append("<body>")

For i = 1 To 100
  '*** call Append 100 times to generate HTML page content...
Next

sb.Append("</body>")
sb.Append("</html>")

'*** convert string data to String object
Dim WebPage As String = sb.ToString()
```

Using the `StringBuilder` class takes a little more effort than concatenating strings together using the `&` operator. Nevertheless, it's critical that you learn to work with the `StringBuilder` class. The code in Listing 3.5 is far more efficient than that in Listing 3.4, simply because it reduces the number of temporary `String` objects created as a side effect of the `&` operator.

`String.Format` is another efficient mechanism for building strings, as it uses the `StringBuilder` class internally to generate a result. Here's a quick example of building a string from three components—s1, s2, and s3:

```
result = String.Format("{0}{1}{2}", s1, s2, s3)
```

The `String.Format` method is discussed further in the section "Formatting Strings" later in this chapter.

Comparing Strings Using `String` Class Methods

It is a very common programming task to compare two strings to determine whether they are equal. You can compare two strings for equality in several ways. The most straightforward approach is to use the `Equals` instance method of the `String` class:

```
Dim s1 As String = "Rosebud"
Dim s2 As String = "rosebud"

If s1.Equals(s2) Then
  '*** do something if strings are equal
Else
  '*** do something else
End If
```

In this example, the string comparison returns `False` because the `Equals` method conducts the comparison in a case-sensitive fashion. If you want control over whether the comparison is conducted in a case-sensitive or case-insensitive manner, you call the `Compare` method of the `String` class:

```
Dim s1 As String = "Rosebud"
Dim s2 As String = "rosebud"

'*** perform case-insensitive, culture-specific comparison
If String.Compare(s1, s2, True) = 0 Then
  '*** strings are equal
End If

'*** perform case-sensitive, culture-specific comparison
If String.Compare(s1, s2, False) = 0 Then
  '*** strings are equal
End If
```

The `Compare` method returns a value of `0` if the two strings are equal, a negative value if `s1` is less than `s2`, and a positive value if `s1` is greater than `s2`. Normally, a string X is less than a string Y if X appears before Y in the dictionary.

The `Compare` method doesn't simply check whether both strings denote the exact same sequence of characters. Instead, it conducts a more sophisticated test using a set of culture-specific rules. For instance, two strings considered equal in one language such as Spanish or German might not be equal in another language such as English.

The `Compare` method uses a `CultureInfo` object internally to obtain culture-specific information when it conducts its comparison. If you don't pass a `CultureInfo` object explicitly, the `Compare` method creates one automatically from the user's machine settings. Alternatively, you can explicitly pass a `CultureInfo` object as a parameter when calling `Compare`. For example, if you wanted to compare two strings using the cultural rules for U.S. English, you would call `String.Compare` as follows:

```
Dim ci As New System.Globalization.CultureInfo("en-US")
If String.Compare(s1, s2, True, ci) = 0 Then
  '*** strings are equal based on rules of U.S. English
End If
```

Culture-specific comparisons conducted with the `Compare` method are fairly expensive, so you should use this method only when you definitely want to perform a string comparison using culture-specific rules. When you don't need to perform a string comparison using culture-specific rules, select a different comparison technique, such as the `Equals` method or the `CompareOrdinal` method.

The `CompareOrdinal` method is also part of the `String` class. The main difference between the `CompareOrdinal` method and the `Compare` method is that the former never uses culture-specific rules when conducting a string comparison. For this reason, comparisons conducted with the `CompareOr-dinal` method are faster than those conducted with the `Compare` method. Note that the semantics for the return value of `CompareOrdinal` are defined in the exact manner as those for `Compare`—that is, an integer <, =, or > 0:

```
Dim s1 As String = "Rosebud"
Dim s2 As String = "rosebud"

'*** perform case-insensitive comparison
If String.CompareOrdinal(s1, s2, True) = 0 Then
  '*** strings are equal
End If

'*** perform case-sensitive comparison
If String.CompareOrdinal(s1, s2, False) = 0 Then
  '*** strings are equal
End If
```

The `CompareOrdinal` method is also more flexible than the `Equals` method because it provides a `Boolean` parameter that lets you specify whether you want to perform the comparison in a case-sensitive or case-insensitive fashion. For this reason, `CompareOrdinal` provides the fastest way to conduct a case-insensitive comparison.

Comparing Strings Using the = Operator

Many developers who have experience with earlier versions of Visual Basic are accustomed to conducting string comparisons using the = operator. Visual Basic .NET likewise supports the use of the = operator to compare strings, but the behavior of this operator is subtly different in the new language. Let's take a moment to discuss what the Visual Basic .NET compiler does when you conduct a string comparison using the = operator.

The first point to understand about using the = operator to compare strings is that the Visual Basic .NET compiler automatically generates a call to a special helper method named `StrCmp` from the `Microsoft.Visual-Basic` assembly. The `StrCmp` method is defined in the `StringType` class within the `Microsoft.VisualBasic.CompilerServices` namespace.

The second point to understand is that string comparisons conducted using the = operator are affected by a compile-time setting known as `Option Compare`. A unit of code can be compiled using a setting of either `Option Compare Binary` or `Option Compare Text`. The former denotes case-sensitive comparisons, and the latter performs case-insensitive comparisons. You can change the compilation setting on a project-wide basis by using the `Project Properties` dialog. The default setting for new projects is `Option Compare Binary`. You can also adjust the compilation setting for an individual source file by adding an `Option Compare` statement at the top:

```
Option Compare Text
```

The usage of `Option Compare` is identical to that of `Option Explicit` and `Option Strict` discussed in Chapter 2. Placing an `Option Compare` statement at the top of a source file overrides the project-wide setting for the code in that source file. Source files that do not include an `Option Compare` statement are compiled according to the project-wide setting.

When the Visual Basic .NET compiler generates an internal call to the `StrCmp` method, it passes a `Boolean` parameter to indicate whether the code containing the string comparison was compiled using `Option Compare Binary` or `Option Compare Text`. The `StrCmp` method contains conditional logical to conduct the comparison one way for `Option Compare Binary` and a different way for `Option Compare Text`.

Suppose you decide to compare strings with a compile-time setting of `Option Compare Binary`. String comparisons are conducted in a case-sensitive fashion without using culture-specific rules, because the `StrCmp` method calls the `CompareOrdinal` method of the `String` class and inspects the return value for you.

However, unlike a direct call to `Compare` or `CompareOrdinal`, comparing strings with the = operator evaluates to a `Boolean` value. Therefore, using the = operator instead of calling `Compare` or `CompareOrdinal` directly can result in code that's easier to read and write. For example:

```
Dim s1 As String = "Rosebud"
Dim s2 As String = "rosebud"

If s1 = s2 Then
   '*** do something if strings are equal
Else
   '*** do something else if strings are not equal
End If
```

The underlying `StrCmp` method provides extra convenience because it interprets a `String` reference with a value of `Nothing` as equivalent to a `String` reference that points to an empty `String` object. Consider this simple example:

```
Dim s1 As String
Dim s2 As String = String.Empty

If s1 = s2 Then
   '*** this statement block will execute!
End If
```

As you can see, the `String` variable s1 holds a value of `Nothing`. The `String` variable s2 points to an empty `String` object. These two variables compare as equal when you use the = operator.

This behavior is helpful because it eliminates the need to differentiate between `String` references with a value of `Nothing` and `String` references that point to empty `String` objects. The following method definition illustrates this point by conducting a single check to see whether an incoming `String` parameter contains a nonempty string.

```
Public Sub Method1(ByVal param1 As String)
  '*** check that parameter is valid
  If param1 = String.Empty Then
    '*** throw exception due to invalid parameter
  End If

  '*** continue with method execution
End Sub
```

The evaluation of param1 = String.Empty returns True regardless of whether the parameter points to an empty String object or contains a value of Nothing. This behavior is convenient because it eliminates the need to perform two individual tests to ensure that the parameter denotes a String object of length greater than zero.

How do string comparisons with the = operator change when you compile your code using Option Compare Text? First, the string comparisons are conducted in a case-insensitive fashion. Second, the underlying StrCmp method calls the String.Compare method (not CompareOrdinal), which means that strings are compared using culture-specific rules. This behavior can prove valuable when you need to conduct string comparisons in a culture-specific fashion, but it can contribute unnecessary overhead when culture-specific comparisons are unnecessary.

Unfortunately, there is no way to use the = operator to perform a case-insensitive comparison without incurring the overhead of a culture-specific comparison. Remember—you can always conduct case-insensitive comparisons by calling the method String.CompareOrdinal yourself, and do so without incurring the overhead of locale-specific checks. You can also conduct case-sensitive comparisons using the String.Equals method. Some developers prefer these two techniques because the results do not vary according to whether the code was compiled under Option Compare Binary or under Option Compare Text.

String Conversions

The CTS guarantees that you can convert any value or object into a string. The CTS can make this guarantee because the Object class defines a method named ToString that returns a string-based representation. As you may recall from Figure 3.1, every type (except an interface) inherits from the `Object` class. Therefore, every value and every object exposes an implementation of the `ToString` method. Here are just two examples:

```
Dim AccountBalance As Decimal = 2324.31D
Dim s1 As String = AccountBalance.ToString()

Dim TodaysDate As Date = Date.Today
Dim s2 As String = TodaysDate.ToString()
```

In addition to calling `ToString`, you can explicitly convert a primitive value to a string by using the `CStr` or `CType` conversion operator. Using either of these operators has the same effect as calling `ToString` directly.

Converting to and from the `String` type can require more attention than it did in earlier versions of Visual Basic. In the conversion matrix shown in Figure 3.6, for example, notice that the `Char` type is the only type that can be implicitly converted to the `String` type. When strict type checking is enabled, a compile-time error will occur if you attempt to implicitly convert a numeric value to a string, as in the following code fragment:

```
Dim i As Integer = 714
Dim s As String = i    '*** does not compile with Option Strict On
```

Visual Basic .NET does provide a little extra convenience when you use the `&` operator to concatenate strings. When you concatenate values using the `&` operator, the Visual Basic .NET compiler assumes that you are converting any nonstring types to strings. Therefore, the compiler allows for an implicit conversion from a numeric type to the `String` type, as in the following code fragment:

```
Dim i As Integer = 714
Dim s As String = "The magic number is " & i   '*** this does compile
```

You are encouraged to use the `&` operator instead of the + operator when concatenating string values. While both operators can get the job done, the `&` operator is more strongly typed because it can be used for string concatenation only. By comparison, the + operator does not provide as much type safety because it can also be used to perform operations such as addition. When you use the `&` operator to concatenate strings, you gain a stronger guarantee that your code will do what you expect it to do.

Formatting Strings

Some managed types expose a version of the ToString method that allows you to customize the formatting of the returned string. In particular, the ToString method exposed by some types provides a parameter for you to pass a *formatting code*. All of the CTS's primitive types support formatting codes. This makes it very easy to format things such as dates, times, and currency values:

```
Dim AccountBalance As Decimal = 2324.31D
Dim s1 As String = AccountBalance.ToString("$#,##0.00")

Dim TodaysDate As Date = Date.Today
Dim s2 As String = TodaysDate.ToString("MMMM d, yyyy")
```

Each type that supports formatting codes provides its own unique set of codes. You should consult the online documentation for the FCL to see which formatting codes are supported by the types in which you are interested. For example, the documentation for the ToString method of the type System.DateTime includes a list of the formatting codes available for formatting dates and times.

You have just seen one way to make formatting codes available via the ToString method. There is a second technique that you might find equally useful. The String class provides a public shared method named Format that helps turn a set of strings into one string (e.g., when you are building an SQL query string).

When you call the Format method, you must pass a *format string* as the first parameter. A format string contains a mixture of static text and one or more *placeholders*. The Format method dynamically inserts string values into the locations of the format string marked by the placeholders.

To add a placeholder to a format string, you place a zero-based index number between the { and } characters. For example, the first placeholder is {0} and the second placeholder is {1}. A simple example will demonstrate how this technique works. Suppose you want to format a string containing today's date and a user's account balance. The code in Listing 3.6 will perform this function, generating a string such as "Your account balance is 2324.31 as of 12/27/2002 12:00:00 AM". In other words, the call to String.Format in Listing 3.6 converts the second parameter into a string and inserts it into the {0} placeholder, then converts the third parameter into a string and inserts it into the {1} placeholder.

LISTING 3.6: Using `String.Format` to dynamically build a string

```
Dim AccountBalance As Decimal = 2324.31D
Dim TodaysDate As Date = Date.Today

Dim FormatString, Output As String
FormatString = "Your account balance is {0} as of {1}"
Output = String.Format(FormatString, AccountBalance, TodaysDate)
```

The `String.Format` method can prove even more useful, because you can define placeholders using type-specific formatting codes. Let's make the following minor modification to the format string in Listing 3.6:

```
FormatString = "Your account balance is {0:C} as of {1:MM/d/yyyy}"
```

Now the user's account balance will be formatted in the general currency format because the first placeholder has the C formatting code. Similarly, the date will be formatted using custom formatting instructions because the second placeholder contains the formatting code M/d/yyyy. The resulting output string now looks more like `"Your account balance is $2,324.31 as of 12/27/2002"`.

Programming with Arrays

An array is a fixed-length data structure that allows you to store and retrieve elements based on an index number. When you create an array, you get to choose its *length*. The length of an array determines how many elements the array can hold. An array is also a strongly typed data structure. Every array is defined in terms of a specific type such as `Integer`, `String`, or `Object`; this type determines what type of element can be stored within the array.

Most of the Visual Basic .NET syntax for arrays resembles that used in earlier versions of Visual Basic, with a few important exceptions. One of these differences relates to an array's lower bound. In earlier versions of Visual Basic, you could choose the lower bound when you created the array. Some programmers preferred creating arrays with a lower bound of 0; others preferred creating arrays with a lower bound of 1.

In Visual Basic .NET, all arrays have a lower bound of 0. While some programmers will regret the loss of one-based arrays, the fact that arrays are always zero-based promotes a new level of consistency throughout .NET by eliminating any uncertainty about whether a given array is zero-based.

In truth, it's technically possible to create an array in Visual Basic .NET with a lower bound other than zero. Two factors make this strategy impractical, however:

- Arrays that have a lower bound other than 0 are not CLS-compliant.
- The array syntax provided by Visual Basic .NET (and C#) only supports zero-based arrays.

For these reasons, it is reasonable to assume that all the arrays you create and consume will have a lower bound of 0.

Let's start by looking at a simple example of creating an array and initializing all of its elements. The following code creates an `Integer` array with four elements:

```
'*** create four-element integer array
Dim array1(3) As Integer

'*** populate each element
array1(0) = 2
array1(1) = 4
array1(2) = 6
array1(3) = 8
```

This array syntax is unchanged from earlier versions of Visual Basic. When you create an array, you denote the number of elements by specifying the upper bound. In this example, the array has a lower bound of 0, an upper bound of 3, and hence 4 elements. Read and write access to elements within the array is available by enclosing the appropriate index value within parentheses.

In the CTS, all arrays are reference types. Arrays are thus first-class objects in the .NET programming model. In addition, array objects are always created on the managed heap, as shown in Figure 3.11. Like other objects, an array object (and its elements) can be accessed only through a reference.

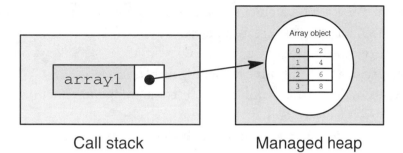

FIGURE 3.11: An array is a heap-based object.

The preceding example created the array object as part of the declaration of the array reference variable. It is also legal to separate these operations into distinct lines of code. Some (including the authors) would argue that separating the declaration of the reference variable from the creation of the array object more closely models reality. To do so, you use the ReDim statement of Visual Basic .NET:

```
'*** declare array reference variable
Dim array1() As Integer

'*** create heap-based array object
ReDim array1(3)
```

Programmers who have experience in earlier versions of Visual Basic will undoubtedly remember the ReDim keyword. The syntax for writing a ReDim statement in Visual Basic .NET remains the same, requiring the name of the array variable and the desired upper bound. However, the behavior of the ReDim statement is somewhat different in Visual Basic .NET.

When the ReDim statement executes in Visual Basic .NET, it creates an array object on the managed heap and assigns a reference to the array reference variable in the ReDim statement. Thus using the ReDim statement to create an array object is similar to using the New operator to create an object from a standard reference type.

The designers of Visual Basic .NET chose to retain the ReDim keyword for creating array objects so that the syntax for array programming would remain similar to that employed in earlier versions of Visual Basic. In reality, the name of the keyword doesn't accurately describe what is really going on. The `ReDim` statement is not used to "redimension" an existing array object, but rather to create a new array object. The Visual Basic .NET language would be more straightforward if the `ReDim` keyword were replaced with a more intuitive keyword, such as `CreateArray`. When you see the `ReDim` keyword or use it in your code, think of the fictitious `CreateArray` keyword instead.

When you create an array object, all elements are initially set to their default values. For example, all elements within a numeric array are initially set to a value of zero. If you want to specify nonzero initialization values, Visual Basic .NET provides a convenient new syntax for initializing the elements of an array. After declaring the array reference variable, you create an array object and initialize its elements by including a list of values enclosed in curly braces, known as an *array initialization list*. The following code demonstrates the use of both integer and string initialization lists:

```
Dim array1() As Integer = {2, 4, 6, 8}
Dim array2() As String = {"Albert", "Mort", "Elvis"}
```

When you use an array initialization list, you cannot include the upper bound of the array in the declaration of the array reference variable. The upper bound is automatically determined by the number of values included in the initialization list. For example, `array2` has an upper bound of 2.

Also note that the array initialization list does not need to be part of the array reference variable declaration. It is perfectly legal to create an array object using an array initialization list and then assign it to an array reference variable that was declared on an earlier line. For example:

```
'*** declare array reference variables
Dim array1() As Integer
Dim array2() As String

'*** create and initialize new array objects
array1 = New Integer() {2, 4, 6, 8}
array2 = New String() {"Moe", "Curly", "Larry"}
```

In the preceding code, this task is accomplished by using the `New` operator followed by the array type name, empty parentheses, and the array initialization list. While this syntax isn't overly intuitive, it seems very handy once you become accustomed to it.

In some situations, you may need to create an array object that has a length of zero. This task requires another syntax that isn't overly intuitive—you must initialize an array reference variable with an empty initialization list. Examine the following two lines of code:

```
Dim array1() As Integer = {}
Dim array2() As Integer
```

A subtle, yet critical difference distinguishes these two lines of code. The array reference variable `array1` references an array object with a length of zero. The array reference variable `array2` is not explicitly initialized and so is auto-initialized to a value of `Nothing`. When you are required to pass an array reference, good programming practice is to pass an array object with a length of zero as opposed to a value of `Nothing`.

Now that you have seen how to create and initialize an array object, let's discuss an aspect of programming arrays in Visual Basic .NET that is very different from previous versions of Visual Basic. As mentioned earlier, arrays are reference types. This means, for example, that you can assign two different array reference variables to point to the same array object:

```
'*** create an array object
Dim array1() As Integer - {2, 4, 6, 8}

'*** create second reference to point to array object
Dim array2() As Integer = array1

'*** inspect same array through both reference variables
Dim i As Integer = array1(3)    '*** i = 8
Dim j As Integer = array2(3)    '*** j = 8
```

Figure 3.12 shows the result of this code—namely, the same array object is accessible through both reference variables `array1` and `array2`. If this outcome seems strange, keep in mind that it is consistent: The behavior of arrays in Visual Basic .NET is no different than the behavior of other reference types when it comes to assigning one reference variable to another. As depicted in Figure 3.12, you are not copying the array object, but rather making a copy of the reference.

The preceding example demonstrates an aspect of programming arrays in Visual Basic .NET that is fundamentally different from previous versions

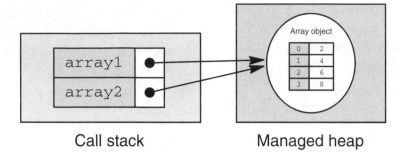

FIGURE 3.12: In Visual Basic .NET, multiple reference variables can point to the same array object.

of Visual Basic. Visual Basic .NET's predecessors do not treat arrays as true reference types. An example will further clarify this distinction.

LISTING 3.7: One array object, or two?

```
'*** create four-element array
Dim array1(3) As Integer

'*** assign value to first element
array1(0) = 100

'*** create another array variable
Dim array2() As Integer

'*** assign first array to second array
array2 = array1

'*** use second array variable to modify first element
array2(0) = 200

'*** can modification be seen through first array variable?
Dim i As Integer
i = array1(0)      '*** does i equal 100 or 200?
```

Consider the code in Listing 3.7. This code compiles and runs in both Visual Basic .NET and earlier versions of Visual Basic, but it does not produce the same behavior under each language. The important question in this example is this: Does i have a value of 100 or 200? When you run this code in Visual Basic .NET, the result is similar to that shown in Figure 3.12—the array1 and array2 reference variables both point to a single array object. Therefore, any modifications made through array2 are visible through array1. As a result, i equals 200.

In earlier versions of Visual Basic, assigning array1 to array2 makes a copy of the actual array. Therefore, array1 and array2 denote entirely different arrays. When you make a modification through the variable array2, you do not see that change when you inspect the array held by the variable array1. As a result, if you run the code in Listing 3.7 with Visual Basic 6, i equals 100.

Using ReDim Preserve

Another form of array syntax that has been retained from previous versions of Visual Basic is the Preserve keyword. It provides a handy technique when you have an array filled to capacity and need to add room for more elements. Using a ReDim statement together with the Preserve keyword can produce a larger array object while retaining all element values from the current array object. Here's an example in which the length of an array is dynamically increased from 2 to 4:

```
'*** create and populate two-element array
Dim array1(1) As Integer
array1(0) = 2
array1(1) = 4

'*** grow the array by two elements
ReDim Preserve array1(3)
array1(2) = 6
array1(3) = 8
```

This code works in Visual Basic .NET as well as in previous versions of Visual Basic. If it had used the ReDim statement without the Preserve keyword, then all elements in the new array would have been initialized to their default values. In particular, the elements array1(0) and array1(1) would both have a value of 0. Using the Preserve keyword ensures that array1(0) retains its value of 2 and array1(1) retains its value of 4.

When you include the Preserve keyword in this fashion, it might seem as though the code is increasing the number of elements in the underlying array object. In reality, this is not the case. Once an array object has been created in the .NET Framework, its number of elements can never change. In other words, the length of an array object is immutable.

Thus a `ReDim` statement that contains the `Preserve` keyword cannot increase the number of elements in the existing array object. Instead, it creates a new array object with the requested number of elements. The `Preserve` keyword then triggers the copying of the elements from the old array object into the new array object.

A `ReDim` statement with the `Preserve` keyword provides the illusion that your code is increasing the length of an array. However, now you know what's really happening behind the scenes. More importantly, you understand that using a `ReDim` statement with the `Preserve` keyword has the potential to trigger a very expensive set of operations. Think carefully about the performance implications whenever you use this syntax.

A simple example illustrates how abusing the `ReDim Preserve` syntax can yield inefficient code. Suppose you need to design a class that will store a collection of `Integer` values. Inside the implementation of this class, you decide to use an array to store your `Integer` values. Examine the following definition of a `CustomIntegerCollection` class:

```
Public Class CustomIntegerCollection
   Private InnerArray() As Integer
   Private NextIndex As Integer = 0

   Public Sub Add(ByVal int As Integer)
     ReDim Preserve InnerArray(NextIndex)
     InnerArray(NextIndex) = int
     NextIndex += 1
   End Sub
End Class
```

This code works, but carries a high price. Each time the `Add` method is called, it uses a `ReDim` statement to create a new array with one more element than the array currently held by the `InnerArray` field. This design isn't very efficient because calling `Add` 1000 times results in the creation of 1000 array objects. Things are even more inefficient because the `Preserve` keyword requires .NET to copy all the elements from the old array object into the new array object. For example, when you call the `Add` method for the one-thousandth time, the `ReDim Preserve` statement not only creates a new array of length 1000, but also copies the existing 999 integer values.

A more efficient design would eliminate the creation of so many new array objects as well as the repeated copying. For example, you could rewrite the `Add` method so that it executes the `ReDim Preserve` statement only once every 100 calls. This goal can be accomplished by growing the array's length with a *chunking interval* of 100 when it reaches maximum capacity. Here's the resulting class definition:

```
Public Class CustomIntegerCollection
  Private InnerArray() As Integer
  Private NextIndex As Integer = 0
  Private MaxIndex As Integer = -1

  Public Sub Add(ByVal int As Integer)
    If MaxIndex < NextIndex Then
      '*** grow array by chunking interval of 100
      MaxIndex += 100
      ReDim Preserve InnerArray(MaxIndex)
    End If
    InnerArray(NextIndex) = int
    NextIndex += 1
  End Sub
End Class
```

The rewritten `CustomIntegerCollection` class demonstrates how using a chunking interval can increase performance. For other applications, you might be better off with a chunking interval that is either larger or smaller than 100. The point is that you shouldn't execute a `ReDim Preserve` statement each time you need to grow an array by a single element.

While arrays are useful in many situations, the .NET Framework offers several other types of data structures that can provide more efficient means for storing data in a given design scenario. Most of these data structures are defined as classes inside the FCL's `System.Collections` namespace. For example, the `ArrayList` class can hold an arbitrary number of elements and, therefore, is ideal when you don't know in advance how many elements the array must hold. The `Hashtable` class provides a dictionary of name-value pairs that makes it very efficient to add and retrieve items from a collection. You should look through the documentation for the `System.Collections` namespace to see what other classes are available.

Defining an Array's Element Type

As the preceding discussion emphasized, arrays always act as reference types. The *element type* of an array, however, can be based on either a value type or a reference type. For example, you might declare an array based on a value type, such as `Integer`, `Double`, or `Date`. Alternatively, you might declare an array based on a reference type, such as `String`, `Object`, or the user-defined class `Human` shown in Listing 3.1.

When you declare an array based on a value type such as `Integer`, the resulting array object is one contiguous piece of memory that holds the values as elements (see Figure 3.11). But what happens when an array is based on a reference type? Then the array object is one contiguous piece of memory that holds references as elements.

To see how this works, let's look at some examples. The following code creates two different arrays of reference type `Human`:

```
'*** create an array with two references
Dim humans1() As Human = {New Human(), New Human()}

'*** create an array with four references
Dim humans2(3) As Human
humans2(0) = New Human()
humans2(1) = New Human()
humans2(3) = humans2(1)
```

Figure 3.13 shows the resulting layout of the reference variables, array objects, and underlying `Human` objects. An array object defined in terms of

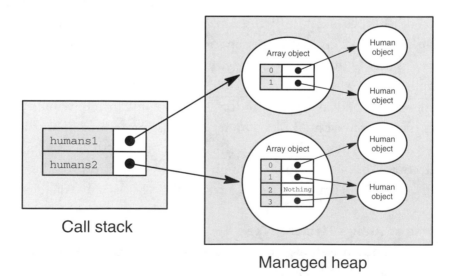

FIGURE 3.13: Array objects based on reference types contain references.

a reference type never contains inner objects, but rather references that can be assigned to point to other objects on the managed heap. If you don't assign an object to one of the references within the array, the reference will retain its default value of Nothing, as in the case of humans2(2) in Figure 3.13. It is also possible for two references within an array to point to the same object, as in the case of humans2(1) and humans2(3).

In addition, it is possible (and not uncommon) to create an array whose element type is defined in terms of the Object class. This structure is surely the most flexible type of array, because it contains a set of references that can be used to store any type of object or any type of value. The following example demonstrates the flexibility of using an Object array to keep track of an integer, string, and Human object:

```
'*** create Object array
Dim items(3) As Object

'*** store some data into array
items(0) = New Human()
items(1) = "Rosebud"
items(3) = 42
```

Figure 3.14 shows the array created by the preceding code. As you can see, you can store anything you want into an Object array. Due to their flexibility, Object arrays are commonly used in the classes of the FCL. You might find good reasons to use them in your own designs as well.

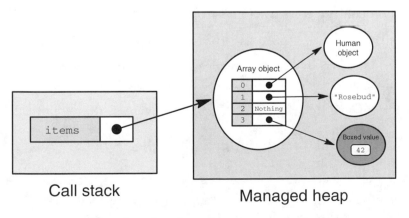

FIGURE 3.14: An array based on the Object type can hold anything.

As always, there's a catch. When dealing with `Object` arrays, and `Object`-based data structures in general, you must note a few important design issues.

First, storing a value type in an `Object` array will result in boxing. For example, the assignment of the integer 42 into `items(3)` yields the boxed value shown in Figure 3.14. This boxing behavior can have implications for your code's efficiency. An `Integer` array will be far more efficient than an `Object` array if you need to store 10,000 `Integer` values.

Second, `Object` arrays make it much harder for the compiler to identify potential bugs in your code because the `Object` type doesn't allow for compile-time type checking. For instance, the compiler cannot detect when you assign the wrong type to an array element or attempt to use an array element incorrectly.

Finally, you will often need to perform explicit type conversions when you retrieve elements from the array:

```
Dim items(3) As Object
items(0) = New Human()
items(1) = "Rosebud"
items(3) = 42

'*** retrieve items from array
Dim human1 As Human = CType(items(0), Human)
Dim s As String = CStr(items(1))
Dim i As Integer = DirectCast(items(3), Integer)
```

Recall that `DirectCast` is used to optimize the unboxing of values.

An Alternative Declaration Syntax for Arrays—Try It, You Might Like It!

Visual Basic .NET offers an alternative syntax for declaring array reference variables. In this case the parentheses are placed not after the variable name, but after the type:

```
Dim items As Object()  '*** declare object reference variable
ReDim items(3)         '***  create array of length 4
```

So? While ultimately it is a matter of programmer preference, learning and using this new syntax offers a number of advantages. First, it reinforces the notion, for example, that `Object` and `Object()` are entirely different types—the former denotes a single object reference while the latter denotes an array of object references. Second, the new syntax is consistent with other usages of array syntax in VB.NET, such as the declaration of methods that return arrays,

```
Public Function GetItems() As Object()
```

and the use of `CType` when type-casting an object reference back into an array reference of the correct type,

```
Dim names As String()
names = CType( GetItems(), String() )
```

Third, the syntax is consistent with that used in other languages such as C#. Finally, the syntax is consistent with the .NET programming model in general, because asking the type of an array reference variable yields this style of answer:

```
Dim t As String
t = names.GetType().Name   '*** what type is names?
```

In other words, `"String[]"` (in C#, arrays are denoted by `[]`). The one disadvantage to this syntactic style is that you lose the ability to declare and create arrays in one line:

```
Dim values As Integer(99)  '*** compile-time error
```

The preceding code is, unfortunately, illegal. But, like the authors, you may become a convert to the new syntax. Try it!

Array Classes and Multidimensional Arrays

Array objects are created from array classes. However, coming to an understanding of what array classes are and how they work can be a little tricky. It's more challenging to conceptualize array classes because their definitions do not exist inside assemblies as other class definitions do. Instead, an array class is synthesized on the fly by both your compiler and the .NET

Framework. For a type such as `Integer`, the .NET Framework can synthe-size a one-dimensional array, a two-dimensional array, a three-dimensional array, and so on. Visual Basic .NET allows you to create arrays with up to 32 dimensions.

Each array class is defined in terms of two specific entities: an element type and a *rank*. The rank is the number of dimensions. A one-dimensional array has a rank of 1, a two-dimensional array has a rank of 2, and so on. The important point is that Visual Basic .NET supports an array class for creating one-dimensional `Integer` array objects that is distinct from the array class for creating two-dimensional `Integer` array objects.

An array reference variable, like an array object, is defined in terms of a specific array class. Let's look at an example of defining three array ref-erence variables denoting arrays of different rank:

```
'*** reference for one-dimensional array
Dim array1() As Integer

'*** reference for two-dimensional array
Dim array2(,) As Integer

'*** reference for three-dimensional array
Dim array2(,,) As Integer
```

When you declare an array reference variable with empty parentheses, you declare the variable in terms of a one-dimensional array class. If you add a single comma inside the parentheses, you declare a reference variable in terms of a two-dimensional array class. Each time you add another comma, you increase the rank by one.

Now suppose you want to create a two-dimensional array of `Integer` values. The following code will accomplish this task:

```
'*** declare 2D array reference variable
Dim array1(,) As Integer

'*** create 2D array object with 2 rows, 2 columns
ReDim array1(1, 1)

'*** assign values to elements
array1(0, 0) = 2
array1(0, 1) = 4
array1(1, 0) = 6
array1(1, 1) = 8
```

Here, the ReDim statement requires an upper bound for each dimension of the array. The preceding code sets the first and second dimensions to both have an upper bound of 1, then initializes all four elements.

Note that you can also use an initialization list to create and initialize a multidimensional array:

```
Dim array1(,) As Integer = {{2, 4}, {6, 8}}
```

An array class with a particular number of dimensions is not compatible with another array class with a different number of dimensions. This is true even when two array classes are defined in terms of the same element type. For example, the two-dimensional Integer array class is not compatible with the one-dimensional Integer array class. It is therefore illegal to assign a two-dimensional Integer array object to a one-dimensional Integer array reference variable, as the following code attempts to do:

```
Dim array1(,) As Integer = {{2, 4}, {6, 8}}
Dim array2() As Integer = array1   '*** compile-time error
```

The array reference variable array2 is defined in terms of the one-dimensional Integer array class. As a result, array2 can reference only one-dimensional Integer array objects—which explains why the preceding code will not compile. On the other hand, the variable array2 can reference any one-dimensional Integer array object, no matter how many elements it has. In essence, an array object's rank is predetermined by its array class, but its length is not.

The System.Array Class

Array classes are unlike other classes in that they are not actually defined within assemblies. Instead, their definitions are synthesized on an as-needed basis according to a set of rules outlined by the programming model of the CTS. One of the most important rules about array classes is that every one inherits from the base class System.Array, as shown in Figure 3.15.

Having all array classes inherit from the System.Array class confers an important advantage: All array objects now automatically provide the set of public methods and properties built into the Array class. For instance, the Array class exposes a public property named Length that allows you

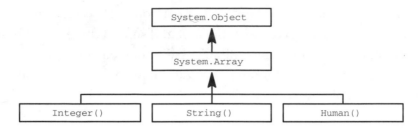

FIGURE 3.15: All array classes inherit from `System.Array`.

to determine the number of elements in an array object. Likewise, the `Array` class exposes a public property named `Rank` that allows you to determine the number of dimensions. For example:

```
Dim array1() As Integer = {2, 4, 6, 8}
Dim len As Integer = array1.Length        '*** 4
Dim r As Integer = array1.Rank            '*** 1
```

The `Length` property makes it easy to enumerate through an array object and access its elements one-by-one using a simple `For` loop. This is typically done by declaring a local `Integer` variable to act as the index counter:

```
Dim array1() As Integer = {2, 4, 6, 8}
Dim index As Integer

For index = 0 To array1.Length - 1
  Console.WriteLine(array1(index))
Next
```

Alternatively, you might prefer enumerating through the elements of the array using a `For Each` loop. Instead of declaring a local variable as an index counter, you would create a local variable based on the array's element type to act as a placeholder. During each iteration of the loop, the local placeholder variable is filled with a copy of the appropriate array element's value or reference:

```
Dim array1() As Integer = {2, 4, 6, 8}
Dim int As Integer

For Each int In array1
  Console.WriteLine(int)
Next
```

Should you prefer the `For` loop style of enumeration or the `For Each` style? The choice largely depends on your personal preference. Many programmers believe that the `For Each` style is easier to read and write. Conversely, the `For` loop provides write access to each array element, and in some cases code using this technique may run slightly faster.

Array objects also expose a public instance method named `Clone` used for duplicating an array object. It is helpful when you need to make a copy of all elements held by an array object. Note that the `Clone` method has a generic return type of `Object`. As a consequence, you'll need to explicitly convert its return value when strict type checking is turned on. Here's an example of cloning a one-dimensional `Integer` array object in the presence of strict type checking:

```
'*** create an array object
Dim array1() As Integer = {2, 4, 6, 8}

'*** create second array object by cloning array1
Dim array2() As Integer = CType(array1.Clone(), Integer())
```

There is a very important point to keep in mind when calling the `Clone` method on an array object whose element type is based on a reference type: Calling the `Clone` method copies the references within the array object, but it does not copy the objects to which those references point. Thus the result of calling `Clone` is two distinct array objects that reference the same set of underlying objects, known as a *shallow copy*. If you need to copy the underlying objects referenced within an array object (i.e., perform a *deep copy*), you must manually do so. Furthermore, the objects to which those references point must also support deep-copy cloning, and so on. We will revisit this topic in Chapter 10 when we examine object cloning in depth.

The `Array` class provides a rich set of shared methods for manipulating and searching the elements within array objects:

- The `Copy` method facilitates the transfer of data from one array object to another.
- The `Clear` method allows you to selectively reinitialize any element or any range of elements in an array object.
- The `Reverse` method rearranges the elements of an array object into reverse order.

- The `Sort` method rearranges the elements of an array object into a sorted order.

Here are examples of using some of these shared methods:

```
Dim women() As String = {"Becky", "Alice", "Dylan", "Cleo"}
Dim men() As String = {"Don", "Bob", "Aaron", "Chris"}

Dim people() As String
ReDim people(women.Length + men.Length - 1)
System.Array.Copy(women, 0, people, 0, women.Length)
System.Array.Copy(men, 0, people, women.Length, men.Length)

System.Array.Sort(people)
System.Array.Reverse(people)
```

As you can see, the shared methods of the `Array` class are designed to take one or more array objects as parameters. In the preceding code, the `Copy` method is called twice to transfer data from two source array objects into a single target array object. The `Sort` method is called to sort the resulting `String` elements into alphabetical order. Finally, the `Reverse` method is called to rearrange the `String` elements into a reverse sorted order.

Note that the `Reverse` method does not perform a reverse sort; it simply reverses the elements. If you want to perform a reverse sort, you must first call `Sort` and then call `Reverse` as shown in this example.

By default, you cannot call the `Sort` method on every type of array object. In particular, the `Sort` method is supported only for array objects whose element type implements a special interface named `IComparable`. Fortunately, all of the core CTS types for numeric values, strings, and dates support this interface. As a result, you can sort arrays based on types such as `Integer`, `Double`, `String`, and `Date`. Furthermore, you can implement the `ICompa-rable` interface on a custom type and then call `Sort` on a custom array type such as `Human()`. Chapter 6 explains how to implement an interface.

The `Array` class also provides useful methods for searching through the elements of an array object. For example, the methods named `IndexOf` and `LastIndexOf` perform linear searches. The `BinarySearch` method performs an optimized array search known as binary search, assuming the array is in sorted order. Consult the documentation of the `System.Array` class for more information on the use of these methods.

Obviously, the CTS and Visual Basic .NET provide rich support for working with arrays. The fact that all array classes are reference types makes array programming in Visual Basic .NET fundamentally different from array programming in earlier versions of Visual Basic. In the .NET Framework you must understand the difference between an array class, an array object, and an array reference variable. Once you do, programming arrays becomes much more intuitive—and much more powerful. The `Array` class provides a good deal of functionality to assist you when you need to perform common chores on the array or its elements.

SUMMARY

The CTS provides a foundation for all managed languages and for the .NET Framework itself. It is complemented by the CLS, which seeks to improve interoperability across managed languages such as Visual Basic .NET and C#. As a result of this improved level of interoperability, the .NET Framework is significantly better than COM at allowing companies to mix and match programming languages as they undertake component-based development.

As a Visual Basic .NET developer, you must become thoroughly familiar with the CTS, because the CTS defines the type system and programming model you will use whenever you write code. In the course of this chapter, it should have become clear that the Visual Basic .NET language differs dramatically from previous versions of Visual Basic. In particular, its underlying type system is vastly different from anything that has come before. To use Visual Basic .NET effectively, you must understand many new concepts such as inheritance, shared members, and the difference between value types and reference types.

This chapter also exposed you to programming with the primitive CTS types as well the `Object` class and the `String` class. You saw how the `Array` class factors into programming with array objects. The next few chapters will build upon the CTS fundamentals introduced here. Now it's time to discuss the new OOP support in Visual Basic .NET, including how to take advantage of it when creating your own classes.

◢ 4 ◾
Classes

THIS CHAPTER COVERS the fundamentals of designing classes with Visual Basic .NET. Even if you have experience designing classes with a previous version of Visual Basic, there's quite a bit more for you to learn, because Visual Basic .NET introduces a number of new concepts and a wealth of new syntax.

The chapter first examines the differences between shared members and instance members. It then considers how the Visual Basic .NET compiler treats `Module` types differently from standard `Class` types. Next, the chapter explains how to design and create specific kinds of class members, such as fields, constructors, methods, and properties. Along the way, you will see how to use some advanced design techniques, such as overloading and nested types.

Designing Classes

Classes are the primary building blocks with which you write and reuse code that targets the .NET Framework. Classes can model abstractions for real-world entities such as customers, invoices, and expense reports. They can also model more task-oriented abstractions such as a processor for handling client requests or a dispatcher for running a series of jobs in sequence or in parallel.

In short, classes make it possible to design in terms of abstractions and then to write implementations for these abstractions that can be compiled into production code and distributed via assemblies. A typical class contains members such as fields and methods. Listing 4.1 presents a simple example of a definition of a class named Human that is designed to model the state and behavior of a human to meet the needs of a particular application.

LISTING 4.1: A Human **class for modeling humans in an application**

```
Public Class Human
  Public Name As String

  Public Function Speak() As String
    Return "I am a human named " & Name
  End Function
End Class
```

Class authors often design their classes as templates to be used by other programmers as a basis for creating objects. It's a fairly simple matter for a programmer to create an object from a class using the New operator. Here's an example of client-side code that creates and uses an object based on the Human class of Listing 4.1:

```
Dim human1 As New Human()
human1.Name = "Brian"
Dim message As String = human1.Speak()
```

This code should be familiar to any programmer who has experience programming with classes in an earlier version of Visual Basic. However, Visual Basic .NET provides some powerful new alternatives when it comes to designing classes.

For example, you can now define the members of a class to be *shared* members; you can initialize objects and shared fields using *constructors;* and you can provide *overloaded* implementations for methods and properties. These are merely some of the topics covered in this chapter. As you will see, the OOP support provided to class authors by Visual Basic .NET is far more powerful than that offered by earlier versions of Visual Basic. Let's start our exploration with a brief discussion of encapsulation.

Encapsulating Types and Members

Encapsulation is a very important concept in object-oriented programming. From a software designer's point of view, encapsulation is the practice of packaging code and data into a single class, and then hiding as many of the implementation details as possible from the class users. A stand-alone class (i.e., one that is not nested within other classes) must be either a public type or a friend type. Public types are exposed to other assemblies and are declared with the `Public` keyword. Friend types are not exposed to other assemblies and are declared with the `Friend` keyword. A class is implicitly declared as a friend type if you do not supply either the `Public` or the `Friend` keyword in its declaration.

When you're designing a public class, it often makes sense to hide some of its members by reducing their accessibility. After all, the less the class users know about the details of the class, the more flexibility you have to evolve the class in the future. Listing 4.2 shows a class definition that contains five fields demonstrating the five possible levels of member accessibility.

LISTING 4.2: The five levels of class member accessibility

```
Public Class Class1
  '*** accessible by all code
  Public Field1 As Integer

  '*** accessible from within the current assembly
  Friend Field2 As Integer

  '*** accessible by this class only
  Private Field3 As Integer

  '*** accessible by this class and by child (derived) classes
  Protected Field4 As Integer

  '*** union of Protected and Friend accessibility
  Protected Friend Field5 As Integer
End Class
```

Let's discuss each level of accessibility in turn. If you define a class member with the `Public` access modifier, it is accessible to all code that also has access to the class. A public member of a public class thus has the highest level of accessibility—it can be accessed by code both inside and outside the containing assembly. If you define a field without an explicit access modifier, then it is implicitly private. If you define a method or a property without an explicit access modifier, then it is implicitly public.

To restrict the accessibility of a member of a public class to its containing assembly, you can define it with the `Friend` access modifier. A friend member is inaccessible to code from external assemblies. As a result, you can always revise or remove a friend member without worrying about how the change will affect code in other assemblies; a modification to a friend member affects only code inside the same assembly. Note that the access modifiers `Public` and `Friend` have the same meaning for a member inside a friend class, because the accessibility of the entire class is already restricted to its containing assembly.

You can achieve the highest levels of encapsulation by defining a class member with the `Private` access modifier. A private member is accessible only to code inside the class itself. That is, private members are off-limits to code in other types.

Defining fields as private members offers several benefits. First, you get the guarantee that no code outside your class can directly access a private field. This means no other programmer can modify your private data in ways that you had not intended. In this way, private fields help to ensure that your data remains valid. Second, a judicious use of private members is very important when you intend to evolve a class definition over time. Private members allow you to change the internal implementation details of a class without the risk of introducing changes that break other code that depends on the class.

You can also define a member using the `Protected` access modifier. Protected accessibility is a little less restrictive than private accessibility. A protected member is accessible not only to code within the containing class but also to code within derived classes that inherit from the containing class. (A detailed discussion of inheritance is deferred until Chapter 5, which covers protected members in more depth.)

Finally, note that the `Protected` access modifier and `Friend` access modifier can be used together when defining a class member. This combination has the accumulative effect of giving the member both friend accessibility and protected accessibility.

Before we move on, note one important restriction that applies when you are defining public members in public types: You cannot define a public member that relies on a friend type. The following code violates this restriction:

```
Friend Class Dog
  '*** definition
End Class

Public Class Human
  Public Pet As Dog    '*** compile-time error
End Class
```

In the preceding code, the Dog class is defined as a friend type and the Human class is defined as a public type. Now consider the Pet field of class Human. It is illegal to add such a public member to the Human class that relies on the Dog class, because a class user would have access to the field but not to its underlying type. As a result, the Human class will not compile because the public Pet field is based on a friend type.

If you were allowed to use friend types within the definition of a public member, it would create a mismatched set of expectations from the perspective of code in other assemblies. Code from other assemblies should have access to each public member, but it can access only public members that are based on other public types. Therefore, friend types cannot be used when defining public members. In general, every type in a member definition must have an accessibility level that is equal to or greater than the accessibility level of the member being defined.

Shared Members versus Instance Members

Shared members have existed in other languages such as C++ and Java for years and are a very welcome addition to Visual Basic. In C#, C++, and Java, shared members are called "static" members. It would be easy to argue that the term "shared" used by Visual Basic .NET is more concise and more in line with reality. That's because the shared members of a class are actually shared across every object created from that class.

Chapter 3 introduced the concept of shared members. Recall that certain members of a type can be associated with the type itself as opposed to being associated with an instance of the type. Let's look at Listing 4.3, which shows a class with two fields—one instance and one shared.

LISTING 4.3: A class with two fields—one instance and one shared

```
Public Class Human
  '*** instance field
  Public Name As String

  '*** shared field
  Public Shared Species As String = "Homo sapiens"
End Class
```

In this class definition, Name is defined as an instance member (because every human has his or her own name). Species is defined as a shared member (because all humans share the same species designator). How do these two kinds of members differ? To access the instance member, you must first create or acquire an object that's been instantiated from the class. Here's the minimum amount of code you have to write to access the Name field:

```
Dim human1 As New Human()
human1.Name = "Bob"
```

Shared methods can be more convenient because they can be accessed without instantiating an object beforehand. You can access a shared member by using the class name followed by the member name:

```
Dim s As String = Human.Species
```

Note that the syntax of Visual Basic .NET allows you to access shared members in two different ways. The technique shown above, which uses the class name, is preferred for the sake of readability. The alternative technique uses an object reference. For example:

```
Dim human1 As New Human()
Dim s As String = human1.Species
```

While this code is acceptable to the compiler, it is recommended that you avoid accessing shared members through reference variables. It can be confusing and lead to reduced readability, because shared members are not really associated with the object behind the object reference; a shared member is associated with the class itself. An example will drive this point home—but be forewarned that an encounter with this technique can be quite confusing the first time around!

Consider the following code fragment, which declares two reference variables but creates only one instance of the Human class:

```
'*** this works
Dim human1 As New Human()
Dim result1 As String = human1.Species

'*** this works, too
Dim human2 As Human
Dim result2 As String = human2.Species
```

In this example, human1 and human2 are reference variables of type Human. In other words, both are reference variables that are capable of pointing to an instance of Human. In addition, both variables can be used to access the shared member Species. Note that human2 has not been assigned to an object and, therefore, is Nothing. Nevertheless, it can still be used to access a shared member without any problems. But what would happen if you attempted to access an instance member through an object reference like human2 that contains a value of Nothing? A runtime exception.

Obviously, accessing a shared member through a reference variable is both confusing and unnecessary. For this reason, it is recommended that you use the ClassName.MemberName syntax whenever you write client-side code to access public shared members. The designers of C# clearly agreed with this point, because they allow access to shared (i.e., static) members only through use of the class name.

Shared members open up several new design possibilities. For example, the memory for a shared field is allocated only once per class, no matter how many objects are ultimately created. This approach is much different than the allocation of the memory for instance fields, which is doled once per object. Figure 4.1 illustrates how instance fields and shared fields are laid out in memory for the Human class given in Listing 4.3. As you can see, shared fields have an advantage in that they can be used to share data across multiple instances of the same class.

Figure 4.1 depicts a design in which a shared field is used to share data across multiple instances of a class. While such a design is usable in many

```
Module MyApp
  Sub Main()

     Dim human1 As New Human()
     human1.Name = "Doug"

     Dim human2 As New Human()
     human2.Name = "Jose"

  End Sub
End Module

Public Class Human
   '*** instance field
   Public Name As String
   '*** shared field
   Public Shared Species As String = "Homo sapiens"
End Class
```

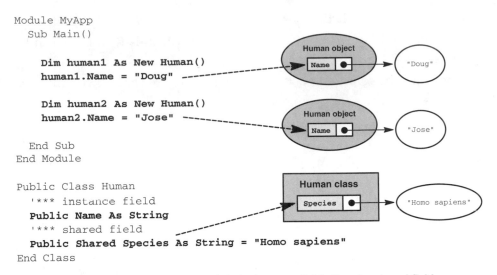

FIGURE 4.1: Memory is allocated differently for instance fields than for shared fields.

situations, you shouldn't make unrealistic assumptions about how the CLR caches shared field data.

The data of a shared field is scoped by an AppDomain. As explained in Chapter 1, an AppDomain is a subdivision of a process on the host platform. If you run a simple console-based application or a simple form-based application, all of your code is likely to run in the default AppDomain. Thus your code will see the same instance of the data for shared fields, and the lifetime of these shared fields will be the same as the lifetime of the hosting application.

By comparison, shared fields act much differently when you use them in a more sophisticated runtime environment such as ASP.NET. The hosting environment for ASP.NET is based on a scheme where multiple AppDomains are automatically spawned and recycled behind the scenes. Whenever ASP.NET recycles an AppDomain, all the data from your shared fields is lost and, therefore, must be reinitialized. Furthermore, there is no guarantee that two client requests will be executed in the same AppDomain, implying that they may see different instances of the shared fields. This is true even when the same client submits two requests.

The point being emphasized here is that you have to know something about the environment in which your code will run before you can determine the scope of how shared fields will actually be shared. Base your assumptions on your knowledge of whether the hosting application will run within a single long-lived AppDomain or whether it may spawn multiple AppDomains during its lifetime.

Designing with Shared Members

Shared members are more convenient than instance members because they alleviate the need to instantiate objects. In particular, they are great for times when you want to create a class that exposes a set of utility functions. Let's examine one class in the FCL that has such as design—`System.Math`. The following client-side code calls a few of the shared methods within the `System.Math` class:

```
Dim result1, result2, result3 As Double
result1 = System.Math.Sqrt(225)
result2 = System.Math.Pow(15, 2)
result3 = System.Math.Log(225)
```

As this code demonstrates, the client does not have to create objects so as to call the methods. The implication: When you are creating a class that doesn't require multiple objects with their own private data layouts, you can elect to design the class so that it contains only shared members. An example might be a low-level data access class. At other times, you may need to create a class that has the full capabilities provided by objects. In these cases, you would design the class solely in terms of instance members. Finally, in more complicated designs, you might create a class that contains a mixture of shared members and instance members.

Keep in mind that the rules for writing code for an instance member differ from the rules for writing code for a shared member. An example will illustrate this difference. Imagine you are rewriting the Human class to contain both an instance method and a shared method:

```
Class Human
  Public Name As String
  Public Shared Species As String = "Homo sapiens"

  '*** instance method
  Public Function GetInfo1() As String
    '*** instance method implementation
  End Function
```

```
'*** shared method
Public Shared Function GetInfo2() As String
    '*** shared method implementation
  End Function
End Class
```

When you implement the instance method `GetInfo1`, you have access to both the instance field `Name` and the shared field `Species`:

```
'*** instance method
Public Function GetInfo1() As String
  Return "This human's name is " & Name & vbCrLf & _
        "This human's species is " & Species
End Function
```

When implementing a shared method, bear in mind that a shared member is not associated with a specific instance (see Figure 4.1). As a result, a shared method is allowed access to any other shared member of the class. This implies that `GetInfo2` can legally access the shared field `Species`:

```
'*** shared method
Public Shared Function GetInfo2() As String
  Return "The species of all humans is " & Species
End Function
```

Because a shared method doesn't execute within the context of any specific instance, however, it doesn't make sense for the implementation to access instance members. In fact, it is illegal for a shared member to access instance members of the class. For example, what would happen if you attempted to access the `Name` field from the shared method `GetInfo2`?

```
Public Shared Function GetInfo2() As String
  Return "This human's name is " & Name       '*** legal?
End Function
```

You will receive a compile-time error message. The compiler will not allow you to access an instance member from a shared member.

Furthermore, it is illegal to use the `Me` keyword within a shared method, because `Me` refers to a particular instance. As should be clear by now, the rules for implementing a shared member are more restrictive than the rules for implementing an instance member. These restrictions derive from the fact that a shared member does not execute within the scope of any particular instance.

To Me or Not to Me?

Consider for a moment the instance method GetInfo1 discussed in the text. This method must be called using an object reference:

```
Dim obj As New Human()
obj.Name = "Jim Bag"
System.Console.WriteLine( obj.GetInfo1() )
```

When implementing GetInfo1, you as a programmer have a choice: You can refer to class members by using the OOP syntax Me.MemberName or simply by using MemberName. Should you prefer one approach over the other?

In most cases the use of the Me keyword is optional, and just a matter of personal taste. For example, here's the instance method GetInfo1 rewritten to use the Me keyword when accessing class members:

```
'*** instance method
Public Function GetInfo1() As String
  Return "This human's name is " & Me.Name & vbCrLf & _
         "This human's species is " & Species
End Function
```

While Me has the advantage of triggering Visual Studio's IntelliSense feature, it also reinforces an object-oriented style of programming. When you see a reference to Name, it could be a local variable, a parameter, or a class member. When you see a reference to Me.Name, however, it immediately tells you that Name is a class member. For this reason, the authors of this book are strong proponents of using the Me keyword.

In some cases the Me keyword is required, not optional. For example, if the method contains a parameter with the same name as a field, the Me keyword is used to disambiguate between parameter and field:

```
Public Class Human
  Public Name As String
  Public Sub SetName(ByVal Name As String)
    Me.Name = Name    '*** assignment parameter to field
  End Sub
End Class
```

Another common situation where the use of Me is required occurs when an object must pass its own reference to some other class or object. Such a design typically involves a class or object that allows other objects to register references for callback purposes. The Me keyword provides the best way for an object to pass a reference to itself to a third party.

What about the implementation of shared methods—is there an equivalent to the Me keyword? The class name serves as the object-oriented equivalent of Me. For example:

```
'*** shared method
Public Shared Function GetInfo2() As String
  Return "This species of all humans is " & Human.Species
End Function
```

Combining Shared Members with Instance Members

When it comes to designing classes that contain both shared members and instance members, the possibilities are limited only by your imagination. One more class design will give you an idea of what is possible. Keep in mind that this class design could not be created in previous versions of Visual Basic.

Suppose you want to design a class that will allow other programmers to instantiate objects such that each object has a unique ID. The easiest solution is to add a shared field to store a class-wide counter for counting objects as they are created. You can then expose a shared method that creates the object for the client, assigns a unique ID, and returns a reference to this object. Such a method is often called a *factory method*. Examine the class definition in Listing 4.4, which implements this design.

As you know, the memory for a shared field is allocated exactly once for the class. For this reason, only one instance of the field NextHuman is defined in Listing 4.4, regardless of whether objects have been created from the class. Therefore, a design with a shared field such as NextHuman makes it possible to track a class-wide state that can be read and modified by the implementation of shared methods such as GetNextHuman.

LISTING 4.4: A class design supporting the notion of a factory method

```
Public Class Human
  '*** instance members
  Private ID As Integer
  Public Function GetInfo() As String
    Return "Human #" & CStr(ID)
  End Function

  '*** shared members
  Private Shared NextHuman As Integer = 1
  Public Shared Function GetNextHuman() As Human  '*** factory method
    Dim temp As New Human()
    temp.ID = NextHuman
    NextHuman += 1
    Return temp
  End Function

End Class
```

In this design, `GetNextHuman` is a shared method that acts as a factory method. A call to `GetNextHuman` returns a new `Human` object with a unique ID. That is, the implementation of `GetNextHuman` creates an instance of the `Human` class and assigns the current value of `NextHuman` to its `ID` field. Then, the implementation of `GetNextHuman` increments the value of the `NextHuman` field to prepare for the next time this factory method is called. Finally, `GetNextHuman` returns a reference to the newly created object back to the caller.

Once you have implemented this kind of design, client-side code should create objects using your factory method instead of the `New` operator. For example, the client should call `GetNextHuman` to create `Human` objects:

```
Dim human1, human2, human3 As Human
Dim info1, info2, info3 As String

'*** call factory method to create new instances
human1 = Human.GetNextHuman()
human2 = Human.GetNextHuman()
human3 = Human.GetNextHuman()

'*** inspect state of instances
info1 = human1.GetInfo()    '*** info1 = "Human #1"
info2 = human2.GetInfo()    '*** info2 = "Human #2"
info3 = human3.GetInfo()    '*** info3 = "Human #3"
```

A design with a factory method like the one shown in Listing 4.4 is just one of countless ways to employ shared members in Visual Basic .NET. One thing you should observe about this example is that all the code associated with the class is defined inside the class itself. Because earlier versions of Visual Basic did not support shared members, programmers often resorted to far less elegant approaches, such as maintaining class-specific code in separate .BAS modules.

The `Module` Type

Now that you have an appreciation for the difference between designing with shared members versus designing with instance members, it's time to discuss the `Module` type in Visual Basic .NET. The first thing to understand about this type is that it is not recognized by the CTS. The `Module` type is an example of a productivity-oriented abstraction that has been created by the Visual Basic .NET language designers.

The `Module` type provides the illusion that members can be defined on a global basis outside the scope of any type. In reality, the members you define in a module type are not defined at a global scope, but rather defined inside the scope of a class that's generated from the module definition. An example will illustrate exactly what is happening. Suppose you compile the following `Module` type definition:

```
Public Module TaxCalculator
  Private TaxRate As Double = 0.075

  Public Function CalculateTax(Price As Decimal) As Decimal
    Return CDec(Price * TaxRate)
  End Function
End Module
```

The Visual Basic .NET compiler takes this `Module` definition and uses it to generate a special `Class` definition. When written in Visual Basic .NET, the `Class` definition looks something like this:

```
<Microsoft.VisualBasic.Globals.StandardModule()> _
Public NotInheritable Class TaxCalculator
  Private Shared TaxRate As Double = 0.075

  Public Shared Function CalculateTax(Price As Decimal) As Decimal
    Return CDec(Price * TaxRate)
  End Function
End Class
```

The first point to notice is that every member in a `Module` type is implicitly shared. The `Shared` keyword is implied on each member and cannot be used explicitly by the programmer—the member is already shared. The second point is that the generated class does not support object instantiation, which means that a module is a noncreatable type. The third point is that the class does not support inheritance. As a result, the `Class` definition generated from a module does not allow other programmers to design classes that inherit from it.

Notice also that the generated class is defined with the `StandardModule` attribute from the `Microsoft.VisualBasic` assembly. Why does the Visual Basic .NET compiler apply this attribute to a `Class` definition generated for a `Module` type? The answer has to do with client-side programmers who are programming against the `Module` type. More specifically, it relates to Visual Basic .NET programmers who are programming against the `Module` type.

The `StandardModule` attribute is recognized by the IntelliSense support in the Visual Studio .NET IDE and by the Visual Basic .NET compiler. In short, the presence of this attribute allows developers who are programming against the `Module` type to call its members without having to include the module name. For example, you can call the `CalculateTax` method from the previous definition of `TaxCalculator` with or without the type name:

```
'*** call method using Module name
Dim tax1 As Decimal = TaxCalculator.CalculateTax(129.95D)

'*** call method without using Module name
Dim tax2 As Decimal = CalculateTax(19.99D)
```

If `CalculateTax` was defined as a `Shared` method inside a standard `Class` definition, you would have to reference it using both the class name and the method name. The use of the `Module` type simply allows other Visual Basic .NET developers to get at its members without having to qualify the name of the member. Therefore, the `Module` type provides the illusion that its members are defined at a global scope.

The Visual Basic .NET language designers added the `Module` type to give developers something with the same look and feel as .BAS modules from earlier versions of Visual Basic. Many of the wrapper methods provided in the `Microsoft.VisualBasic` assembly are defined inside `Module` types, which makes it easier to port code written in Visual Basic 6.

Keep in mind that the convenience of the `Module` type's shortened calling syntax does not extend across languages. Developers using other languages such as C# will see a Visual Basic .NET `Module` definition as a `Class` definition with shared members. Therefore, developers using other languages cannot access a member of a `Module` type without using the type name. In other languages, there is no difference between a method defined in a `Module` type and a shared method defined in a `Class` definition.

There are a few other miscellaneous issues to watch for concerning the use of the `Module` type. These issues might catch you off guard if you're not paying attention.

First, Visual Basic .NET allows the caller to omit the `Module` type name only when there's no ambiguity about which method is being called. The Visual Basic .NET compiler will report a compile-time error if it determines that multiple modules have a candidate method definition with the same name and signature.

Let's look at an example. Suppose you are working with two class library projects: one contains a `Module` type named `TaxCalculator1` and the other contains a `Module` type named `TaxCalculator2`. Further suppose that you are writing code in a Windows application project in which you have referenced both class library projects and imported their namespaces. Now here's the question that demonstrates the problem: Can `Tax-Calculator1` and `TaxCalculator2` both contain a public method named `CalculateTax` with the same calling signature?

The answer is yes. If you write code in the application that attempts to call method `CalculateTax` without using a module name, a compile-time error will result because the compiler recognizes the ambiguity. You can easily resolve this kind of ambiguity by rewriting the call to include the correct `Module` name—for example, `TaxCalculator2.CalculateTax`.

While this example demonstrates one way to get into trouble with modules, things can become even more complicated. The Visual Basic .NET compiler examines the `Module` type in the caller's assembly first before it decides whether it needs to look elsewhere for the desired method. If the compiler doesn't find this method in the caller's assembly, it continues to search through the modules of other assemblies. The important point is that the Visual Basic .NET compiler doesn't search through the Module types of external assemblies if it finds a matching method in a module of the assembly currently being built. In other words, the current assembly takes priority.

An example will illustrate this point. Suppose you are writing a Windows application project and a class library project, where the Windows application project references the class library project. Assume that you have imported the namespace from the class library that contains the external Module definition. Now you can write code in the application that accesses types in the class library project without using full namespace qualification.

Now imagine that the Windows application project contains a Module type named TaxCalculator1 and the class library project contains a Module type named TaxCalculator2; each of these modules contains a public method named CalculateTax with the same calling signature. What happens if you call the CalculateTax method without qualifying it with a Module name? You might expect a compile-time error to be generated due to the obvious ambiguity. This is not the case, however. The Visual Basic .NET compiler actually generates a call to the CalculateTax method in the Module type of the Windows application project. The compiler doesn't care whether matching public methods exist in the Module types of external assemblies.

The key point here is that you have to be careful. You don't want to be tricked into calling the method from a local Module type when you really want to call a method from an external Module type. Once again, you can avoid such problems by always qualifying a call with the Module type name. In some situations, you may even need to fully qualify the call with the namespace in which the Module type is defined.

Developers often debate whether to design in terms of Module types or in terms of Class definitions with shared members. The choice really comes down to a matter of taste and programming style. Some developers like to use Module types because they make it a little easier to call methods. Other developers avoid the use of these types because modules relax the rules of name qualification, increase the risk of problems from naming conflicts, and work only in Visual Basic .NET.

Class Members

If you have experience working with classes in an earlier version of Visual Basic, you already understand the purpose of class members such as fields, methods, and properties. Your previous experience with classes gives you the foundation for learning all the new OOP features that have been added to Visual Basic .NET.

Many of these new features make the language more powerful for programmers who are authoring classes. You have already seen that adding shared members to a class creates design possibilities that did not exist in Visual Basic .NET's predecessors. At this point, we will delve into the different kinds of members you can add to a class. We start by discussing how to add fields and constructors, then consider ways to add methods and properties to a class. The chapter concludes by explaining why and how a class might contain a nested class.

Fields

A field is a named, typed unit of storage. Every field in a class must have a unique name. Every field must be defined using a system-defined or a user-defined type. Furthermore, every field must be defined as either a shared member or an instance member.

Fields are like local variables in that they are auto-initialized to a well-known value in cases where they're not explicitly initialized by the programmer. For example, fields based on numeric types auto-initialize to a value of 0, while fields based on reference types auto-initialize to a value of Nothing.

As mentioned earlier, you can initialize both instance fields and shared fields using an inline syntax called a *field initializer*. Field initializers make it fairly easy to write and read the code for initializing fields. The following code fragment initializes two fields using field initializers:

```
Public Class Class1
  Public Field1 As Integer = 24
  Public Shared Field2 As Integer = 48
End Class
```

In this case the field initializers are simple integer constants. Initializers can be more complex, however. For example, the initializer for an instance field can call a shared method in the same class, such as the initializer for the field ID in the following code fragment:

```
Public Class Human
  '*** instance field with initializer
  Public ID As Integer = GetNextID()

  '*** shared members for generating unique IDs
  Private Shared NextID As Integer = 0
  Private Shared Function GetNextID() As Integer
    NextID += 1
    Return NextID
  End Function
End Class
```

Here, the initializer calls a shared method to generate a unique ID at object creation time. As you might expect, an initializer also has the flexibility of calling an instance method in the same class, or shared methods in other classes.

A field must be defined as either a value type or a reference type. (Chapter 3 outlined some of the important differences between these two types.) A field instance based on a value type holds the actual data for the type. A field based on a reference type holds a reference that may or may not point to a valid object holding the data for the type. Figure 4.2 presents a complete program and the resulting set of objects to highlight the difference between fields as value types and fields as reference types. Study this figure carefully.

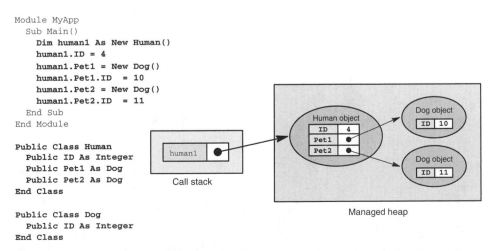

FIGURE 4.2: The fields of an object may contain values as well as references to other objects.

The term *object graph* is frequently used to describe the set of objects that can be accessed directly or indirectly through a particular reference variable. Figure 4.2 shows the object graph for the local reference variable human1, which consists of three objects. In less trivial scenarios, the object graph might contain hundreds or even thousands of objects.

Const *and* ReadOnly *Fields*

Both the programming model of the CLR and Visual Basic .NET support the concepts of Const and ReadOnly fields. The use of these kinds of fields in a design can prove valuable when you are working with values that will remain immutable throughout the lifetime of an object or program. The use of the Const and ReadOnly keywords allows you to document certain assumptions about when field values can and cannot be modified. This, in turn, allows the Visual Basic .NET compiler to perform optimizations and extra compile-time checks to ensure your data is not being used in unintended ways.

The difference between a Const field and a ReadOnly field is that the value of a Const field must be known at compile time, whereas the value of a ReadOnly field can be calculated at runtime. For this reason, Const fields must be initialized using expressions such as literal values that can be fully evaluated by the compiler. Here's an example of a custom class with a Const field:

```
Public Class MathClass
  Public Const PI As Single = 3.141592
End Class
```

As Const values are known at compile time, the value of a Const field cannot vary between different instances of the class. For this reason, the Visual Basic .NET compiler modifies the definition of each Const field so that implicitly it is a shared field. It is unnecessary—and inefficient—for Visual Basic .NET to allocate a separate instance of a Const field for each object created from the class.

When you want to write client-side code that uses a public Const field, you simply use the same syntax that you would use to access any other public shared field. For example, you can access the PI constant shown earlier with the following code:

```
Dim radius As Double = 2.5
Dim area As Double = MathClass.PI * (radius ^ 2)
```

One very important issue concerning the use of `Const` fields must be acknowledged. Managed compilers (including the compiler for Visual Basic .NET) perform an optimization at compile time when you write code that references a `Const` field. The literal value of the constant is compiled directly into the client-side code. This approach provides an optimization in that the value of the `Const` field need not be queried at runtime.

While `Const` fields often yield optimizations that make your code run faster, their use does require a little extra attention. In fact, you can easily get into trouble using `Const` fields. Suppose you create a class library project that contains a public class, and this public class contains a public `Const` field named `InterestRate`. Now imagine you create a Windows application project that references the class library project. You write code in this application that uses the value of the `InterestRate` field to perform a calculation. When you finish testing the application and the class DLL, you release both assemblies into production.

What happens later, when you need to change the interest rate to a different value? It's not enough to simply update the class library project and rebuild the DLL. The value of the old interest rate is embedded within the IL of the Windows application. Therefore, you must recompile the Windows application after you recompile the DLL so that the application will use the new interest rate.

As this example demonstrates, you must be very careful when exposing public `Const` fields as part of public types. It is an appropriate thing to do when you have a constant value that isn't expected to change, such as the mathematical value of pi. By contrast, attempting to maintain values in public `Const` fields that will likely change over time can create problems. Just remember that changing a public `Const` field in a later version of a class library will introduce breaking changes to existing clients.

If some values will be immutable through the lifetime of a program but might change across versions of the assembly for a component library, you have a few different options at your disposal. In this case, you don't want the client application's compiler to perform the optimization of embedding the actual value inside the client application. Instead, the client application should query the DLL for the value at runtime. One way to accomplish this task is to use a private Const field combined with a public method or property to return the constant value to the client. Another technique is to use a public shared ReadOnly field instead of a public Const field.

Instance fields that are defined as ReadOnly differ from Const fields in that their initialization values do not need to be known at compile time. Instead, their values can be calculated at object creation time. As a consequence, a ReadOnly instance field can be different for each object created from the same class. Of course, the compiler cannot automatically transform a ReadOnly field into a shared field as it does for a Const field. You decide whether a ReadOnly field is defined as a shared field or an instance field by choosing to use or omit the Shared keyword.

A ReadOnly field offers advantages in a design because its value cannot be modified once it has been initialized. A ReadOnly instance field can be modified only while the object is being constructed; you should use such a field when you have a value that will remain constant throughout the lifetime of an object. A ReadOnly shared field can be modified only at class initialization time; you should use such a field when you have a value that will remain constant through the lifetime of a program.

ReadOnly fields protect your data against being used in unexpected ways. In that spirit, the compiler will raise an error if a programmer attempts to modify a ReadOnly field inside the implementation of a method or property. In this way, the compiler helps enforce the rules you have documented about how your data should be used.

Let's revisit the definition of the Human class shown earlier. Recall that it included an instance field named ID whose value was calculated during object construction. This field is an ideal candidate for a ReadOnly field.

```
Class Human
  '*** ReadOnly field with initializer
  Public ReadOnly ID As Integer = GetNextID()

  '*** shared members for generating unique IDs
  Private Shared NextID As Integer = 0
  Private Shared Function GetNextID() As Integer
    NextID += 1
    Return NextID
  End Function
End Class
```

In the example, the public `ID` field has been defined with read-only semantics. After a client has created a `Human` object, it can query the `ID` field but cannot update it. A key point to keep in mind is that you can only assign a value to a `ReadOnly` field in two ways: (1) with an initializer or (2) inside a *constructor*. At this point, your next question should be, "What's a constructor?"

Constructors

A constructor is a special kind of class member that's used to initialize objects—in particular, their fields. A constructor is like a method in that it contains executable code and may be defined with parameters. It is different from a method in that it is not called by clients in the same fashion .

Two different kinds of constructors exist:

- Instance constructors are used to initialize objects.
- Shared constructors are used to initialize the shared fields of a class.

Instance Constructors

An instance constructor runs whenever the CLR creates an object from a class. Such a constructor provides the class author with an opportunity to execute code that ensures that objects are constructed in a valid state. Note that instance constructors are often called simply "constructors." When this book uses the term "constructor," it is referring to an instance constructor as opposed to a shared constructor.

A constructor is an executable unit of code inside a class definition that is called automatically by the CLR whenever a client instantiates an object. For example, if a client program creates an object from your class using the `New` operator, your constructor executes and gives you a chance to initialize the fields within your object. In Visual Basic .NET, you add a constructor to a class by adding a sub procedure with the name `New`. Listing 4.5 presents a simple example of two classes, each with its own constructor.

The constructor in the `Human` class of Listing 4.5 has been defined with a parameter. For this reason, it is known as a "parameterized constructor." The constructor in the `Dog` class of Listing 4.5 has been defined without parameters. A nonparameterized constructor goes by several names, including "default constructor" and "no-arg constructor." In this book, we will refer to a nonparameterized constructor as the default constructor.

LISTING 4.5: Examples of classes with parameterized and default constructors

```
Public Class Human
  Private Name As String

  '*** parameterized constructor to initialize object
  Public Sub New(Name As String)
    Me.Name = Name
  End Sub
End Class

Public Class Dog
  Private Name As String

  '*** default constructor to initialize object
  Public Sub New()
    Me.Name = "Spot"
  End Sub
End Class
```

Let's examine some client-side code that creates objects from the Human
and Dog classes using the New operator:

```
'*** different ways to create objects via the parameterized constructor
Dim human1 As Human = New Human("Josie")
Dim human2 As New Human("Fernando")

'*** different ways to create objects via the default constructor
Dim dog1 As Dog = New Dog
Dim dog2 As Dog = New Dog()
Dim dog3 As New Dog
Dim dog4 As New Dog()
```

As you can see from this client-side code, Visual Basic .NET syntactically
supports multiple ways to call both parameterized and default constructors. The parameters defined inside a constructor's parameter list determine how the client uses the New operator. When you instantiate an object
using the New operator and a parameterized constructor (e.g., the Human
class), you must pass the appropriate parameters enclosed in parentheses
after the name of the class. When you instantiate an object using the New
operator and a default constructor (e.g., the Dog class), use of parentheses
after the class name is optional.

Parameterized constructors allow the class author to exert a much greater degree of control over field initialization. While the Human class in Listing 4.5 allows a client-side programmer to pass initialization data in the call to New, it also prohibits calls to New that don't pass the initialization values required by the constructor(s). For example, given the definition of class Human in Listing 4.5, it is illegal for the client-side programmer to write the following code:

```
'*** this doesn't compile because Human has no default constructor
Dim human1 As New Human()
```

A client-side programmer using the New operator is always calling a constructor. When you call the New operator, the class must include a constructor with a parameter list that matches the parameter list passed to the New operator. If no such constructor is found, you'll receive a compile-time error message.

Several aspects of the creation and use of constructors merit some special attention. For example, a class can only be created if it contains one or more accessible constructors. This restriction sometimes seems confusing because it's possible to create an object from a class without an apparent constructor. That is, the Visual Basic .NET compiler automatically adds a default constructor to your class if you haven't defined one explicitly. Suppose you create a class definition like the following and compile it into a DLL:

```
Public Class Dog
  Private Name As String
End Class
```

Because your class doesn't have a constructor of its own, the Visual Basic .NET compiler adds a default constructor for you. If you wrote the equivalent constructor yourself, it would look something like this:

```
Public Class Dog
  Private Name As String

  Public Sub New()
    '*** empty implementation
  End Sub
End Class
```

If you're skeptical or simply curious, you can verify this behavior by compiling a Visual Basic .NET class into a DLL and inspecting its metadata using the utility `ILDASM.EXE` discussed in Chapter 2. This utility reveals the class definition that's been generated by the Visual Basic .NET compiler; note that constructors are always named `.ctor`. When you look at a class definition with `ILDASM.EXE`, you will be able to verify that the Visual Basic .NET compiler adds a public default constructor to any class whose definition lacks an explicit constructor.

Any constructor that's automatically added by the Visual Basic .NET compiler is always a default constructor. It's important to recognize the effect that a default constructor has on clients that want to create objects from your class. When your class exposes a public default constructor, a client-side programmer can create an object without passing any initialization data:

```
Dim dog1 As New Dog   '*** call to default constructor
```

As mentioned earlier, the Visual Basic .NET compiler automatically adds a default constructor to your class when you do not add a constructor of your own. Conversely, the compiler doesn't supply such a constructor when you explicitly add a parameterized constructor to your class. That explains why a class with a single parameterized constructor (such as the Human class in Listing 4.5) does not have a default constructor.

It is perfectly legal to define a class with more than one constructor, a technique known as *overloading* constructors. If you want to include a default constructor as well as a parameterized constructor, you must explicitly define both constructors in your class:

```
Public Class Dog
  Private Name As String

  '*** parameterized constructor
  Public Sub New(ByVal Name As String)
    Me.Name = Name
  End Sub

  '*** default constructor
  Public Sub New()
    Me.Name = "Spot"
  End Sub
End Class
```

Whether you want both a default constructor and a parameterized constructor depends on the kind of class being designed. In cases where the client should pass initialization data in every call to the New operator, a default constructor is not necessary. In cases where you want to provide meaningful default values for all your fields, adding a public default constructor is very convenient.

When overloading constructors, you have the flexibility to add more than one parameterized constructor to a class. In some cases, providing client-side programmers with multiple constructors can prove more convenient because they can choose between several different parameter lists. Consider the Dog class, which has been rewritten here to define two parameterized constructors:

```
Public Class Dog
   Private Name As String
   Private Age As Integer

   '*** 1st parameterized constructor
   Public Sub New(ByVal Name As String, ByVal Age As Integer)
     Me.Name = Name
     Me.Age = Age
   End Sub

   '*** 2nd parameterized constructor
   Public Sub New(ByVal Name As String)
     Me.Name = Name
     Me.Age = -1  '*** -1 means age unknown
   End Sub
End Class
```

The design of this class is based on the assumption that it is illegal to create a Dog object without a valid name. That's why no default constructor is provided. At the same time, the class allows a client to create a Dog object without a valid age. Given this class definition, a Dog object can be created in either of two ways:

```
Dim dog1 As New Dog("Lassie", 10)
Dim dog2 As New Dog("Snoopy")
```

In other words, the design of this class assumes that the age of the dog is an optional piece of data. Consequently, the class includes logic to determine that the age is unknown if the Age field has a value of -1. The point of this design is that some initialization data is required while other initialization data is optional. When using the New operator to create a Dog object, a client must pass the Name parameter, but passing the Age parameter is optional.

When designing and implementing larger classes, you'll probably overload constructors. Indeed, classes that contain four or five constructors are not especially uncommon. Such a design provides more flexibility to your clients.

While each overloaded constructor in a class must have its own implementation, you might want to create several constructors in a class that all need to run common initialization code. To avoid writing and maintaining duplicate code across several constructors, you should learn how to call one constructor from another. Here's a modified version of the Dog class in which one constructor calls another:

```
Public Class Dog
   Private Name As String
   Private Age As Integer

   '*** first parameterized constructor
   Public Sub New(ByVal Name As String, ByVal Age As Integer)
     Me.Name = Name
     Me.Age = Age
   End Sub

   '*** second parameterized constructor
   Public Sub New(ByVal Name As String)
     Me.New(Name, -1)  '*** forward call to constructor
   End Sub
End Class
```

As this code demonstrates, it's a fairly simple matter to call one constructor from another. You simply call Me.New as if you were calling a method. Of course, calling one overloaded constructor from another constructor requires you to pass the appropriate parameter list of the target constructor. In other words, the call to Me.New must be made using a parameter list that matches the parameter list of the overloaded constructor you want to call. Also, note that the call to another constructor must be the first statement in the overloading constructor; you cannot do initialization work first and then call another constructor.

Occasionally, you may want to prohibit clients from creating any objects from your class—for example, if you've designed a class that contains only shared members. One way to prevent programmers from creating objects based on your class is to make sure the class doesn't contain an accessible constructor. This means you cannot define a public constructor, and you must ensure that the Visual Basic .NET compiler doesn't add a public constructor automatically. You can accomplish this goal by explicitly defining a private constructor in your class:

```
'*** a class with no public constructors
Public Class Human
  Private Sub New()
  End Sub

  '*** other members omitted for clarity
End Class
```

Although this design prohibits clients from creating objects themselves using the New operator, the restriction doesn't mean the class itself is not creatable. In fact, the class is still creatable by code that can access the constructor. For example, shared methods in the Human class could create Human objects using the New operator.

Where have we seen something like this before? Listing 4.4 showed the Human class with a shared factory method. Think what would happen if you added a private constructor to that class. You could prevent clients from creating objects by any means other than your shared factory method. In some cases this is a very useful design technique.

Sometimes it's useful to define constructors using the Friend access modifier. Recall that a friend member is only accessible to code within the containing assembly. Therefore, a class design that contains only friend constructors effectively makes a class creatable from inside the containing assembly but noncreatable to code in other assemblies.

Initializers and Constructors

So far, this chapter has discussed two techniques for assigning an initial value to a field: using a field initializer and writing code in a constructor. The following class definitions demonstrate these two approaches:

```
Public Class Class1
  Public Field1 As Integer = 10
  Public Field2 As Double = 2.14
```

```
End Class

Public Class Class2
  Public Field1 As Integer
  Public Field2 As Double

  Public Sub New()
    Me.Field1 = 10
    Me.Field2 = 2.14
  End Sub
End Class
```

Both techniques produce the same effect. In fact, these two classes are essentially identical once they are compiled. This similarity reflects the manner in which the Visual Basic .NET compiler handles field initializers.

At compile time, the Visual Basic .NET compiler deals with field initializers by adding executable code to the beginning of each constructor in the class. Therefore, when you write a class definition such as that shown above for Class1, the compiler transforms it into the class definition shown for Class2.

The Visual Basic .NET compiler is guaranteed to execute field initializers in the order in which they are defined. In other words, initializers at the top of a class definition will always run before the ones at the bottom. Also, field initializers are guaranteed to execute before any explicit code you've written in the constructor. For this reason, it is probably a mistake to create the following class:

```
Public Class Class3
  Public Field1 As Integer = 10

  Public Sub New()
    Field1 = 20  '*** overrides field initializer of Field1
  End Sub
End Class
```

The code inside the constructor runs after the field initializer, so the value of 10 assigned by the field initializer is overwritten in the constructor with the value 20. This result highlights why you should initialize a field either with an initializer or within a constructor. Don't try to do both, because the assignment in the constructor will always overwrite the assignment of the initializer. This will obviously create problems with respect to readability and maintainability.

When choosing between field initializers and a constructor for initializing your fields, there are a few factors you should consider. Field initializers can help to improve both readability and maintainability, especially when a class has several different constructors. By comparison, writing code inside a constructor provides more flexibility, because you can write as much as code as needed to complete the initialization process.

Shared Constructors

As the preceding discussion has emphasized, instance constructors initialize objects. In addition, Visual Basic .NET allows you to provide shared constructors (also known as class constructors). Shared constructors are most often used to initialize class-level data such as shared fields.

Unlike an instance constructor, a shared constructor is not called directly by clients. Instead, it is called by the CLR before any other code in the class is allowed to execute. Note that a shared constructor cannot take parameters, and thus cannot be overloaded. To create a shared constructor, you add a shared sub procedure named New with no parameters. Listing 4.6 presents a simple class with a shared constructor.

LISTING 4.6: A class with a shared constructor

```
Public Class Class1
  Public Shared Private LastTimeIGotLoaded As Date

  '*** shared constructor
  Public Shared Sub New()
    LastTimeIGotLoaded = Date.Now
  End Sub
End Class
```

Exactly when the CLR calls a shared constructor is undefined. Nevertheless, when you supply a shared constructor, you are guaranteed that the CLR will execute its implementation exactly once and that it will run sometime between the time when the program starts and the time when a client first uses the class. Thus the shared constructor will run before any client can access any member of the class. You are also guaranteed that the shared constructor will run before any instance constructor runs.

Field initializers work the same way with shared fields as they do with instance fields. When you add an initializer to a shared field, the Visual Basic .NET compiler simply adds code to the beginning of the shared constructor to perform the assignment. As in the case of instance field initializers, the initializers for shared fields are guaranteed to run in the order in which they are defined. They are also guaranteed to run before any explicit code in the shared constructor executes.

Methods

Programmers write the majority of their code in the form of method implementations. The methods of a class define which operations may be performed on that class or on objects created from that class. Any method definition includes three parts:

- *Method signature.* The method signature defines the client-side calling syntax. The signature, which is always the first part of any method definition, includes the method's name, its parameter list, and the return type if present.
- *Method semantics.* The method semantics define what happens when the method is called. These semantics should be well defined by the author of the method, because their definition and documentation provide other programmers with an expectation of what should happen when the method is called. Note that the method semantics cannot be captured in source code or compiled into the metadata of your assemblies. Instead, they must be communicated by some other means, such as word of mouth or written documentation that you distribute along with the assembly that contains your code.
- *Method implementation.* The method implementation is where you write your lines of executable code that make good on the promise extended to other programmers by the method semantics.

We'll use the class definition in Listing 4.7 to illustrate a few important points about methods.

LISTING 4.7: A simple class with two methods—a function and a sub

```
Public Class Class1

  '*** method defined as a function
  Public Function Method1(ByVal i As Integer) As String
    '*** method implementation
  End Function

  '*** method defined as a sub procedure
  Public Sub Method2(ByVal s As String, ByRef x As Double)
    '*** method implementation
  End Sub

End Class
```

Each method must be defined using either the `Function` keyword or the `Sub` keyword. A method defined with `Function` must have a typed return value and its signature should be defined with an `As` clause at the end. A method defined with `Sub` does not have a return value and cannot have an `As` clause at the end. Methods written in C# with a return type of `void` are equivalent to `Sub` methods in Visual Basic .NET.

When passing parameters to a method, the method's signature determines whether the parameters will be passed by reference or by value (see Listing 4.7). Parameters defined with the `ByVal` keyword are passed by value; parameters defined with the `ByRef` keyword are passed by reference. If you define a parameter without using either the `ByVal` or `ByRef` keyword, the default convention for parameter passing is by value. In contrast, in earlier versions of Visual Basic the default parameter-passing convention was by reference.

There's more to say on parameter passing with respect to using the `ByVal` and `ByRef` keywords. However, let's wait until Chapter 10 to go into these details.

Optional Parameters

In Visual Basic .NET, methods can be defined with optional parameters. If you have used optional parameters in earlier versions of Visual Basic, you will want to take note of some important differences regarding how they work in Visual Basic .NET. Specifically, their use is more restricted in Visual Basic .NET. Consider the following class definition:

```
Public Class Class1
  Public Sub Method3(Optional ByVal i As Integer = 1)
    '*** implementation
  End Sub
End Class
```

Unlike in previous versions of Visual Basic, the use of an optional parameter now requires a default value. Furthermore, Visual Basic .NET does not support the IsMissing function. This lack of support means that within the method implementation, you cannot differentiate between a call that omits the parameter and a call that happens to pass the default value for the parameter.

Note that optional parameters are not really recognized by the programming model of the CLR. Instead, optional parameters are a compile-time feature that is supported by the Visual Basic .NET compiler. When you compile an assembly that includes a method with an optional parameter, the Visual Basic .NET complier adds extra metadata to the method's definition. To do so, the Visual Basic .NET compiler uses a custom attribute from the FCL to mark the parameter as optional and to cache its default value in the component metadata of your assembly.

When other Visual Basic .NET programmers write code that uses your assembly, they can call methods with or without the optional parameters. But what *really* happens when a programmer calls your method and omits the optional parameter? The client-side compiler inspects the metadata in your assembly and determines that the parameter is optional. The compiler then obtains the default value from the metadata and embeds this value directly into the IL generated for the client-side code. Therefore, the use of optional parameters brings up the same issue as the use of Const fields—namely, when you change the default value of an optional parameter, you must recompile all client applications that use that value.

As you can see, optional parameters are supported by the Visual Basic .NET compiler through attributes and everything about their use is completely resolved at compile time. Although the Visual Basic .NET compiler can deal with optional parameters from the client-side perspective, it's important to recognize that many other compilers cannot (including the C# compiler). This restriction means that optional parameters are, for the most part, a feature that remains exclusive to Visual Basic .NET programmers.

Use of optional parameters does not violate the rules of the CLS, however. In fact, a programmer who is using another managed language such as C# can call methods that have been defined in Visual Basic .NET with optional parameters. The C# programmer will then see these as mandatory parameters rather than optional parameters.

Parameter Arrays

Methods in Visual Basic .NET can also be defined with parameter arrays. A method can have at most one parameter that's defined as a parameter array, which must be the rightmost parameter in the parameter list. Here's an example of such a method:

```
Public Class Class1
  Public Sub Method4(ByVal ParamArray data() As String)
    '*** implementation
  End Sub
End Class
```

At compile time, the signature for `Method4` is compiled into component metadata as a standard array parameter along with a custom attribute signifying that it is a parameter array. When you write the implementation for a method like `Method4`, you can handle the incoming parameter for the parameter array just as you would deal with any other standard array. On the client side, however, you can write code using any of the following techniques to call a method with a parameter array:

```
Dim obj As New Class1()
obj.Method4()
obj.Method4("Bob")
obj.Method4("Moc", "Curly", "Larry")
obj.Method4("A", "B", "C", "D", "E", "F", "G")
```

As this example demonstrates, a Visual Basic .NET programmer who calls a method with a parameter array can pass any number of parameters. On the client side, the Visual Basic .NET compiler simply generates the code to package the parameters being passed into a standard array when calling the method.

Parameter arrays resemble optional parameters in the sense that they are a convenience feature added by the compiler. Unlike optional parameters, however, parameter arrays are supported in C# as well as Visual Basic .NET.

As a consequence, designs that use parameter arrays in public method signatures can be used interchangeably across these two languages.

Overloading Methods

Earlier, we saw how overloading works with constructors. Now, let's conduct a more thorough examination of how overloading works with methods in general. Method overloading is a design technique in which a class author creates two or more methods with the same name inside the same class. You can overload both shared methods and instance methods.

The primary motivation for overloading a method name with multiple implementations is to provide client-side programmers with more flexibility and more convenience. Consider the code in Listing 4.8.

LISTING 4.8: A class with overloaded methods

```
Public Class HumanManager

  Public Function GetHuman(ID As Integer) As Human
    '*** method implementation
  End Function

  Public Function GetHuman(Name As String) As Human
    '*** method implementation
  End Function

End Class
```

The definition of the HumanManager class contains two method definitions named GetHuman. Thus the GetHuman method has been overloaded with two different implementations. What differentiates these two method implementations from each other is their signature—in particular, their parameter lists. One has a single parameter based on the Integer type, and the other has a single parameter based on the String type. Now look at an example of some client-side code written against this HumanManager class:

```
Dim mgr As New HumanManager()

'*** call GetHuman(Integer)
Dim human1 As Human = mgr.GetHuman(23)

'*** call GetHuman(String)
Dim human2 As Human = mgr.GetHuman("Bob")
```

Given the design of the HumanManager class, it doesn't matter whether the client has an integer value with a human's ID or a string value with a human's name—the client can still call the GetHuman method and obtain the human object. Note that both implementations of GetHuman adhere to very similar semantics. This should always be the case when you overload a method name.

When you overload a set of methods to the same name, each individual method must have a unique parameter list. For two parameter lists to be unique, they must differ in terms of the number of their parameters and/or the sequence of their parameter types. It is illegal to overload two methods based simply on their return type. It is also illegal to overload two methods where the parameter lists differ only by the use of ByVal and ByRef, or by the names of the parameters themselves.

In short, when considering method signatures for the purposes of overloading, you should think only in terms of the method name and the parameter types. For example, you could view the method signatures from the HumanManager class in Listing 4.8 in this format:

```
GetHuman(Integer)
GetHuman(String)
```

Viewing method signatures in this way emphasizes that these two methods have different parameter lists. Once you start thinking about method signatures in these terms, it becomes easier to understand the rules of overloading.

As another example, look at the following class definition:

```
Public Class Class1
  Public Function Method1(ByVal x As Integer) As String
    '*** definition
  End Function

  Public Sub Method1(ByVal y As Integer)
    '*** definition
  End Sub

  Public Sub Method1(ByRef z As Integer)
    '*** definition
  End Sub
End Class
```

This class definition will not compile, because all three methods have the same signature for the purposes of method overloading. That is, the signature for all three methods can be expressed in the following form:

```
Method1(Integer)
```

It is illegal to use any two of these definitions for `Method1` inside the same class. It doesn't matter whether a method is defined with the `Function` keyword or the `Sub` keyword. Likewise, it doesn't matter whether a method's parameters have different names or differ in their use of the `ByVal` and `ByRef` keywords. You must make the parameter list of each overloaded member unique with respect to the number and/or type of its parameters.

From the client-side perspective, how does the Visual Basic .NET compiler deal with overloaded methods? When you call a method that has been overloaded, the compiler determines which method implementation to invoke by matching the parameter list of the caller's syntax with the parameter list of an available implementation. When strict type checking is enabled, the decision about which method implementation to call is always made by the compiler at compile time. No performance penalty is imposed as would occur if the decision was deferred until runtime.

If it fails to identify an exact match between the parameter list of the caller and the parameter lists of the overloaded method, the Visual Basic .NET compiler will try to find a match using a set of promotion rules. For example, the compiler knows it can promote a `Short` to an `Integer`. Examine the following code, based on the class definition of Listing 4.8:

```
Dim human1 As Human
Dim ID1 As Short = 48
human1 = mgr.GetHuman(ID1)   '*** calls GetHuman(Integer)
```

When the Visual Basic .NET compiler cannot find any match, it generates a compile-time error. For example, with `Option Strict` enabled, the caller cannot pass a `Long` when the overloaded method's parameter is based on an `Integer`:

```
Dim human2 As Human
Dim ID2 As Long = 48
human2 = mgr.GetHuman(ID2)   '*** compile-time error
```

When you are designing a class, you might find that several overloaded methods require a common implementation. Obviously you don't want to write and maintain redundant code, so it's important that you learn to call one implementation of an overloaded method from another. Consider the following class with an overloaded method:

```
Public Class BarFly
  Public Sub Speak(ByVal message As String)
    MsgBox(message)           '*** common implementation
  End Sub

  Public Sub Speak()
    Me.Speak("How ya doing")  '*** forward call
  End Sub
End Class
```

As this example demonstrates, one overloaded method implementation can simply call another by name. Just make sure you pass the appropriate parameter list for the target method when making the call.

In the preceding example, the implementation of the Speak method with no parameters forwards the call to the other overloaded implementation of Speak. In essence, the parameter-less implementation of Speak simply supplies a default parameter value and then delegates the work to the other implementation of Speak. Now consider the following client-side code:

```
Dim bob As New BarFly()

'*** call Speak(String)
bob.Speak("Good afternoon")

'*** call Speak()
bob.Speak()
```

These two calls to Speak use different entry points into the class, so each call is directed to a different method implementation. Nevertheless, the design of Speak allows both calls to leverage a common implementation. The implication is that overloaded methods can be used to simulate optional parameters with default values. This tactic represents a valuable design technique that you should add to your bag of tricks. In fact, you will usually prefer this design technique over a design that uses optional parameters, for the reasons explained in the next subsection.

Method Overloading versus Optional Parameters

Now that you understand the basics of member overloading, it's important to recognize why you should prefer overloading for creating optional parameters as opposed to using the `Optional` keyword.

The first problem with `Optional` parameters is that they are not supported across all languages. For example, programmers using C# cannot take advantage of the `Optional` parameters you define inside your methods. A C# programmer sees an `Optional` parameter as a mandatory parameter. However, if you use overloaded methods to simulate `Optional` parameters, you can achieve the desired result in a language-neutral fashion.

The second problem with `Optional` parameters is that the default value is compiled into the client's executable image, which can produce unexpected results. Imagine you have a DLL that includes a method with an `Optional` parameter whose default value is 10. When you compile a client that calls this method and omits the parameter, the client contains the logic to make the call and pass a value of 10 for the parameter.

But suppose you modify the method inside the DLL to change the parameter's default value from 10 to 20. When you recompile the DLL and rerun the old client, what value do you expect for the parameter? The client still passes a value of 10—and that's what you should expect because 10 was the default value when the client was compiled. Your change within the DLL to the default value is not used unless the client is recompiled against the new version of the DLL. Once again, if you design using overloaded methods instead of `Optional` parameters, you can avoid this problem.

A final issue that arises with `Optional` parameters is their tendency to create versioning problems for a class DLL project. Suppose you have the following `Class` definition inside a DLL:

```
Public Class BarFly
  Public Sub Speak()
    MsgBox("How ya doing")
  End Sub
End Class
```

Assume you've compiled this class into a DLL and compiled several client applications against it. These client applications now have a dependency on a method named `Speak` that takes no parameters. What would happen if you added an `Optional` parameter to the `Speak` method and recompiled the DLL? There is no longer a method named `Speak` that takes no parameters. Therefore, the new version of your assembly has introduced breaking changes to existing client applications. If you keep the implementation of `Speak` that takes no parameters and simply add a second overloaded version of `Speak` that takes a parameter, versioning is far more elegant. This technique also eliminates the need to recompile any client applications.

You will inevitably encounter times when you have to decide between using `Optional` parameters and using overloaded methods. While you might already be familiar with the use of `Optional` parameters, they don't always produce the best results. Clearly, there are several good reasons to prefer method overloading instead of `Optional` parameters. If you or another programmer on your team find yourselves creating methods with `Optional` parameters, reconsider whether method overloading offers a better design approach.

Properties

For historical reasons, many developers prefer the syntactic simplicity of using public fields when they program against a class definition. Unfortunately, using public fields weakens the encapsulation of the class and makes it more difficult to evolve the class implementation over time. The programming model of the .NET Framework provides properties as a way to provide the illusion of public fields to the client while maintaining the encapsulation of private fields in the class.

Many class authors like to expose properties over fields because this technique allows them to intercept a client's request to read or modify data. Unlike a field, a property definition can include executable code to perform actions such as calculations and data validation. While properties often correspond to private fields of a class, such a relationship is not a requirement. Rather, properties can be used to expose a public facade that is entirely different from the actual layout of your private fields. Internally, property implementations may use calculations or lazy evaluation to return the appropriate value to the client.

Inside a class definition, a property is a named member that includes one or two inner method declarations. One of these inner methods is defined using a `Get` block and is called the *get method* or *accessor*. The other inner method is defined using a `Set` block and is called the *set method* or *mutator*.

Listing 4.9 shows an example of a class that exposes the data from a private field using a public property named `Name`. The definition of the `Name` property contains a `Set` block and a `Get` block. You should think of these two inner blocks as individual methods. Note the presence of the parameter named `Value` in the property's set method. Visual Basic .NET uses this intrinsic parameter to pass the property value assigned by the client to your property implementation inside the property's set method.

LISTING 4.9: A class with a public property mapped to a private field

```
Public Class Human

  '*** private field
  Private m_Name As String

  '*** property provides controlled access to private field
  Public Property Name As String
    Get
      '*** perform calculations here if necessary
      Return m_Name
    End Get

    Set(ByVal Value As String)
      '*** perform validation here if necessary
      m_Name = Value
    End Set
  End Property

End Class
```

Every property is based on a specific type. For example, the `Name` property in Listing 4.9 is based on the `String` type. The type of a property applies to the return type of the get method and the `Value` parameter of the set method.

The way properties work internally is not as straightforward as the mechanism employed by other class members such as fields and methods. Their more complex operation reflects the fact the Visual Basic .NET compiler works hard to create an illusion—namely, to make a method or a pair of methods appear as a field to the client. How does the compiler accomplish this goal?

Let's examine the compiled version of the Human class from Listing 4.9 to see how the code is compiled into a class definition. Figure 4.3 shows what the class looks like from the perspective of the ILDASM.EXE utility. The compiler creates individual method definitions when you create a property with a Get block and a Set block. There is one method definition for the get method and another for the set method. The implementation for these two methods is created from the code inside the Get block and the Set block.

These two methods are named using a standard naming convention:

- The get method for a property is named using the property name together with a prefix of get_.
- The set method for a property is named using the property name together with a prefix of set_.

In the preceding example, the two methods created for the Name property are therefore named get_Name and set_Name.

Take another look at Figure 4.3. Observe that the compiler has created a third member that represents the property itself. Locate the member named Name, which has an upward-facing triangle to its left. This property member isn't really a physical member like the get method and the set method; rather, it is a metadata-only member.

The value of this metadata-only member derives from its ability to inform compilers and other development tools that the class supports the

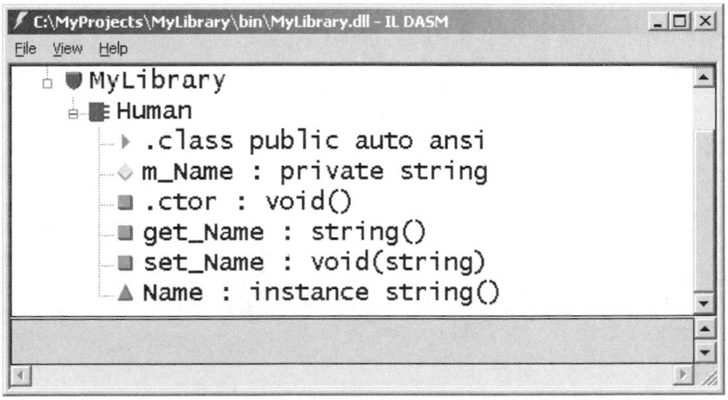

FIGURE 4.3: A property is implemented with methods and a metadata-only member.

.NET pattern for properties. The property member also contains the names of the get and set methods. Compilers for managed languages such as Visual Basic .NET and C# use the property member to discover the name of its internal get and set methods at compile time.

When a class contains a public property like the one just discussed, client code is free to access this member like a field. To access a shared property, a caller would use the same syntax as for any other shared member: the class name, followed by the property name. To access an instance property, a caller must use an object reference. Here's an example of accessing the Name property of the Human class from Listing 4.9:

```
Dim human1 As New Human()

'*** triggers call to set_Name("Bob")
human1.Name = "Bob"

'*** triggers call to get_Name()
Dim s As String = human1.Name
```

Three kinds of properties exist: read/write properties, read-only properties, and write-only properties. The property in Listing 4.9 is a read/write property because it has both a Get block and a Set block. In contrast, the following class definition contains both a read-only property and a write-only property:

```
Public Class Customer

  Private m_FirstName As String
  Private m_LastName As String
  Private m_Password As String

  '*** property contains getter but no setter
  Public ReadOnly Property FullName as String
    Get
        Return m_FirstName & " " & m_LastName
    End Get
  End Property

  '*** property contains setter but no getter
  Public WriteOnly Property Password as String
    Set
      m_Password = Value
    End Set
  End Property

End Class
```

As demonstrated in this example, a read-only property must contain a `Get` block but cannot contain a `Set` block. Likewise, a write-only property must contain a `Set` block but cannot contain a `Get` block. You must also use the `ReadOnly` keyword when you define a read-only property, and the `WriteOnly` keyword when you define a write-only property. The Visual Basic .NET compiler generates compile-time errors if you don't use the `ReadOnly` and `WriteOnly` keywords when appropriate.

Parameterized and Default Properties

A property is like a method in the sense that it can be defined with one or more parameters. When a property has a parameter, that parameter works like an index into a collection. As a result, a parameterized property is able to exhibit collection-like qualities. Let's examine a class definition that demonstrates how to create a parameterized property. Listing 4.10 shows a class with a `Members` property that is indexed using a string.

LISTING 4.10: A class with a parameterized property

```
Public Class BridgeClub
  Private m_President As New Human("Marsha")
  Private m_Secretary As New Human("Randy")
  Private m_Treasurer As New Human("Nicole")

  Public ReadOnly Property Members(ByVal Title As String) As Human
    Get
      Select Case Title
        Case "President"
          Return m_President
        Case "Secretary"
          Return m_Secretary
        Case "Treasurer"
          Return m_Treasurer
        Case Else
          '*** no match: throw exception to caller
          Throw New ApplicationException("Unknown title")
      End Select
    End Get
  End Property
End Class
```

The `Members` property of the `BridgeClub` class in Listing 4.10 provides access to three private fields. Each of these private fields holds a reference to a specific member of the bridge club. A client of the `BridgeClub` class can obtain a reference to any of these objects by querying the `Members` property and passing the appropriate string value of the desired member. Here's an example of client-side code accessing the `Members` property:

```
Dim club As New BridgeClub()
Dim pres As Human = club.Members("President")
Dim sec As Human = club.Members("Secretary")
```

Taking this example one step further, you can define a parameterized property so that it's recognized as the default property. As you will see, default properties can provide an additional convenience to client-side programmers. You can define a parameterized property as a default property by adding the `Default` keyword to its definition:

```
Default ReadOnly Property Members(ByVal Title As String) As Human
    '*** same property implementation as shown before
End Property
```

Once you've defined a parameterized property using the `Default` keyword, client-side code can omit the property name when accessing it. For example, assuming that the `Members` property definition of Listing 4.10 has been extended with the `Default` keyword, a client has the option of accessing the property with or without the property's name:

```
Dim club As New BridgeClub()
Dim pres, sec As Human

'*** access parameterized property by name
pres = club.Members("President")

'*** access parameterized property as default
sec = club("Secretary")
```

As this example demonstrates, when you want to access a parameterized default property, you can access it by name or you can access it as a default property. Interestingly, C# supports only parameterized properties that are marked as a default property. In that language's terminology, such properties are called "indexers." On the other hand, C# does not support accessing parameterized properties by name. If you need to write code that might be used by C# programmers, make sure that you define each public parameterized property using the `Default` keyword.

Visual Basic .NET supports overloading properties in much the same way that it supports overloading methods. For example, one overloaded implementation of the `Members` property could accept a string parameter, while another overloaded implementation could accept an integer parameter. Therefore, one implementation of the `Members` property could return a `Human` object based on the friendly string value, while another implementation could return a `Human` object based on the ordinal number.

One important restriction applies to default properties. Unlike in earlier versions of Visual Basic, in Visual Basic .NET a property without parameters cannot be defined as a default property. This restriction follows from some of the cleanup efforts made to the Visual Basic .NET language. Recall from Chapter 3 that the `Set` statement is no longer supported for the assignment of object references. Once the `Set` statement was removed from the language, nonparameterized default properties created an ambiguity that could not be resolved, so they had to be removed as well.

Let's conclude this discussion of properties by exploring some fun syntax that is sure to inspire a sense of nostalgia in any long-time Visual Basic programmer. If you have a default property that accepts a single string parameter, the client can access this property by using the `!` syntax. Therefore, you can rewrite the client-side code from the previous example as follows:

```
Dim club As New BridgeClub()
Dim pres As Human = club!President
Dim sec As Human = club!Secretary
```

When you use the `!` operator, the Visual Basic .NET compiler looks for a default property that takes a single string parameter. If it finds such a property, it calls the property's get method, passing whatever comes after the `!` operator as the value of the string parameter. If the compiler cannot locate a default property that takes a single string parameter, it generates a compile-time error.

From the beginning of time, Visual Basic programmers have referred to the `!` operator as the *bang operator*. You have to admit that the bang operator adds to the personality of Visual Basic .NET and helps to differentiate it from any other managed language. You could say that this sort of syntax is *very VB*.

Nested Types

As discussed previously, a class definition can contain members such as fields, constructors, methods, and properties. With Visual Basic .NET, it is also possible to create a class definition that contains a nested definition for another type. A type that is defined inside the scope of another class definition is known as a *nested type.* Listing 4.11 shows two examples of nesting one class definition within another.

LISTING 4.11: Nested types

```
Public Class CustomerList
   Private Class Enumerator
     '*** class definition
   End Class
End Class

Public Class EmployeeList
   Public Class Enumerator
     '*** class definition
   End Class
End Class
```

Nested types provide a convenient way to manage and encapsulate code. For example, the CustomerList class and the EmployeeList class in Listing 4.11 each have a nested class named Enumerator. Even though two different classes are named Enumerator, no naming conflict arises because each is defined within the scope of a different class. If you create a utility class that is used by only one other class, nesting can help encapsulate the utility class from other code inside the same assembly. In general, nesting helps to avoid cluttering a namespace with extra type names.

A nested type resembles other class members in that its level of visibility controls how other code can use it. When you add a nested class to a public class, the nested class is public by default. If you choose to use nested classes, you have the option of defining them using a more restrictive level of visibility.

A class definition that is not nested in another class definition must be defined as either a `Public` type or a `Friend` type. In contrast, a class that's nested inside another class is like other kinds of class members in that you can define it using the `Private` keyword or the `Protected` keyword.

How do nested classes work? A programmer who is new to this concept can easily become confused about when objects from a nested class are instantiated. A quick example will clarify this issue. Imagine you have a `Dog` class that contains a nested `Flea` class:

```
Public Class Dog
  Private Class Flea
    '*** class definition
  End Class
End Class
```

Let's write some client-side code to create a new object from the `Dog` class:

```
Dim fido As New Dog()
```

Here's the question: Was a `Flea` object created when the `Dog` object was created? The answer is no. The `Dog` class and the `Flea` class are separate class definitions—it just so happens that the `Flea` class was defined within the `Dog` class. Each class must be instantiated individually. If you want to create a `Flea` object, some code must perform this operation explicitly. Here's a modified version of the `Dog` class that instantiates some `Flea` objects using field initializers:

```
Public Class Dog
  '*** private fields
  Private flea1 As New Flea()
  Private flea2 As New Flea()

  '*** nested class
  Private Class Flea
    '*** class definition
  End Class

End Class
```

Don't be fooled into thinking that the concepts involved with nested types are any more complicated than they really are. Like a namespace, a class simply provides an additional level of scoping in which you can define other types.

SUMMARY

Even if you have years of experience using a previous version of Visual Basic, it may take some effort on your part to embrace all of the new OOP support provided in Visual Basic .NET. After all, using fields, constructors, methods, and properties effectively requires an understanding of some nontrivial concepts. Nevertheless, learning these concepts and the syntax that goes along with them is the price of admission that must be paid when you decide to design and write software with Visual Basic .NET. This chapter introduced the many kinds of members you can add to a class, with one exception—events. We will defer the discussion of events until Chapter 8.

The redesign of the Visual Basic language to be a first-class citizen in terms of support for OOP brings with it a new set of responsibilities. This chapter examined the class as a stand-alone type. The next two chapters will build on this chapter by examining type relationships that are created when you begin to program with inheritance and interfaces. As you will see, the rules for operations such as creating constructors and overloading methods will become more complex when you begin to design and program types that are related through inheritance. Your firm understanding of how to design a class as a stand-alone entity is an essential prerequisite to learning the material that lies ahead.

5

Inheritance

M ANY PROGRAMMERS HAVE long considered inheritance to be one of
the most significant design features of OOP. Inheritance was made
popular more than two decades ago by languages such as C++ and
Smalltalk. Since then, new languages (e.g., Java) have come along and
refined the features and syntax for using inheritance. Now with the emer-
gence of the .NET Framework, Microsoft has designed a platform from the
ground up that offers support for what is arguably one of the most elegant
forms of inheritance to date.

The more you use the .NET Framework, the more you will realize just
how extensively it takes advantage of inheritance. For example, as discussed in Chapter 3, the CTS relies heavily on inheritance. When you use
the Windows Forms package, your new forms will inherit from an existing
form-based class in the FCL. When you use ASP.NET, your Web pages and
Web services will inherit from preexisting classes in the FCL. As a developer building applications or component libraries based on the .NET
Framework, you will find that familiarity with inheritance is an absolute
necessity.

Inheriting from a Class

Inheritance allows you to derive a new class from an existing class. Suppose
that class C inherits from class B. Then class B is typically called the *base*

class, and class C is called the *derived* class. Note that this terminology is not necessarily standard; some refer to B and C as *superclass* and *subclass*, or as *parent* and *child* classes, respectively. This book will stick with the terms "base" and "derived."

A derived class definition automatically inherits the implementation and the programming contract of its base class. The idea is that the derived class starts with a reusable class definition and modifies it by adding more members or by changing the behavior of existing methods and properties.

One of the primary reasons for designing with inheritance is that it provides an effective means for reusing code. For example, you can define a set of fields, methods, and properties in one class, and then use inheritance to reuse this code across several other classes. Inheritance is particularly beneficial in scenarios that require multiple classes with much in common but in which the classes are all specialized in slightly different ways. Examples include the following familiar categories: employees (administrative, technical, sales), database tables (customers, orders, products), and graphical shapes (circle, rectangle, triangle).

LISTING 5.1: A simple base class

```
'*** base class
Public Class Human

  '*** private implementation
  Private m_Name As String

  '*** public members
  Public Property Name() As String
    '*** provide controlled access to m_Name
  End Property

  Public Function Speak() As String
    Return "Hi, I'm a human named " & m_Name
  End Function

End Class
```

Let's start by looking at a simple example to introduce the basic syntax of inheritance. Listing 5.1 defines a class named Human that we would like to use as a base class. In Visual Basic .NET, when you want to state explicitly that one class inherits from another, you follow the name of the class with the `Inherits` keyword and the name of the base class. For example, here are two derived class definitions for `Manager` and `Programmer`, both with `Human` as their base class:

```
'*** first derived class
Public Class Manager
        Inherits Human
   '*** code to extend Human definition
End Class

'*** second derived class
Public Class Programmer : Inherits Human
   '*** code to extend Human definition
End Class
```

For the `Programmer` class, the preceding code fragment uses a colon instead of an actual line break between the class name and the `Inherits` keyword. As you might recall from earlier versions of Visual Basic, the colon acts as the line termination character. This colon-style syntax is often preferred because it improves readability by keeping the name of a derived class on the same line as the name of its base class.

The `Human` class serves as a base class for both the `Manager` class and the `Programmer` class. It's now possible to write implementations for these classes that are quite different as well as to add new members to each class to further increase their specialization. Nevertheless, these two classes will always share a common set of implementation details, and both support a unified programming contract defined by the `Human` class.

By default, every class you create in Visual Basic .NET can be inherited by other classes. If for some reason you don't want other programmers to inherit from your class, you can create a *sealed* class. A sealed class is defined in the Visual Basic .NET language using the keyword `NotInheritable`. The compiler will generate a compile-time error whenever a programmer attempts to define a class that inherits from such a sealed class:

```
Public NotInheritable Class Monkey   '*** sealed class definition
   '*** implementation
End Class

Public Class Programmer : Inherits Monkey   '*** compile-time error!
End Class
```

Figure 5.1 shows a common design view of class definitions known as an *inheritance hierarchy*. The Human class is located at the top of the hierarchy. The Manager class and the Programmer class inherit from the Human class and are consequently located directly below it in the inheritance hierarchy. Notice the direction of the arrows when denoting inheritance.

As shown in Figure 5.1, an inheritance hierarchy can be designed with multiple levels. Consider the two classes at the bottom of the hierarchy in Figure 5.1, SeniorProgrammer and JuniorProgrammer. These classes have been defined with the Programmer class as their base class. As a consequence, they inherit indirectly from the Human class. Thus a class in a multilevel inheritance hierarchy inherits from every class reachable by following the inheritance arrows upward.

An important design rule should always be applied when designing with inheritance. Two classes that will be related through inheritance should be able to pass the *is-a* test. In short, the test goes like this: If it makes sense to say "C is a B," then it makes sense for class C to inherit from class B. If such a sentence doesn't make sense, then you should reconsider the use of inheritance in this situation.

For example, you can correctly say that a programmer "is a" human. You can also correctly say that a senior programmer "is a" programmer. As you can see, the purpose of the is-a test is to ensure that a derived class is designed to model a more specialized version of whatever entity the base class is modeling.

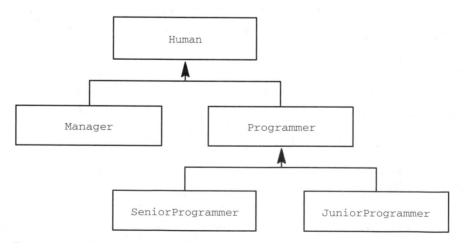

FIGURE 5.1: An inheritance hierarchy

You should try never to establish an inheritance relationship between two classes that cannot pass the is-a test. Imagine you saw a novice programmer trying to make the `Bicycle` class inherit from the `Wheel` class. You should intervene because you cannot correctly say that a bicycle "is a" wheel. You can correctly say that a bicycle "has a" wheel (or two), but that relationship calls for a different design technique that doesn't involve inheritance. When you determine that two entities exhibit the "has a" relationship, the situation most likely calls for a design using *containment*, in which the `Wheel` class is used to define fields within the `Bicycle` class. In other words, the `Bicycle` class *contains* the `Wheel` class.

Base Classes in the .NET Framework

Now that you've seen some of the basic principles and the syntax for using inheritance, it's time to introduce a few important rules that have been imposed by the .NET Common Type System (CTS).

The first rule is that you cannot define a class that inherits directly from more than one base class. In other words, the CTS does not support *multiple inheritance*. It is interesting to note that the lack of support for multiple inheritance in the .NET Framework is consistent with the Java programming language.

The second rule imposed by the CTS is that you cannot define a class that doesn't have a base class. This rule might seem somewhat confusing at first, because you can write a valid class definition in Visual Basic .NET (or in C#) that doesn't explicitly declare a base class. A little more explanation is required to clarify this point.

When you define a class without explicitly specifying a base class, the compiler automatically modifies the class definition to inherit from the `Object` class in the FCL. Once you understand this point, you can see that the following two class definitions have the same base class:

```
'*** implicitly inherit from Object
Public Class Dog
End Class

'*** explicitly inherit from Object
Public Class Cat : Inherits System.Object
End Class
```

These two CTS-imposed rules of inheritance can be summarized as follows: Every class (with the exception of the `Object` class) has exactly one base class. Of course, it's not just classes that have base types. For example, every structure and every enumeration also has a base type. Recall from Chapter 3 that the inheritance hierarchy of the CTS is *singly rooted* because the system-defined `Object` class serves as the ultimate base type (see Figure 3.1). Every other class either inherits directly from the `Object` class or inherits from another class that inherits (either directly or indirectly) from the `Object` class.

Inheriting Base Class Members

Although a derived class inherits the members of its base class, the manner in which certain kinds of members are inherited isn't completely intuitive. While the way things work with fields, methods, and properties is fairly straightforward, the manner in which constructors are inherited brings up issues that are a bit more complex.

Inheritance and Fields, Methods, and Properties

Every field, method, and property that is part of the base class definition is inherited by the derived class definition. As a result, each object created from a derived type carries with it all the states and behaviors that are defined by its base class. However, whether code in a derived class has access to the members inherited from its base class is a different matter altogether.

As mentioned in Chapter 4, each member of a class is defined with a level of accessibility that determines whether other code may access it. There are five levels of accessibility:

- *Private.* A base class member defined with the `Private` access modifier is not accessible to either code inside the derived class or client-side code using either class.

- *Protected.* A base class member defined with the `Protected` access modifier is accessible to code inside the derived class but is not accessible to client-side code. Private and protected members of a base class are similar in that they are not accessible to client-side code written against either the base class or the derived class.

- *Public*. A base class member defined with the `Public` access modifier is accessible to code inside the derived class as well as all client-side code. Public members are unlike private and protected members in that they add functionality to the programming contract that a derived class exposes to its clients.

- *Friend*. A member that is defined with the `Friend` access modifier is accessible to all code inside the containing assembly but inaccessible to code in other assemblies. The friend level of accessibility is not affected by whether the accessing code is part of a derived class.

- *Protected Friend*. The protected friend level of accessibility is achieved by combining the `Protected` access modifier with the `Friend` access modifier. A protected friend is accessible to all code inside the containing assembly *and* to code within derived classes (whether the derived class is part of the same assembly or not).

Listing 5.2 presents an example that summarizes the discussion of what is legal and what is not legal with respect to accessing fields of varying levels of accessibility.

LISTING 5.2: The meaning of access modifiers in the presence of inheritance

```
'*** base class
Public Class BettysBaseClass
   Private Field1 As Integer
   Protected Field2 As Integer
   Public Field3 As Integer
End Class

'*** derived class
Public Class DannysDerivedClass : Inherits BettysBaseClass
   Public Sub Method1()
     Me.Field1 = 10   '*** illegal (compile-time error)
     Me.Field2 = 20   '*** legal
     Me.Field3 = 30   '*** legal
   End Sub
End Class

'*** client-side code
Module BobsApp
```

continues

```
Public Sub Main()
  Dim obj As New DannysDerivedClass()
  obj.Field1 = 10   '*** illegal (compile-time error)
  obj.Field2 = 20   '*** illegal (compile-time error)
  obj.Field3 = 30   '*** legal
End Sub
End Module
```

Now that we have outlined the rules of member accessibility, it's time to discuss how to properly encapsulate base class members when designing for inheritance. *Encapsulation* is the practice of hiding the implementation details of classes and assemblies from other code. For example, a protected member is encapsulated from client-side code. A private member is encapsulated from client-side code and derived classes. A friend member is encapsulated from code in other assemblies.

Imagine you are designing a component library that you plan to sell to other companies. You will update this component library from time to time and send the newest version to your customers. If your design involves distributing base classes that other programmers will likely extend through the use of inheritance, you need to think very carefully through the issues of defining various base class members as private versus protected.

Any member defined as private is fully encapsulated and can be modified or removed without violating the original contract between a base class and any of its derived classes. In contrast, members defined as protected are a significant part of the contract between a base class and its derived classes. Modifying or removing protected members can introduce breaking changes to your customer's code.

To keep your customers happy, you must devise a way to maintain and evolve the base classes in your component library without introducing breaking changes. A decade's worth of experience with inheritance has told the software industry that this challenge can be very hard to meet.

When authoring base classes, it's critical to start thinking about *versioning* in the initial design phase. You must determine how easy (or how difficult) it will be to modify derived classes if modifications to base classes cause breaking changes. It helps to design with the knowledge that it's a common mistake to underestimate the importance of encapsulating base class members from derived classes.

Another important consideration is whether it makes sense to use inheritance across assembly boundaries. While the compilers and the plumbing of the CLR are more than capable of fusing a base class implementation from one assembly together with the derived class implementation in a second assembly, you should recognize that versioning management grows ever more difficult as the scope of the inheritance increases.

That doesn't mean that you should never use cross-assembly inheritance. Many experienced designers have employed this strategy very effectively. For example, when you leverage one of the popular .NET frameworks such as Windows Forms or ASP.NET, you're required to create a class in a user-defined assembly that inherits from a class in a system-defined assembly. But understand one thing: The designers at Microsoft who created these frameworks thought long and hard about how to maintain and evolve their base classes without introducing breaking changes to your code.

If you plan to create base classes for use by programmers in other development teams, you must be prepared to think through these same issues. It is naive to ponder encapsulation only in terms of stand-alone classes, and only in terms of a single version. Inheritance and component-based development make these issues much more complex. They also make mistakes far more costly. In general, you shouldn't expose base class members to derived classes and/or other assemblies if these members might ever change in name, type, or signature. Following this simple rule will help you maintain backward compatibility with existing derived classes while evolving the implementation of your base classes.

Inheritance and Constructors

The way in which constructors are inherited isn't as obvious as for other kinds of base class members. From the perspective of a client attempting to create an object from the derived class, the derived class definition does not inherit any of the constructors defined in the base class. Instead, the derived class must contain one or more of its own constructors to support object instantiation. Furthermore, each constructor defined in a derived class must call one of the constructors in its base class before performing any of its own initialization work.

Recall from Chapter 4 that the Visual Basic .NET compiler will automatically create a public default constructor for any class definition that does not define a constructor of its own. This default constructor also contains code to call the default constructor of the base class. As an example, consider the following class definition:

```
'*** a class you write
Public Class Dog
End Class
```

Once compiled, the definition of this class really looks like this:

```
'*** code generated by compiler
Public Class Dog : Inherits System.Object

  '*** default constructor generated by compiler
  Public Sub New()
    MyBase.New()  '*** call to default constructor in System.Object
  End Sub

End Class
```

As this example reveals, the compiler will generate the required constructor automatically along with a call to the base class's default constructor. But what about the situation in which the base class does not have an accessible default constructor? In such a case, the derived class definition will not compile because the automatically generated default constructor is invalid. As a result, the author of the derived class must provide a constructor of his or her own, with an explicit call to a constructor in the base class.

The only time a derived class author can get away with not explicitly defining a constructor is when the base class provides an accessible default constructor. As it turns out, the Object class contains a public default constructor, which explains why you don't have to explicitly add a constructor to a class that inherits from the Object class. Likewise, you don't have to explicitly add a constructor to a class that inherits from another class with an accessible default constructor.

Sometimes, however, you must inherit from a class that doesn't contain a default constructor. Consider the following code, which includes a revised definition of the Human class discussed earlier. In particular, note that the Human class now contains a parameterized constructor:

```
Public Class Human
  Protected m_Name As String

  Public Sub New(ByVal Name As String)
    m_Name = Name
  End Sub

  Public Function Speak() As String
    Return "Hi, I'm a human named " & m_Name
  End Function
End Class

Public Class Programmer : Inherits Human
  '*** this class definition will not compile
End Class
```

Because this definition contains a single parameterized constructor, the compiler doesn't automatically add a default constructor to class Human. As a result, when you try to define the Programmer class without an explicit constructor, your code will not compile because Visual Basic .NET cannot generate a valid default constructor. To make the Programmer class compile, you must add a constructor that explicitly calls an accessible constructor defined in the Human class:

```
Public Class Programmer : Inherits Human

  Public Sub New(Name As String)
    MyBase.New(Name) '*** call to base class constructor
    '*** programmer-specific initialization goes here
  End Sub

End Class
```

As shown in the preceding code, you make an explicit call to a base class constructor by using MyBase.New and passing the appropriate list of parameters. Note that when you explicitly call a base class constructor from a derived class constructor, you can do it only once and the call must be the first statement in the constructor's implementation.

Of course, you never *have* to rely on compiler-generated calls to the default constructor. In some cases you might prefer to call a different constructor. An explicit call to MyBase.New can always be used at the top of a derived class constructor to call the exact base class constructor you want. Some programmers even add explicit calls to the default constructor by using `MyBase.New`. Even though such calls can be automatically generated by the compiler, making these calls explicit can serve to make your code self-documenting and easier to understand.

Let's take a moment and consider the sequence in which the constructors are executed during object instantiation by examining the scenario where a client creates an object from the `Programmer` class using the `New` operator. When the client calls `New`, a constructor in the `Programmer` class begins to execute. Before this constructor can do anything interesting, however, it must call a constructor in the `Human` class. The constructor in the `Human` class faces the same constraints. Before it can do anything interesting, it must call the default constructor of the `Object` class.

The important observation is that constructors execute in a chain starting with the least-derived class (i.e., `Object`) and ending with the most-derived class. The implementation for the constructor of the `Object` class always runs to completion first. In the case of creating a new `Programmer` object, when the constructor for the `Object` class completes, it returns and the constructor for the `Human` class next runs to completion. Once the constructor for the `Human` class returns, the constructor for the `Programmer` class runs to completion. After the entire chain of constructors finishes executing, control finally returns to the client that started the sequence by calling the `New` operator on the `Programmer` class.

Limiting Inheritance to the Containing Assembly

Now that you understand the basics of how constructors must be coordinated between a base class and its derived classes, let's explore a useful design technique that prevents other programmers in other assemblies from inheriting from your base classes. The benefit of using this technique is that you can take advantage of inheritance within your assembly, but prevent cross-assembly inheritance. This approach eliminates the need to worry about how changes to the protected members in the base class might introduce breaking changes to code in other assemblies. Why would you want to do this? An example will describe a situation in which you might find this technique useful.

Suppose you're designing a component library in which you plan to use inheritance. You've already created an assembly with a base class named `Human` and a few other classes that derive from `Human`, such as `Manager` and

Programmer. In this scenario, you will benefit from the features of inheritance inside the scope of your assembly. In an effort to minimize your versioning concerns, however, you want to limit the use of inheritance to your assembly alone. To be concise, you'd like to prevent classes in other assemblies from inheriting from your classes.

Of course, it's a simple matter to prevent other programmers from inheriting from the derived classes such as Programmer and Manager: You simply declare them as sealed classes using the NotInheritable keyword. Such a declaration makes it impossible for another programmer to inherit from these classes. However, you cannot define the Human class using the NotInheritable keyword because your design relies on it serving as a base class. Also, you cannot define a base class such as Human as a friend class when public classes such as Programmer and Manager must inherit from it. The CTS doesn't allow a public class to inherit from a friend class, because in general the accessibility of an entity must be equal to or greater than the accessibility of the new entity being defined (a new entity can restrict access, but cannot expand access).

To summarize the problem, you want the Human class to be inheritable from within the assembly and, at the same time, to be non-inheritable to classes outside the assembly. There is a popular design technique that experienced software designers often use to solve this problem—they create a public base class with constructors that are only accessible from within the current assembly. You accomplish this by declaring the base class constructors with the Friend keyword:

```
'*** only inheritable from within the current assembly!
Public Class Human

  Friend Sub New()
    '*** implementation
  End Sub

End Class
```

Now the definition of the Human class is inheritable from within its assembly but not inheritable to classes in other assemblies. While this technique is not overly intuitive at first, it can prove very valuable. It allows the compiler to enforce your design decision so as to prohibit cross-assembly inheritance. Again, the reason to use this technique is to help simplify a design that involves inheritance. Remember that cross-assembly inheritance brings up many issues that are often best avoided when they're not a requirement.

Polymorphism and Type Substitution

In the first part of this chapter, inheritance was presented as an effective way to reuse the implementation details of a base class across many derived classes. While reuse of implementations is valuable, another aspect of inheritance is equally important—its support for polymorphic programming.

Polymorphism

Every derived class inherits the programming contract that is defined by the public members of its base class. As a result, you can program against any object created from a derived class by using the same programming contract that's defined by the base class. In other words, inheritance provides the ability to program against different types of objects using a single programming contract. This *polymorphic* programming style is a powerful programming technique because it allows you to write generic, client-side code. That is, the client-side code, which is written against the base class, is also compatible with any of the derived classes, because they all share a common, inherited design. The derived classes are thus plug-compatible from the perspective of the client, making the client's code more applicable to a wider range of situations.

Poly-whatism?

Polymorphism is one of the authors' favorite computer science terms. While precise definitions vary, polymorphism can be envisioned as the notion that an operation (method) supports one or more types (classes). For example, you can write "X + Y", and this operation will work in .NET whether X and Y are both integers, reals, or strings. Hence the operator "+" is polymorphic, and the code "X + Y" represents polymorphic programming. Expressing this in OOP terms, it might be easier to think of this code as "X.plus(Y)". At the end of the day, "X.plus(Y)" is more generic because it works in multiple situations.

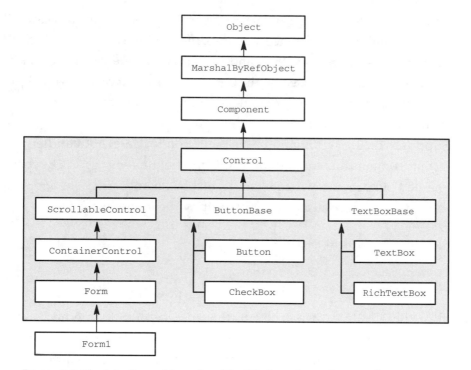

FIGURE 5.2: The inheritance hierarchy of the Windows Forms framework

Let's look at an example of writing generic client-side code based on the principle of polymorphism. This example will use classes within an inheritance hierarchy that has been designed by the Windows Forms team at Microsoft. Figure 5.2 shows some of the more commonly used classes in the Windows Forms framework that provide the implementations for forms and various controls.

The hierarchy depicted in Figure 5.2 contains a class named `Control` that serves as a base class for several other classes. Let's write a method definition called `FormatControl` against this `Control` class:

```
Imports System.Windows.Forms
Imports System.Drawing

Public Class ControlManager

  Public Sub FormatControl(ByVal ctrl As Control)
    '*** generic code using Control class
    ctrl.BackColor = Color.Blue
    ctrl.ForeColor = Color.Red
  End Sub

End Class
```

This implementation of `FormatControl` is truly generic code. You can call this method and pass a reference to many different types of objects, including `Button`, `CheckBox`, `TextBox`, and `Form`. When a method such as this one defines a parameter based on the `Control` class, you can pass an object of any type that inherits either directly or indirectly from the `Control` class in the inheritance hierarchy.

Suppose you are writing an implementation for an event handler in a form that contains a command button named `cmdExecuteTask`, a check box named `chkDisplayMessage`, and a text box named `txtMessage`. You can achieve polymorphic behavior by writing the following code:

```
Dim mgr As New ControlManager()
mgr.FormatControl(cmdExecuteTask)
mgr.FormatControl(chkDisplayMessage)
mgr.FormatControl(txtMessage)
```

Each of these calls is dispatched to the `FormatControl` method. Even though each call passes a distinct type of object, the `FormatControl` method responds appropriately because each object "is a" control. The important lesson you should draw from this example is that objects created from a derived class can always be substituted when an instance of the base class is expected.

Method overloading adds yet another dimension to polymorphic programming. For example, you could overload the `FormatControl` method of the `ControlManager` class with a more specialized definition in the case of `TextBox` objects:

```
Public Class ControlManager

  Public Sub FormatControl(ByVal txt As TextBox)
    '*** process object as a text box
  End Sub

  Public Sub FormatControl(ByVal ctrl As Control)
    '*** process other objects as a generic control
  End Sub

End Class
```

The Visual Basic .NET compiler will dispatch the call to the implementation of `FormatControl(TextBox)` when it determines that the caller is passing a `TextBox` reference. It will call `FormatControl(Control)` when it determines that the `Control` class is the most-derived class compatible with the type of reference being passed:

```
Dim mgr As New ControlManager()

'*** this call invokes FormatControl(TextBox)
mgr.FormatControl(txtMessage)

'*** these calls invoke FormatControl(Control)
mgr.FormatControl(cmdExecuteTask)
mgr.FormatControl(chkDisplayMessage)
```

As the discussion here reveals, polymorphism is very powerful because it allows you to program in more generic terms and to substitute different compatible implementations for one another. To design, write, and use class definitions in Visual Basic .NET that benefit from polymorphism, however, you must understand a number of additional concepts. The first is the difference between an object type and a reference variable type.

Converting between Types

It's important that you distinguish between the type of object you're programming against and the type of reference you're using to interact with that object. This consideration is especially critical when you are working with classes in an inheritance hierarchy, because you will commonly access derived objects using a base class reference. For example, a `TextBox` object can be referenced through a variable of type `TextBox` or a variable of type `Control`:

```
Dim textbox1 As TextBox = txtMessage
textbox1.Text = "test 1"

Dim control1 As Control = txtMessage
control1.Text = "test 2"
```

In the preceding code, the same `TextBox` object is being accessed through two types of reference variables. The subtle but critical observation here is that an object—and the reference variables used to access that object—can be based on different types. The only requirement is that the reference variable type must be compatible with the object type. A base class reference variable is always compatible with an object created from that base class, or any class that inherits directly or indirectly from that base class. In this example, the `control1` reference variable is compatible with a `TextBox` object because the `TextBox` class inherits (indirectly) from the `Control` class.

As you see, inheriting one class from another creates an implicit compatibility between the two types. If you can reference an object using a `TextBox` reference variable, you are guaranteed that you can also reference that object using a `Control` reference variable. This is consistent with the is-a rule because a text box "is a" control. Due to this guaranteed compatibility, the Visual Basic .NET compiler allows you to implicitly convert from the `TextBox` type to the `Control` type, even with strict type checking enabled. This technique, which is sometimes referred to as *up-casting* (i.e., casting up the inheritance hierarchy), is always legal.

Trying to convert a base class reference to a derived class reference—that is, down the inheritance hierarchy—is an entirely different matter. Known as *down-casting*, this technique is not always legal. For example, if you can reference an object using a `Control` reference variable, you cannot necessarily also reference that object using a `TextBox` reference variable. While this type of reference might be permitted in some situations, it's definitely not legal in all cases. What if the object is actually a `Button` and not a `TextBox`?

When strict type checking is enabled, the Visual Basic .NET compiler will not allow you to implicitly convert down an inheritance hierarchy (e.g., from `Control` to `TextBox`). The following code demonstrates how to convert back and forth between `Control` and `TextBox` references:

```
Dim textbox1, textbox2, textbox3 As TextBox
Dim control1, control2, control3 As Control

'*** (1) compiles with or without Option Strict
textbox1 = txtMessage
control1 = textbox1

'*** (2) doesn't compile unless Option Strict is disabled
control2 = txtMessage
textbox2 = control2    '*** error: illegal implicit conversion

'*** (3) compiles with or without Option Strict
control3 = txtMessage
textbox3 = CType(control3, TextBox)
```

No problem arises if you want to implicitly convert from the `TextBox` class to the `Control` class (1). However, the automatic compatibility between these two types works only in a single direction—upward. It is therefore illegal to perform an implicit conversion from a `Control` reference to a `TextBox` reference (2). You cannot implicitly convert to a type located downward in the inheritance hierarchy. Therefore, the conversion from `Control` to `TextBox` must be made explicitly by using the `CType` conversion operator (3).

The Visual Basic .NET compiler never worries about the type of the actual object when it decides whether to allow an implicit conversion. Instead, it always relies on the static types of the reference variables being used when deciding whether implicit conversion should be permitted.

Keep in mind that an attempt to convert between types will not always be successful. For example, suppose you attempt to convert a reference variable that is pointing to a `CheckBox` object into a reference variable of type `TextBox`:

```
Dim control1 As Control = chkDisplayMessage
Dim textbox1 As TextBox = CType(control1, TextBox)
```

This code will compile without error because the `CType` operator is used to perform the conversion explicitly. It will fail at runtime, however, because a `CheckBox` object is not compatible with the programming contract defined by the `TextBox` class. In particular, the CLR will determine that the type-cast is illegal and throw an exception. A more detailed discussion of throwing and handling exceptions is deferred until Chapter 9.

If you aren't sure whether an attempt to convert a reference downward to a more-derived type will succeed, you can always perform a runtime test using the `TypeOf` operator. For example, you can test whether a `Control` reference variable points to a `TextBox`-compatible object using the following code:

```
Public Sub FormatControl(ByVal ctrl As Control)
  '*** check whether object is a TextBox
  If TypeOf ctrl Is TextBox Then  '*** safe to convert!
    Dim txt As TextBox = CType(ctrl, TextBox)
    '*** program against control as TextBox
    txt.TextAlign = HorizontalAlignment.Center
  End If
End Sub
```

It's not always necessary to write code that performs this kind of run-time test. You could instead overload the `FormatControl` method with a more specialized implementation to handle the case of a `TextBox` object. Nevertheless, sometimes you cannot predict the type of object you'll be dealing with until runtime.

Consider the situation in which you'd like to enumerate through all the controls on a form and perform a specific action only with the text boxes. The form provides a `Controls` collection that you can enumerate through using a `For Each` loop, but you cannot determine which controls are `TextBox` objects until runtime. This scenario offers a perfect example of when you should perform a runtime test using the `TypeOf` operator:

```
'*** code in a form's event handler
Dim ctrl As Control
For Each ctrl In Me.Controls
  If TypeOf ctrl Is TextBox Then
    Dim txt As TextBox = CType(ctrl, TextBox)
    '*** program against control as TextBox
    txt.TextAlign = HorizontalAlignment.Center
  End If
Next
```

You have just seen how polymorphism works with a set of classes defined in an existing inheritance hierarchy like the Windows Forms framework. Now it's time to turn your attention to how you can create an inheritance hierarchy of your own and produce the same effect. As part of this discussion, we'll continue with the example started earlier in this chapter, which included the `Human` base class and the `Programmer` derived class (see Figure 5.1).

Replacing Methods in a Derived Class

Now that you have seen the high-level motivation for polymorphism, it's time for a low-level explanation of the mechanics of how members are accessed at runtime. To use inheritance to add polymorphic behavior to your designs, you must first understand the differences between *static binding* and *dynamic binding*.

Static binding and dynamic binding represent two different ways in which a client can invoke a method or property of an object. Static binding is usually more straightforward and results in better performance. Dynamic binding yields greater flexibility and is the underlying mechanism that allows a derived class to replace behavior inherited from a base class. The latter type of binding is one of the crucial ingredients of polymorphic programming.

Static Binding

LISTING 5.3: A simple base class with a statically bound method

```
Public Class Human
  Public Function Speak() As String
    Return "I am a human"
  End Function
End Class


Public Class Programmer : Inherits Human
  '*** inherits Speak from base class
End Class
```

First, let's tackle static binding. Suppose you are designing the Human and Programmer classes and come up with the two class definitions shown in Listing 5.3. Now imagine someone writes code that creates a Programmer object and invokes the Speak method. The caller can invoke the Speak method through a reference variable of type Programmer or through a reference variable of type Human:

```
Dim programmer1 As Programmer = New Programmer()
Dim human1 As Human

Dim message1, message2 As String
message1 = programmer1.Speak()   '*** calls Human.Speak()
message2 = human1.Speak()        '*** calls Human.Speak()

Console.WriteLine(message1)      '*** "I am a human"
Console.WriteLine(message2)      '*** "I am a human"
```

Both method invocations work via static binding, which is the default method invocation mechanism used by Visual Basic .NET and by the CLR. Static binding is based on the type of the reference variable, not the type of object being referenced. For example, if you are accessing a Programmer object through a reference variable of type Human, the type information from the definition of Human is used to bind the client to the correct member definition.

Another important aspect of static binding is that the decision about where to locate the definition for the method being invoked is always made at compile time—that is, statically. This decision-making process is different than in dynamic binding, in which the decision about where to locate the method definition is made at runtime. With static binding, the compiler can perform more of the work at compile time. For this reason, static binding can provide a measurable performance advantage over dynamic binding.

Dynamic Binding and Overridable Methods

One of the most valuable features of inheritance is the fact that the designer of a base class can provide default behavior that can optionally be replaced by a derived class author. For example, a base class author can provide a default implementation for a method. A derived class author can then choose whether to use the base class implementation or to write a more specialized implementation. In some cases, a derived class author even has the option of extending the base class implementation by adding extra code to the derived class.

Using a derived class to replace the implementation of a method or a property defined in a base class is known as *overriding*. Method overriding relies on dynamic binding, not static binding. Dynamic binding takes into account the type of an object at runtime, which gives the CLR a chance to locate and call the overriding method. In this way dynamic binding supports more flexible code, albeit with a runtime cost. Interestingly, dynamic binding is the default in the Java programming language and, in fact, the only option in Java in most cases.

An example will illustrate why dynamic binding is so important. Imagine you have written the following client-side code that uses the programming contract defined by the Human class shown in Listing 5.3:

```
Public Class Reporter
  Public Sub InterviewHuman(ByVal target As Human)
    Dim Message As String = target.Speak()
    MessageBox.Show(Message)
  End Sub
End Class
```

A caller could invoke the InterviewHuman method by passing a Human object or by passing a Programmer object. Whichever type of object is passed to the InterviewHuman method must, however, provide an implementation of the Speak method as defined by the programming contract of the Human class.

An important aspect of polymorphism is that any Human-derived class should be able to provide a behavior for the Speak method that differs from the behavior of other Human-derived classes. For example, a Programmer class should be able to provide an implementation of Speak that is different from that in the Human class. You cannot take advantage of these different behaviors if static binding is being used. Because the InterviewHuman method programs against the Human type, static binding would result in every call to Speak being dispatched to the implementation defined in the Human class. Therefore, true polymorphic behavior is not possible with static binding. Your class design must contain methods that are invoked through dynamic binding.

Of course, the features of dynamic binding don't apply to all kinds of class members. When you add methods and properties to a base class, you have the option of defining them to be invoked through either static binding or dynamic binding. You don't have the same option when you add fields to a base class. In the CTS, fields can be accessed only through static binding. In other words, method and properties can be declared as *overridable* but fields cannot. This restriction gives public methods and properties yet another advantage over public fields from a design perspective.

Now that you've learned the fundamental concepts behind dynamic binding, it's time to see the Visual Basic .NET syntax that's required to support it. You enable dynamic binding by defining overridable methods and properties.

LISTING 5.4: A simple base class with a dynamically bound method

```
Public Class Human
  Public Overridable Function Speak() As String
    '*** default implementation
    Return "I am a human"
  End Function
End Class
```

The first requirement to enable overriding is that a base class must define the method or property as overridable. To do so, you declare the member definition using the `Overridable` keyword (equivalent to the `virtual` keyword in C# and C++), as shown in Listing 5.4. It's important to understand the implications of defining a method with the `Overridable` keyword. In this case, it means that every invocation of the `Speak` method through a reference variable of type `Human` will result in dynamic binding. Also, classes that inherit from `Human` will have the option of overriding the `Speak` method to provide a more specialized implementation.

Because a dynamically bound call is potentially slower than a statically bound call, it makes sense that a base class author must ask for it explicitly. Languages such as Visual Basic .NET and C# require a base class author to be very explicit about declaring methods that are overridable for another reason, too: When a method is overridable, the design becomes more challenging because the method overriding complicates the contract between a base class and its derived classes. We will revisit this topic later in this chapter. For now, just take it on faith that declaring a method or property as overridable increases your responsibilities as a base class author.

Let's finish our example by creating a derived class that overrides a method implementation defined within its base class. First, the derived class must contain a method with the same name and the same signature as the overridable method in its base class. Second, the overriding method must be explicitly declared to override the base class implementation using the `Overrides` keyword. In the following code fragment, the `Programmer` class overrides the `Speak` method inherited from the `Human` class of Listing 5.4:

```
Public Class Programmer : Inherits Human
   Public Overrides Function Speak() As String
     '*** overriding implementation
     Return "I am a programmer"
   End Function
End Class
```

Now that we've written a derived class definition that overrides a method implementation in its base class, we are ready to see an example of dynamic binding in action. Examine the following client-side code:

```
Dim programmer1 As Programmer = New Programmer()
Dim human1 As Human = programmer1
Dim message1, message2 As String

message1 = programmer1.Speak()   '*** calls Programmer.Speak
message2 = human1.Speak()        '*** calls Programmer.Speak

Console.WriteLine(message1)      '*** "I am a programmer"
Console.WriteLine(message2)      '*** "I am a programmer"
```

As this code demonstrates, it doesn't matter whether you access the `Programmer` object through a reference variable of type `Programmer` or of type `Human`. The dynamic binding scheme employed by the CLR always locates the appropriate method implementation by looking up the inheritance hierarchy for the most-derived class that holds a definition for the method in question. In the preceding code, `Programmer` is the most-derived class that contains an implementation of the `Speak` method.

Chaining Calls from a Derived Class to a Base Class

When you override a method, it's fairly common practice to chain a call from your overriding implementation in the derived class to the overridden implementation in the base class. This technique allows you to leverage the implementation provided by the base class and extend it with extra code written in the derived class. Consider the following reimplementation of the `Programmer` class:

```
Public Class Programmer : Inherits Human
  Public Overrides Function Speak() As String
    '*** chain call to Speak method in base class
    Return MyBase.Speak() & " who is a programmer"
  End Function
End Class
```

The Visual Basic .NET keyword `MyBase` is used in a derived class to explicitly access public or protected members in its base class. In this example, the `Programmer` definition of `Speak` makes an explicit call to the `Human` implementation of `Speak`. This approach allows the derived class author to reuse and extend the method implementation provided by the base class author.

As shown in the preceding example, the `MyBase` keyword allows a derived class author to chain a call to the base class author's implementation. A chained call doesn't have to be made at the beginning of the derived class implementation, however. It can be made at any point in the overriding implementation.

Design Issues with Overridable Methods

You've just seen the syntax for creating overridable methods. You've also seen the syntax for overriding a method and for chaining a call to an overridden base class implementation. As a result of the discussion, you might have concluded that the syntax required for method overriding isn't especially complicated.

In reality, mastering the syntax is the easy part. Making sure you get the semantics correct is a much tougher job. Anyone who has managed a large software project using inheritance and method overriding can tell you that managing the semantics of overridable methods and properties requires a high level of expertise and attention to detail.

An overridable method complicates the programming contract of a base class because a derived class author can use any of three possible approaches:

- A derived class author can inherit a base class implementation and reuse it without modification.
- A derived class author can provide an overriding implementation that chains a call back to the base class implementation.
- A derived class author can provide an overriding implementation that does not chain a call back to the base class implementation.

Consider these three approaches for dealing with an overridable method from a design perspective. You might say that there are really three options: reusing, extending, and replacing. When a derived class inherits a method, it *reuses* the base class implementation. When a derived class overrides a method and chains a call back the base class, it *extends* the base class implementation. When a derived class overrides a method and does not chain a call back the base class, it *replaces* the base class implementation.

While the CLR's support for method overriding allows for reusing, extending, and replacing, many overridable methods have semantics that do not support all three approaches. The overridable `Finalize` method of the `Object` class, for instance, is a real-world example of an overridable method that does not allow replacing. If you elect to override the `Finalize` method in a user-defined class, your implementation must chain a call back to the `Finalize` implementation of the base class. If you fail to chain a call to the base class implementation, you have broken the semantic contract of this overridable method and your code will likely exhibit problematic behavior. Chapter 10 discusses when and how to override the `Finalize` method; for now, just recognize that replacing the implementation for an overridable method creates problems.

As you can see, some overridable methods only support reusing or extending the base class implementation. An overridable method may also have semantics that allow for reusing and replacing yet disallow extending. In general, the semantics of overridable methods and properties require extra attention.

The semantics involved with chaining can become even more complicated because the semantics of some overridable methods require an overriding implementation to chain a call back to the base class implementation at a specific point in time. For example, the semantics of one overridable method might require overriding method implementations to chain a call to the base class implementation before doing any work in the derived class. The semantics of another overridable method might require overriding method implementations to chain a call to the base class implementation after all work has been completed in the derived class implementation.

This discussion should lead you to two important observations:

- The semantics of method and property overriding are often sensitive to whether an overriding method should chain a call to its base class.
- The semantics of overriding can be affected by whether the chained call should be made at the beginning or at the end of the overriding method or property implementation.

If you must ever design a base class, it is your responsibility to document the semantics for each overridable method and property. Your documentation should specify for each overridable method and property whether chaining a call back to your base class implementation is required. You should also point out any occasion where a chained call must be made at the beginning or at the end of the overriding implementation in the derived class.

Even if you never design or write a base class definition, you must keep these rules in mind. As a .NET programmer, you will almost certainly encounter situations in which you must create classes that inherit from one of the base classes provided by the .NET Framework.

When you are working with inheritance, semantic errors can be much more challenging to find than syntax errors. The compiler will catch syntax errors and identify their exact locations in your code, but it cannot catch semantic errors. This factor makes semantic errors related to inheritance far more difficult to locate. Making sure the semantics for overridable methods are well defined and adhered to requires a lot of discipline. It may also require coordination across different development teams.

Declaring a Method as `NotOverridable`

Recall that a class created with Visual Basic .NET is inheritable by default. If you create a class named `Programmer` that inherits from `Human`, another programmer can create a third class, `SeniorProgrammer`, that inherits from your derived class:

```
Public Class SeniorProgrammer : Inherits Programmer
  '*** can this class override Speak?
End Class
```

Given the class definitions for `Human`, `Programmer`, and `SeniorProgrammer` (which now form the inheritance hierarchy shown in Figure 5.1), ask yourself the following question: Should the author of `SeniorProgrammer` be able to override the `Programmer` implementation of `Speak`? The answer is yes. A method that is declared with the `Overrides` keyword is itself overridable. The author of `SeniorProgrammer` can override the implementation of `Speak` in `Programmer` with the following code:

```
Public Class SeniorProgrammer : Inherits Programmer
  Public Overrides Function Speak() As String
    '*** overriding implementation
  End Function
End Class
```

You can take this example one step further by creating a class named `SuperSeniorProgrammer` that inherits from `SeniorProgrammer`. `Super-`

`SeniorProgrammer` would be able to override the `SeniorProgrammer` definition of the `Speak` method with yet another implementation.

If you take this example to the logical extreme, you can create as many classes as you want in the inheritance hierarchy, with each class inheriting from the one above it and overriding the `Speak` method with a new implementation. There isn't really a theoretical limitation on how many levels you can design in an inheritance hierarchy. In reality, practical limitations often determine how many levels of inheritance you should allow. A few examples will demonstrate how you can limit the use of inheritance to keep a complicated design from getting out of hand.

Suppose you've created a definition for `Programmer` by inheriting from `Human`. From your perspective, you are the beneficiary of inheritance because you were able to reuse code from `Human` and you saved yourself a good deal of time in doing so. However, if you allow other programmers to inherit from your derived class, you must also live up to the responsibilities of a base class author. That includes documenting the semantics for all of your overridable methods.

When you override a method using the `Overrides` keyword, your method definition becomes overridable by default. You can reverse this default behavior by adding the `NotOverridable` keyword before the `Overrides` keyword. This technique is used here to prevent the continued overriding of the `Speak` method:

```
Public Class Programmer : Inherits Human
  Public NotOverridable Overrides Function Speak() As String
    '*** overriding implementation
  End Function
End Class

Class SeniorProgrammer : Inherits Programmer
  '*** this class cannot override Speak
End Class
```

The author of `SeniorProgrammer` is no longer allowed to override the `Speak` method. As this example illustrates, when you declare an overriding method implementation with the `NotOverridable` keyword, that choice simplifies your design. You don't have to worry about other classes inheriting from your class and breaking the semantics of your method.

Using the `NotOverridable` keyword allows you to disallow overriding on a method-by-method or a property-by-property basis, but another option can make life even easier. Recall that you can disallow inheriting altogether by using the `NotInheritable` keyword. This keyword is applicable to base classes as well as derived classes such as `Programmer`:

```
Public NotInheritable Class Programmer : Inherits Human
  Public Overrides Function Speak() As String
    '*** overriding implementation
  End Function
End Class
```

Now classes may no longer inherit from `Programmer`. This choice really simplifies things because you don't have to worry about a contract of behavior between `Programmer` and derived classes. Sometimes it makes sense to define overridden methods and properties as `NotOverridable`; at other times it's better to define a derived class as `NotInheritable`. Both techniques simplify the overall design of a derived class.

Most software developers agree that keeping a design as simple as possible is beneficial. But there's another good reason to apply the `NotOverridable` and `NotInheritable` keywords whenever you can: They can also improve performance.

Recall that overridable methods require the use of dynamic binding and, therefore, may incur a runtime cost. Judicious use of the `NotOverridable` and `NotInheritable` keywords allows the Visual Basic .NET compiler to employ static binding rather than dynamic binding at times, thereby reducing execution time.

For example, imagine `Programmer` is defined with the `NotInheritable` keyword. The Visual Basic .NET compiler can make the assumption that a reference variable of type `Programmer` will only reference an object created from the `Programmer` class. That is, the client will never use a `Programmer` reference variable to access an object of some class derived from `Programmer`. Because `Programmer` is sealed, a `Programmer` reference variable can only be used to access objects created from `Programmer`. There is no opportunity for polymorphism and, consequently, no need to use dynamic binding. In such a case, the compiler will optimize calls by using static binding instead of dynamic binding.

MyBase **versus** MyClass **versus** Me

While we're on the topic of static binding versus dynamic binding, it makes sense to discuss some subtle differences between the keywords Me, MyClass, and MyBase. All three can be used inside a method implementation of a class to refer to a class member, but they can exhibit quite different behavior.

Listing 5.5 summarizes the class definitions we have discussed so far: Human, Programmer, and SeniorProgrammer. Study the listing, and determine which methods are invoked using static binding and which are invoked using dynamic binding.

LISTING 5.5: An inheritance hierarchy with statically and dynamically bound methods

```
Public Class Human
  Public Overridable Function Speak() As String
    Return "I am a human"
  End Function
End Class

Public Class Programmer : Inherits Human
  Public Overrides Function Speak() As String
    Return "I am a programmer"
  End Function

  Public Sub GetInfo()
    '*** what happens when you call Speak from this method?
  End Sub
End Class

Public Class SeniorProgrammer : Inherits Programmer
  Public Overrides Function Speak() As String
    Return "I am a senior programmer"
  End Function
End Class
```

Listing 5.5 includes three different definitions of the Speak method. The Programmer class overrides the definition of Speak from its base class, then is itself overridden again by the derived class SeniorProgrammer. Notice that the Programmer class now contains an additional method named Get-Info. Imagine you wrote the following definition for this method:

```
'*** method definition in Programmer class
Public Sub GetInfo()
  Dim message1, message2, message3, message4 As String
  message1 = MyBase.Speak()
  message2 = MyClass.Speak()
  message3 = Me.Speak()
  message4 = Speak()

  Console.WriteLine(message1)    '*** ?
  Console.WriteLine(message2)    '*** ?
  Console.WriteLine(message3)    '*** ?
  Console.WriteLine(message4)    '*** ?
End Sub
```

As you can see, there are four different ways to call the Speak method. The question is, What does the method output? The answer: The output depends on the type of object. First, suppose you call GetInfo using a reference variable of type Human:

```
Dim h1 As Human = New Human
h1.GetInfo()
```

This code fails to compile because the Human class does not contain a method called GetInfo—just making sure you were awake! Next, suppose you call GetInfo using a reference variable of type Programmer that refers to a Programmer object:

```
Dim p1 As Programmer = New Programmer
p1.GetInfo()
```

The method call outputs the following to the console window:

```
I am a human
I am a programmer
I am a programmer
I am a programmer
```

That should make sense, because the base class of a Programmer is Human. Finally, suppose you call GetInfo using a reference variable of type Programmer that refers to a SeniorProgrammer object:

```
Dim p2 As Programmer = New SeniorProgrammer()
p2.GetInfo()
```

Here is the resulting output:

```
I am a human
I am a programmer
I am a senior programmer
I am a senior programmer
```

The explanation of this result is a little more subtle. While the object is of type `SeniorProgrammer`, the method being called is defined inside the `Programmer` class. Therefore, this example illustrates a case where the `Programmer` class has other classes both above it and below it in the inheritance hierarchy that can affect what happens at runtime.

What happens when this call to `p2.GetInfo` executes?

- When `GetInfo` calls `MyBase.Speak`, the Visual Basic .NET compiler uses static binding to invoke the implementation of `Speak` within the base class—in this case the `Human` class, because `Programmer` inherits from `Human`.
- When it calls `MyClass.Speak`, the compiler use static binding to invoke the implementation of `Speak` in the calling method's class—in this case `Programmer` because `GetInfo` is defined within `Programmer`.
- When it calls `Me.Speak`, the compiler uses dynamic binding to invoke the most-derived implementation of `Speak`—in this case it is defined in `SeniorProgrammer`.

If you call `Speak` without using one of these three keywords, it has the exact same effect as calling `Me.Speak`—namely, it uses dynamic binding.

Calls through the `MyBase` and `MyClass` keywords always result in static binding to the base class and the current class, respectively. Calls through the `Me` keyword result in dynamic binding whenever the method being called is declared as overridable. Each of these keywords can be useful in certain scenarios.

Shadowing Methods

While most uses of static binding are relatively straightforward, this is not always the case. In certain situations, static binding can become complex and non-intuitive. In particular, it can be tricky when a base class and a derived class have one or more member definitions with the same name. An example will demonstrate this point.

Suppose we return to Listing 5.3, where the Human class defines Speak as a statically bound method. What would happen if the Programmer class also supplied a method called Speak? In other words:

```
Public Class Human
  Public Function Speak() As String
    Return "I am a human"
  End Function
End Class

Public Class Programmer : Inherits Human
  Public Function Speak() As String
    Return "I am a programmer"
  End Function
End Class
```

Both class definitions contain a method named Speak with the same calling signature. When a member in a derived class is defined in this manner with the same name as a non-overridable member in its base class, the technique is called *member shadowing*. That is, the Programmer class definition of Speak shadows the Human class definition of Speak.

LISTING 5.6: A derived class that shadows a method of its base class

```
Public Class Human
  Public Function Speak() As String
    Return "I am a human"
  End Function
End Class

Public Class Programmer : Inherits Human
  Public Shadows Function Speak() As String
    Return "I am a programmer"
  End Function
End Class
```

The Visual Basic .NET compiler produces a compile-time warning when you shadow an inherited member. This warning is meant to raise a red flag so you can avoid shadowing if you have stumbled upon it accidentally. If you want to deliberately shadow a member from a base class, you can suppress the compiler warning by making your intentions explicit with the Shadows keyword, as shown in Listing 5.6.

In a few rare situations, an experienced class designer may decide to use shadowing. The most common scenario where shadowing occurs is when the base class author adds new members to a later version. Imagine that you created the `Programmer` class by inheriting from an earlier version of the `Human` class that did not contain a `Speak` method. Therefore, at the time when you added the public `Speak` method to the `Programmer` class, it did not conflict with any of the methods inherited from its base class.

What would happen if the author of the `Human` class decided to add a public `Speak` method in a later version of the class? You would then face the dilemma of either removing the `Speak` method from the `Programmer` class or shadowing the `Speak` method from the `Human` class. A few other scenarios call for shadowing, but this one is probably the most common.

You should do your best to avoid shadowing members from a base class, because member shadowing creates ambiguities that make it easy for a client-side programmer to get into trouble. The problem with member shadowing is that it is based on static binding and, consequently, produces inconsistent results.

The following example will demonstrate where shadowing a member in a base class can create a good deal of confusion. Imagine you're writing client-side code in which you will create an object of type `Programmer`. Assume the `Programmer` class is defined as shown in Listing 5.6, where `Programmer` contains a `Speak` method that shadows the `Speak` method in the `Human` class.

To understand what's going on, you must remember how static binding works: The reference variable's type controls method invocation. Now look at the following code:

```
Dim programmer1 As Programmer = New Programmer
Dim human1 As Human

Dim message1, message2 As String
message1 = programmer1.Speak()   '*** calls Programmer.Speak()
message2 = human1.Speak()        '*** calls Human.Speak()
```

The reference variable named `programmer1` is of type `Programmer`. Therefore, invoking the `Speak` method through `programmer1` will result in invoking the implementation defined in the `Programmer` class. Likewise, the reference variable named `human1` is of type `Human`. Therefore, invoking the Speak method through human1 will result in invoking the implementation defined in the Human class. The strange thing about this example is that a single object responds in different ways to a call of Speak depending on the type of reference that is used to access the object. Dynamic binding produces much more intuitive results because the type of object—not the type of reference—determines which method is actually executed.

To make matters worse, it is legal to shadow an overridable method. However, shadowing an overridable method is something you rarely want to do. This possibility is mentioned here only as a warning that sloppy syntax can result in shadowing by mistake. This kind of mistake is likely to lead to trouble. For example, what happens when a base class defines an overridable method, and a derived class author attempts to override it but forgets to use the Overrides keyword? The compiler produces a warning but still compiles your code as if you had used the Shadows keyword:

```
Public Class Human
   Public Overridable Function Speak() As String
     '*** default implementation
   End Function
End Class

Public Class Programmer : Inherits Human
   '*** author forgot to use Overrides keyword
   Public Function Speak() As String
      '*** method shadows Human.Speak
   End Function
End Class
```

Shadowing Overloaded Methods and Properties

Shadowing can become even more complicated when it involves methods and properties that have been overloaded. Recall that the name for a method or property can be overloaded with multiple implementations that differ in terms of their parameter lists. Let's look at an example in which the Human class contains two overloaded methods named Speak, and then the Programmer class inherits from Human and defines Speak so that it shadows one of the inherited methods:

```
Public Class Human
   Public Function Speak() As String
     Return "I am a human"
   End Function
```

```
    Public Function Speak(ByVal message As String) As String
      Return "I am a human who says " & message
    End Function
End Class

Public Class Programmer : Inherits Human
    Public Function Speak() As String
      Return "I am a programmer"
    End Function
End Class
```

In this example, the definition of the Speak method in the Programmer class will shadow the definition of the Speak method in the Human class with the matching signature. What you might not expect is that the other overloaded definition of Speak within Human is hidden as well. Thus the method with the signature Speak(String) is not part of the Programmer class definition. For this reason, the semantics of shadowing in Visual Basic .NET are sometimes referred to as *hide-by-name*.

If you try to compile these two class definitions, you will receive another compiler warning. As before, you can suppress this warning by adding the Shadows keyword to the definition of the Speak method in Programmer, as depicted in Listing 5.7.

LISTING 5.7: Shadowing an overloaded method

```
Public Class Human
    Public Function Speak() As String
      Return "I am a human"
    End Function

    Public Function Speak(ByVal message As String) As String
      Return "I am a human who says " & message
    End Function
End Class

Public Class Programmer : Inherits Human
    Public Shadows Function Speak() As String
      Return "I am a programmer"
    End Function

    '*** hides Speak(String) from base class
End Class
```

You might ask why the Visual Basic .NET compiler requires you to use the Shadows keyword to suppress the compiler warning in this situation. To understand the motivation behind this requirement, ask yourself the following question: Should the definition for the method with the signature Speak() in the Programmer class hide every definition of Speak in the Human class, or should it just shadow the one with the matching signature? In this case the Shadows keyword indicates that every implementation of Speak in the Human class should be hidden from clients programming against the definition of Programmer.

There's a subtle yet important difference between shadowing a method and hiding a method. In Listing 5.7, the method Speak() is shadowed, whereas the method Speak(String) is hidden. The shadowed method is still accessible to clients through the derived class definition, but the hidden method is not. Take a look at the following client-side code to see the difference. This code creates only one object of type Programmer, yet accesses this same object through two different reference variables:

```
Dim programmer1 As Programmer = New Programmer
Dim human1 As Human

Dim message1, message2, message3, message4 As String

'*** access object through derived class reference
message1 = programmer1.Speak()          '*** calls Programmer.Speak()
message2 = programmer1.Speak("Hello")   '*** error: method doesn't exist

'*** access object through base class reference
message3 = human1.Speak()               '*** calls Human.Speak()
message4 = human1.Speak("Hello")        '*** calls Human.Speak(String)
```

As this example reveals, member hiding has a strange side effect. An object created from the Programmer class still provides a definition for Speak(String)—as evidenced by the fact that human1.Speak("Hello") works. However, the Speak(String) method is accessible only to clients that are accessing the object through a reference variable of type Human. As this example involves static binding, a call to Speak() through a reference variable of type Human will use the method definition from Human. Thus hiding doesn't remove a method or property definition from an object; it simply makes a member inaccessible to clients that use reference variables based on the derived class.

You've just seen how Visual Basic .NET allows you to shadow and hide methods using hide-by-name semantics with the `Shadows` keyword. It also allows you to use the `Overloads` keyword instead of the `Shadows` keyword in situations in which you would rather achieve *hide-by-signature* semantics. With this technique, you can shadow an overloaded method from a base class without hiding other method definitions of the same name. Let's revisit Listing 5.7 and make one minor modification:

```
Public Class Human
  Public Function Speak() As String
    Return "I am a human"
  End Function

  Public Function Speak(ByVal message As String) As String
    Return "I am a human who says " & message
  End Function
End Class

Public Class Programmer : Inherits Human
  Public Overloads Function Speak() As String
    Return "I am a programmer"
  End Function

  '*** inherits Speak(String) from base class
End Class
```

The only change that has been made to this code from Listing 5.7 is that the `Overloads` keyword has replaced the `Shadows` keyword in the `Programmer` class definition of `Speak()`. This change has the effect of shadowing a method by signature as opposed to hiding it by name. The result is that class `Programmer` now makes the definition of `Speak(String)` accessible to clients:

```
Dim programmer1 As Programmer = New Programmer
Dim human1 As Human

Dim message1, message2, message3, message4 As String

'*** access object through derived class reference
message1 = programmer1.Speak()          '*** calls Programmer.Speak()
message2 = programmer1.Speak("Hello")   '*** calls Human.Speak(String)

'*** access object through base class reference
message3 = human1.Speak()               '*** calls Human.Speak()
message4 = human1.Speak("Hello")        '*** calls Human.Speak(String)
```

It's now possible to call Speak() and Speak(String) using a reference variable of type Programmer or a reference variable of type Human. One of these method signatures is shadowed, and the other is inherited directly from Human to Programmer. Calls to Speak() are dispatched to either the Human class definition or the Programmer class definition depending on the type of reference variable used. Calls to Speak(String) are always dispatched to the definition in the Human class.

The Overloads keyword should be used on some occasions that do not involve any form of hiding or shadowing. For example, you might want to add a method to a derived class that shares the same name as one or more methods in its base class but doesn't match any of their parameter lists. Suppose you wanted to create a new class that inherits from our running definition of Human (see Listing 5.7). What if you decided to add a third method named Speak that had a signature that was different from the two signatures of Speak inherited from Human? This scenario does not involve either shadowing or hiding, but you can and should use the Overloads keyword:

```
Class Programmer : Inherits Human
  '*** inherits Speak() from base class
  '*** inherits Speak(String) from base class

  Public Overloads Function Speak(ByVal excited As Boolean) As String
    If excited Then
      Return "Oh boy, I am an excited programmer"
    Else
        Return "I am a programmer"
    End If
  End Function
End Class
```

Now the Programmer class supports three overloaded versions of Speak. Two implementations of Speak are inherited from Human, and a third implementation is added to the Programmer class. Notice that you would get very different results if you do not use the Overloads keyword in the Speak(Boolean) method definition of the Programmer class. If you omit this keyword, the Visual Basic .NET compiler would once again default to using the Shadows keyword. In that case, the Programmer class would contain only one definition of Speak, not three.

Clearly, a design in which members are shadowed and/or hidden has the potential to catch programmers off guard. The shadowing of fields, methods, and properties results in multiple definitions with the same name. Confusion may arise because different types of reference variables produce inconsistent results when accessing the same object.

While most of this discussion has dealt at length with the complexities of shadowing and hiding, you most likely will not have to deal with these topics on a regular basis. In fact, the complexities discussed over the last several pages explain why most designers try their best to avoid designs involving shadowing and hiding. You are well advised to follow suit and avoid the use of shadowing and hiding when you design and implement your own classes.

SUMMARY

As you read through this chapter, one theme probably became clear: The use of inheritance increases your responsibilities both during the design phase and during the coding phase. If you decide to create a class from which other classes will inherit, you must make several extra design decisions. If you make these decisions incorrectly, you can get yourself into hot water pretty quickly. This is especially true when you need to revise a base class after other programmers have already begun to use it.

The first question you should address is whether it makes sense to use inheritance in your designs. In other words, should you be designing and writing your own base classes to be inherited by other classes? Once you've made a decision to use inheritance in this manner, you take on all the responsibilities of a base class author. It's your job to make sure that every derived class author understands the programming contract your base class has defined for its derived classes.

While you may never create your own base class, you will more than likely create custom classes that inherit from someone else's base class. It's difficult to imagine that you could program against the classes of the FCL without being required to inherit from a system-provided base class such as the Form class, the Page class, or the WebService class. Because so many of the class libraries in the .NET Framework have designs that involve base classes, every .NET developer needs to understand the responsibilities of a derived class author. If you don't have a solid understanding of the issues at hand, you will find it difficult to implement a derived class correctly.

■ 6 ■
Abstract Classes and Interfaces

C HAPTER 5 INTRODUCED the concept of inheritance. Inheritance enables you to write common code in a base class that can be reused across many derived classes. It also enables you to create software designs based on the principles of polymorphism and type substitution. Chapter 6 extends the discussion of inheritance and polymorphism to include two advanced topics: abstract classes and interfaces.

This chapter begins with a discussion of abstract classes, explaining why it is sometimes helpful to define a base class as an abstract class. It then describes how and why you might want to add abstract methods to an abstract base class. As you will see, an abstract base class enables you to define a programming contract with a partially completed implementation. The remaining part of the implementation must be filled in by the classes that inherit from it.

After covering abstract base classes, the chapter then turns to interfaces. Interfaces add an extra dimension to inheritance and polymorphism. An interface is like a base class in that it enables you to create a programming contract that represents a unified type. However, it provides the means to achieve polymorphism without some of the limitations that are imposed on inheriting base classes.

For a .NET developer, the ability to think and program in terms of interfaces is an essential skill. You will undoubtedly be required to create classes that implement system-defined interfaces of the .NET Framework Class

Library, but sometimes you will benefit from creating a custom interface in one of your own designs.

Abstract Classes

All classes can be separated into two categories: classes that are creatable and classes that are not creatable. Classes are creatable if they support object instantiation using the New operator. Classes are not creatable if they do not support object instantiation. In object-oriented terminology, creatable classes are referred to as *concrete classes*, whereas noncreatable classes are referred to as *abstract classes*.

The term "concrete class" reinforces the notion that you must have a class definition with a concrete implementation to create an object. Conversely, the term "abstract class" implies that the class definition does not have a concrete implementation. Instead, an abstract class defines a programming contract along with a partially completed implementation. It makes sense that an abstract class is not a creatable type because you cannot create an object from an incomplete implementation.

Let's revisit a software design that was used as an example in Chapter 5. In that design, the Manager class and the Programmer class inherited from the base class Human. This example demonstrated how two derived classes can reuse a set of implementation details from a common base class. A base class such as Human can serve to define a unified type that makes it possible to substitute different types of objects for one another, such as Programmer objects and Manager objects. In short, the Human class (see Listing 5.4) enables polymorphic programming like this:

```
Dim humans As Human(), h As Human
ReDim humans(N)

   .
   .   '*** fill array with Managers, Programmers, etc.
   .

For Each h In humans
   h.Speak()   '*** let each type of human speak in his or her own way
Next
```

For a quick review, see Figure 5.1 and the Chapter 5 section, "Polymorphism and Type Substitution."

Now consider the following question: Should all three of the classes from this example be defined as concrete classes? Obviously, if your application will use `Programmer` objects and `Manager` objects, the `Programmer` class and the `Manager` class must be defined as concrete classes. The answer is not quite so clear as to whether the `Human` class should be defined as a concrete class or an abstract class.

First, ask yourself whether it's necessary to create objects of type `Human`. While a base class such as `Human` enables you to achieve reuse and polymorphism, the base class itself often models an entity that's too generic to be instantiated. If you plan to make the design assumption that the `Human` class is to be used only as a base class, then it should be defined as an abstract class. This definition will prevent other programmers from instantiating it directly and using the `Human` class in a manner you did not intend.

The use of abstract base classes is fairly common in the design of an inheritance hierarchy. In this style of development, an abstract base class defines a unified programming contract and some percentage of the implementation required to fulfill that programming contract. It doesn't provide any value unless it is complemented by concrete classes that inherit from it. Figure 6.1 depicts the concrete classes `Manager` and `Programmer` inheriting from the abstract base class `Human`.

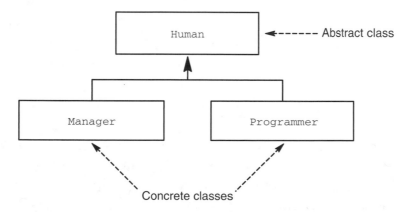

Figure 6.1: An abstract base class must be complemented by concrete classes that inherit from it.

Let's examine the Visual Basic .NET syntax required to create an abstract class. When you create the definition for a base class, you must add the `MustInherit` keyword to make it abstract:

```
'*** abstract class
Public MustInherit Class Human
  Public Overridable Function Speak() As String
    Return "I am a human"
  End Function

  '*** other class members omitted for clarity
End Class
```

A class defined with the `MustInherit` keyword is abstract and, therefore, cannot be directly used to create an object. A client program that attempts to create an object from a `MustInherit` class using the `New` operator will experience a compile-time error:

```
Dim human1 As Human = New Human("Bob")  '*** compile-time error
```

Defining the `Human` class as an abstract class helps to enforce a design-time assumption about how the class should be used by other classes. The designers of the Visual Basic .NET language selected the `MustInherit` keyword because it conveys the idea that an abstract class is useful only in designs that involve inheritance. A `MustInherit` class such as `Human` has no value until someone writes at least one concrete class that inherits from it.

Although an abstract class cannot be used to create an object, it can be used to declare variables, parameters, and fields. Recall that a reference variable declared using a base class can always be used to access objects created from classes that inherit from it, either directly or indirectly. In this example, a `Human` reference variable is used to access an object of type `Programmer`:

```
Dim human1 As Human = New Programmer("Bob")
txtMessage.Text = human1.Speak()
```

From the perspective of polymorphism and overridable methods, there is no difference between an abstract base class and a concrete base class. Because the `Human` class defines an overridable method named `Speak`, the author of the `Programmer` class decides whether to inherit the implementation or to override it.

An abstract base class is similar to a concrete base class in that it can contain both overridable methods and non-overridable methods. However, when you author an abstract base class, you can do something that is not possible when you author a concrete base class: You can add abstract members.

An abstract member is a method or property that has no associated implementation. Instead, the definition for an abstract member contains only a calling signature. This signature makes it possible for other programmers to determine the syntax required to call the member. The actual responsibility for implementing an abstract member is delegated to those authors who create concrete classes that inherit from the abstract base class.

A short example will help you to put things into perspective. Imagine you are designing the Human class as an abstract base class, and you want the Speak method to be part of the programming contract defined by Human. You have decided that it is impractical to provide a generic implementation of the Speak method in the Human class. Instead, you want to force any class that inherits from Human to provide its own custom implementation of Speak. You can accomplish this goal by adding the Speak method as an abstract member to the Human class definition, as shown in Listing 6.1.

LISTING 6.1: An abstract base class with an abstract method

```
Public MustInherit Class Human
   Public MustOverride Function Speak() As String

   '*** other class members omitted for clarity
End Class
```

To define a method or property as an abstract member, you use the MustOverride keyword. When you do so, you are neither responsible for nor allowed to provide an associated implementation. You simply define the calling signature for the member.

Given the definition in Listing 6.1 for the Human class, any concrete class that inherits from the Human class must provide an implementation of Speak. Keep in mind that an abstract member can exist only within the definition of an abstract class. It is illegal to use the MustOverride keyword within a class that has not been defined with the MustInherit keyword.

What happens when a class inherits from an abstract class with one or more abstract members? The inheriting class must either implement every abstract member or be defined as abstract itself. In other words, the inheriting class must implement every MustOverride method or it must be defined using the MustInherit keyword. Let's look at the definitions for two concrete classes that inherit from the Human class of Listing 6.1 to see how these rules are enforced:

```
Public Class Programmer : Inherits Human
  Public Overrides Function Speak() As String
    Return "I am a programmer"
  End Function

  '*** other class members omitted for clarity
End Class

Public Class Manager : Inherits Human
  '*** does not compile without an implementation for Speak
End Class

Public MustInherit Class Administrator : Inherits Human
  '*** compiles correctly, because also an abstract class
End Class
```

The Programmer class inherits from Human and provides its own implementation for the abstract method Speak. The Manager class—a concrete class—does not contain its own implementation of the Speak method, so it will not compile. The Administrator class is an abstract class, so it does not require an implementation of Speak. As you can see, the compiler enforces the rule that any concrete class that inherits from an abstract base class must provide an implementation of every abstract member.

To summarize a few points about abstract classes:

- Defining a class as an abstract class enables you to document your intention to use the class exclusively as a base class.
- An abstract base class is like a concrete base class in that it may contain both overridable and non-overridable methods.
- Abstract base classes are more flexible than concrete base classes because they can also contain abstract members.

One final comment about concrete base classes versus abstract base classes: The use of either kind of base class is constrained by the .NET Framework's model of single inheritance. As explained in Chapter 5, a class is limited to a single base class. Thus a class cannot use inheritance to support the programming contracts defined by more than one potential base class. Recognizing this limitation, software designers often seek out a more flexible approach when designing applications and infrastructures based on polymorphism and type substitution. Their search brings us to our next topic: interfaces.

Interfaces

An interface is a type that defines a programming contract—nothing more. You can think of an interface as an abstract class that consists purely of abstract members. This definition implies that an interface defines the calling signatures for a set of methods and properties, and that it never contains any form of implementation.

Let's begin our exploration of interfaces by comparing them to concrete base classes and abstract base classes. Recall that a concrete base class is a type that defines a programming contract along with a complete implementation, and an abstract base class is a type that defines a programming contract along with a partially completed implementation. An interface is a type that defines a programming contract without any implementation at all.

Interfaces are especially useful in getting beyond the limitations imposed by the .NET Framework's model of single inheritance. Whereas a class definition can inherit from only a single base class, a class can implement as many interfaces as desired. The inclusion of interfaces in the programming model of the .NET Framework means that an object can support any number of programming contracts, which adds a tremendous amount of flexibility when you are designing applications and components in terms of polymorphism. For this reason, interfaces are commonly used within the FCL.

For example, the `System` namespace contains several interfaces, including `ICloneable` and `IDisposable`. (By convention, interface names start with the letter "I".) Many .NET developers create classes that implement these system-defined interfaces.

The purpose of this chapter is to build your understanding of interfaces from the ground up, so we will examine a series of examples based on a custom interface. As you will see, there are three important aspects to working with interfaces:

- Someone must define an interface.
- One or more programmers must create classes that implement this interface.
- Some client-side code must be written against the interface type.

Once you see how these three pieces fit together, you will have a newfound appreciation for how elegantly interfaces can support polymorphism within a system design.

Defining an Interface

Before we create our first interface definition, let's cover a few rules. An interface definition usually contains the signatures for a set of methods and properties. However, you cannot include any form of implementation, such as data layout details or executable code. For instance, it is illegal to create an interface definition that contains fields or constructors. Likewise, an interface cannot contain a method or property whose definition includes an implementation.

To create an interface definition, you use the `Interface` construct. Inside the `Interface` construct, you can declare the signatures for methods and properties. Here's a simple definition for an interface named `IHourlyEmployee`:

```
Public Interface IHourlyEmployee
  ReadOnly Property TaxID() As String
  Function CalculateWages(ByVal hours As Single) As Decimal
End Interface
```

The `IHourlyEmployee` interface defines the calling signature for a property named `TaxID` and a method named `CalculateWages`. Note that all members of an interface type are implicitly public and abstract. To this end, it is illegal to use the `Public` keyword or the `MustOverride` keyword on a member inside an interface definition. Remember, however, that interface members are always defined with the semantics implied by these two keywords.

Interfaces themselves can be marked as either `Public` (for inter-assembly use) or `Friend` (for intra-assembly use). If you define an interface without using either the `Public` keyword or the `Friend` keyword, the interface's visibility remains restricted to its containing assembly—just as if you had defined it using the `Friend` keyword. In this respect, interface definitions follow the same rules as other types.

Implementing an Interface

The second aspect to programming with interfaces is creating a class that implements the interface. After all, an interface is an abstract type, which means it has no value until it is implemented by at least one concrete class.

Your first step toward implementing an interface is to use the `Implements` keyword within a class definition. The following example shows the starting point for the definition of a class named `MailClerk` that implements the `IHourlyEmployee` interface:

```
Public Class MailClerk
        Implements IHourlyEmployee

   '*** implementation omitted
End Class
```

This definition for the `MailClerk` class contains the `Implements` keyword. You place the `Implements` keyword, followed by the name of the interface, on a separate line underneath the class name. If you like, you can join the lines using a colon, as shown here:

```
Public Class MailClerk : Implements IHourlyEmployee
   '*** implementation omitted
End Class
```

Next, you must map each interface member to a specific implementation. Listing 6.2 shows a complete example, including both the `IHourlyEmployee` interface and its implementation in the `MailClerk` class. Look carefully at the end of each method signature in the `MailClerk` class.

LISTING 6.2: A class must use `Implements` **clauses to map each interface member to an implementation.**

```
Public Interface IHourlyEmployee
  ReadOnly Property TaxID() As String
  Function CalculateWages(ByVal hours As Single) As Decimal
End Interface

Public Class MailClerk : Implements IHourlyEmployee
  Protected m_TaxID As String

  Public Sub New(ByVal TaxID As String)
    m_TaxID = TaxID
  End Sub

  Public ReadOnly Property TaxID() As String _
                  Implements IHourlyEmployee.TaxID
    Get
      Return m_TaxID
    End Get
  End Property

  Public Function CalculateWages(ByVal hours As Single) As Decimal _
        Implements IHourlyEmployee.CalculateWages
    Return CDec(hours * 50)   '*** calculate rate of $50/hour
  End Function
End Class
```

As shown in Listing 6.2, each member of an interface must be explicitly wired up to a member inside the implementing class by adding an `Implements` clause at the end of the member signature. For example, the definition of the `TaxID` property requires the `Implements` clause to provide an entry point for clients that have programmed against the `IHourlyEmployee` interface:

```
Public ReadOnly Property TaxID() As String _
                    Implements IHourlyEmployee.TaxID
```

Likewise, the implementation of the `CalculateWages` method requires the `Implements` clause:

```
Public Function CalculateWages(ByVal hours As Single) As Decimal _
              Implements IHourlyEmployee.CalculateWages
```

The definition for a class that implements an interface will not compile until the class author has added an `Implements` clause to map each interface member to an implementation within the class. This restriction makes sense because implementing an interface is an all-or-nothing proposition: If a class implements an interface, it must provide an implementation for each interface member to satisfy the interface's programming contract.

Implementing Interfaces with Visual Studio .NET

The Visual Studio .NET IDE provides a handy feature when you are writing a class that implements an interface. Its code editor window provides a code generator that can yield skeletons for the methods and properties of an interface. This convenient feature enables you to avoid the tedious job of typing the method and property signatures and their required `Implements` clauses by hand. Here's a quick overview of how the code generator works.

The Visual Basic .NET code editor window provides two combo boxes located on the top border directly above your code. Once you have added the `Implements` clause to the class definition, you should be able to use the drop-down combo box on the left to view the name of each class defined in that source file. Under the class name, you should see an indented list of interfaces that have been associated with the class through the `Implements` keyword. Select the name of the interface you are implementing in the left-hand combo box.

Next, use the drop-down combo box on the right to view a list of members defined by that interface. Selecting a method or property from the right-hand combo box will cause the code editor to generate a code skeleton for that member. The code editor defines the skeleton with the proper `Implements` clause, and you simply provide the implementation.

It is perfectly legal to leave a member implementation empty if desired. Your only requirement is to provide a concrete, callable member for each interface member—the member doesn't have to actually do anything if that makes sense. The implementation is up to you.

Programming against an Interface

An interface is similar to an abstract class in that it does not represent a creatable type. As a consequence, a compile-time error will result if you place an interface name after the New operator in a misguided attempt to create an object:

```
'*** this will not compile
Dim employee1 As IHourlyEmployee = New IHourlyEmployee
```

Although an interface is not a creatable type, you can use it to declare variables, parameters, and fields. You can then use these variables, parameters, and fields to reference any type of object that implements that interface. This makes it possible to write generic, reusable code against the interface type. For example, you could write a class named PayrollManager that is designed to work with any object implementing the IHourlyEmployee interface:

```
Public Class PayrollManager

  Function GetPaycheckInfo(ByVal emp As IHourlyEmployee) As String
    '*** calculate payroll information based on 40-hour work week
    Return emp.TaxID & " is owed " & _
          emp.CalculateWages(40).ToString("$#,##0.00")
  End Function

End Class
```

When you call the GetPaycheckInfo method on a PayrollManager object, you can pass any object that implements the IHourlyEmployee interface. Because the MailClerk class implements the IHourlyEmployee interface, you can call GetPaycheckInfo and pass a MailClerk object:

```
Dim mgr As New PayrollManager()

'*** create and use IHourlyEmployee-compatible object
Dim employee1 As IHourlyEmployee = New MailClerk("123-45-6789")
Dim info As String = mgr.GetPaycheckInfo(employee1)
```

In Listing 6.2, you saw how to write the definition for a concrete class that implements the IHourlyEmployee interface. It wouldn't be too difficult to write other classes to support this interface. The good news is that no matter how many different types of objects implement IHourlyEmployee, the `PayrollManager` class treats all of them in a uniform fashion. The only requirement is that any object passed to the `GetPaycheckInfo` method must implement `IHourlyEmployee`.

In fact, the `PayrollManager` class is not tightly coupled to any concrete implementation of the `IHourlyEmployee` interface. In other words, the `PayrollManager` class is *decoupled* from the concrete classes with which it interacts. The decoupling of classes is desirable because it promotes polymorphic programming and code reuse. Indeed, the fact that the `Payroll-Manager` class is decoupled from any concrete class makes it more reusable. Code written in the definition of the `PayrollManager` class can be used with any concrete class that implements the `IHourlyEmployee` interface.

CLR Internals

What happens when you invoke a method or a property through an interface-based reference? Recall that interfaces are based on abstract members. Therefore, it is not possible to use static binding when accessing a member through an interface reference. Whenever you access a method or a property through an interface reference, the CLR uses dynamic binding to locate the correct member implementation at runtime.

The Interface Contract versus the Class Contract

When a class implements an interface, the class itself supports two distinct and unrelated programming contracts: one defined by the interface and the other defined by the public members of the class and its base classes. These programming contracts are known as the *interface contract* and the *class contract*, respectively.

In the `MailClerk` class shown in Listing 6.2, the `TaxID` property and the `CalculateWages` method are supported as public members in both the interface contract and the class contract. For example, you can access the `CalculateWages` method using the interface type:

```
Dim employee1 As IHourlyEmployee
employee1 = New MailClerk("123-45-6789")
Dim wages As Decimal = employee1.CalculateWages(40)
```

Alternatively, you can access the `CalculateWages` method using the class type, through a reference variable of type `MailClerk`:

```
Dim clerk1 As MailClerk
clerk1 = New MailClerk("987-65-4321")
Dim wages As Decimal = clerk1.CalculateWages(40)
```

As you can see, you can access a `MailClerk` object using a reference of type `IHourlyEmployee` or a reference of type `MailClerk`. It's important to recognize that rules govern the conversion between these two types. When a class implements an interface, an is-a relationship is established. This relationship is similar to the relationship between a derived class and its base class. From a design perspective, you can say that a mail clerk "is an" hourly employee. Then, from a coding perspective, you can implicitly convert from the `MailClerk` type to the `IHourlyEmployee` type:

```
Dim clerk1 As MailClerk = New MailClerk("987-65-4321")
Dim employee1 As IHourlyEmployee  = clerk1
```

Strict type checking doesn't allow you to implicitly convert from the `IHourlyEmployee` type to the `MailClerk` type. After all, some objects that implement the `IHourlyEmployee` interface might not be compatible with the `MailClerk` class contract. Strict type checking requires an explicit conversion when you want to assign the value of an `IHourlyEmployee` reference to a `MailClerk` reference. For example, the following code will not compile with strict type checking enabled:

```
Dim employee1 As IHourlyEmployee = New MailClerk("987-65-4321")
Dim clerk1 As MailClerk = employee1 '*** does not compile
```

To assign the value of an `IHourlyEmployee` reference to a `MailClerk` reference, you must perform an explicit conversion using the `CType` operator:

```
Dim employee1 As IHourlyEmployee = New MailClerk("987-65-4321")
Dim clerk1 As MailClerk = CType(employee1, MailClerk)
```

Keep in mind that an explicit conversion performed using either the `CType` operator or the `DirectCast` operator is not guaranteed to succeed. For example, a call to the `CType` operator will fail at runtime if you attempt to convert an `IHourlyEmployee`-compatible object that is not an object of type `MailClerk`. If you want to perform a runtime check to ensure that the target object supports a certain type before you attempt a conversion, apply the `TypeOf` function together with the `Is` operator using the syntax shown in Chapter 5, in the section "Converting between Types."

Visualizing Interfaces

One key to understanding interfaces is having a way to visualize them. Return for a moment to the code in which a *single* `MailClerk` object (defined by Listing 6.2) is referenced by two different variables:

```
Dim clerk As MailClerk = New MailClerk("123")
Dim emp As IHourlyEmployee = clerk
```

Here `clerk` is of type `MailClerk`, and `emp` is of type `IHourlyEmployee`—this realization is critical. To visualize what is going on, look at Figure 6.2. Each "antenna" coming out of the object represents a separate contract you can use to communicate with that object. A `MailClerk` has two antennas: one representing its class contract, and the other representing its `IHourlyEmployee` contract. How you declare your reference variables determines which antenna—that is, contract—you program against.

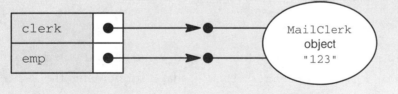

FIGURE 6.2: Interfaces viewed as object "antennas" can help you visualize what's going on.

Hiding and Renaming Interface Members

In most cases, when you implement an interface you should also expose the interface members as public members of the class contract. This practice is consistent with the example in Listing 6.2. There the members `TaxID` and `CalculateWages` were accessible through the definitions of both the interface and the class. Sometimes, however, you might want to hide or rename interface members within the class definition.

Let's examine a situation in which you might want to implement an interface but refrain from exposing the interface members as public members of the class. Visual Basic .NET provides the capability to implement interface members while renaming them or hiding them from the list of public members offered by the class. To see how this process works, imagine you have created a class named `Receptionist` with the following definition:

```
Public Class Receptionist
  Protected m_SocialSecurityNumber As String

  Public Sub New(ByVal SocialSecurityNumber As String)
    m_SocialSecurityNumber = SocialSecurityNumber
  End Sub

  Public ReadOnly Property SocialSecurityNumber() As String
    Get
      Return m_SocialSecurityNumber
    End Get
  End Property
End Class
```

The `Receptionist` class defines a single public member, a property named `SocialSecurityNumber`. You can write code to access this property in the following manner:

```
Dim receptionist1 As Receptionist = New Receptionist("918-27-3645")
Dim ssn As String = receptionist1.SocialSecurityNumber
```

Now let's add a twist to this scenario. What should you do if you need to modify the `Receptionist` class so that it implements the `IHourlyEmployee` interface? You realize that the interface contains a read-only property named `TaxID` that maps to the same underlying data as the `SocialSecurityNumber` property.

As you can see, there's an issue with member naming: Two properties with different names really should map to a single implementation. The good news is that the Visual Basic .NET syntax enables you to rename a member of an interface so that the class member that implements it can have a different name. In Listing 6.3, for example, both the `SocialSecurityNumber` property of the `Receptionist` class and the `TaxID` property of the `IHourlyEmployee` interface map to a common implementation through the `Implements` clause.

LISTING 6.3: Interface members can be renamed or hidden in the class contract.

```
Public Class Receptionist : Implements IHourlyEmployee
  Protected m_SocialSecurityNumber As String

  Public Sub New(ByVal SocialSecurityNumber As String)
    m_SocialSecurityNumber = SocialSecurityNumber
  End Sub

  Public ReadOnly Property SocialSecurityNumber() As String _
                 Implements IHourlyEmployee.TaxID
    Get
      Return m_SocialSecurityNumber
    End Get
  End Property

  Protected Function CalculateWages(ByVal hours As Single) As Decimal _
        Implements IHourlyEmployee.CalculateWages
    Return CDec(hours * 50)
  End Function
End Class
```

In addition to renaming the `TaxID` property to `SocialSecurityNumber`, the class definition in Listing 6.3 shows an example of hiding an interface member. The `CalculateWages` method has been defined as protected, which means the programming contract supplied by the `Receptionist` class does not contain this method. Hence the `CalculateWages` method is accessible to clients that are programming against the interface, but inaccessible to clients that are programming against the class.

In summary, method renaming and hiding has no effect on clients that program against the interface type when accessing your objects:

```
Dim employee1 As IHourlyEmployee
employee1 = New Receptionist("918-27-3645")
Dim TaxID As String = employee1.TaxID
Dim wages As Decimal = employee1.CalculateWages(40)
```

Instead, method renaming and hiding affects only those clients that program against the class itself. As Listing 6.3 demonstrates, clients programming against the interface continue to access members using the names as they're defined in the interface. Clients programming directly against the class definition access renamed members using their public names, if they are accessible at all:

```
'*** this code works as expected
Dim receptionist1 As Receptionist
receptionist1 = New Receptionist("918-27-3645")
Dim ssn As String = receptionist1.SocialSecurityNumber

'*** this code will not compile
Dim receptionist2 As Receptionist
receptionist2 = New Receptionist("546-37-2819")
Dim TaxID As String = receptionist2.TaxID                '*** error
Dim wages As Decimal = receptionist2.CalculateWages(40)  '*** error
```

The techniques just demonstrated for renaming and hiding interface members can be useful in a few situations. Renaming is helpful when methods and properties of differing names require a common implementation. Hiding is helpful when a member of an interface should not show up in the class definition, or when doing so would generate conflicts due to the presence of identical member signatures (e.g., when you are releasing a new version of a class). It is suggested that you use these techniques sparingly. In general, a class is more convenient to use if its class contract mirrors all the functionality that's available through each interface contract it implements.

Using Interfaces Together with Inheritance

On many occasions, a class definition will contain both the `Inherits` keyword and the `Implements` keyword. This approach enables you to inherit from a base class while simultaneously implementing one or more interfaces. To accomplish this goal, you must place the `Inherits` keyword and the base class name on the second line and then place the `Implements` keyword and the interface name(s) on the third line. The `Inherits` keyword always goes before the `Implements` keyword:

```
Public Class Programmer
      Inherits Human
      Implements IHourlyEmployee
  '*** implementation omitted
End Class
```

Listing 6.4 shows a complete definition for the `Programmer` class, with support for the `IHourlyEmployee` interface. As you can see, the `Programmer` class is a bit more complicated than the `MailClerk` class in Listing 6.2 because `Programmer` inherits from a specific base class (whereas `Mail-`

Clerk implicitly inherited from Object). However, Programmer objects and MailClerk objects both implement the same interface. Objects of either type can be substituted for one another in a design based on the IHourlyEmployee interface.

LISTING 6.4: Class definitions often contain the Inherits **and** Implements **keywords.**

```
Public Class Programmer : Inherits Human
                          Implements IHourlyEmployee
  Protected m_TaxID As String

  Public Sub New(ByVal Name As String, ByVal TaxID As String)
    MyBase.New(Name)
    m_TaxID = TaxID
  End Sub

  Public ReadOnly Property TaxID() As String _
             Implements IHourlyEmployee.TaxID
    Get
      Return m_TaxID
    End Get
  End Property

  Public Function CalculateWages(ByVal hours As Single) As Decimal _
       Implements IHourlyEmployee.CalculateWages
    Return CDec(hours * 125)  '*** rate is $125/hour
  End Function
End Class
```

Now consider what happens when a class inherits from a base class that implements an interface. As you might recall from Chapter 5, when one class inherits from another, the public members defined in the base class contract are automatically added to the contract of the derived class. The list of interfaces implemented by the base class is inherited as well. In other words, a derived class automatically implements any interface that is implemented by its base class.

You may find yourself in a situation where you have to author several classes, all of which implement the same interface. In such a scenario, it can be helpful to create a base class that contains a default implementation for each member of the interface. That way, derived classes can inherit the default implementation and simply override any behavior that needs to be specialized.

Let's look at another example. In Listing 6.4, the `Programmer` class implements the `IHourlyEmployee` interface. If you create a derived class named `JuniorProgrammer` that inherits from `Programmer`, there is no need to explicitly implement `IHourlyEmployee`. The `JuniorProgrammer` class implicitly implements `IHourlyEmployee` because it inherits from `Programmer`:

```
Public Class JuniorProgrammer : Inherits Programmer
  '*** inherits implementation of IHourlyEmployee.TaxID
  '*** inherits implementation of IHourlyEmployee.CalculateWages
End Class
```

Things couldn't be easier if you're satisfied with the way the `Programmer` class implements the members of the `IHourlyEmployee` interface. But what if you want to create a class named `SeniorProgrammer` that overrides the `Programmer` implementation of the `CalculateWages` method? This step can be a little tricky.

By default, a method definition is not overridable. The same is true of method definitions that contain an `Implements` clause. The `CalculateWages` method in the `Programmer` class of Listing 6.4 is not declared using the `Overridable` keyword, for instance, so its implementation cannot be overridden by derived classes.

To allow for the overriding of a method in a base class, you must define the member using the `Overridable` keyword. Let's modify the `CalculateWages` method of the `Programmer` class so that derived classes can override its behavior:

```
Public Class Programmer : Inherits Human
                        Implements IHourlyEmployee

  Public Overridable Function CalculateWages(ByVal hours As Single) _
          As Decimal Implements IHourlyEmployee.CalculateWages
    Return CDec(hours * 125)
  End Function

  '*** other class members omitted for clarity
End Class
```

Now you can write the definition for the derived class `SeniorProgrammer` with an implementation that overrides the `CalculateWages` method:

```
Public Class SeniorProgrammer : Inherits Programmer

  '*** overrides implementation of IHourlyEmployee.CalculateWages
  Public Overrides Function CalculateWages(ByVal hours As Single) _
          As Decimal Implements IHourlyEmployee.CalculateWages
    Return CDec(hours * 175)  '*** senior programmers make more
  End Function

End Class
```

Implementing Multiple Interfaces

When you create the definition for a class, you have the option of implementing as many interfaces as you'd like. You can implement multiple interfaces by adding a comma-delimited list of interface names after the `Implements` keyword, as follows:

```
Public Class Programmer
      Inherits Human
      Implements IHourlyEmployee, ICloneable, IDisposable
  '*** implementation omitted
End Class
```

When you define a class in this manner, you must also add code to map every member of every interface to a specific implementation using `Implements` clauses. This capability to implement multiple interfaces gives you plenty of power and flexibility. Naturally, there's a catch: It also creates a few potential problems with respect to the names of interface members.

Suppose you want to implement two interfaces in a class, where each interface contains a method that has been designed to do the exact same thing. For example, imagine you want to define a class that implements the following two interfaces:

```
Public Interface IScreenPainter
  Sub Render()
End Interface

Public Interface IArtist
  Sub Draw()
End Interface
```

What if you decide that the implementation for `IScreenPainter.Render` should be the same as the implementation for `IArtist.Draw`? You could write two separate implementations for these two interface members, but that would result in redundant code in your class. Alternatively, you could write one implementation to forward to the other, which avoids the code redundancy. Visual Basic .NET provides a third alternative—an easier and more elegant solution to this problem. That is, you can map both interface members to a single implementation as long as both members have an identical calling signature.

You accomplish this by providing a comma-delimited list of interface members in the `Implements` clause for the method definition:

```
Public Class GraphicDevice
  Implements IScreenPainter, IArtist

  '*** map multiple members to one implementation
  Public Sub Render() _
        Implements IScreenPainter.Render, IArtist.Draw
    '*** code to write to display
  End Sub

End Class
```

In the preceding code, a call to the `Render` method through a reference variable of type `IScreenPainter` will be dispatched to the same method implementation as a call to the `Draw` method through a reference variable of type `IArtist`. You can map as many interface members as desired to this implementation as long as each interface member has the same calling signature.

In this example, the class contract for the `GraphicDevice` class exposes the implementation using the public name `Render`. Alternatively, you could rename the method to `Draw` or any other name. Either way, you must decide which name to use in the class contract.

Mapping multiple interface members with different names to a common implementation enables you to resolve situations in which two methods with different names were designed to do the same thing. But what if the situation were reversed? That is, what if you had to implement two methods that have the same name but were designed to do different things?

The following example highlights the potential problem. Suppose you want to create a class that implements an interface named `IArtist` and an interface named `ICowboy`. Assume that these two interfaces are based on the following definitions:

```
Public Interface IArtist
  Sub Draw()
End Interface

Public Interface ICowboy
  Sub Draw()
End Interface
```

Both interfaces contain a method named `Draw`, but these versions of the `Draw` method have very different semantics. What it means for an artist to draw is very different from what it means for a cowboy to draw. Although it's possible to join both interface members to the same implementation, you would not want to do so. Instead, your class requires two separate implementations of the `Draw` method. Examine the following definition for a class named `ArtisticCowboy`:

```
Public Class ArtisticCowboy : Implements IArtist, ICowboy

  '*** map members of same name to different implementations
  Public Sub DrawPicture() Implements IArtist.Draw
    '*** code to draw picture
  End Sub

  Public Sub DrawGun() Implements ICowboy.Draw
    '*** code to draw gun
  End Sub

End Class
```

The syntax of Visual Basic .NET enables you to map the two different entry points for `Draw` to their own separate implementations. This way you can avoid problems created by naming conflicts across interfaces.

Note also that the definition for the `ArtisticCowboy` class does not expose a public method named `Draw`. Instead, each implementation of the `Draw` method has been renamed in the class contract to differentiate between the intended behaviors of these two method implementations.

Interface Inheritance

It's possible to define an interface that inherits from another interface. In fact, it's possible to define an interface that inherits from two or more interfaces. Let's keep our discussion of this advanced topic as simple as we can, however, by limiting it to an interface that inherits from one other interface.

When one interface inherits from another interface, the contract defined by the derived interface will include all members defined by the contract of the base interface. In addition, the contract of the derived interface will include any members that are defined within the body of the derived interface. An example will illustrate how this process works. Assume you start with an interface named IDog:

```
Public Interface IDog
   Sub Bark()
End Interface
```

IDog is a (somewhat contrived) interface designed to model the behavior of a dog. What if you wanted to create a new interface that was an extended version of IDog? You could use IDog as a base interface and create a second interface that inherits from it. When you want to inherit one interface from another, you use the Inherits keyword as you would expect:

```
Public Interface ISuperDog : Inherits IDog
   Sub FetchSlippers()
End Interface
```

The derived interface ISuperDog contains the Bark method as well as the FetchSlippers method. When an interface such as ISuperDog inherits from another interface such as IDog, the two interfaces take on a formalized is-a relationship. By definition, all objects that implement ISuperDog must also implement IDog. There can be no object that implements ISuperDog that does not also implement IDog.

Next, let's look at an example of a class that explicitly implements both the base interface IDog and the derived interface ISuperDog. Examine the following definition for the Beagle class:

```
Public Class Beagle : Implements IDog, ISuperDog
   Sub Bark() Implements IDog.Bark
     '*** implementation
   End Sub

   Sub FetchSlippers() Implements ISuperDog.FetchSlippers
     '*** implementation
   End Sub
End Class
```

The `Beagle` class explicitly declares support for `IDog` and `ISuperDog`. Because the `Beagle` class explicitly implements `IDog`, its implementation includes an entry point for the method `IDog.Bark`. In this case, the Visual Basic .NET compiler makes the assumption that the entry point for `IDog.Bark` will also serve as the entry point for `ISuperDog.Bark`. The `FetchSlippers` method is defined by the `ISuperDog` interface and not defined by `IDog`. Therefore, the `Beagle` class definition must explicitly map `ISuperDog.FetchSlippers` to a specific implementation.

Now let's examine a different approach to writing a class that implements both interfaces. Examine the following definition for the `Terrier` class:

```
Public Class Terrier : Implements ISuperDog
  Sub Bark() Implements ISuperDog.Bark
    '*** implementation
  End Sub

  Sub FetchSlippers() Implements ISuperDog.FetchSlippers
    '*** implementation
  End Sub
End Class
```

The `Terrier` class differs from the `Beagle` class in that it does not declare explicit support for the `IDog` interface. However, the `Terrier` class implements the derived interface `ISuperDog`, which means it implicitly implements `IDog` as well. You can reference a `Terrier` object through a reference variable of type `IDog` or a reference variable of type `ISuperDog`.

Although the implementation details of the `Terrier` class vary from those of the `Beagle` class, these differences remain hidden from client-side code. Both classes implement `IDog` and `ISuperDog`. Objects created from either class can be used in any situation that calls for an `IDog` object or an `ISuperDog` object.

SUMMARY

Designing effectively with inheritance and polymorphism requires expertise and insight. A designer has many options at his or her disposal, including concrete base classes, abstract base classes, and interfaces. Knowing when to choose one of these design approaches over the others is possible only when you have achieved a reasonable understanding of the topics presented in Chapters 5 and 6.

A design that involves inheriting from an abstract class or a concrete class has an obvious advantage over a design that involves an interface. That is, you can reuse implementation details from a base class—such as field definitions and method implementations—across many derived classes. An interface definition, by contrast, rules out reuse of these kinds of implementation details.

A design that relies an interface has an advantage because it is not limited by the .NET Framework's model of single inheritance. Therefore, interfaces provide a more flexible means to achieve the benefits of polymorphism and type substitution. For this reason, interfaces are used throughout the .NET Framework.

As a .NET developer, you must be fluent with the concepts and syntax associated with programming interfaces. Subsequent chapters describe scenarios in which you must implement system-defined interfaces such as `ICloneable` and `IDisposable`. Of course, you always have the option of creating custom interfaces and integrating them into your designs as well.

■ 7 ■
Delegates

D ELEGATES PLAY AN important role in the programming model of the
.NET Framework. They provide valuable support for developers who
need to design and write software that uses callback notifications. Knowing
how to work with delegates is critical because the use of callbacks is wide-
spread throughout the .NET Framework. For example, the event-driven
model of the Windows Forms framework is based on delegates.

This chapter will build your understanding of delegates from the
ground up. It begins with a general discussion of how callbacks are used
in application design. Once you fully appreciate the design problems that
can be solved using callbacks, the chapter introduces and explains the .NET
programming construct known as a delegate. As part of this coverage, you
will see the architectural details of how delegates work as well as the syntax for programming with delegates. Several other factors should motivate
you to learn about them. First, events in the .NET Framework are layered
on top of delegates. When you use an event-driven application framework
such as Windows Forms or ASP.NET, your knowledge of programming
delegates will make you a much stronger developer. Second, delegates provide a straightforward mechanism in .NET for executing a method asynchronously on a secondary thread. Therefore, delegates provide one of the
easiest ways to become involved in multithreading.

The Callback: A Simple Design Pattern

Application software is often designed around the programming technique known as callbacks. In a callback, one part of an application sends out notifications to alert other parts of the application when something interesting has occurred. More specifically, a *callback* is a call from a notification source back to a method implemented by one or more *handlers*.

Most Visual Basic programmers are already familiar with the concept of callbacks because of the manner in which Visual Basic has always supported event handling. An event handler is a simple example of a callback method. When you write an event handler for the `Click` event of a command button, you are really writing the implementation for a callback method. However, you are not required to explicitly call this event handler. Instead, the Windows Forms framework acts as a notification source and calls your event handler automatically at exactly the right time.

To fully appreciate the value of a design based on callbacks, it can be helpful to draw an analogy to something that might occur in everyday life. Imagine your boss has just assigned a task to you. This task will take several hours to complete and your boss wants to know the minute you are done. It would probably become very annoying to you if your boss called you on the phone every few minutes to ask you whether you had finished the task. It would be far more reasonable for you to make the following suggestion to your boss: "Don't call me; I'll call you and tell you when I'm done."

As long as you notify your boss the moment you have completed the task, your boss can react and take any appropriate actions in a timely fashion. As you can imagine, the use of a callback in this particular scenario will be much more efficient (and far less annoying) than having your boss poll you every few minutes to see whether you have finished your work.

Let's look at another example of using a callback, this one involving code. Imagine you are designing an application with a class named `BankAccount` that contains a method named `Withdraw`. Another part of the application should react whenever a `BankAccount` object experiences a withdrawal of an amount greater than $5000. The starting point for your class might look something like this:

```
Public Class BankAccount
  Public Sub Withdraw(ByVal Amount As Decimal)
    If (Amount > 5000) Then
      '*** send notification to interested parties
    End If

    '*** perform withdrawal
  End Sub
End Class
```

In this example, a `BankAccount` object acts as a notification source. That means a `BankAccount` object must provide a way for a listener object to express its interest in receiving notifications. In other words, a `BankAccount` object must allow a listener object to register a callback method.

Let's continue with our design by creating a listener class that contains a handler method. The following definition for the `AccountAuditor` class contains a method named `OnLargeWithdrawal` that accepts a parameter named `Amount`:

```
'*** listener class
Public Class AccountAuditor
  '*** handler method
  Public Sub OnLargeWithdrawal(ByVal Amount As Decimal)
    '*** perform action in response to large withdrawal
  End Sub
End Class
```

The `AccountAuditor` class acts as a listener and handles the notifications sent from a `BankAccount` object whenever a large withdrawal is made. When a large withdrawal occurs, a `BankAccount` object calls the `OnLargeWithdrawal` method on a `AccountAuditor` object.

Now you can write and maintain the logic for what has to happen when a large withdrawal is made in the `OnLargeWithdrawal` method. What kinds of things might an application need to do whenever a large withdrawal occurs? The application might be required to record the details of the withdrawal into a special log file. In another scenario, it might be required to block the request for the withdrawal until it is approved by a bank manager. Undoubtedly you can think of many other tasks to perform in a handler method such as `OnLargeWithdrawal`.

The next step in implementing this callback is to modify the BankAccount class so that a BankAccount object can track a reference to an AccountAuditor object. A BankAccount object will use this reference to an AccountAuditor object to access the OnLargeWithdrawal method when it's time to send a notification. This aspect of implementing a callback can be accomplished by adding two new members to the BankAccount class, listener and RegisterListener:

```
Public Class BankAccount
  Private listener As AccountAuditor

  Public Sub RegisterListener(ByVal listener As AccountAuditor)
    Me.listener = listener
  End Sub

  '*** Withdraw method omitted for clarity
End Class
```

The BankAccount class now contains a private field named listener that can be used to access the handler method on an AccountAuditor object. The BankAccount class has also been given a method named RegisterListener that can connect a listener to a notification source. In other words, an application should call the RegisterListener method to set up an AccountAuditor object to receive callback notifications from a BankAccount object.

At this point we can modify the Withdraw method of the BankAccount class to perform a callback notification by using the listener field:

```
Public Class BankAccount
  .
  . '*** listener and RegisterListener omitted
  .

  Public Sub Withdraw(ByVal Amount As Decimal)
    '*** send notifications if required
    If (Amount > 5000) AndAlso (Not listener Is Nothing) Then
      listener.OnLargeWithdrawal(Amount)
    End If

    '*** perform withdrawal
  End Sub
End Class
```

Note that the `Withdraw` method tests whether the `listener` field contains a valid reference to an `AccountAuditor` object. This step is important because the `listener` field will have a value of `Nothing` until the `RegisterListener` method is called with a reference to an `AccountAuditor` object. You must prevent your code from attempting to invoke an instance method on an uninitialized reference. After all, it doesn't make sense to make the callback if nobody is listening.

The final step in putting all the pieces together is adding code that creates a notification source object and a listener object, then wires them together by calling `RegisterListener`. Listing 7.1 shows an entire application that implements the callback design we have developed so far.

LISTING 7.1: A class-based design for single-listener callback notifications

```
'*** notification listener class
Public Class AccountAuditor
   Public Sub OnLargeWithdrawal(ByVal Amount As Decimal)
     '*** write info about withdrawal to log file
   End Sub
End Class


'*** notification source class
Public Class BankAccount
   Private listener As AccountAuditor

   Public Sub RegisterListener(ByVal listener As AccountAuditor)
     Me.listener = listener
   End Sub

   Public Sub Withdraw(ByVal Amount As Decimal)
     '*** send notifications if required
     If (Amount > 5000) AndAlso (Not listener Is Nothing) Then
       listener.OnLargeWithdrawal(Amount)
     End If

     '*** perform withdrawal
   End Sub
End Class

'*** application that registers listener to receive notifications
Module MyApp
   Sub Main()
     Dim account1 As New BankAccount()
     Dim listener1 As New AccountAuditor()
```

continues

```
'*** register listener for callback notifications
account1.RegisterListener(listener1)

'*** do something that triggers callback
account1.Withdraw(5001)
End Sub
End Module
```

In Listing 7.1, the code that responds to callback notifications has been decoupled from the code that sends the notification. The `BankAccount` class doesn't require any logic dealing with what has to happen when a large withdrawal occurs. Instead, the logic related to large withdrawals can be maintained within the `AccountAuditor` class. This separation means that you don't need to modify the `BankAccount` class whenever you modify the application logic for dealing with large withdrawals. Therefore, a design based on callbacks and handler methods provides an easy way to customize and extend the behavior of an existing application.

The preceding example has demonstrated how to decouple the code for handling large withdrawals from the `BankAccount` class, but its design could still use some improvement. Currently, the `BankAccount` class is dependent on a listener object created from the `AccountAuditor` class. If we now modified the design so that the callback method `OnLargeWithdrawal` is defined inside an interface, the `BankAccount` class would no longer be dependent on any particular listener class. As an example, suppose we create an interface named `IAccountAuditor` and modify the `BankAccount` class to use this interface to track its current listener:

```
Public Interface IAccountAuditor
  Sub OnLargeWithdrawal(ByVal Amount As Decimal)
End Interface

Public Class BankAccount
  Private listener As IAccountAuditor

  Public Sub RegisterListener(ByVal listener As IAccountAuditor)
    Me.listener = listener
  End Sub

  '*** Withdraw method omitted for clarity
End Class
```

This new design allows a `BankAccount` object to send notifications to any type of listener object that implements the `IAccountAuditor` interface. Now the `BankAccount` class can send callback notifications in an anonymous fashion where it doesn't have to be concerned about what type of object is acting as a listener. As this example demonstrates, the use of an interface enables you to create a callback design based on polymorphism where different types of listener objects can be easily substituted for one another. A callback design based on interfaces and polymorphism is often referred to as a *loosely coupled* design.

We should take one more step to improve the design of the `BankAccount` class. The current implementation allows for the registration of only a single listener object. We would like a `BankAccount` object to have the ability to send notifications to several listeners at once. You can modify the `BankAccount` class to track multiple listeners by using an internal `ArrayList` and then modifying the `RegisterListener` method as follows:

```
Public Class BankAccount
   Private listeners As New ArrayList

   Public Sub RegisterListener(ByVal listener As IAccountAuditor)
     listeners.Add(listener)
   End Sub

   '*** Withdraw method omitted for clarity
End Class
```

In this code, the `listener` field from the previous example has been replaced with a new field named `listeners`. The `listeners` field is based on the `ArrayList` collection class and is initialized with a new `ArrayList` object whenever a `BankAccount` object is created. The `RegisterListener` method has been rewritten to add the new listener object to the existing list of listeners.

To complete the implementation of our new `BankAccount` class, we must rewrite the `Withdraw` method so that it enumerates through the collection of listeners and calls the `OnLargeWithdrawal` method of each listener object individually:

```
Public Sub Withdraw(ByVal Amount As Decimal)

  '*** send notifications when required
  If (Amount > 5000) Then
    '*** enumerate through ArrayList
    Dim listener As IAccountAuditor
    For Each listener In listeners
      '*** send notification to each listener
      listener.OnLargeWithdrawal(Amount)
    Next
  End If

  '*** perform withdrawal
End Sub
```

Listing 7.2 shows the entire application rewritten to use our new design. In this case, the application creates a BankAccount object and two listener objects. The application then registers both listener objects to receive callbacks so that they can react when a large withdrawal occurs. A BankAccount object is able to treat the two listener objects in the same way because both of them implement the IAccountAuditor interface.

LISTING 7.2: An interface-based design for multilistener callback notifications

```
'*** notification interface
Public Interface IAccountAuditor
  Sub OnLargeWithdrawal(ByVal Amount As Decimal)
End Interface

'*** notification source class
Public Class BankAccount
  Private listeners As New ArrayList()

  Public Sub RegisterListener(ByVal listener As IAccountAuditor)
    listeners.Add(listener)
  End Sub

  Public Sub Withdraw(ByVal Amount As Decimal)
    '*** send notifications if required
    If (Amount > 5000) Then
      Dim listener As IAccountAuditor
      For Each listener In listeners
        listener.OnLargeWithdrawal(Amount)
      Next
    End If

    '*** perform withdrawal
  End Sub
End Class
```

```
'*** listener classes
Public Class AccountAuditor1 : Implements IAccountAuditor
   Public Sub OnLargeWithdrawal(ByVal Amount As Decimal) _
       Implements IAccountAuditor.OnLargeWithdrawal
     '*** handler1 implementation
   End Sub
End Class

Public Class AccountAuditor2 : Implements IAccountAuditor
   Public Sub OnLargeWithdrawal(ByVal Amount As Decimal) _
       Implements IAccountAuditor.OnLargeWithdrawal
     '*** handler2 implementation
   End Sub
End Class

Module MyApp
   Sub Main()
     Dim account1 As New BankAccount()
     '*** create listeners
     Dim listener1 As New AccountAuditor1()
     Dim listener2 As New AccountAuditor2()

     '*** register listener for callback notifications
     account1.RegisterListener(listener1)
     account1.RegisterListener(listener2)

     '*** do something that triggers callback
     account1.Withdraw(5001)
   End Sub
End Module
```

It should be clear that the design in Listing 7.2 is superior to the design in Listing 7.1 in several ways. First, the BankAccount class has been decoupled from the type of classes to which it must send notifications. This decoupling makes it easy to create and substitute different types of listener objects. Second, the new design can accommodate multiple listeners. A BankAccount object can be set up to send notifications to as many listener objects as you'd like. It would not be very difficult to modify the main program in Listing 7.2 by adding third and fourth listener objects to perform additional actions when a large withdrawal occurs. Extending the application's behavior in this manner is a simple matter because it doesn't require any modifications to the BankAccount class.

A Trip Down Memory Lane with C++ Function Pointers

C++ programmers have been implementing callbacks in their applications since long before the advent of the .NET Framework. In C++, a callback is often implemented not with the use of an interface, but rather with a *function pointer*. While you don't need to know the low-level details of how to program using function pointers, it's valuable for you to understand them at a higher level because of their influence on the architecture of the .NET Framework.

A function pointer is the memory address of a method implementation. At the assembly language level, it points to a set of instructions that represent the executable logic for a method. To use a function pointer, one part of the application must initialize it to point to a particular method. Another part of an application then uses this function pointer to execute the method to which it points.

Function pointers are useful in C++ because they provide an efficient way to implement a callback between a notification source and a listener. As long as a notification source can obtain a function pointer that points to the implementation for a handler method, it can send out notifications in an anonymous fashion. Like a callback design based on an interface, the use of function pointers allows the notification source to be loosely coupled to its listeners.

When it comes to modeling callbacks, function pointers enjoy a few distinct advantages over interfaces:

- Function pointers don't require a notification source and its listeners to agree on the names of callback methods. The only requirement is that a handler method have the same calling signature as the notification source when executing the callback. In an interface-based design, a notification source and each handler method must adhere to the method names as defined by the interface.
- Function pointers provide a finer degree of granularity than interfaces. When a set of callback methods is modeled in terms of an interface, a listener object must provide an implementation for each method in the interface. Because an interface represents a programming contract that is an all-or-nothing proposition, you cannot imple-

ment a single callback method from an interface that defines several other methods. Modeling a set of callback methods in terms of function pointers provides a finer degree of control because you can register handlers to receive callbacks on a method-by-method basis.

- Function pointers offer greater flexibility. While interfaces require you to work in terms of objects and instance methods, function pointers do not. In this way, they make it possible to implement callbacks in which handler methods are defined as shared methods or instance methods.

Implementing callback notifications using function pointers also has a few notable disadvantages:

- The use of function pointers requires an application to access memory directly. The CLR prohibits direct access to memory to any code that is running in safe mode, so it doesn't make sense to have function pointers play a major role in the programming model of the .NET Framework.

- In C++, function pointers are not guaranteed to be used in a type-safe manner. Suppose you were designing a callback in a C++ application using function pointers. What would happen if you passed a function pointer that pointed to a handler method and then called the method behind it using an incorrect parameter list? This possibility poses a serious problem because the C++ compiler does not always detect this kind of programming error. Instead, the C++ compiler may generate compiled code in which a handler method and its caller don't agree on how parameters are passed at runtime. Such code is likely to crash an application whenever it runs.

The use of C++ function pointers would be much more reliable if the C++ compiler could perform type safety checks in all cases to ensure that the parameter list expected by a handler method always matches the parameter list used by its callers. From the perspective of type safety, it is clear that implementing a callback with an interface is better than using function pointers, because the use of an interface guarantees that the compiler can detect programming errors in the calling sequence.

Delegates

When the architects of the .NET Framework team began to design their new platform, they knew they wanted to provide rich support for implementing callbacks. They weighed the pros and cons of implementing callback methods in terms of interfaces versus implementing them in terms of function pointers. In the end, the.NET Framework architects decided to create a hybrid technique that combines the type safety and polymorphism of interfaces with the efficiency and flexibility of function pointers. This innovation relies on the use of *delegates*.

A delegate is a special kind of type within the programming model of the .NET Framework. The architects of the .NET Framework added delegates to provide a convenient binding mechanism to connect one or more handler methods to a notification source. As you will see, delegates can be used to implement the same kinds of callback designs employed in Listings 7.1 and 7.2. The good news is that a design based on delegates often requires less code and provides more features than an explicit design based on classes or interfaces.

In Visual Basic .NET, you define a delegate type by using the `Delegate` keyword. Each delegate definition you create must include a type name and the calling signature for a handler method. Here are three delegate type definitions:

```
Public Delegate Sub BaggageHandler()
Public Delegate Sub MailHandler(ItemID As Integer)
Public Delegate Function QuoteOfTheDayHandler(Fun As Boolean) As String
```

As shown in this code, you define the calling signature of a delegate type by using the standard Visual Basic syntax for defining a method definition. Like a method, a delegate type must be defined using either the `Sub` keyword or the `Function` keyword. A delegate definition is also similar to a method definition in that it can optionally define a parameter list and a return value.

Delegate types are like other types in Visual Basic .NET in that they can be defined using either the `Public` access modifier or the `Friend` access modifier. If you create a delegate type at the source file level and do not explicitly define it with an access modifier, the delegate is defined as a friend type and will be accessible only to code within the containing assembly. You should define a delegate type as `Public` whenever it will implement callbacks across assembly boundaries.

When you compile code that contains a delegate type definition, the Visual Basic .NET compiler performs some extra work behind the scenes. In particular, it automatically generates a class definition for each delegate type. The class generated for each delegate type is a creatable class that inherits from a system-provided class named `MulticastDelegate`. Using ILDASM.EXE, Figure 7.1 shows what the three delegate types given earlier look like after compilation; the `QuoteOfTheDayHandler` delegate has been expanded to reveal its class members.

Take a moment to examine the definition of the `QuoteOfTheDayHandler` delegate type shown in Figure 7.1. In addition to creating a class that inherits from `MulticastDelegate`, the Visual Basic .NET compiler added a public constructor (`.ctor`) and three public methods (`BeginInvoke`, `EndInvoke`, and `Invoke`).

The Visual Basic .NET compiler adds a public constructor to each delegate definition to make it a creatable type. Once you acknowledge that delegates are creatable types, it becomes easier to understand how they are used in an application. Programming with delegates requires that you create delegate objects from delegate types. Furthermore, each delegate object must be initialized to point to a target method implementation. In just a moment, you will see the syntax for creating a delegate object that is bound to a particular target handler method.

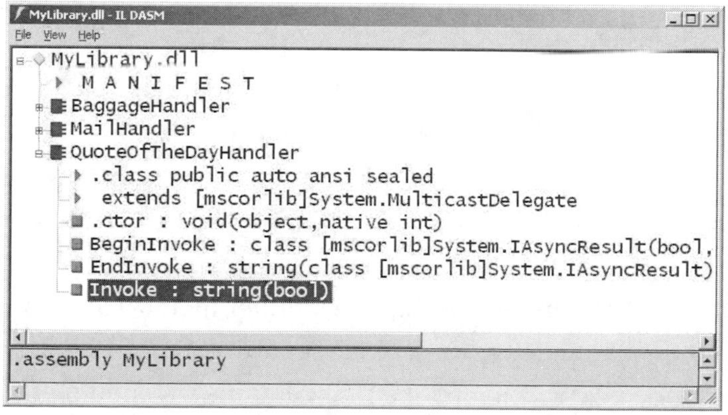

FIGURE 7.1: The Visual Basic .NET compiler creates classes from delegate definitions.

In addition to creating a public constructor, the compiler automatically adds a public method named Invoke whenever it generates a delegate type definition. The Invoke method allows a notification source that is holding a reference to a delegate object to call the target handler method to which the delegate object is bound. When you call Invoke on a delegate object, it simply forwards the call to its target handler method.

Note that the calling signature for the Invoke method of QuoteOfThe-DayHandler matches the calling signature of the delegate type itself. This is always standard procedure; the compiler will always generate an Invoke method whose calling signature matches the calling signature of the containing delegate type. Any input parameters that you pass in a call to Invoke will be forwarded in the call to the target handler method. If the target handler method has any output parameters or a return value, these values will be returned to the caller of the delegate object's Invoke method.

You probably noticed that the definition for type QuoteOfTheDayHandler contains two additional methods, BeginInvoke and EndInvoke. These methods provide a basis for executing a delegate object's target handler method on a separate thread in an asynchronous fashion. The fact that delegates can be used to execute certain tasks asynchronously makes delegates even more powerful. You are encouraged to consider the use of delegates if you plan to develop multithreaded code.

Creating a Delegate Object

When you want to create a delegate object, you typically use the New operator followed by the name of the delegate type. When you create a delegate object using the New operator, you must provide the delegate with the information it needs to bind to a target handler method. Let's step through an example using the QuoteOfTheDayHandler delegate.

Before you can create a delegate object, you must determine the handler method to which it should bind. A handler method can be either a shared method or an instance method. The name of the handler method doesn't matter—the only requirement is that the handler method's calling signature must match the delegate type's calling signature. Suppose you have written a class named JennysHandlers that contains a shared method written to be a handler method for the QuoteOfTheDayHandler delegate type:

```
Public Class JennysHandlers
   Public Shared Function GetQuote(ByVal Fun As Boolean) As String
     '*** custom handler implementation
   End Function
End Class
```

In this code, the shared method `GetQuote` has the correct calling signature to be used with the `QuoteOfTheDayHandler` delegate.

When you want to create a delegate object, you use the `New` operator and pass a parameter value with the information that allows the CLR to bind the new delegate object to a target method implementation. In Visual Basic .NET, you do so by using the `AddressOf` operator followed by the method name. Let's create a delegate object that is bound to the `GetQuote` method:

```
Dim handler1 As QuoteOfTheDayHandler
handler1 = New QuoteOfTheDayHandler(AddressOf JennysHandlers.GetQuote)
```

The Visual Basic .NET compiler will generate a compile-time error if the calling signature of the `GetQuote` method does not match the calling signature of the delegate type `QuoteOfTheDayHandler`. These compile-time checks make programming with delegates far less error prone than programming with C++ function pointers. The strongly typed nature of delegates ensures that a notification source and its handler methods will all agree on the calling signature.

You might remember the `AddressOf` operator from earlier versions of Visual Basic. This operator was introduced in Visual Basic 5 to provide a means for passing actual function pointers to low-level functions in the Win32 API. The `AddressOf` operator plays a somewhat different role in Visual Basic .NET. Its primary purpose is now to initialize delegate objects.

The Visual Basic .NET language provides a convenient shorthand syntax for creating a delegate object. To see this shortcut in action, review the preceding code sample, now rewritten in a more concise syntax:

```
Dim handler1 As QuoteOfTheDayHandler
handler1 = AddressOf JennysHandlers.GetQuote
```

As you see, the call to the `New` operator can be omitted for convenience. In this example the Visual Basic .NET compiler is smart enough to create a new object from the `QuoteOfTheDayHandler` delegate type and assign a reference to this delegate object to the variable `handler1`. In general, whenever the compiler expects a delegate object of type `QuoteOfTheDayHandler`, you can simply pass the following expression:

```
AddressOf JennysHandlers.GetQuote
```

The Visual Basic .NET compiler automatically expands this expression into code that creates a new `QuoteOfTheDayHandler` object that's bound to the handler method `GetQuote`. While the longer syntax makes it more obvious as to what is really going on, the shorthand syntax is more concise and easier to write.

Now that you know how to bind a new delegate object to a handler method, let's call the handler method to which the delegate object is bound. One approach is to apply the `Invoke` method on the delegate object:

```
'*** create and bind delegate object
Dim handler1 As QuoteOfTheDayHandler
handler1 = AddressOf JennysHandlers.GetQuote

'*** execute target method
Dim quote As String = handler1.Invoke(True)
```

In this example, the call to `Invoke` requires a single parameter of type `Boolean` and has a return value based on the `String` type. When you call `Invoke` on the delegate object, it simply forwards the call to the target handler method `GetQuote`. Of course, the call to `Invoke` returns the same value that was returned from the underlying call to `GetQuote`.

The Visual Basic .NET language provides another convenient shorthand syntax for programming delegates: You have the option of omitting the call to the delegate's `Invoke` method. If you don't provide an explicit call to `Invoke`, the Visual Basic .NET compiler automatically adds this call for you. Look at the following example:

```
'*** this code
Dim quote1 As String = handler1.Invoke(True)

'*** is the same as this code
Dim quote2 As String = handler1(True)
```

In the second case the call to `Invoke` is made implicitly. When you replace the syntax `handler1.Invoke(True)` with the syntax `handler1(True)`, the Visual Basic .NET compiler automatically adds the call to `Invoke`. Therefore, you can treat a reference variable or field based on a delegate type as if it were the name of an actual method.

Whether you make explicit calls to `Invoke` or allow the compiler to provide these calls comes down to a stylistic preference on your part. Your choice has no effect on your code once it is compiled. Some programmers prefer explicit calls to `Invoke` because they believe this technique makes their code easier to read and understand. Other programmers prefer implicit calls to `Invoke` because that approach requires less typing.

Interestingly, the C# compiler doesn't allow for explicit calls to a delegate's `Invoke` method. Instead, it requires that programmers use the implicit style in which a delegate reference is treated as though it were an actual method name. If you plan to switch back and forth between Visual Basic .NET and C#, you should consider using the implicit style of calling `Invoke` because it promotes greater consistency across these two languages.

Binding a Delegate to an Instance Method

So far, you have bound a delegate object to a shared method by using the `AddressOf` operator followed by the class name together with the shared method name. It's also possible to bind a delegate to an instance method.

Instance methods differ from shared methods in that the former must execute within the context of an object created from the class in which they are defined. Therefore, binding a delegate object to an instance method requires the delegate object to track a target object as well as the target method implementation. After all, a delegate object could not call an instance method unless it knew which object to use for the method's execution context.

To create a delegate object that is bound to an instance method, you start by creating or acquiring a reference to an object created from the class that defines the instance method. Suppose you have created a class named `JerrysQuotes` that contains an instance method named `NextQuote`:

```
Public Class JerrysQuotes
  Public Function NextQuote(ByVal Fun As Boolean) As String
    '*** implementation
  End Function
End Class
```

To bind a delegate object to the instance method `NextQuote`, you must first create an object from the class `JerrysQuotes`. Once you have acquired an object reference, you can create and bind a delegate object to one of its instance methods. You do so by using the `AddressOf` operator together with the object reference followed by the method name:

```
Dim quotes As New JerrysQuotes()
Dim handler2 As QuoteOfTheDayHandler = AddressOf quotes.NextQuote
```

The difference between this example and the shared method example is that the delegate object must now keep track of the target object. Figure 7.2 reveals some of the private implementation details of a delegate object. As you can see, every delegate object contains a private field that holds a function pointer to a method implementation. Delegate objects that are bound to an instance method also track a reference to a target object that will be used when the target instance method executes.

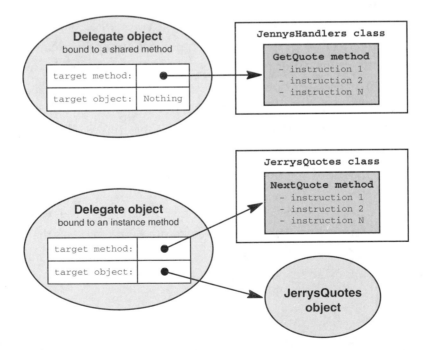

FIGURE 7.2: A delegate object is bound to a handler method and, if appropriate, the handler object.

From a lower-level perspective, a delegate object is nothing more than a friendly, type-safe wrapper around a function pointer. From a higher-level perspective, delegates open up many possibilities for designing an application with callbacks. They provide a flexible and efficient way to implement a loosely coupled design in which a notification source sends notifications to a set of listeners.

A Delegate-Based Design for Implementing Callbacks

Now that you've seen the basics of programming with delegates, let's revisit the callback design developed earlier involving the `BankAccount` class and its `Withdraw` method. In particular, let's redesign the callback method using a delegate instead of an interface (see Listing 7.2). We'll start by defining a new delegate type named `LargeWithdrawalHandler`:

```
Public Delegate Sub LargeWithdrawalHandler(ByVal Amount As Decimal)
```

Next, let's modify the `BankAccount` class to act as a notification source. We can do so by adding two members: (1) a private field named `handler` of delegate type `LargeWithdrawalHandler` and (2) a method named `RegisterHandler` that allows other code to register a delegate object to receive callback notifications. Here's the resulting class definition:

```
Public Class BankAccount
  Private handler As LargeWithdrawalHandler

  Public Sub RegisterHandler(ByVal handler As LargeWithdrawalHandler)
    Me.handler = handler
  End Sub

  '*** other class members omitted
End Class
```

Recall that the examples developed earlier included a registration method named `RegisterListener`, because callback designs based on classes and interfaces require you to work in terms of listener objects and instance methods. The registration method in our new design has been renamed `RegisterHandler` to emphasize the fact that shared methods can also be registered as handlers.

The `RegisterHandler` method accepts a single parameter of type `LargeWithdrawalHandler`. The implementation of `RegisterHandler` assigns this parameter value to the private field `handler` so that a `BankAccount` object can track a delegate object and call its handler method.

Once the `RegisterHandler` method has been called with a delegate object, any method within the `BankAccount` class can execute the handler method by calling `Invoke` on the registered delegate object. Here's an example of executing the `Invoke` method from within the `Withdraw` method of the `BankAccount` class:

```
Public Sub Withdraw(ByVal Amount As Decimal)
  '*** send notifications if required
  If (Amount > 5000) AndAlso (Not handler Is Nothing) Then
    handler.Invoke(Amount)
  End If

  '*** perform withdrawal
End Sub
```

In this code, the `Withdraw` method conducts a check to confirm that the `handler` field contains a valid reference and not a value of `Nothing`. Recall that the `handler` field has a value of `Nothing` until a call to `RegisterHandler` occurs. You must prevent your code from attempting to execute the `Invoke` method on an uninitialized reference.

The `BankAccount` class has been now been rewritten to send out a delegate-based notification whenever a withdrawal of more than $5000 occurs. Now it's time to connect a handler method that can accept these notifications. Examine the following class, which defines a number of possible handler methods:

```
Public Class AccountHandlers
  Public Shared Sub GetApproval(ByVal Amount As Decimal)
    '*** block until manager approves withdrawal amount
  End Sub

  Public Shared Sub LogWithdrawalToDB(ByVal Amount As Decimal)
    '*** write withdrawal info to a database
  End Sub

  Public Shared Sub LogWithdrawalToFile(ByVal Amount As Decimal)
    '*** write withdrawal info to a log file
  End Sub
End Class
```

The `GetApproval`, `LogWithdrawalToDB`, and `LogWithdrawalToFile` methods have all been written with the proper calling signatures to serve as handler methods for the notifications sent by a `BankAccount` object.

Now let's write a simple application that hooks everything together. First, the application must create a `BankAccount` object. Next, it must create a delegate object that is bound to a target handler method such as `GetApproval`. Finally, a call to the `RegisterHandler` method must be made, passing a reference to the delegate object. Here goes:

```
Module MyApp
  Sub Main()
    '*** create bank account object
    Dim acc1 As New BankAccount()

    '*** create delegate object and register callback method
    acc1.RegisterHandler(AddressOf AccountHandlers.GetApproval)

    '*** do something that triggers callback
    acc1.Withdraw(5001)
  End Sub
End Module
```

This code example doesn't use the `New` operator when creating a delegate object, but rather the more convenient shorthand syntax. Because the `RegisterHandler` method expects a parameter of type `LargeWithdrawalHandler`, you can simply use the `AddressOf` operator followed by the method name as shown in the preceding code. The `GetApproval` method is shared, so we didn't need to use the `New` keyword to create an instance of class `AccountHandlers`.

At this point, we have created a simple application that performs a callback notification using a delegate. When the `Main` method calls the `Withdraw` method on the `BankAccount` object and passes a parameter value of `5001`, the implementation of the `Withdraw` method uses the delegate object held by the `handler` field to execute the method `GetApproval`.

This application provides a good example of a loosely coupled design. The `BankAccount` class doesn't know or care what type of handler method is used. Thus it would be very easy to replace the handler method `GetApproval` with the handler methods `LogWithdrawalToDB` or `LogWithdrawalToFile`. It would also be easy to create another method in a different class and use this new method as the callback method. From this discussion, you should be able to conclude that a delegate-based design can provide polymorphism in the same fashion as an interface-based design.

One more important design issue still needs to be addressed. The current implementation of the BankAccount class only provides callbacks to a single listener. A better design would modify the BankAccount class so that it could provide callbacks to more than one listener at a time. In the design shown in Listing 7.2, we used an ArrayList object to keep track of multiple listeners. Fortunately, delegates also provide built-in support for dealing with multiple listeners through a feature known as *multicasting*.

Multicasting

All delegate types have built-in support for dealing with multiple handler methods. They gain this support by inheriting from the MulticastDelegate class that's defined in the System namespace. Multicasting enables you to combine several handler methods in a list so that all of them are bound to the same delegate object. When Invoke is called on the delegate object, the MulticastDelegate class provides the code to execute each handler method in the list.

An example will help you see exactly how this process works. Suppose you want to link two different handler methods to a single delegate object. You can accomplish this task by calling a shared method in the System.Delegate class named Combine. If you call the Combine method and pass two delegate objects to it, this method will return a new delegate object that is a multicast of the other two. The following example illustrates taking the handler methods for two different delegate objects and combining them into a multicast delegate object:

```
'*** create two individual delegates
Dim handler1, handler2 As LargeWithdrawalHandler
handler1 = AddressOf AccountHandlers.GetApproval
handler2 = AddressOf AccountHandlers.LogWithdrawalToDB

'*** combine delegates into multicast delegate
Dim result As [Delegate] = [Delegate].Combine(handler1, handler2)

'*** convert reference to LargeWithdrawalHandler type
Dim handlers As LargeWithdrawalHandler
handlers = CType(result, LargeWithdrawalHandler)

'*** execute BOTH handler methods in multicast list
handlers.Invoke(5001)
```

Note the use of the square brackets around the name of the [Delegate] class. These square brackets are required because Delegate is also a keyword in the Visual Basic .NET language. They serve as escape characters, telling the Visual Basic .NET compiler that you intend to use Delegate as a class name and not as the keyword. If you don't like the square brackets, simply refer to the Delegate class by its fully qualified name System.Delegate.

The call to Combine returns a reference to a newly created multicast delegate object. Note that the Combine method has a generic return type of Delegate, which must be converted to the more specific delegate type LargeWithdrawalHandler in this case. This conversion is required if you want to call the Invoke method.

How are multicast delegates implemented? A multicast delegate is simply a linked list of delegate objects (jump ahead and take a peek at Figure 7.3). The private implementation of each delegate object contains a field designed to hold a reference to the previous delegate object in the list. You might think it would be more intuitive if a delegate object held a reference to the "next" delegate object in the list as opposed to the "previous" delegate object. However, the multicast delegate design uses the notion of the previous delegate because of the sequence in which the handler methods are executed. The reason that each delegate object tracks a previous delegate will become clear in the next few paragraphs.

When you have created a multicast delegate that contains multiple handler methods, the delegate at the head of the list holds a reference to the previous delegate. That delegate in turn holds a reference to the previous delegate, and so on. For the delegate object at the tail of the list, the field for the previous delegate has a value of Nothing. As you will see, the position in which a delegate object is placed in the list is important and non-intuitive—the delegate at the head of the list actually executes last.

When you call Combine, it links two or more delegate objects together and returns a reference to the delegate object at the head of the list. The previous example called the overloaded implementation of Combine that accepts two delegate parameters. This implementation of Combine creates a multicast list that places the delegate object passed as the second parameter at the head of the list. As a result, in the previous example the delegate at the head of the list is bound to the LogWithdrawalToDB method. This delegate object in turn contains a private field that references the previous delegate object, which is bound to the GetApproval method.

Another version of Combine accepts an array of delegate objects. When you pass an array of delegate objects to this Combine method, it places the delegate object in array position 0 at the head of the list. You can call whichever overloaded version of Combine you prefer—but just make sure you pay attention to how each delegate object is placed in the list. The positioning of delegates in the list gives you control over which handler method executes first.

When you call Invoke on the delegate object at the head of the list, the MulticastDelegate class provides the code to enumerate through the list and execute the Invoke method on each delegate object in the list (much in the same way that our earlier design in Listing 7.2 iterated through the ArrayList object). The individual handler methods are processed one after another, executing in a serialized and synchronous fashion. Take note of which handler methods are executed first.

The delegate object at the head of a multicast list does not execute its handler method until after it has called the Invoke method on the previous delegate object. That explains why the MulticastDelegate design pattern refers to it as the "previous" delegate object as opposed to the "next" delegate object. Control passes from the delegate object at the head of the list to the delegate object at the tail of the list before any handler methods are executed.

As a result, the delegate object at the tail of a multicast list always executes its handler method first. Therefore, execution always occurs from back to front. You should conclude that the delegate object at the head of the multicast list always executes its handler method last. In our example involving a multicasting of two delegate objects, the GetApproval method will execute before the LogWithdrawalToDB method.

Implementing Callbacks with a Multicast Delegate

Let's revisit the example involving the BankAccount class and add support for multiple listeners via multicasting. We will modify the class implementation so that a BankAccount object can make callbacks to a list of handler methods. Here's the revised class definition:

```
Public Class BankAccount
  Private handlers As LargeWithdrawalHandler

  Public Sub RegisterHandler(ByVal handler As LargeWithdrawalHandler)
    '*** add new handler to head of multicast list
    Dim NewList As [Delegate] = [Delegate].Combine(handlers, handler)
    handlers = CType(NewList, LargeWithdrawalHandler)
  End Sub

  Public Sub Withdraw(ByVal Amount As Decimal)
    '*** send notifications if required
    If (Amount > 5000) AndAlso (Not handlers Is Nothing) Then
      handlers.Invoke(Amount)
    End If

    '*** perform withdrawal
  End Sub
End Class
```

Notice that the `handler` field has been renamed to `handlers`, signifying that it can be used to hold a reference to a multicast delegate object. In reality, this is nothing more than a renaming issue since the field is still based on the `LargeWithdrawalHandler` delegate type.

The implementation of the `RegisterHandler` method has also been updated to support multicasting. The implementation of `RegisterHandler` now calls the `Combine` method to add the new delegate object to the existing list of delegate objects. This implementation of `RegisterHandler` passes the new delegate object as the second parameter in its call to `Combine`, so the new delegate object will become the head of the list and will, therefore, be executed last. You could easily rewrite `RegisterHandler` to place a new delegate object at the tail of the multicast list by reversing the two parameters sent to the `Combine` method, like this:

```
Public Sub RegisterHandler(ByVal handler As LargeWithdrawalHandler)
  '*** add new handler to tail of multicast list
  Dim NewList As [Delegate] = [Delegate].Combine(handler, handlers)
  handlers = CType(NewList, LargeWithdrawalHandler)
End Sub
```

This code would cause the new delegate object to execute its handler method first, before any other delegate object in the list. The end result is that you can control the order in which the handler methods of a multicast list are executed.

You might have also observed that the `Withdraw` method did not require any modifications, with the exception of updating the name of the `handler` field to `handlers`. The call to `Invoke` is made in the exact same way as before. This illustrates one of the most valuable aspects of using multicast delegates—a notification source doesn't have to be concerned with how many target methods are bound to a delegate object. It simply calls `Invoke` and each handler method is automatically executed.

Now that the `BankAccount` class has been updated to support multi-casting, let's rewrite the main program of the application to register three different handler methods to respond to large withdrawal notifications in different ways:

```
Sub Main()
  '*** create bank account object
  Dim acc1 As New BankAccount()

  '*** create register handler methods
  acc1.RegisterHandler(AddressOf AccountHandlers.GetApproval)
  acc1.RegisterHandler(AddressOf AccountHandlers.LogWithdrawalToDB)
  acc1.RegisterHandler(AddressOf AccountHandlers.LogWithdrawalToFile)

  '*** do something that triggers callbacks
  acc1.Withdraw(5001)
End Sub
```

At this point you have seen the entire design for implementing callback notifications using delegates. Listing 7.3 gives a complete application based on this design. This application is identical in functionality to the interface-based design in Listing 7.2—it provides a type-safe approach to creating plug-compatible handler methods involving multiple listeners. However, the delegate-based design is a little more flexible in that you can use handlers that are defined as shared methods. A delegate-based approach allows you to be more productive because it also supplies the code needed to manage multiple listeners.

LISTING 7.3: A delegate-based design for callback notifications involving multiple listeners

```
Imports System

Public Delegate Sub LargeWithdrawalHandler(ByVal Amount As Decimal)

Public Class BankAccount
  Private handlers As LargeWithdrawalHandler
```

```vb
   Public Sub RegisterHandler(ByVal handler As LargeWithdrawalHandler)
     '*** add new handler to head of multicast list
     Dim NewList As [Delegate] = [Delegate].Combine(handlers, handler)
     handlers = CType(NewList, LargeWithdrawalHandler)
   End Sub

   Public Sub Withdraw(ByVal Amount As Decimal)
     '*** send notifications if required
     If (Amount > 5000) AndAlso (Not handlers Is Nothing) Then
       handlers.Invoke(Amount)
     End If

     '*** perform withdrawal
   End Sub
End Class

Public Class AccountHandlers
   Public Shared Sub GetApproval(ByVal Amount As Decimal)
     '*** block until manager approval
   End Sub

   Public Shared Sub LogWithdrawalToDB(ByVal Amount As Decimal)
     '*** write withdrawal info to database
   End Sub

   Public Shared Sub LogWithdrawalToFile(ByVal Amount As Decimal)
     '*** write withdrawal info to log file
   End Sub
End Class

Module MyApp
   Sub Main()
     '*** create bank account object
     Dim acc1 As New BankAccount()

     '*** register callback methods
     acc1.RegisterHandler(AddressOf AccountHandlers.GetApproval)
     acc1.RegisterHandler(AddressOf AccountHandlers.LogWithdrawalToDB)
     acc1.RegisterHandler(AddressOf AccountHandlers.LogWithdrawalToFile)

     '*** do something that triggers callbacks
     acc1.Withdraw(5001)
   End Sub
End Module
```

Finally, multicasting allows you to place the handler methods so they execute in a predictable sequence. Given the application in Listing 7.3, Figure 7.3 shows how the delegates are laid out in memory. The GetApproval method will execute first because it has been placed at the tail of the list.

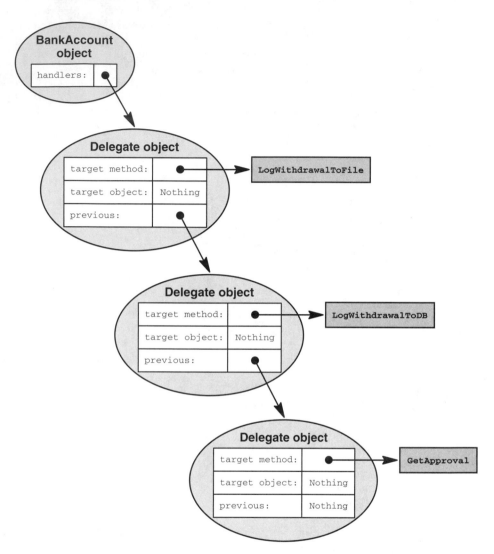

FIGURE 7.3: A multicast delegate list executes its handler methods from back to front.

Next, the LogWithdrawalFromDB method will execute. Because the Log-WithdrawalToFile method was registered last, it will be placed at the head of the list and, consequently, execute last.

Calling the GetInvocationList Method

In many cases, a notification source can simply call Invoke to execute all the target handler methods associated with a multicast delegate object. At other times, you need more control. For example, you might need to determine how many target handler methods have been added to the multicast delegate. You also might be required to write code that can gracefully catch exceptions thrown by handler methods in the list.

The `Delegate` class provides a public instance method named `Get-InvocationList`. When you call this method on a multicast delegate, it returns an array of references to individual delegate objects. This array makes it possible to determine how many handler methods are currently bound to a multicast delegate via its `Length` property:

```
'*** determine number of target handler methods
Dim HandlerCount As Integer = handlers.GetInvocationList().Length
```

A call to `GetInvocationList` also makes it relatively simple to enumerate through the individual delegate objects and explicitly call each handler method. Since a call to `GetInvocationList` returns an array of references to delegate objects, a `For Each` loop then makes it easy to enumerate through the list of delegates. Here the `Withdraw` method makes explicit calls to each handler method in the multicast list:

```
Public Sub Withdraw(ByVal Amount As Decimal)
  '*** send notifications if required
  If Not (Amount > 5000) AndAlso (Not handlers Is Nothing) Then
    Dim handler As LargeWithdrawalHandler
    For Each handler In handlers.GetInvocationList()
      handler.Invoke(Amount)
    Next
  End If

  '*** perform withdrawal
End Sub
```

The preceding code doesn't really provide any more control than simply executing the `Invoke` method on the `handlers` field. Given that fact, why would you ever need to call `GetInvocationList` to enumerate through the delegate objects in the list? One reason is that you might want more control if one of the handler methods throws an exception during its execution.

Let's look at one last example. Imagine you are holding on to a multicast delegate object that is bound to 10 handler methods. What happens if you call `Invoke` and the seventh handler method throws an exception? The first six handler methods have already executed successfully. The exception thrown by the seventh handler method causes the `Invoke` method to terminate unexpectedly. The problem is that the eighth, ninth, and tenth handler methods never execute at all.

Now you see the problem. There's really no way to know which handler methods executed successfully, which handler method failed, and which handler methods never executed. The solution is to restructure your code to explicitly call the `Invoke` method on each delegate within a `Try` block, like this:

```
Dim handler As LargeWithdrawalHandler

For Each handler In handlers.GetInvocationList()
  Try
    handler.Invoke(Amount)
  Catch ex As Exception
    '*** handle exception and continue
  End Try
Next
```

Now you can deal with any possible exceptions, continue executing handler methods, and so on.

A second reason you might need to call `GetInvocationList` and enumerate through the delegate objects individually is that this approach makes it possible to retrieve return values and reference parameters from more than one handler method. If you call `Invoke` on a multicast delegate object and it involves an output parameter or a return value, the results you get are somewhat arbitrary. The reference parameter or return value you receive is supplied by the last handler method that executes. Obviously, you will have more control if you enumerate across the delegate objects in the list and explicitly call `Invoke` on each one. This technique gives you the ability to capture separate output parameters and return values for each handler method call.

The `GetInvocationList` method returns an array that represents a snapshot in time. In other words, `GetInvocationList` returns the list of delegate objects that were present at the time the method was called. If you add a new delegate object to a multicast delegate, then an array generated with an earlier call to `GetInvocationList` will be out of synch. You must call `GetInvocationList` again to return a new array that represents the updated list of delegate objects.

SUMMARY

A delegate is a programming construct that provides support for implementing callback notifications. Delegates provide a binding mechanism for connecting a notification source to one or more handler methods. They allow you to implement callback notifications in a manner that is both type safe and loosely coupled. As a result, you can create an application in which handler methods are easily added and substituted for one another to change the application's behavior.

The information presented in this chapter is an important prerequisite to the discussion in Chapter 8, which focuses on events. Events are really just a productivity layer built on top of delegates. Now that you understand how delegates work, you are ready for an advanced discussion of how events and delegates coexist.

8
Events

IF YOU HAVE previous experience with Visual Basic, you are probably already familiar with the basic concepts involved with programming events. However, events in the .NET Framework are not the same as events in previous versions of Visual Basic—they are based on the concepts and architectural details involved with delegates.

In Chapter 7, you learned about the roles that delegates play in the .NET Framework. You also learned what's required to program with delegates. This chapter will build on this knowledge by discussing how events are implemented internally using delegates.

Your understanding of the .NET event model is particularly important as a developer using the .NET Framework, because popular application frameworks such as Windows Forms and ASP.NET rely heavily on events. Much of the work you will do to customize the behavior of these types of application involves creating and registering event handlers. Possessing a knowledge of how delegates are used to implement events allows you to take advantage of some advanced programming techniques.

A Short History of Event-Based Programming

Events have been a significant aspect of the Visual Basic programming model ever since the very first version shipped back in the early 1990s. In fact, Visual Basic's initial rise to fame and fortune was largely driven by the fact that it provided an intuitive event-based paradigm for building GUI applications on the Windows platform. Most programmers who are experienced with Visual Basic agree that events provide a very straightforward approach for writing code that responds to a user's actions.

But what exactly is an event? An event is just a formalized software pattern in which a notification source makes callbacks to one or more handler methods. In this sense, events are very similar to the callback designs discussed in Chapter 7 on delegates. They are valuable, however, because they can implement callbacks in a simpler fashion. Events are easier to work with because the compiler and the Visual Studio .NET IDE can perform much of the delegate-based work automatically behind the scenes.

In the mid-1990s, the architects of COM added events to their programming model to improve COM's integration with Visual Basic. Events were formalized in COM through a set of standard interfaces known as the connection point interfaces. These interfaces made it possible to register a listener object to receive COM-based callbacks from a notification source. This, in turn, made it possible to use COM events across application and component library boundaries.

Recognizing the burgeoning popularity of event-based programming in Visual Basic and COM, the .NET architects decided to include events as a formal part of the Common Type System (CTS). They knew that events would be valuable because events allow application framework designers (e.g., the Windows Forms team and the ASP.NET team) to provide an event-based paradigm for rapid application development.

The .NET architects knew it did not make sense to reuse any of the implementation details from COM or previous versions of Visual Basic in the .NET Framework's version of events. After all, these existing implementations were written with unmanaged code. It made far more sense to redesign and reimplement support for events from the ground up. As a result, the .NET Framework relies on delegates to provide the underlying plumbing for making events work.

A design that involves events is based on an *event source* and one or more *event handlers*. An event source can be either a class or an object. An event handler is a delegate object that's bound to a handler method. Figure 8.1 shows an event source with two event handlers forming a multicast delegate.

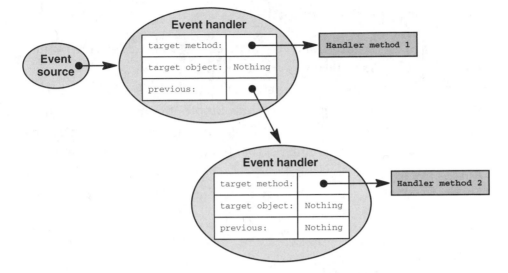

FIGURE 8.1: A .NET event is implemented in terms of a multicast delegate.

Every event is defined in terms of a particular delegate type. For each event defined by an event source, there is a private field that is based on the event's underlying delegate type. You use this field to track a multicast delegate object. An event source also provides a public registration method that allows you to register as many event handlers as desired.

When you create an event handler (i.e., a delegate object) and register it with an event source, the event source simply appends the new event handler to the end of the list. An event source then uses the private field to call Invoke on the multicast delegate, which will in turn call the registered event handlers.

What's really nice about events is that much of the work to set them up is done behind the scenes. The Visual Basic .NET compiler automatically adds a private delegate field and a public registration method whenever you define an event. Visual Studio .NET provides a code generator that can automatically emit the skeleton definitions for your handler methods. As a consequence, you don't have to write the code to create or register your handler methods; you are responsible only for writing handler method implementations.

Programming with Events

Because .NET events are built on top of delegates, their underlying plumbing details differ dramatically from the way things used to work in previous versions of Visual Basic. Nevertheless, the designers of Visual Basic .NET did a good job in keeping the syntax for programming events consistent with earlier versions of Visual Basic. In many cases, programming events involves the same familiar Visual Basic syntax that you used in the past. For example, keywords such as Event, RaiseEvent, and WithEvents behave almost identically to the way their counterparts behaved in previous versions of Visual Basic.

Defining an Event

Let's start by creating a simple callback design based on an event. First, we need to define an event within a class definition using the Event keyword. Recall that every event must be defined in terms of a specific delegate type. Here's an example of the definition of a custom delegate type and a class that uses it to define an event.

```
Public Delegate Sub LargeWithdrawalHandler(ByVal Amount As Decimal)

Public Class BankAccount
  Public Event LargeWithdrawal As LargeWithdrawalHandler

  '*** other members omitted
End Class
```

Here the LargeWithdrawal event is defined as an instance member. In this design a BankAccount object will act as the event source. If you want a class to act as an event source instead of an object, you should define events as shared members using the Shared keyword.

When you program with events, it's important to acknowledge that the compiler does a good deal of extra work for you behind the scenes. For example, what actions does the compiler take when you compile the definition of our latest BankAccount class into an assembly? Using ILDASM.EXE, Figure 8.2 shows the resulting class definition. It provides a revealing look at how the Visual Basic .NET compiler assists you.

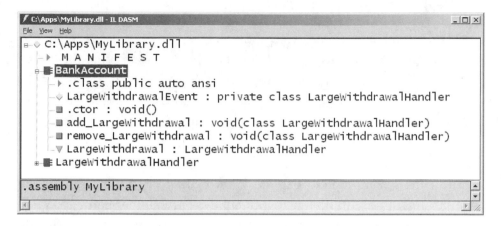

FIGURE 8.2: The compiler generates four special members whenever you define an event.

When you define an event, the compiler generates four members inside the class definition. The first member, a private field based on the delegate type, is used to track a reference to a delegate object. The compiler generates the name for this private field by taking the name of the event itself and adding the suffix `Event`. Thus, creating an event named `LargeWithdrawal` results in the creation of a private field named `LargeWithdrawalEvent` (see Figure 8.2).

The compiler also generates two methods to assist with the registration and unregistration of delegate objects that serve as event handlers. These second and third members that are added to the class definition are named according to a standard naming convention:

- The method for registering an event handler is named after the event together with a prefix of `add_`.
- The method for unregistering an event handler is named after the event together with a prefix of `remove_`.

Thus the registration and unregistration methods created for the `LargeWithdrawal` event are named `add_LargeWithdrawal` and `remove_LargeWithdrawal`.

The Visual Basic .NET compiler generates an implementation for `add_LargeWithdrawal` that accepts a delegate object as a parameter and adds it to the list of handlers by calling the `Combine` method of the `Delegate` class. The implementation supplied by the compiler is almost identical to the implementation of the `RegisterHandler` method shown in Listing 7.3. The compiler generates an implementation for `remove_LargeWithdrawal` that removes a handler method from the list by calling another method in the `Delegate` class named `Remove`.

The fourth member that is added to the class definition represents the event itself. You should be able to locate the event member named `LargeWithdrawal` in Figure 8.2; it is the member with an upside-down triangle next to it. This event member isn't really a physical member like the other three, but rather a metadata-only member. It can inform compilers and other development tools that the class supports the .NET pattern for event registration. It also contains the names of the registration and unregistration methods. For example, compilers for managed languages such as Visual Basic .NET and C# use the event member to discover the name of the registration method at compile time.

Visual Studio .NET also looks for this metadata-only event member. When Visual Studio .NET sees that a class definition contains events, it can automatically generate both the skeleton definitions for handler methods and the registration code to register these methods as event handlers.

Before we move on to the topic of raising events, let's examine a few miscellaneous issues involved with creating a delegate type to use for defining events. First, a delegate type cannot be used to define an event if it has a return value. This restriction means you must define the delegate type using the `Sub` keyword instead of the `Function` keyword:

```
'*** can be used for events
Public Delegate Sub BaggageHandler()
Public Delegate Sub MailHandler(ItemID As Integer)

'*** cannot be used for events
Public Delegate Function QuoteOfTheDayHandler(Fun As Boolean) As String
```

There's a good reason for this restriction: It's more difficult to work with return values in a case involving a multicast delegate that's bound to several handler methods. A call to `Invoke` on a multicast delegate returns the same value as the last handler method in the invocation list, but capturing the return values of handler methods that appear earlier in the list isn't so straightforward. Eliminating the need to capture multiple return values makes events easier to use.

The Visual Basic .NET language also supports an older style of syntax in which you can define an event without explicitly defining it in terms of a delegate type. The following class definition might look similar to what you would have written in Visual Basic 6:

```
Public Class BankAccount
   Public Event LargeWithdrawal(ByVal Amount As Decimal)

   '*** other members omitted
End Class
```

At first glance, you might think an event defined using this in-line syntax is not based on a delegate type, but that is not the case. Remember that every event must be based on a delegate type. Therefore, the Visual Basic .NET compiler must create a delegate type definition for you behind the scenes. If you compile the preceding code, the compiler will generate the definition of a delegate type named `LargeWithdrawalEventHandler` as a nested type inside the `BankAccount` class. You would get the same result if you explicitly nested the delegate type:

```
Public Class BankAccount
   Public Delegate Sub LargeWithdrawalHandler(ByVal Amount As Decimal)

   Public Event LargeWithdrawal As LargeWithdrawalHandler

   '*** other members omitted
End Class
```

When you use the in-line syntax for defining an event with an implicit delegate type, you do not use the `Sub` keyword. Because delegate types for events cannot be defined with the `Function` keyword, the Visual Basic .NET language designers felt that it was appropriate to make the `Sub` keyword implicit. Another motivation for keeping the `Sub` keyword implicit is that it makes it easier to port code written in previous versions of Visual Basic.

Raising an Event

Let's modify the `BankAccount` class so that it raises an event when a withdrawal exceeds the $5000 threshold. The easiest way to fire the `LargeWithdrawal` event is use the `RaiseEvent` keyword within the implementation of a method, property, or constructor. The following code fires the `LargeWithdrawal` event from the `Withdraw` method:

```
Public Class BankAccount
  Public Event LargeWithdrawal As LargeWithdrawalHandler

  Public Sub Withdraw(ByVal Amount As Decimal)
    '*** send notifications if required
    If (Amount > 5000) Then
      RaiseEvent LargeWithdrawal(Amount)
    End If

    '*** perform withdrawal
  End Sub
End Class
```

When you fire an event using the `RaiseEvent` keyword, the Visual Basic .NET compiler automatically generates the code required to execute each event handler. For example, what do you think happens when you write the following code?

```
RaiseEvent LargeWithdrawal(Amount)
```

The Visual Basic .NET compiler expands this expression to code that calls `Invoke` on the private field that holds the multicast delegate object (see Figure 8.2). In other words, using the `RaiseEvent` keyword has the same effect as writing the following code:

```
If (Not LargeWithdrawalEvent Is Nothing) Then
  LargeWithdrawalEvent.Invoke(Amount)
End If
```

The code generated by the Visual Basic .NET compiler conducts a check to ensure that the `LargeWithdrawalEvent` field contains a valid reference to a object. Why? Because the `LargeWithdrawalEvent` field will have a value of `Nothing` until the first handler method is registered. For this reason, the generated code doesn't attempt to call `Invoke` unless at least one handler method is currently registered.

When raising an event, it usually doesn't matter whether you use the `RaiseEvent` keyword or whether you program directly against the private `LargeWithdrawalEvent` field that is automatically created by the compiler. Both approaches produce equivalent code:

```
'*** this code
RaiseEvent LargeWithdrawal(Amount)

'*** is the same as this code
If (Not LargeWithdrawalEvent Is Nothing) Then
  LargeWithdrawalEvent.Invoke(Amount)
End If
```

You might prefer the syntax of the `RaiseEvent` keyword because it requires less typing and results in more concise code. In less trivial cases where you need more control, however, it might make sense to explicitly program against the private `LargeWithdrawalEvent` field. An example will illustrate this possibility.

Imagine a scenario where a `BankAccount` object has three event handlers that have been registered to receive notifications for the `LargeWithdrawal` event. What would happen if you triggered the event using the `RaiseEvent` keyword and the second event handler in the invocation list threw an exception? The line of code containing the `RaiseEvent` statement would experience a runtime exception, but you would have no way to determine which event handler threw the exception. Furthermore, there would be no way to handle the exception thrown by the second event handler and allow the normal processing to continue where the third event handler is executed as expected.

If you are willing to program in terms of the private `LargeWithdrawalEvent` field, you can deal with an exception thrown by an event handler in a more graceful manner. Examine the following code:

```
Public Sub Withdraw(ByVal Amount As Decimal)
  '*** send notifications if required
  If (Amount > 5000) AndAlso (Not LargeWithdrawalEvent Is Nothing) Then
    Dim handler As LargeWithdrawalHandler
    For Each handler In LargeWithdrawalEvent.GetInvocationList()
      Try
        handler.Invoke(Amount)
      Catch ex As Exception
```

```
            '*** deal with exceptions as they occur
        End Try
    Next
  End If

  '*** perform withdrawal
End Sub
```

This approach provides an extra measure of control because you can explicitly call the target method for each event handler. Therefore, you can handle an exception and go on to execute event handlers that appear later in the multicast list. This strategy is better than using the `RaiseEvent` syntax, where an exception thrown by an event handler may prevent the execution of subsequent event handlers in the invocation list.

Creating and Registering an Event Handler

Visual Basic .NET provides two ways to create an event handler and register it with an event source:

- *Dynamic event binding,* which involves the use of the `AddHandler` keyword
- *Static event binding,* which involves the use of the `WithEvents` keyword

Dynamic Event Binding Using the `AddHandler` Keyword

Recall that an event handler is a delegate object. To create an event handler, you instantiate a delegate object from the delegate type on which the event is based. When you create this delegate object, you must bind it to the target handler method that will serve as the event handler.

You register the event handler with a specific event by calling the special registration method on the event source. In the example application, the registration method for the `LargeWithdrawal` event is named `add_LargeWithdrawal`. When you call the `add_LargeWithdrawal` method and pass a delegate object as a parameter, the event source adds the delegate object to the list of event handlers that are to receive event notifications.

One point might be a little confusing: You never directly call an event registration method such as `add_LargeWithdrawal`. In fact, the Visual

Basic .NET compiler will raise a compile-time error if you try to access an event registration method by name. Instead, you must use an alternate syntax involving the `AddHandler` keyword. When you use an `AddHandler` statement, the Visual Basic .NET compiler automatically generates code to call the event registration method.

Let's look at an example in which we connect a few event handlers using dynamic event registration. Imagine we are working with the following set of shared handler methods from the `AccountHandlers` class:

```
Public Class AccountHandlers
  Public Shared Sub LogWithdrawal(ByVal Amount As Decimal)
    '*** write withdrawal info to log file
  End Sub

  Public Shared Sub GetApproval(ByVal Amount As Decimal)
    '*** block until manager approval
  End Sub
End Class
```

We must now create an event handler that's bound to the handler method `LogWithdrawal`. First, create the delegate object that will serve as an event handler:

```
Dim handler1 As LargeWithdrawalHandler
handler1 = AddressOf AccountHandlers.LogWithdrawal
```

Next, register this new delegate object with an event source using the `AddHandler` statement. You are required to pass two parameters to `AddHandler`:

```
AddHandler <event>, <delegate object>
```

The first parameter is an expression that evaluates to an event of a class or object. The second parameter is a reference to the delegate object that will serve as the event handler.

Now we can complete the example by registering the handler we just created with the `LargeWithdrawal` event of a `BankAccount` object:

```
'*** create bank account object and add handler to event
Dim account1 As New BankAccount()
AddHandler account1.LargeWithdrawal, handler1
```

When you use the `AddHandler` keyword to register an event handler for the `LargeWithdrawal` event, the Visual Basic .NET compiler expands this code to call the registration method `add_LargeWithdrawal`. Once the code containing the `AddHandler` statement has executed, your event handler is in place and ready to receive event notifications. The `LogWithdrawal` method will now execute whenever the `BankAccount` object raises a `LargeWithdrawal` event.

The preceding example used a longer form of syntax to illustrate exactly what happens when you create and register an event handler. Once you understand how things work, you might appreciate the following, more concise syntax that accomplishes the same goal:

```
'*** create bank account object
Dim account1 As New BankAccount()

'*** register event handlers
AddHandler account1.LargeWithdrawal, _
        AddressOf AccountHandlers.LogWithdrawal
AddHandler account1.LargeWithdrawal, _
        AddressOf AccountHandlers.GetApproval
```

Since the `AddHandler` statement expects a reference to a delegate object as the second parameter, you can use the shorthand syntax of the `AddressOf` operator followed by the name of the target handler method. The Visual Basic .NET compiler then generates the extra code required to create the delegate object serving as the event handler.

The `AddHandler` statement of the Visual Basic .NET language is complemented by the `RemoveHandler` statement. `RemoveHandler` takes the same two parameters as `AddHandler`, but has the opposite effect. That is, it removes the target handler method from the list of registered event handlers by calling the `remove_LargeWithdrawal` method supplied by the event source. Here's an example:

```
Dim account1 As New BankAccount()

'*** register event handler
AddHandler account1.LargeWithdrawal, _
        AddressOf AccountHandlers.LogWithdrawal

'*** unregister event handler
RemoveHandler account1.LargeWithdrawal, _
        AddressOf AccountHandlers.LogWithdrawal
```

Now you have seen all the steps required to implement a callback design using events. Listing 8.1 gives a complete application in which two event handlers are registered to receive callback notifications from the `LargeWithdrawal` event of a `BankAccount` object. As an exercise to improve your understanding, compare the application in Listing 8.1 to the applications in Listings 7.2 and 7.3. You should see that the use of an event in a class definition can produce the same result as the other designs, but the event-based `BankAccount` class design requires less code to achieve the same goal.

LISTING 8.1: An event-based design for callback notifications using dynamic event binding

```
Public Delegate Sub LargeWithdrawalHandler(ByVal Amount As Decimal)

Public Class BankAccount
  Public Event LargeWithdrawal As LargeWithdrawalHandler

  Public Sub Withdraw(ByVal Amount As Decimal)
    '*** send notifications if required
    If (Amount > 5000) Then
      RaiseEvent LargeWithdrawal(Amount)
    End If

    '*** perform withdrawal
  End Sub
End Class

Public Class AccountHandlers
  Public Shared Sub LogWithdrawal(ByVal Amount As Decimal)
    '*** write withdrawal info to log file
  End Sub

  Public Shared Sub GetApproval(ByVal Amount As Decimal)
    '*** block until manager approval
  End Sub
End Class

Module MyApp
  Sub Main()
    '*** create bank account object
    Dim account1 As New BankAccount()

    '*** register event handlers
    AddHandler account1.LargeWithdrawal, _
            AddressOf AccountHandlers.LogWithdrawal
```

continues

```
        AddHandler account1.LargeWithdrawal, _
                AddressOf AccountHandlers.GetApproval

    '*** do something that triggers callbacks
    account1.Withdraw(5001)
  End Sub
End Module
```

Static Event Binding Using the WithEvents Keyword

Programmers with previous experience in Visual Basic usually find static event binding fairly easy to use, because it involves familiar syntax based on the WithEvents keyword. Let's look at a simple example.

Imagine you want to create a new class named AccountAuditor1 to act as an event listener using static event binding. You can define a class as an event listener by adding one or more fields defined with the WithEvents keyword:

```
Public Class AccountAuditor1
    Private WithEvents account As BankAccount

    '*** other members omitted
End Class
```

A field defined using the WithEvents keyword must be based on a class that defines one or more instance events. In this example, the field named account can be defined using the WithEvents keyword because the BankAccount class defines an instance event named LargeWithdrawal. Defining the account field in this way allows methods defined within the AccountAuditor1 class to be registered as event handlers for events raised by a BankAccount object.

Next, let's create a method that will act as an event handler for the LargeWithdrawal event. Such a method must have the appropriate calling signature. For example, a method that will act as an event handler for the LargeWithdrawal event must have a calling signature that matches the calling signature of the delegate type LargeWithdrawalHandler. Consider the revised AccountAuditor1 class definition:

```
Public Class AccountAuditor1
    Private WithEvents account As BankAccount
```

```
Public Sub Handler1(ByVal amount As Decimal) _
                    Handles account.LargeWithdrawal
   '*** handler method implementation
   End Sub
End Class
```

We have added a new method named `Handler1`. As you can see, the calling signature of this handler method matches the calling signature of the delegate type `LargeWithdrawalHandler`.

Notice that the definition of the `Handler1` method ends with a `Handles` clause:

```
Public Sub Handler1(...) Handles account.LargeWithdrawal
```

The `Handles` clause is based on a `WithEvents` field and an event. It is important because it provides a hint to the Visual Basic .NET compiler. More specifically, the presence of a `Handles` clause triggers the Visual Basic .NET compiler to generate extra code that will create and register an event handler. In this particular case, the compiler generates code to create an event handler of type `LargeWithdrawalHandler` bound to the `Handler1` method. The compiler also generates code to register this event handler with the `BankAccount` object assigned to the `account` field.

The `Handles` keyword is new in Visual Basic .NET. Earlier versions of Visual Basic required you to use a specific naming convention for event handler methods. For example, Visual Basic 6 would require the handler method in the previous example to be named `account_LargeWithdrawal`. In contrast, in Visual Basic .NET the name of the handler method no longer matters; what is important is that the handler method is defined with an appropriate `Handles` clause.

The real magic happens when you assign an event source object to a `WithEvents` field. We will defer the discussion of how the compiler supplies this magic until later in this chapter. Instead, we will make one more addition to the `AccountAuditor1` class so that it can be used as an event listener.

A listener object needs an event source object. For example, it doesn't make sense to create an `AccountAuditor1` object unless you have a `BankAccount` object that will act as an event source. Let's add a constructor so that every `AccountAuditor1` object is initialized with a `BankAccount` object as its event source:

```
Public Class AccountAuditor1
   Private WithEvents account As BankAccount

   Public Sub Handler1(ByVal amount As Decimal) _
                      Handles account.LargeWithdrawal
     '*** handler method implementation
   End Sub

   Public Sub New(ByVal source As BankAccount)
     Me.account = source  '*** triggers binding of event handler
   End Sub
End Class
```

This constructor assigns the source parameter to the WithEvents field named account. This line of code is where the automatic binding of the event handler takes place.

Now the AccountAuditor1 class can be used to create a listener object. Consider the following code fragment:

```
'*** create event source
Dim account1 As New BankAccount

'*** create listener object and bind event handler
Dim listener1 As New AccountAuditor1(account1)

'*** do something that triggers event
account1.Withdraw(5001)
```

When the constructor of the AccountAuditor1 class executes, the Visual Basic .NET compiler generates the code needed to create an event handler object that's bound to the Handler1 method. The compiler also generates code to register the event handler with the BankAccount object by calling the registration method add_LargeWithdrawal. Now the Handler1 method will execute whenever the Withdraw method raises the Large-Withdrawal event.

You have just seen the fundamentals of how to create a listener class using static event binding. Listing 8.2 summarizes this discussion by showing a complete application that uses static event binding to implement a callback design similar to our earlier callback designs. Clearly, static event binding and dynamic event binding are two different approaches that achieve the same goal.

LISTING 8.2: An event-based design for callback notifications using static event binding

```
Public Delegate Sub LargeWithdrawalHandler(ByVal Amount As Decimal)

Public Class BankAccount
  Public Event LargeWithdrawal As LargeWithdrawalHandler

  Public Sub Withdraw(ByVal Amount As Decimal)
    '*** send notifications if required
    If (Amount > 5000) Then
      RaiseEvent LargeWithdrawal(Amount)
    End If

    '*** perform withdrawal
  End Sub
End Class

Public Class AccountAuditor1
  Private WithEvents account As BankAccount

  Public Sub Handler1(ByVal amount As Decimal) _
                   Handles account.LargeWithdrawal
    '*** handler method implementation
    MsgBox("Handler1")
  End Sub

  Public Sub New(ByVal source As BankAccount)
    Me.account = source   '*** triggers binding of event handler
  End Sub
End Class

Public Class AccountAuditor2
  Private WithEvents account As BankAccount

  Public Sub Handler2(ByVal amount As Decimal) _
                   Handles account.LargeWithdrawal
    '*** handler method implementation
    MsgBox("Handler2")
  End Sub

  Public Sub New(ByVal source As BankAccount)
    Me.account = source   '*** triggers binding of event handler
  End Sub
End Class

Module MyApp
  Sub Main()
    '*** create bank account object
    Dim account1 As New BankAccount()
```

continues

```
'*** register event handlers
Dim listener1 As New AccountAuditor1(account1)
Dim listener2 As New AccountAuditor2(account1)

'*** do something that triggers callbacks
account1.Withdraw(5001)
End Sub
End Module
```

Static versus Dynamic Event Binding

After these explorations of static event binding and dynamic event binding, you might be wondering which one you should use. In truth, you should learn how to use both. The Visual Studio .NET IDE uses static event binding when you ask it to generate skeleton definitions for your event handler methods, so understanding this kind of event binding will be important when you are working with an event-driven application framework such as Windows Forms or ASP.NET WebForms.

On the other hand, dynamic event binding can be much more flexible than static event binding. For example, static event binding can be used only when the event source is an object; it cannot be used when the event source is a class. In other words, static event binding can be used with instance events but not with shared events. Dynamic event binding will allow you to bind to either shared events or instance events.

Moreover, sometimes the Visual Studio .NET IDE cannot generate all the event-handling code you need for an application. On such occasions, you must write the code to create and register event handlers by hand. In that situation, dynamic event binding is likely to be more straightforward and easier to use than static event binding. After all, it takes only a single `AddHandler` statement to create an event handler from any method and bind it to any event. The only requirement is that the handler method have the proper calling signature required for the event in question.

One final point: Static event binding is a special programming feature that is unique to Visual Basic .NET. Other managed languages such as C# support dynamic event binding but do not support the equivalent of static event binding. If you plan to switch back and forth between managed languages or need to port code from C# to Visual Basic .NET, you should consider using dynamic event binding instead of static event binding.

The Magic behind Static Event Binding

Earlier, we promised to reveal the details of how the Visual Basic .NET compiler supports static event binding. Of course, you can use static event binding without understanding all the details, but some readers may be curious about what the compiler is doing behind the scenes. If you don't want to peek behind the curtain, you can safely skip ahead to the next section.

Let's look first at what happens when you compile a class definition with a `WithEvents` field. To illustrate the discussion, we'll continue to use the `AccountAuditor` class developed earlier:

```
Public Class AccountAuditor
  Private WithEvents account As BankAccount

  '*** other members omitted
End Class
```

What happens when you compile this class? The Visual Basic .NET compiler generates the class definition shown in Figure 8.3. As you can see, the class definition generated by the compiler is very different from the class definition that you wrote. After the class definition has been compiled, there is no longer a field named `account`. Instead, it is replaced by a private field named `_account` and a read/write property named `account`. The compiler has also generated special implementations for the account prop-

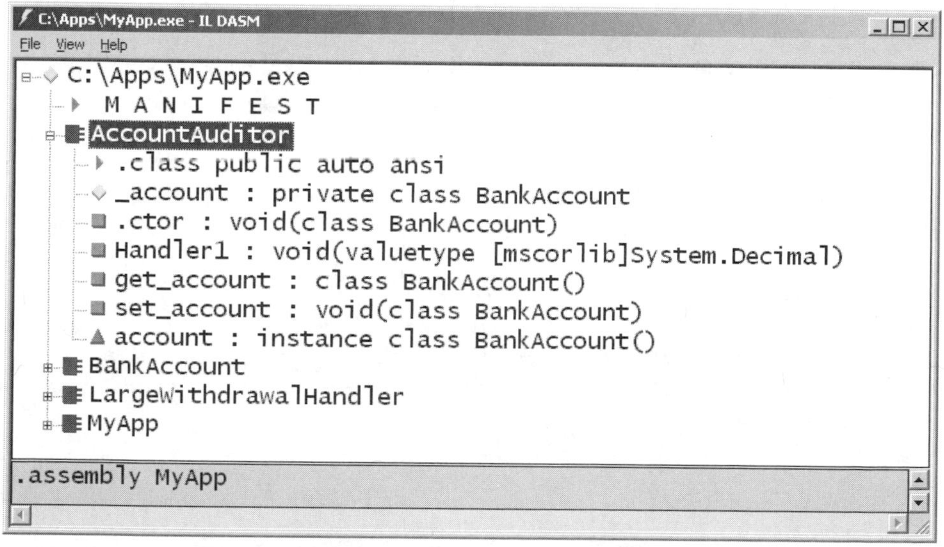

FIGURE 8.3: The compiler-generated details of static event binding

erty's `Set` and `Get` methods. The implementation for the `Set` method is where all the magic occurs.

What really happens when you assign an event source object to a `With-Events` field? For example, what happens when you assign a `BankAccount` object to the `account` field in the constructor of the `AccountAuditor` class?

```
Public Class AccountAuditor
   Private WithEvents account As BankAccount

   Public Sub Handler1(ByVal amount As Decimal) _
                      Handles account.LargeWithdrawal
     '*** handler method implementation
   End Sub

   Public Sub New(ByVal source As BankAccount)
     Me.account = source  '*** triggers call to add_LargeWithdrawal
   End Sub
End Class
```

In reality, you are not assigning the event source object to a field. Instead, you are assigning the event source object to a property that causes the `Set` method named `set_account` to execute. The implementation for `set_account` is generated to create and register an event handler for each method defined with the appropriate `Handles` clause. Listing 8.3 shows how the Visual Basic .NET compiler translates the original class definition during compilation.

LISTING 8.3: Static event binding is implemented using a compiler-generated property.

```
'*******************************************************
'**** here's the class as you originally wrote it ***
'*******************************************************
Public Class AccountAuditor
   Private WithEvents account As BankAccount

   Public Sub Handler1(ByVal amount As Decimal) _
                      Handles account.LargeWithdrawal
     '*** handler method implementation
   End Sub

   Public Sub New(ByVal source As BankAccount)
     Me.account = source  '*** triggers call to add_LargeWithdrawal
   End Sub
End Class
```

```
'***************************************************************
'*** the code that actually gets compiled looks like this ***
'***************************************************************
Public Class AccountAuditor
  Private _account As BankAccount

  Private Property account() As BankAccount
    Get
      Return _account
    End Get

    '*** magic code starts here ****************************
    Set(ByVal Value As BankAccount)
      If (Not _account Is Nothing) Then
        _account.remove_LargeWithdrawal(AddressOf Me.Handler1)
      End If
      If (Not Value Is Nothing) Then
        _account = Value
        _account.add_LargeWithdrawal(AddressOf Me.Handler1)
      End If
    End Set
    '*** magic code ends here ****************************
  End Property

  Public Sub New(ByVal source As BankAccount)
    Me.account = source
  End Sub

  Public Sub Handler1(ByVal amount As Decimal) _
                      Handles account.LargeWithdrawal
    '*** handler implementation
  End Sub
End Class
```

There's a lot to digest in Listing 8.3, so take matters slowly and focus first on the code generated by the compiler for the Set method of the AccountAuditor class. This code checks whether an existing event source object is being referenced by the _account field. If so, the code unregisters it by calling the event's unregistration method, remove_LargeWithdrawal. Next, the Set method checks the Value parameter to see whether the assigned value is a valid reference to an event source object or a value of Nothing. If the Value parameter holds a valid reference to an event source object, the Set method creates an event handler bound to the Handler1 method and registers it by calling add_LargeWithdrawal.

As you see, there's no real magic involved. When you assign a valid object reference to a `WithEvents` field, the compiler generates the code to create delegate objects and bind them to each method defined with a `Handles` clause. It also generates the code to register these delegate objects by calling the event registration methods defined by the notification source.

With this property-based design, you are not required to bind a listener object to an event source during initialization. You can assign a value to a `WithEvents` field at any time during the lifetime of a listener object. Consider the following revised class definition with two additional methods, `StartListening` and `StopListening`:

```
Public Class AccountAuditor
   Private WithEvents account As BankAccount

   Public Sub Handler1(ByVal amount As Decimal) _
                     Handles account.LargeWithdrawal
     '*** handler method implementation
     MsgBox("Handler1")
   End Sub

   Public Sub StartListening(ByVal source As BankAccount)
     Me.account = source '*** triggers add_LargeWithdrawal
   End Sub

   Public Sub StopListening()
     Me.account = Nothing '*** triggers remove_LargeWithdrawal
   End Sub
End Class
```

With this new design, an `AccountAuditor` object will not be bound to an event source object when it is first created. However, you can call `Start-Listening` at any time to bind a listener object to an event source object. Also, a call to `StartListening` will politely disconnect the listener object from an existing event source. A call to `StopListening` will politely disconnect the listener object from an existing event source and leave the listener object in an unbound state.

Obviously, the Visual Basic .NET compiler does a good deal of work behind the scenes when you use static event binding. Keep in mind that this simple example involved only a single handler method. In the real world, you will often have many handler methods associated with a single `With-`

`Events` field. In such a case, the Visual Basic .NET compiler generates the code required to hook up as many event handlers as you need.

Using `WithEvents` Fields in Inherited Classes

In the .NET Framework, a base class often raises events that should be handled by derived classes. The idea behind this practice is that a derived class author should be able to customize the application's behavior by adding event handlers that respond to events raised by a base class. This design technique provides an alternative to the use of overridable methods. It's important that you understand this design technique because it is used extensively by application frameworks such as Windows Forms and ASP.NET.

A simple example will give you an idea how this approach works. You have already seen that a `Handles` clause can be written in terms of a `With-Events` field. You can also write a `Handles` clause using the `MyBase` keyword to handle an event defined within a base class:

```
Public Class CheckingAccount : Inherits BankAccount
   Public Sub Handler1(ByVal amount As Decimal) _
                      Handles MyBase.LargeWithdrawal
     '*** handler method implementation
   End Sub
End Class
```

Once again, the Visual Basic .NET compiler generates all of the code required to create and register an event handler. The code for a base class event, however, is generated in a slightly different fashion than the code for an event associated with a `WithEvents` field. In this example, the compiler adds the code for binding to the `LargeWithdrawal` method into the constructor of the `CheckingAccount` class.

You should keep one other point in mind when you are working with a base class that exposes events: While a derived class can handle a base class event, a derived class cannot raise an event defined by its base class. Look at the following example:

```
Public Class CheckingAccount : Inherits BankAccount
  Public Sub SomeOtherMethod()
    RaiseEvent LargeWithdrawal(5001) '*** compile-time error
  End Sub
End Class
```

Because the implementation for an event involves a private field, the event can be raised only from within the class in which it is defined. A compile-time error will result if you try to raise a base class event using a `RaiseEvent` statement or attempt to access the private field by name.

Handling Events Raised by the .NET Framework

At this point you should have a firm understanding of how events work. You should also be comfortable reading and writing code that uses both static event binding and dynamic event binding. This chapter concludes with practical examples of handling some of the common events raised by various frameworks within the .NET Framework Class Library.

The `System.EventHandler` Delegate

When you build applications using Windows Forms or ASP.NET, you will observe that a significant percentage of events you encounter are defined in terms of a generic delegate type named `EventHandler`. The `EventHandler` type exists in the `System` namespace and has the following definition:

```
Public Delegate EventHandler(sender As Object, e As EventArgs)
```

The delegate type `EventHandler` defines two parameters in its calling signature:

- The first parameter, `sender`, is based on the generic `Object` type. It is used to pass a reference that points to the event source object. For example, a `Button` object acting as an event source will pass a reference to itself whenever it raises an event based on the `EventHandler` delegate type.
- The second parameter, `e`, is defined by `EventHandler` in terms of a class named `EventArgs`. In many cases, an event source passes a parameter value equal to `EventArgs.Empty`, indicating there is no additional parameterized information. If an event source wants to pass extra parameterized information in the `e` parameter, it should pass an object created from a class that derives from the `EventArgs` class.

Listing 8.4 shows an example involving two event handlers in a Windows Forms application that are connected using static event binding. Both the `Load` event of the `Form` class and the `Click` event of the `Button` class are defined in terms of the delegate type `EventHandler`.

LISTING 8.4: Windows Forms events handled using static event binding

```
Imports System
Imports System.Windows.Forms

Public Class MyApp : Inherits Form

    '*** static event handler for base class event
  Private Sub Form1_Load(ByVal sender As Object, _
                    ByVal e As EventArgs)_
                  Handles MyBase.Load
    '*** event handler code
  End Sub

  '*** button defined as WithEvents field
  Friend WithEvents cmdDoTask As Button

    '*** static event handler for button
  Private Sub cmdDoTask_Click(ByVal sender As Object, _
                    ByVal e As System.EventArgs) _
                  Handles cmdDoTask.Click
    '*** event handler code
  End Sub

End Class
```

Notice that the names and formats of the two event handler methods in Listing 8.4 are consistent with those generated automatically by the Visual Studio .NET IDE. For example, if you double-click on a form or on a button while you are in design view, Visual Studio .NET will automatically create skeleton event handler methods that look like those in Listing 8.4. You can then fill in the implementations for these methods to give your event handlers the desired behavior.

The Visual Studio .NET IDE generates handler methods using the naming scheme that was required by Visual Basic 6. In Visual Basic .NET, of course, the names of handler methods don't really matter with static event binding; it's the `Handles` clause that is important. Feel free to rename handler methods to anything you want.

You could rewrite the two event handlers in Listing 8.4 so they are connected using dynamic event binding instead of static event binding. For example, the `Form`-derived class in Listing 8.5 provides the exact same event-binding behavior as the `Form`-derived class in Listing 8.4. The only difference is that the code in Listing 8.5 uses dynamic event binding and thus does not require use of the `WithEvents` or `Handles` keyword.

LISTING 8.5: Windows Forms events handled using dynamic event binding

```
Imports System
Imports System.Windows.Forms

Public Class MyApp : Inherits Form
  Friend cmdDoTask As Button

  Public Sub New()
    '*** other initialization code omitted
    AddHandler MyBase.Load, AddressOf Me.Handler1
    AddHandler cmdDoTask.Click, AddressOf Me.Handler2
  End Sub

  Private Sub Handler1(ByVal sender As Object, _
                       ByVal e As EventArgs)
    '*** event handler code
  End Sub

  Private Sub Handler2(ByVal sender As Object, _
                       ByVal e As System.EventArgs)
    '*** event handler code
  End Sub
End Class
```

In many cases, you will write implementations for handler methods based on the `EventHandler` delegate type without referencing either the `sender` parameter or the `e` parameter. For example, these parameter values are of no real use when you are writing a handler for the `Load` event of a `Form`-derived class. The `sender` parameter doesn't provide any value because it denotes the form object itself—which is already available via `Me`. The `e` parameter passes `EventArgs.Empty`. As a consequence, the following `Boolean` variables are always `True`:

```
Sub Form1_Load(sender As Object, e As EventArgs) Handles MyBase.Load
  '*** these tests are always true
  Dim test1 As Boolean = sender Is Me
  Dim test2 As Boolean = e Is EventArgs.Empty
End Sub
```

You might wonder why the calling signature of the `Load` event isn't more highly customized for its needs. After all, it would be less confusing if the `Load` event didn't include any parameters at all. It's fairly easy to find other examples of events based on the `EventHandler` delegate type in which neither the `sender` parameter nor the `e` parameter passes anything of value.

Ask yourself the following questions: Why have so many events been modeled in terms of the `EventHandler` when this delegate type has such a generic calling signature? Why didn't the .NET Framework designers model each event in terms of a custom delegate with a calling signature that was fine-tuned for its needs? As it turns out, a design goal in the development of the .NET Framework called for restricting the number of delegates used for event handling. A little more explanation is in order.

The first motivation for minimizing the number of delegate types relates to more efficient utilization of memory. Loading more types requires more memory. If every event defined by the classes within the Windows Forms framework was based on a custom delegate, hundreds of delegate types would have to be loaded into memory every time you ran a Windows Forms application. The Windows Forms framework can achieve much better memory utilization by relying on only a handful of delegate types for its many events.

The second motivation for minimizing the number of delegate types relates to the desire to achieve polymorphism with pluggable handler methods. When you write a handler method with a calling signature that matches the `EventHandler` delegate, you can bind it to the majority of the events raised by a form and its controls.

Let's look at a few generic event handlers. In the first example, you want to respond to the `TextChanged` event of several text boxes on a form by changing the user's input to uppercase. There's no need to create a separate event handler for each control. Instead, you can create a single event handler and bind it the `TextChanged` event of several different text boxes.

```
Public Class MyApp : Inherits Form
  Friend WithEvents TextBox1 As TextBox
  Friend WithEvents TextBox2 As TextBox
  Friend WithEvents TextBox3 As TextBox

  '*** create event handler bound to several TextChanged events
```

```
    Private Sub TextChangedHandler(ByVal sender As System.Object, _
                                   ByVal e As System.EventArgs) _
                                Handles TextBox1.TextChanged, _
                                        TextBox2.TextChanged, _
                                        TextBox3.TextChanged
    '*** convert sender to TextBox
    Dim txt As TextBox = CType(sender, TextBox)
    txt.Text = txt.Text.ToUpper()
  End Sub
End Class
```

As this code illustrates, a `Handles` clause isn't limited to a single event. You can include as many events as necessary by placing a comma-delimited list after the `Handles` keyword. In this case, the `TextChangedHandler` method creates three different event handlers. Therefore, this method will execute whenever the user changes the text in any of the three text boxes (`TextBox1`, `TextBox2`, and `TextBox3`).

When the `TextChangedHandler` method executes, how do you know which `TextBox` object is raising the event? The `sender` parameter resolves this question. Recall that the `sender` parameter is passed in terms of the generic type `Object`. You must convert it to a more specific type before you can program against it. In this example, the `sender` parameter must be converted to `TextBox` to access its `Text` property.

If you have experience building form-based applications with earlier versions of Visual Basic, you are undoubtedly familiar with control arrays. A primary advantage of using control arrays was that they support the creation of a single handler method that responds to events raised by several different controls. Although Visual Basic .NET does not support control arrays, you should not be overly alarmed. The new language provides an alternate technique for binding a single handler method to several different events. Here's an example of a handler method that's bound to three different events on three different control types:

```
Public Class MyApp : Inherits Form
  Friend WithEvents TextBox1 As TextBox
  Friend WithEvents CheckBox1 As CheckBox
  Friend WithEvents ListBox1 As ListBox

  '*** define form-wide dirty flag
  Friend DirtyFlag As Boolean

  '*** create handler to set dirty flag when various events occur
```

```
  Private Sub DirtyFlagHandler(ByVal sender As Object, _
                              ByVal e As EventArgs) _
          Handles TextBox1.TextChanged, _
                  CheckBox1.CheckedChanged, _
                  ListBox1.SelectedIndexChanged
    '*** set form-wide dirty flag
    DirtyFlag = True
  End Sub
End Class
```

As you can see, the scheme for binding handler methods to events is relatively flexible. All that's required is that a handler method and the events to which it is bound be based on the same delegate type. The fact that so many events in the .NET Framework are based on the `EventHandler` delegate type makes it easy to write generic handler methods.

When you write a generic handler method, it's sometimes necessary to write code to perform conditional operations that execute only when the event source is a certain type of object. For example, your handler method can inspect the `sender` parameter using the `TypeOf` operator. This inspection allows your handler method to execute one set of operations if the event source is a `Button` object and another set of operations if the event source is a `Checkbox` object:

```
Private Sub GenericHandler1(sender As Object, e As EventArgs)
  If (TypeOf sender Is Button) Then
    Dim btn As Button = CType(sender, Button)
    '*** program against btn
  ElseIf (TypeOf sender Is CheckBox) Then
    Dim chk As CheckBox = CType(sender, CheckBox)
    '*** program against chk
  End If
End Sub
```

Customized Event Parameters

An event notification based on the `EventHandler` delegate typically doesn't send any meaningful information in the parameter named e. In fact, the e parameter is often useless because it contains either a value of `Event-Args.Empty` or a value of `Nothing`. Nevertheless, the .NET Framework designers created a convention for passing parameterized information from an event source to its event handlers; it relies on the creation of a custom event argument class and a custom delegate type.

The mouse events raised by the `Form` class provide a good example of how this convention should be used. Parameterized information about the mouse position and the mouse button that has been clicked is modeled in a class named `MouseEventArgs`. The `MouseEventArgs` class contains an `X` and a `Y` property to track the mouse position as well as a `Button` property to indicate which mouse button has been clicked. By convention the `MouseEventArgs` class must inherit from the generic class `EventArgs`.

The convention for passing parameterized information in an event notification requires a custom delegate to complement the custom event argument class. For instance, a delegate named `MouseEventHandler` complements the class `MouseEventArgs`:

```
Delegate MouseEventHandler(sender As Object, e As MouseEventArgs)
```

Suppose you would like to respond to a mouse-related event such as the `MouseDown` event of the `Form` class. You can write a handler method that looks like this:

```
Private Sub Form1_MouseDown(ByVal sender As Object, _
                            ByVal e As MouseEventArgs) _
                            Handles MyBase.MouseDown
  '*** capture mouse position
  Dim x_position As Integer = e.X
  Dim y_position As Integer = e.Y

  '*** take action depending on which button was clicked
  Select Case e.Button
    Case MouseButtons.Left
      '*** do something
    Case MouseButtons.Right
      '*** do something else
  End Select

End Sub
```

The `e` parameter is very useful in the implementation of this handler method; it is used to determine where the mouse is located as well as which mouse button was clicked. All this parameterized information has been made possible by the design of the `MouseEventArgs` class.

Other examples of this parameterization convention are found in the Windows Forms framework. For example, a class named `KeyPressEventArgs` is complemented by a delegate type named `KeyPressEventHandler`. A class named `ItemChangedArgs` is complemented by a delegate type named

`ItemChangedHandler`. You will likely encounter other events with parameterized information that follow this same convention.

As an exercise to build your understanding, let's redesign the event raised by the `BankAccount` class to follow this convention. First, create a new event argument class that inherits from the `EventArgs` class:

```
Public Class LargeWithdrawalArgs : Inherits EventArgs
  Public Amount As Decimal

  Public Sub New(ByVal Amount As Decimal)
    Me.Amount = Amount
  End Sub
End Class
```

Note that a custom event argument class should be designed to contain a public field for each value that an event source needs to pass to its event handler. In this case, the `LargeWithdrawalArgs` class has been designed with a `Decimal` field named `Amount`.

Next, create a new delegate type to complement the new event argument class:

```
Public Delegate Sub LargeWithdrawalHandler(ByVal sender As Object, _
                          ByVal e As LargeWithdrawalArgs)
```

By convention, this delegate type is defined with an `Object` parameter named `sender` as the first parameter. The second parameter named `e` is based on the new custom event argument class `LargeWithdrawalArgs`.

Now that we have created the custom event argument class and a complementary delegate type, we can put them to use. Examine the following class definition:

```
Public Class BankAccount
  Public Event LargeWithdrawal As LargeWithdrawalHandler

  Public Sub Withdraw(ByVal Amount As Decimal)
    '*** send notifications if required
    If (Amount > 5000) Then
      Dim args As New LargeWithdrawalArgs(Amount)
      RaiseEvent LargeWithdrawal(Me, args)
    End If

    '*** perform withdrawal
  End Sub
End Class
```

The `LargeWithdrawal` event has been modified to follow the standard .NET convention for passing parameterized information in an event notification. When it comes time to raise a `LargeWithdrawal` event in the `Withdraw` method, it's necessary to create a new instance of the `Large-WithdrawalArgs` class and pass it as a parameter to the handler method(s):

```
Dim args As New LargeWithdrawalArgs(Amount)
RaiseEvent LargeWithdrawal(Me, args)
```

Now let's create a handler method for this event. A handler method will be able to retrieve the parameterized information it needs through the `e` parameter. In this case, a handler method will use the `e` parameter to retrieve the value of the `Amount` field:

```
Public Sub Handler1(sender As Object, e As LargeWithdrawalArgs)
  '*** retrieve parameterized information
  Dim Amount As Decimal = e.Amount
End Sub
```

Listing 8.6 shows a complete application in which a `BankAccount` object sends out event notifications when a large withdrawal occurs. This application differs from those you have seen previously in that parameterized information containing the withdrawal amount is passed using the standard .NET convention.

LISTING 8.6: Application that uses .NET convention for custom parameterized events

```
'*** custom event arguments class
Public Class LargeWithdrawalArgs : Inherits EventArgs
  Public Amount As Decimal

  Public Sub New(ByVal Amount As Decimal)
    Me.Amount = Amount
  End Sub
End Class

'*** delegate to complement custom event arguments class
Public Delegate Sub LargeWithdrawalHandler(ByVal sender As Object, _
                                ByVal e As LargeWithdrawalArgs)

Public Class BankAccount
  Public Event LargeWithdrawal As LargeWithdrawalHandler

  Public Sub Withdraw(ByVal Amount As Decimal)
```

```
      '*** send notifications if required
     If (Amount > 5000) Then
       Dim args As New LargeWithdrawalArgs(Amount)
       RaiseEvent LargeWithdrawal(Me, args)
     End If

       '*** perform withdrawal
   End Sub
End Class

Public Class AccountAuditor
   Private WithEvents account As BankAccount

   Sub Handler1(ByVal sender As Object, _
               ByVal e As LargeWithdrawalArgs) _
               Handles account.LargeWithdrawal
     '*** retrieve parameterized information
     Dim Amount As Decimal = e.Amount
   End Sub

   Public Sub New(ByVal source As BankAccount)
     Me.account = source  '*** triggers binding of event handler
   End Sub
End Class

Module MyApp
   Sub Main()
     '*** create bank account object
     Dim account1 As New BankAccount()

     '*** register event handlers
     Dim listener1 As New AccountAuditor(account1)

     '*** do something that triggers callbacks
     account1.Withdraw(5001)
   End Sub
End Module
```

SUMMARY

Events are a programming construct built on top of delegates that is intended to provide an easier mechanism to implement callback notifications. This compiler-supported abstraction allows an application to register one or more handler methods to receive callbacks from a notification source. Events are also an important aspect of rapid application development, because you can use the Visual Studio .NET IDE to automatically create and register the event handler methods for your applications.

An understanding of delegates and events is important to any developer who plans to use an event-based application framework such as Windows Forms or ASP.NET. As a Visual Basic .NET developer, you should thoroughly understand the differences between dynamic event binding and static event binding. Each technique is more useful than the other in certain situations. You should also become thoroughly familiar with commonly used delegate types supplied by the FCL such as `EventHandler`. In certain situations, you should be prepared to create your own custom delegate types and define your own events.

9

Structured Exception Handling

T HE .NET FRAMEWORK supports the reporting and handling of error conditions through an OOP feature known as *structured exception handling*. Chapter 2 presented a brief introduction to structured exception handling, along with a high-level overview of throwing and catching exceptions. This chapter discusses structured exception handling in more detail and examines how it affects the way you write code.

Learning the rules and syntax for structured exception handling represents a fairly significant change for programmers who are migrating to the new language from an earlier version of Visual Basic. The underlying mechanisms used by Visual Basic .NET for reporting and handling errors are much different from anything that has come before. Consequently, the syntax and style you use to write your error-handling code differ dramatically from anything you have used in earlier versions of Visual Basic.

As you begin to read this chapter, it will actually be helpful if you can forget everything you know about how to report and handle errors from previous versions of Visual Basic. Moving to the new convention will take some time, but in the long run things will be much better because your code for handling errors will be more readable and more easily maintained.

The Fundamentals of Structured Exception Handling

An exception is a type of object that is used to report error conditions. A method can *throw* an exception to send a signal to the hosting application that something has gone wrong during program execution. The CLR itself will also throw an exception when it fails to perform a requested operation. When a method is executing and an exception occurs, the method is given a chance to *catch* the exception and branch off into contingency code that has been written to handle various kinds of error conditions.

Throwing and Catching Exceptions

Throwing an exception is the one and only official way to report an error condition in the .NET Framework. If you call a method and it does not throw an exception, you can assume that the method was able to do what you expected it to do. In other words, you can assume that the method succeeded in its mission. When a method cannot succeed in its mission, it should not return to the caller in the normal fashion. Instead, it should report an error condition by throwing an exception back to its caller.

Let's look at a simple example. Imagine you are writing a method and you determine that under a certain condition you need to report an error. You can accomplish this by throwing an exception back to your method's caller with the following code:

```
Throw New System.Exception("Oh no!")
```

When you write a `Throw` statement in Visual Basic .NET, you are required to pass a reference to an exception object. This task is often accomplished by using the `New` operator within the `Throw` statement to create a new exception object, as in the preceding code. Alternatively, you can create an exception object in one line and include a reference to that object in a `Throw` statement in another line:

```
Dim ex As New System.Exception("Oh no!")
Throw ex
```

When a method executes a `Throw` statement, the CLR knows that the method is reporting an error condition. This action causes the CLR to instantly terminate the method's execution and to throw the exception object back to the method's caller. You should always assume that a method's output parameters and return value are invalid whenever it has thrown an exception.

Of course, methods are not the only things that can throw exceptions. The CLR will also throw an exception when a method attempts to perform an operation that fails at runtime. To see how this process works, examine the following code:

```
Dim i As Integer = Integer.MaxValue
i += 1
```

This code attempts to assign a value that is too large to fit inside an `Integer` value, so the CLR will throw an exception to a method that tries to execute it. The CLR throws exceptions under many other conditions as well, such as when your method attempts to divide an integer by zero or attempts to convert between incompatible types. The documentation supplied by the .NET Framework SDK provides a reference guide to FCL methods, including a list of which exceptions they throw.

It is not realistic to think that your software will always run in a perfect world. For this reason, applications and component libraries should be designed and written under the assumption that things can and will go wrong. Error conditions will occur at some point, and your code must be prepared to deal with them. Therefore, it is critical that you anticipate certain types of exceptions and that you supply error-handling code to recover from these exceptions in as graceful a manner as possible. The way to accomplish this goal is by structuring your code within `Try` statements.

Let's start by discussing what happens when a line of code that is not placed inside a `Try` statement experiences an exception. Imagine you have written a method that adds two `Integer` values together and assigns the resulting sum to an `Integer` variable, but you did not perform these operations inside a `Try` statement. If your method experiences an `OverflowException`, you have no backup plan. The CLR deals with this situation by instantly terminating your method's execution and throwing the `OverflowException` object back to your method's caller. In many cases, you want to avoid this result.

A `Try` statement allows you to perform operations and to call other methods within a `Try` block. The `Try` block is often referred to as a *guarded block* because it gives the CLR an associated backup plan for what to do when things go wrong. For example, a `Try` block can be complemented by one or more `Catch` blocks that execute conditionally when certain types of exceptions occur. Listing 9.1 shows a simple example of a `Try` statement that contains a `Try` block and two associated `Catch` blocks.

LISTING 9.1: A `Try` statement can contain one or more `Catch` blocks that act as error handlers.

```
Try

  '*** guarded block to perform operations and call methods

Catch ex As OverflowException

  '*** handle OverflowException
  Console.WriteLine(ex.Message)

Catch ex As InvalidCastException

  '*** handle InvalidCastException
  Console.WriteLine(ex.Message)

End Try
```

When the CLR encounters a `Try` statement like the one shown in Listing 9.1, it starts by executing the code within the `Try` block. If all the code within the `Try` block executes successfully, the CLR ignores the `Catch` blocks and continues by executing the next line of code that appears after the `End Try`. Matters are much different, however, when code executing within the `Try` block experiences an exception. In such a case, the CLR stops executing code within the `Try` block and begins to inspect the `Catch` blocks in an effort to find an error handler. If the CLR finds a `Catch` block that matches the type of the exception that has been thrown, it executes this `Catch` block. As you see, a `Catch` block represents a contingency plan that executes conditionally when things go wrong.

The CLR will never execute more than one `Catch` block within a `Try` statement. Thus, once the CLR finds a `Catch` block with a compatible exception type, it does not continue looking for any other compatible `Catch` blocks.

Also, the CLR always inspects `Catch` blocks from top to bottom. As a result, the order in which `Catch` blocks appear within a `Try` statement is significant.

The manner in which you trap and handle error conditions in Visual Basic .NET is very different from that used in earlier versions of Visual Basic. In particular, you no longer trap exceptions based on error numbers, as in the case of `Err.Number`. Instead, you trap exceptions based on their underlying type. For this reason, you can say that structured exception handling in Visual Basic .NET relies on a strongly typed model, whereas earlier versions of Visual Basic do not.

Now let's ask another important question: What happens when an exception occurs within a `Try` block and the CLR cannot find a `Catch` block within the enclosing `Try` statement to deal with that particular type of exception? If the CLR starts looking for a compatible `Catch` block and cannot find one, it assumes that your code isn't prepared to deal with the error condition. It therefore instantly terminates your method's execution and throws the exception to your method's caller. In essence, if an exception occurs within a `Try` statement and no compatible `Catch` block exists, the CLR provides the same behavior as if you had never written your code within a `Try` statement in the first place.

One other critical aspect of the fundamental behavior of a `Catch` block warrants attention. When the CLR finds a compatible `Catch` block and begins to execute to the code within it, the CLR assumes that the code inside the `Catch` block will fix whatever problem caused the exception. If the code within your `Catch` block can rectify the problem at hand, things work out well. After the CLR executes your `Catch` block, it resumes the method's execution in a normal fashion, starting with the first line of code that appears after the `End Try`.

But what happens when the code within a `Catch` block cannot remedy the problem? If the code within a `Catch` block cannot recover from the exception, it probably means that the method containing the `Catch` block cannot succeed in its mission. In other words, the method cannot complete the task that its caller has asked it to do. In such a case, it should report an error to its caller by throwing an exception. However, this response doesn't happen automatically when the CLR has started to execute the code in a `Catch` block.

Let's look at an example of a method that does not take this behavior into account. Examine the following definition of the `Add` method:

```
Function Add(ByVal x As Integer, ByVal y As Integer) As Integer
  Try
    Dim temp As Integer
    temp = x + y
    Return temp
  Catch ex As OverflowException
    System.Diagnostics.EventLog.WriteEntry("Bob's App", ex.Message)
  End Try
End Function
```

Look at the line of code that adds the values for two `Integer` parameters together and assigns their sum back to the `Integer` variable `temp`. This line of code might very well experience an `OverflowException`. As you can see, the programmer has provided an appropriate `Catch` block to deal with this kind of exception. The `Catch` block responds to the exception by writing a diagnostic entry to the Windows event log using the `EventLog` class that is defined within the `System.Diagnostics` namespace.

While writing this entry to the Windows event log can be very helpful in diagnosing problems within an application, it's not enough. The `Catch` block in this example has not fixed the problem at hand. The method cannot succeed in its mission because it cannot return the correct value to the caller, so it has a bug. Whenever the `Add` method experiences an `OverflowException`, the method returns a value of `0` and gives the caller no indication that anything went wrong.

Let's rewrite this method to remove the bug. After the `Catch` block has written the entry to the Windows event log, it should throw an exception to indicate that the method was not able to fix the problem. A `Catch` block can then *rethrow* the current exception. Alternatively, it can create and throw a new exception.

When you throw an exception from within a `Catch` block, it has the effect of terminating the enclosing `Try` statement. As long as the `Try` statement is not nested within another `Try` statement, throwing the exception from within a `Catch` block also terminates the execution of the current method and throws the exception back to the method's caller. The following code rewrites the example `Catch` block so it rethrows the current exception:

```
Function Add(ByVal x As Integer, ByVal y As Integer) As Integer
  Try
    Dim temp As Integer
    temp = x + y
    Return temp
  Catch ex As OverflowException
    EventLog.WriteEntry("Bob's App", ex.Message)
    Throw  '*** rethrow exception to caller
  End Try
End Function
```

As this code demonstrates, you can write a `Throw` statement inside a `Catch` block that doesn't include a reference to an exception object. A `Throw` statement without a reference to a specific exception object instructs the CLR to rethrow the current exception. (As discussed later in this chapter, it sometimes makes more sense to create and throw a new exception object than to rethrow the current exception object when reporting an error condition from within a `Catch` block.)

It isn't strictly necessary to catch every possible exception in every method. For example, it doesn't make sense to catch an exception if you plan to simply rethrow the same exception to your caller. In that case, you shouldn't structure your code to use a `Try` statement in the first place. Instead, you can design your applications so that exceptions propagate up the call chain to the code that makes up the user interface. The user interface code can then supply an exception handler that interacts with the application's user. The point is that a method should catch an exception only if it plans to do something interesting with that exception.

Now you have learned the fundamentals of throwing and catching exceptions:

- You use the `Throw` statement to throw exceptions.
- You use `Try` statements containing `Catch` blocks to handle exceptions.
- When you write a `Catch` block, you must either fix the problem that caused the exception or proactively throw an exception to inform your caller that the method could not succeed in its mission.

If you are not paying attention, it's easy to write `Catch` blocks that inadvertently sweep error conditions under the rug. That's a sure-fire way to introduce bugs into your code that are very hard to track down.

Nesting Try Statements

Sometimes it is necessary to nest a Try statement inside another Try statement—for example, to handle the situation in which a Try statement that experiences an exception within a Catch block will instantly terminate its execution. At other times, you will want to write code within a Catch block that can handle an exception in a more graceful manner. Achieving this goal requires placing a second, inner Try statement within a Catch block of the outer Try statement.

Let's look at a simple example in which one Try statement is nested within another Try statement. Listing 9.2 shows an inner Try statement nested within an enclosing Catch block. This style of coding provides an extra degree of protection if the code within a Catch block fails. You are able to catch the exception in the inner Catch block and prevent the outer Try statement from terminating abnormally.

LISTING 9.2: A Try statement can be nested within another Try statement.

```
Try
  '*** first exception occurs here
Catch outerEx As OverflowException
  Try
    '*** handle first exception
    Dim msg1 As String = outerEx.Message
    Console.WriteLine(msg1)
  Catch innerEx As Exception
    '*** handle second exception if it occurs
    Dim msg2 As String = innerEx.Message
    Console.WriteLine(msg2)
  End Try
End Try
```

Note that the variables within the outer and inner Catch blocks must be given different names. In Listing 9.2, the exception object in the outer Catch block is named outerEx, and the exception object in the inner Catch block is named innerEx. You must give these two objects different names when you nest one Catch block inside another because the two variables overlap in scope.

Exception **Classes**

The .NET Framework's model for structured exception handling centers on a class named Exception that is defined in the System namespace. The Exception class is particularly important because of one specific rule that is imposed by the Common Language Specification (CLS): Every exception object must be created from either the Exception class or a class that inherits from Exception. As a consequence, every CLS-compliant exception object shares a programming contract and an underlying implementation that is defined by the Exception class.

Why did the architects of the .NET Framework choose to employ an inheritance-based model for structured exception handling? The use of inheritance makes it possible to create different types of exceptions that have been specialized to report on different kinds of error conditions. Specialized exception classes extend the standard Exception class by adding extra members to their programming contracts and their underlying implementations. In this way, an exception object that is used to report one kind of error condition can track different kinds of information from an exception object that is used to report another kind of error condition.

The Exception class is itself a concrete implementation, but its primary purpose is to serve as a base class for more specialized exception classes. The core libraries of the FCL contain many other exception classes that inherit from Exception. Figure 9.1 shows a high-level view of how the

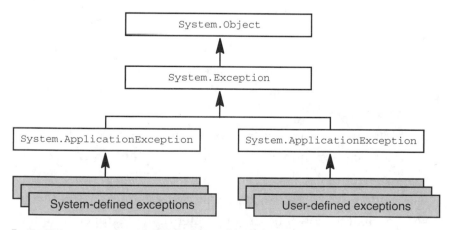

FIGURE 9.1: Exception **class inheritance hierarchy**

.NET exception classes fit into a single inheritance hierarchy in which the `Exception` class appears at the top.

As shown in Figure 9.1, the .NET exception classes are partitioned into two high-level categories:

- *System-defined exceptions.* These exceptions are created by Microsoft and are considered to be part of the .NET Framework and the FCL. By convention, system-defined exceptions inherit from the `System-Exception` class.
- *User-defined exceptions.* These exceptions include all classes that inherit from `ApplicationException`. The creation and usage of user-defined exception classes is discussed toward the end of this chapter.

You will rarely throw or catch exception objects that are created directly from the generic `Exception` class. Instead, you will typically throw and catch exception objects that are created from more specific exception types. There are several system-defined exception classes that you will encounter on a frequent basis. You will probably use some of these system-defined exception classes when you need to report error conditions from your methods as well. Figure 9.2 shows a sampling of some of the system-defined exception classes found within the `System` namespace.

Because the CLR and various libraries within the FCL often throw the system-defined exceptions shown in Figure 9.2, you should become accustomed to writing `Try` statements that handle these exception types. A few examples will highlight when these system-defined exceptions can occur:

- If you attempt to invoke an instance method using a reference variable that has a value of `Nothing`, the CLR will throw a `NullReferenceException`.
- If your attempt to convert from one type to another with the `CType` operator fails at runtime, the CLR will throw an `InvalidCastException`.
- If you attempt to access an item in an array using an index that is smaller than the lower bound or greater than the upper bound, the CLR will throw an `IndexOutOfRangeException`.

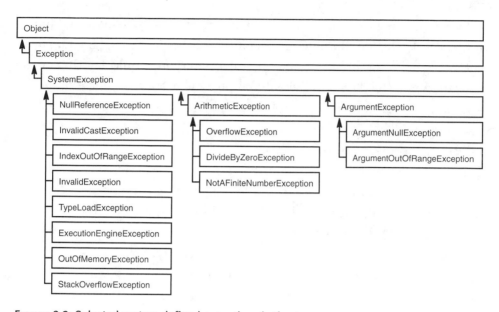

FIGURE 9.2: Selected system-defined exceptions in the `System` namespace

The `System` namespace contains a system-defined exception class named `InvalidOperationException`. A method throws an exception of this type when it needs to report an error indicating that the current object is not in a valid state to perform a specific operation. For example, a `BankAccount` object could be written to throw an `InvalidOperationException` if its `Withdraw` method is called with a withdrawal amount that exceeds the account balance.

As you know, an assembly EXE that represents an application has a set of dependent assemblies. The CLR loads each of these dependent assemblies when the application first uses that assembly. But what happens if you deploy an application but forget to deploy one of its dependent assemblies? The CLR will be unable to locate this dependent assembly at runtime and will throw a `TypeLoadException`. An application should typically handle a `TypeLoadException` by (1) informing the user that the application has not been properly installed on the target machine and (2) gracefully shutting down the application.

The CLR can throw three system-defined exception types that are considered to be nonrecoverable exceptions: `ExecutionEngineException`, `OutOfMemoryException`, and `StackOverflowException`. When your application experiences one of these exceptions, there are too many uncertainties for the application to continue running in a predictable manner. If your application experiences a nonrecoverable exception, you should log diagnostic information to the Windows event log, provide a polite notification to the user, and then shut down the application as gracefully as possible.

Filtering Exceptions Based on Type

Take another look at the inheritance hierarchy of exception classes shown in Figure 9.2. Note that some system-defined exception types do not inherit from the SystemException class directly, but rather inherit from an intermediate base class that inherits from SystemException. For example, the exception classes OverflowException, DivideByZeroException, and NotAFiniteNumberException inherit from the base class ArithmeticException. The exceptions classes ArgumentNullException and ArgumentOutOfRangeException inherit from a base class named ArgumentException.

You have already seen that you handle exception objects by adding Catch blocks within a Try statement. The inheritance hierarchy of exception classes factors into how Catch blocks work. Let's look at an example of a Try statement with two Catch blocks to see how this relationship affects error handling:

```
Try
   '*** guarded block
Catch ex As ArithmeticException
   '*** handler 1
Catch ex As Exception
   '*** handler 2
End Try
```

In the preceding code, the Try statement contains one Catch block for the ArithmeticException class and a second Catch block for the generic Exception class. If the Try block experiences an exception of type ArithmeticException, the CLR will execute the first Catch block because it finds an exact match. However, the CLR will also execute the same Catch block if an exception is thrown whose underlying class inherits from the ArithmeticException class. As a result, the Catch block defined in terms of the

ArithmeticException class will catch an exception of type OverflowException, DivideByZeroException, or NotAFiniteNumberException.

As you can see, the CLR does not require an exact match when it looks for a Catch block to handle an exception. It simply searches for a compatible type that includes all exception classes that inherit from the exception type defined in the Catch block. The manner in which inheritance affects the behavior of a Catch block is very different from the behavior of earlier versions of Visual Basic, where you trap errors based on error numbers.

Think about what happens when you have a Catch block based on the generic Exception class. A Catch block defined in terms of the Exception class will serve as a *catch-all exception handler,* because the CLS rule states that all exception objects must inherit from the Exception class. Therefore, every exception object is compatible with a Catch block that is defined in terms of the generic Exception class.

For this reason, a Catch block defined in terms of the Exception class should always be defined last in a Try statement. To see how this works on a practical level, look at the following code and determine why it doesn't make any sense:

```
Try
  '*** guarded block
Catch ex As Exception
  '*** handler 1
Catch ex As ArithmeticException
  '*** handler 2
End Try
```

In this code, the second Catch block serves no purpose, because it will never execute. The CLR inspects Catch blocks from top to bottom, and the first Catch block is based on the Exception class, so it will catch every exception. Under no circumstances will the second Catch block execute.

It is fairly common practice to create Catch blocks based on the Exception class, because this technique allows you to react to problems that you did not anticipate. However, there are a few special considerations to keep in mind whenever you create a Catch block based on the Exception class. First, a Catch block based on the Exception class is a generic, catch-all handler that should be placed after all other Catch blocks. Second, a Catch block based on the Exception class catches everything including the non-recoverable exceptions discussed earlier. Don't forget your responsibilities within a Catch block. You must either fix the problem or throw an exception to make it your caller's problem. Catch blocks based on the Exception type should usually rethrow the exception to make sure that the exception is not swept under the rug.

```
Try
  '*** guarded block
Catch ex As Exception
  '*** write diagnostic entry to Windows event log
  Throw ' rethrow exception to caller
End Try
```

Using a When Clause in a Catch Block

The Visual Basic .NET language allows you to add a When clause when you write a Catch block. This feature provides a filtering mechanism that gives you an extra degree of control as to when a Catch block will execute. Note that When clauses are unique to the Visual Basic .NET language; other managed languages (e.g., C#) do not provide an equivalent feature.

A When clause allows you to add a filtering expression to the end of the first line of a Catch block. The filtering expression within a When clause should be written to evaluate to a Boolean value of either True or False. The idea is that this filtering expression must evaluate to a value of True for the Catch block to execute. Here's a simple example:

```
Dim i As Integer
Try
  '*** guarded block
  '*** change the value of i
Catch ex As Exception When (i >= 10)
  '*** handler #1
Catch ex As Exception When (i < 0)
  '*** handler #2
Catch ex As Exception
  '*** handler #3
End Try
```

Two conditions must occur before the CLR will execute a Catch block with a When clause:

- The exception type caught by the `Catch` block must be compatible with the exception object thrown from the `Try` block.
- The filtering expression defined within the `Catch` block's `When` clause must evaluate to a value of `True`.

If both of these conditions are met, the CLR will execute the `Catch` block. If either or both of these conditions are not met, the CLR will ignore the `Catch` block and continue looking for another `Catch` block to handle the current exception.

Note that you have the ability to inspect the `Message` property of the current exception object within a `When` clause. Suppose you wanted to handle an exception within a specific `Catch` block only when the current exception object's `Message` property contains the word "overflow." You could accomplish this goal by adding a `Catch` block with the following `When` clause:

```
Catch ex As Exception When (ex.Message.IndexOf("overflow") <> -1)
```

This `When` clause searches through the `Message` property of the current exception object. If this error message contains the word `"overflow"`, the `IndexOf` method of the `String` class returns the index of the starting character, which will have a value of `0` or greater. The `IndexOf` method returns a value of `-1` if the string value held by the `Message` property does not contain the word `"overflow"`. Therefore, this `Catch` block will execute in response to any exception object that has a `Message` property that contains the word `"overflow"`.

Your ability to inspect an exception object within a `When` clause is somewhat limited because you cannot inspect any property of an exception object other than its `Message` property. This restriction reflects the way in which Visual Basic .NET and the CLR implement `When` clauses implemented internally. Unfortunately, this constraint means that you cannot inspect other potentially useful properties that are discussed in the next section, such as `StackTrace`, `Source`, and `TargetSite`. `When` clauses would be even more powerful if they gave you complete access to all of the public members exposed by an exception object.

Members of the `System.Exception` Class

When you write a `Catch` block to handle a specific type of error condition, you have the ability to access the current exception object that contains the pertinent error information. Because all exception objects inherit from the `Exception` class, you will always be able to access the public members of the `Exception` class whenever you access an exception object inside a `Catch` block.

Let's take a moment to inspect the programming contract defined by the `Exception` class. Listing 9.3 shows its most commonly used public members. As you can see, the `Exception` class provides a useful set of public constructors, methods, and properties.

When you create an exception object using the `New` operator, it's common practice to use one of the constructors that accepts an error message. After an exception object has been initialized, its error message is available through the read-only `Message` property.

LISTING 9.3: The `System.Exception` class defines a common programming contract for all exceptions.

```
'*** defined in mscorlib.dll
Namespace System
  Public Class Exception

     '*** public constructors
     Public Sub New()
     Public Sub New(message As String)
     Public Sub New(message As String, innerException As Exception)

     '*** public properties/methods
     Public ReadOnly Property Message() As String
     Public ReadOnly Property StackTrace() As String
     Public Property Source() As String
     Public ReadOnly Property TargetSite() As MethodBase
     Public ReadOnly Property InnerException() As Exception
     Public Function GetBaseException() As Exception

  End Class
End Namespace
```

An error message is a text-based description of what went wrong. Because application developers often display error messages to the application's users, it's a good idea to create error messages that are as user-friendly as possible. In some cases, the error message might suggest a remedy as to how the problem can be fixed—for example, "You cannot withdraw $100 because you have only $60 in your account." Such a message will give the user a hint about how to overcome the problem at hand.

The Exception class also provides a public read-only String property named StackTrace. This property is helpful for diagnosing problems in the development phase because it indicates which methods were in the current call chain when the exception occurred. This list starts with the method that threw the exception and ends with the method that caught the exception. For example, suppose the method named Main called Method1, which in turn called Method2. What would happen if Method2 throws an exception to Method1, and Method1 doesn't handle it? The exception would then propagate back to Main. If a Catch block in Main catches the exception thrown by Method1, the StackTrace property would return the following value:

```
at Method2()
at Method1()
at Main()
```

As you can see, the StackTrace property provides information about which methods were in the call chain at the time when the exception occurred. This sort of diagnostic information can prove handy when you need to find and fix a bug in your code. The StackTrace property can be especially helpful when the call chain includes 10 or more methods, because it allows you to see exactly where the current exception originated.

The StackTrace property provides even more information when you are working in debug mode. In particular, it provides the names of the source files that contain the method definitions as well as the line numbers where exceptions occurred:

```
at Method2() in C:\Apps\DataAccess.vb:line 142
at Method1() in C:\Apps\BusinessLogic.vb:line 738
at Main() in C:\Apps\MyApp.vb:line 67
```

There is one more interesting point to note concerning the StackTrace property. Earlier in this chapter, you saw how to rethrow an exception from within a Catch block—by using a Throw statement without explicitly including a reference to an exception:

```
Try
  '*** guarded block
Catch ex As OverflowException
  '*** write diagnostic entry to Windows event log
  Throw  '*** rethrow current exception to caller
End Try
```

Alternatively, you can rethrow the current exception from inside a `Catch` block by explicitly passing a reference to the current exception object:

```
Try
  '*** guarded block
Catch ex As OverflowException
  '*** write diagnostic entry to Windows event log
  Throw ex '*** rethrow current exception to caller
End Try
```

These two examples are almost identical. The only difference is that the first one uses a `Throw` statement without including an explicit reference to an exception object, whereas the second one uses a `Throw` statement that includes the reference variable `ex` that points to the current exception object. What's the importance of this difference? While both examples rethrow the current exception from within a `Catch` block, there is a subtle difference with respect to what happens to the `StackTrace` property. The first example does not reset the `StackTrace` property. The second example does reset the `StackTrace` property and has the potential to lose some diagnostic information. Therefore, it is recommended that you use the syntax of the first example, in which you rethrow the current exception from within a `Catch` block by using a `Throw` statement but omitting a reference to any exception.

The `Source` property of an exception is used to track which body of code initially threw the exception. By default, the CLR initializes the `Source` property to track the name of the assembly that threw the exception. However, `Source` is a read/write property that you can also use to track application-specific data, such as an identifier for a named object or a custom framework that extends across several assemblies. Here's an example of overwriting the `Source` property before throwing an exception:

```
'*** throw an exception with a user-defined source value
Dim ex As New InvalidOperationException("An error has occurred!")
ex.Source = "AcmeCorp Application Framework"
Throw ex
```

The `Exception` class contains a handy read-only property named `TargetSite` that allows you to obtain information about the method that threw the exception. This valuable feature was sorely missed in previous versions of Visual Basic, in which you had to explicitly propagate information about the name of the method that raised the error. In the .NET Framework, you can always get information about the method that threw the exception by querying the exception object's `TargetSite` property. Examine the `Try` statement shown in Listing 9.4 to see how this technique works.

LISTING 9.4: The `TargetSite` property provides information about where the exception occurred.

```
Try
  '*** guarded code block
Catch ex As Exception
  Dim MethodName, TypeName, AssemblyName As String
  MethodName = ex.TargetSite.Name
  TypeName = ex.TargetSite.ReflectedType.Name
  AssemblyName = ex.TargetSite.ReflectedType.Assembly.FullName
  '*** now write diagnostic information to the Windows event log
  Throw
End Try
```

The code in Listing 9.4 demonstrates the use of the `TargetSite` property to retrieve the name of the method that threw the exception. Note that the `TargetSite` property also allows you to get the name of the containing type and the containing assembly. This information can be very useful when you are writing diagnostic messages to the Windows event log.

Inner Exceptions

Earlier in this chapter, your responsibility when writing a `Catch` block was identified: You must either fix the problem at hand or throw an exception to your caller indicating that the problem has not been fixed. When you take the latter path, you must also decide whether to rethrow the current exception object or whether to create and throw a new exception object.

Suppose you are writing a `Catch` block and decide that you would like to create and throw a new exception. This scenario involves two different exception objects:

- The current exception object that has been caught by the `Catch` block
- The new exception object that you are creating and throwing to the caller

What should you do with the error information that is stored within the current exception? Inner exceptions are intended to help out in this situation. When you create and throw a new exception object, you can include the current exception object as an inner exception. Under this scenario, your caller gains the ability to get error information about both exceptions.

The .NET Framework's support for inner exceptions makes it easy to link together multiple exceptions within a single call chain. Listing 9.5 shows an example of a method that creates and throws a new exception while including the current exception as the inner exception.

LISTING 9.5: When throwing a new exception, you can pass the current exception as an inner exception.

```
Function Add(ByVal x As Integer, ByVal y As Integer) As Integer
  Try
    Dim temp As Integer
    temp = x + y
    Return temp
  Catch ex As OverflowException
    EventLog.WriteEntry("Bob's App", ex.Message)
    Dim msg As String = "Your numbers are too big"
    Throw New InvalidOperationException(msg, ex)
  End Try
End Function
```

Examining this implementation of the `Add` method, you can see that it attempts to add two `Integer` values and assign the resulting sum to the method's return value. This method will experience an `OverflowException` if the caller passes input parameters that are too large. However, the `Add` method does not rethrow an `OverflowException` in this situation. Instead, it creates and throws an exception of type `InvalidOperationException`.

The most important aspect of this example centers on how the `Catch` block creates the new `InvalidOperationException` object—namely, it uses a constructor that accepts a current exception object as the inner exception object. A reference to the inner exception object is passed as the second argument in the constructor of the `InvalidOperationException` class:

```
Throw New InvalidOperationException(msg, ex)
```

Now let's look at some code that catches an exception object that contains a reference to an inner exception object. Imagine that you called the `Add` method, which then threw an `InvalidOperationException`. You could handle that exception and examine the inner exception by querying the read-only `InnerException` property:

```
Try
  Add(Integer.MaxValue, 1)
Catch ex As InvalidOperationException
  If(Not ex.InnerException Is Nothing)
    '*** query inner exception
    Dim inner As Exception = ex.InnerException
    Console.WriteLine(inner.Message)
  End If
End Try
```

When you catch an exception, you can query it to see whether an inner exception exists by testing whether the `InnerException` property has a value of `Nothing`. Of course, an inner exception could itself have an inner exception. Indeed, when an error condition propagates up a long call chain, a chain of three or four inner exceptions becomes possible.

The innermost exception object in the chain will have a `InnerException` property equal to a value of `Nothing`. You can always find this exception by calling the `GetBaseException` method. Think of the innermost exception object as the one that started all of the trouble in the first place; it is typically the first exception thrown in the current call chain.

Examples of Throwing System-Defined Exceptions

Although you can always create user-defined exceptions, this effort isn't always necessary. You can often find a system-defined exception class that meets your needs. Let's work through an example in which you define a class that throws system-defined exceptions in certain situations. Examine the following definition of the `BankAccount` class:

```
Public Class BankAccount
  Protected m_Balance As Decimal
  Sub New(ByVal StartingBalance As Decimal)
    m_Balance = StartingBalance
  End Sub
```

```
Sub Deposit(ByVal Amount As Decimal)
  m_Balance += Amount
End Sub
Sub Withdraw(ByVal Amount As Decimal)
  m_Balance -= Amount
End Sub
End Class
```

Currently, the `BankAccount` class doesn't throw any exceptions. However, let's make the following design assumption about the behavior of a `BankAccount` object: A `BankAccount` object can never have a balance that is a negative value. As a consequence of this assumption, it would be illegal for another programmer to call the constructor for this class and pass a negative number for the `StartingBalance` parameter. Therefore, it would make sense to add code at the beginning of the constructor's implementation to ensure that the `StartingBalance` parameter has a valid value. Listing 9.6 shows such a constructor implementation.

LISTING 9.6: Throwing an exception when invalid parameter input is found

```
Sub New(ByVal StartingBalance As Decimal)

  '*** verify account is not created with negative balance
  If (StartingBalance < 0) Then
    Dim msg As String = "Initial account balance cannot be negative"
    Throw New ArgumentOutOfRangeException("StartingBalance", msg)
  End If

  '*** continue with operation as normal
  m_Balance = StartingBalance

End Sub
```

A constructor has a mission to initialize an object in a valid state. If it cannot accomplish this mission, it should throw an exception. In Listing 9.6, the constructor of the `BankAccount` class throws an `ArgumentOutOfRange` exception if the caller passes a negative value for the starting balance of a new account.

When a constructor throws an exception, the exception is propagated back to the method that called the `New` operator. If the call to `New` was made from within a `Try` statement with an appropriate `Catch` block, the exception can be caught and handled gracefully. If the call to `New` was not made from within a `Try` statement, the method that called `New` will terminate abnormally and the exception will be thrown to its caller. As you can see, calls to constructors follow the same rules as standard methods when it comes to catching and handling exceptions.

This example should demonstrate the importance of validating the input parameters passed by the caller. After all, it will be difficult—if not impossible—for a method to complete its mission if the caller passes input parameters containing invalid data. Therefore, a method should inspect input parameter values and throw an exception if one or more of these parameter values are in an invalid state.

In Listing 9.7, the `Withdraw` method conducts two integrity checks on the `Amount` parameter. In the first check, the `Withdraw` method definition inspects the `Amount` parameter to verify that it is a positive number. The method throws an exception of type `ArgumentOutOfRangeException` if the `Amount` parameter is not positive; after all, it doesn't make sense to have a withdrawal amount that has a negative value or a value of `0`.

LISTING 9.7: A method should throw an exception when passed an invalid input parameter.

```
Sub Withdraw(ByVal Amount As Decimal)

  '*** verify Amount is a positive value
  If (Amount <= 0) Then
    Dim msg As String = "Amount for withdrawal must be a positive number: "
    Throw New ArgumentOutOfRangeException("Amount", amount, msg)
  End If

  '*** verify withdrawal does not create negative account balance
  If (Amount > m_Balance) Then
    Dim msg As String = "Withdrawal request exceeds available funds"
    Throw New InvalidOperationException(msg)
  End If

  '*** continue with operation as normal
  m_Balance -= Amount

End Sub
```

In the second verification check, the `Withdraw` method checks the `Amount` parameter to confirm that it doesn't exceed the current account balance. If the requested withdrawal amount exceeds the current balance, it throws an `InvalidOperationException` so that the account is never left with a negative balance.

User-Defined Exceptions

Sometimes you need to report an error condition that doesn't map to an existing system-defined exception class. In such a case you can design a custom exception class for creating and throwing user-defined exceptions by creating a new class that inherits from the `ApplicationException` class.

Creating a custom exception class offers two benefits:

- You can design exception objects that contain application-specific error information.
- User-defined exception objects can be trapped and handled separately in their own independent `Catch` block.

Let's revisit the example from earlier in this chapter that involved the `BankAccount` class. Recall that the `Withdraw` method for a `BankAccount` object was written to throw an `InvalidOperationException` whenever a withdrawal is attempted for an amount that exceeds the account balance. Let's change things so that a `BankAccount` object throws a user-defined exception instead of a system-defined exception to report this particular type of error condition.

We will start by creating a custom class named `InsufficientFundsException` that inherits from the `ApplicationException` class. Listing 9.8 shows a starting point for this user-defined exception class.

LISTING 9.8: A user-defined exception class should inherit from the `ApplicationException` class.

```
'*** definition for user-defined exception
Public Class InsufficientFundsException
      Inherits ApplicationException

  '*** add a default constructor for convenience
  Sub New()
    MyBase.New("Error occurred due to insufficient funds")
  End Sub

  '*** add a single-parameter constructor
```

```
Sub New(ByVal msg As String)
  MyBase.New(msg)
End Sub

'*** add a two-parameter constructor
Sub New(ByVal msg As String, inner As Exception)
  MyBase.New(msg, inner)
End Sub

'*** add user-defined fields, methods, and properties

End Class
```

The user-defined exception class in Listing 9.8 has three constructors:

- The first constructor supplies a default error message.
- The second constructor accepts a single parameter named msg, which is used to pass the exception's error message to the base class constructor.
- The third constructor accepts a message and an inner exception and directly passes these two parameters to the base class constructor.

If you do not add the third constructor with a parameter for the inner exception, your user-defined exception class will not be able to accommodate other programmers who want to pass inner exceptions.

Your imagination is the only limit as to what fields, methods, and properties you can add to your own custom exception classes. Just keep in mind that user-defined exceptions make it possible to pass any kind of information you like when you need to report an error condition. Also keep in mind that you can (and should) add other constructors to initialize any fields you have added to your user-defined exception class.

When it's time to throw a user-defined exception, you do the same thing as when you throw a system-defined exception. That is, you use the New operator to create an exception object and then you use a Throw statement to throw it:

```
Sub Withdraw(ByVal Amount As Decimal)

  '*** verify withdrawal does not create negative account balance
  If (Amount > m_Balance) Then
```

```
        Throw New InsufficientFundsException
    End If

    '*** continue with operation as normal
    m_Balance -= Amount

End Sub
```

When you call a method that might throw a user-defined exception, you can handle it as you would handle any other exception. In particular, a user-defined exception class can be given its own `Catch` block within a `Try` statement:

```
Sub WithdrawFromAccount(Source As BankAccount, Amount As Decimal)
    Try
        Source.Withdraw(Amount)
    Catch ex As InsufficientFundsException
        '*** handle exception
    End Try
End Sub
```

One last point about user-defined exceptions: It is common practice to design a set of user-defined exception classes within a component library DLL so that all of them inherit from a single user-defined exception class. For example, suppose that the `BankAccount` class threw two user-defined exceptions named `InsufficientFundsException` and `AccountDisabledException`. It might be helpful to create a common base class for both of these exception classes.

Figure 9.3 shows an inheritance hierarchy in which these two user-defined exception classes thrown by the `BankAccount` class inherit from a user-defined base class named `BankAccountException`. Note that the `BankAccountException` class follows the convention of inheriting from `ApplicationException`.

The reason you would design an inheritance hierarchy of exception classes in this manner has to do with convenience. When you throw exceptions, other programmers will inevitably catch them. With this design, one programmer using the `BankAccount` class can create a single `Catch` block based on the `BankAccountException` class that will catch an `InsufficientFundsException` as well as an `AccountDisabledException`. This approach allows the programmer to provide a single generic error handler for all user-defined exceptions thrown by a `BankAccount` object.

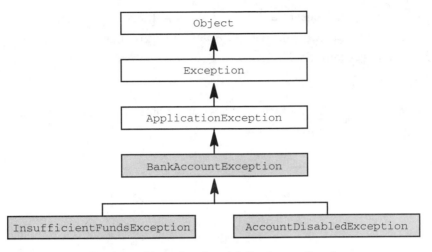

FIGURE 9.3: An inheritance hierarchy of user-defined exception classes

Another programmer might choose to provide one Catch block based on the InsufficientFundsException and a second Catch block based on the AccountDisabledException. That way, each specific type of user-defined exception can have its own unique error handler. As you can see, a design that employs a common base class like the one in Figure 9.3 simply provides more flexibility to other programmers who use your code.

Finally **Blocks**

Much of this chapter has focused on how to write Try statements that contain Catch blocks. As you know, a Catch block is a piece of code that executes conditionally when things go wrong. A Try statement can also contain another construct known as a Finally block:

```
Try
   '*** Try block
Finally
   '*** Finally block
End Try
```

Unlike a Catch block, a Finally block doesn't execute conditionally when things go wrong. Rather, it executes unconditionally regardless of whether the Try block experiences an exception. In other words, the code within a Finally block executes in all situations.

A `Finally` block serves a different purpose than a `Catch` block. Because its code always executes, a `Finally` block is a great place for cleaning up and releasing resources. Listing 9.9 shows an example of using a `Finally` block to close a database connection.

LISTING 9.9: A `Finally` **block usually contains cleanup code that releases resources.**

```
Dim conn As SqlConnection
Try
  conn = New SqlConnection("<your connection string here>")
  conn.Open()
  '*** use connection to perform work
Finally
  '*** check whether connection object is valid and open
  If (Not conn Is Nothing) AndAlso _
    (conn.State <> ConnectionState.Closed) Then
    '*** close connection if necessary
    conn.Close()
  End If
End Try
```

The `Finally` block in Listing 9.9 contains code to close a database connection that was opened in the `Try` block. Note that this `Finally` block works properly in times of success as well as in times of failure. The `Finally` block checks whether a valid connection object exists and then determines whether the connection object is in a connected state. If both of these conditions are true, then the `Finally` block executes the proper code to close the database connection.

A `Try` statement with a `Finally` block does not require a `Catch` block. You have already seen an example of this in Listing 9.9. Nevertheless, it's important to understand that a `Try` statement without a `Catch` block doesn't handle exceptions. Consider the following definition for `Method1`:

```
Sub Method1()
  Try
    '*** perform work
  Finally
    '*** release resources
  End Try
  '*** additional code here
End Sub
```

What happens if an exception occurs while `Method1` is performing work in the `Try` block? The CLR redirects the flow of execution to the `Finally` block. This Try statement doesn't handle any exceptions, however, so it terminates abnormally after the Finally block has executed, which in turn causes Method1 to terminate and throw the exception to its caller. As a consequence, additional code in Method1 that appears after the End Try does not execute.

A Try statement with a Finally block can (and often does) contain one or more Catch blocks. This technique allows you to place one or more error handlers and a Finally block together within the same Try statement. When you write a Try statement, you must always place Catch blocks before the Finally block.

```
Try
   '*** guarded block
Catch ex As OverflowException
   '*** error handler 1
Catch ex As Exception
   '*** error handler 2
Finally
   '*** cleanup code
End Try
```

It's important to understand the flow of execution within a Try statement that contains both Catch blocks and a Finally block. The CLR doesn't execute a Catch block unless an exception has occurred within the Try block, but it always executes the Finally block.

If the CLR does execute a Catch block, it happens before the Finally block executes. The execution of the Finally block always occurs last—that's why it's called the Finally block. The CLR is guaranteed to execute the Finally block even if code within the Try block or a Catch block executes a Return statement. Examine the following definition for Method2:

```
Function Method2() As Integer
   Try
      '*** guarded code here
      Return 0
   Catch ex As Exception
      '*** return to caller normally
      Return -1
   Finally
      '*** this code always executes
   End Try
End Function
```

In this code, there is a Return statement in the Try block and another Return statement in the Catch block. In most situations, a Return statement will be the last line of code to execute within a method before the CLR returns control to the method's caller. This is not the case when a Try statement with a Finally block begins executing, however. The CLR guarantees that the Finally block will execute after the execution of a Return statement but before the CLR returns control to the method's caller. A compile-time error will occur if you place a Return statement within a Finally block .

You have just seen that a Return statement does not prevent a Finally block from executing. What about the case in which a Catch block executes a Throw statement? The CLR treats this case in a similar manner. Examine the following definition for Method3:

```
Sub Method3()
  Try
    '*** guarded code here
  Catch ex As Exception
    '*** write diagnostic info to event log
    '*** rethrow exception to caller
    Throw
  Finally
    '*** this code always executes
  End Try
End Function
```

The Catch block in Method3 rethrows the current exception using a Throw statement. In most cases, a Throw statement will be the last line of code to execute within a method before the CLR throws the exception back to the method's caller. This is not the case when throwing an exception from within a Try statement that also contains a Finally block, however. Once the CLR begins to execute the Try statement, it guarantees that the Finally block will execute.

You should be able to answer one last question about how a Finally block works: What happens if an exception occurs while a Finally block is executing? This situation can cause serious problems because the Try statement that contains the Finally block will terminate abnormally. Examine the following definition for Method4:

```vbnet
Sub Method4()
  Try
    '*** perform work
  Finally
    '*** bad code that triggers OverflowException
    Dim i As Integer = Integer.MaxValue
    i += 1
  End Try
End Sub
```

What happens in this example after the Try block has executed success-fully? The CLR executes the Finally block, which experiences an unhan-dled exception. This problem causes the Try statement to terminate abnormally, which in turn results in Method4 throwing an OverflowExcep-tion to its caller. You should see that this is an undesirable situation.

Think about the case where you are writing a Try statement that con-tains both a Catch block and a Finally block. What if you throw or rethrow an exception from within a Catch block and then another excep-tion occurs inside the Finally block? Examine the following definition for Method5:

```vbnet
Sub Method5()
    Try
      '*** perform work
    Catch ex As Exception
      '*** write diagnostic info to event log
      '*** rethrow exception to caller
      Throw
    Finally
      '*** bad code here
      Dim i As Integer = Integer.MaxValue
      i +- 1
    End Try
  End Sub
```

Here code within the Catch block of Method5 has rethrown the exception that occurred within the Try block. But that's not the exception that Method5 throws to its caller. Instead, Method5 throws the exception that occurs inside the Finally block. In this unfortunate situation, the excep-tion you wanted to throw has been replaced by another exception.

The bottom line is that you must rewrite the code in a Finally block to be bulletproof. If code within a Finally block could potentially experience an exception, that code should be written within an inner `Try` statement that is nested inside the `Finally` block.

```
Try
  '*** perform work
Catch ex As Exception
  '*** write diagnostic info to event log
  '*** rethrow exception to caller
  Throw
Finally
  Try
    '*** cleanup code
  Catch ex As Exception
    '*** error handler
  End Try
End Try
```

Once you structure your code in this fashion, you can throw an exception to the caller from within a `Catch` block without the risk of having that exception replaced by an exception that occurs inside the `Finally` block.

SUMMARY

Exceptions are a way of life in the .NET Framework and the CLR. For this reason, a thorough understanding of throwing and catching exceptions is a prerequisite to writing robust and maintainable code with Visual Basic .NET.

In Visual Basic .NET, all exceptions support the universal programming contract defined by the `System.Exception` class. As a consequence, all exceptions can be dealt with in a uniform fashion. You will encounter many system-defined exceptions on a frequent basis. In addition, you may need to create user-defined exceptions to deal with the specific needs of an application or component library; this kind of custom exception class can inherit from the `ApplicationException` class.

`Finally` blocks are critical when code should execute regardless of whether an exception occurred. A `Finally` block provides a elegant way to structure your code while simultaneously guaranteeing that the CLR will execute the code within the block.

■ 10 ■
Values and Objects

C HAPTER 3 OUTLINED the fundamental differences between value types and reference types. Values are instances created from value types. The CLR treats a value as a simple, formatted chunk of memory. Objects are instances created from reference types. The CLR treats objects much differently than values; it allocates memory for objects on the managed heap and allows you to access them only through the use of references.

This chapter focuses on how the creation of values and objects affects the way that the CLR manages memory within a running application. It begins with a discussion of creating user-defined values types using the Enum construct and the Structure construct. The chapter also explains how designing in terms of value types can provide efficiencies and conveniences that are not available when designing strictly in terms of objects and classes.

The second half of this chapter considers how the CLR manages memory for objects on the managed heap. In particular, it describes how to copy an object by designing a class that supports object cloning. The CLR uses a garbage collector to manage the lifetime of objects on the managed heap; its exploration will lead to an important discussion of how to write the code to clean up after an object when its lifetime ends.

Creating User-Defined Value Types

Let's start by asking a fundamental question: What criteria does the CLR use to determine whether a type is a value type or a reference type? The CLR uses a simple rule: Every type that inherits either directly or indirectly from System.ValueType is a value type. Any type that does not follow this rule is a reference type.

Figure 10.1 shows how value types fit into the CTS's inheritance hierarchy. Many system-provided primitive types such a Boolean, Int32, Double, and DateTime are defined as value types. Notice that all enumerations and structures are defined as value types as well because they inherit from ValueType.

Visual Basic .NET allows you to create two kinds of user-defined values types: enumerations and structures. You create an enumeration using the Enum construct. You create a structure using the Structure construct.

Note that when you create an enumeration or a structure, you are neither required nor allowed to explicitly inherit from ValueType. Instead, the Visual Basic .NET compiler performs the required translation behind the

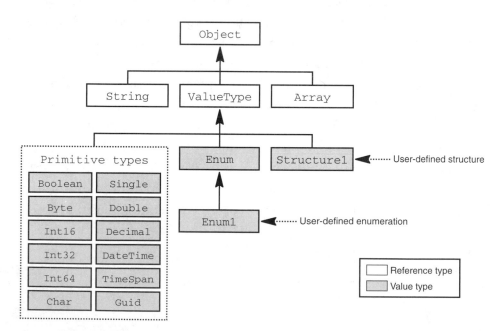

FIGURE 10.1: All types that inherit from System.Value type are considered value types.

scenes. For example, when you create a user-defined value type using the `Structure` construct, the Visual Basic .NET compiler emits a class definition that inherits from `ValueType`. This approach allows the Visual Basic .NET compiler to emit types that the CLR treats as having value type semantics.

The CTS places one important restriction on value types: All value types are sealed. In other words, value types cannot be inherited by other types. If you want to create a type that can be inherited by other types, you should create a new class instead of using a new enumeration or structure.

Creating Enumerations

An *enumeration* is a value type that contains a set of named values. Enumerations are useful in a situation where the value of a parameter or a field should be restricted to a set of predefined states. Suppose you are writing the code for a concrete class named `Burger`. Imagine your application requires that each `Burger` object be initialized in one of three different states: beef, turkey, or veggie. You could complement the design of the `Burger` class with an enumeration that looks like this:

```
Enum BurgerTypeEnum
   Beef
   Turkey
   Veggie
End Enum
```

The Visual Basic .NET compiler does some translation when this enumeration definition is compiled because the resulting type must inherit from `ValueType`. As a result, the definition that is actually compiled into the assembly looks as if it had been defined with the following code:

```
NotInheritable Class BurgerTypeEnum
              Inherits System.Enum
   '*** shared constant fields added for named values
   Public Const Beef As Integer = 0
   Public Const Turkey As Integer = 1
   Public Const Veggie As Integer = 2
End Class
```

Note that this code will not actually compile; it is provided here just to give you a theoretical view of what your code would look like if the Visual Basic

.NET compiler did not do the translation automatically. As you can see, the compiler translates the named values within an enumeration definition into constant fields based on the `Integer` type. As part of this operation, it supplies values for the named constants starting with a value of 0. If you prefer, you can explicitly assign the numeric values to the named constants. For example, if you would rather start at 1 and not 0, you can rewrite the enumeration definition to look like this:

```
Enum BurgerTypeEnum
   Beef = 1
   Turkey
   Veggie
End Enum
```

By default, the Visual Basic .NET compiler uses the 32-bit `Integer` type for the named values within the definition for an enumeration. You have the option of defining an enumeration so that its named values are based on different integer types such as `Byte`, `Short`, or `Long`. You can accomplish this by supplying an `As` clause in the definition. For example, you can rewrite the previous enumeration definition so that its named values are based on the 16-bit `Short` type:

```
Enum BurgerTypeEnum As Short
   Beef
   Turkey
   Veggie
End Enum
```

A key advantage to using an enumeration is that you can design method parameters and fields in terms of a strongly typed set of named values. For example, given the `BurgerTypeEnum`, you can now define the `Burger` class with a constructor that allows the caller to pass one of these enumeration values:

```
Class Burger
   Sub New(ByVal BurgerType As BurgerTypeEnum)
     '*** initialize burger
   End Sub
End Class
```

The named values in `BurgerTypeEnum` are designed to be mutually exclusive. When code is written to create a new `Burger` object, a call to the `New` operator must initialize the new object in one of the three possible states:

```
Dim BobsLunch As New Burger(BurgerTypeEnum.Beef)
Dim BettysLunch As New Burger(BurgerTypeEnum.Turkey)
Dim BerniesLunch As New Burger(BurgerTypeEnum.Veggie)
```

There are several good reasons to use enumerations in this manner:

- The use of enumerations can make your code more readable.
- The IntelliSense feature of Visual Studio .NET supplies a drop-down list of named values when you are making an assignment based on the enumeration type.
- It's easy to determine the friendly string name for an enumeration value.

The `System.Enum` class defines an overridden implementation of `ToString` that provides a convenient way to retrieve the text-based name for an enumeration value. It can prove helpful when you need a string representation of an enumeration value for display purposes. The following code shows how easy it is to obtain the string name of a named value:

```
Dim value1 As BurgerTypeEnum = BurgerTypeEnum.Turkey
Dim name1 As String = value1.ToString() '*** name1 = "Turkey"
```

While the use of an enumeration as a parameter type can help to prevent the passing of invalid parameter values, it doesn't really enforce restrictions as tightly as you might expect. For example, what if a programmer calls the constructor for the `Burger` class and strict type checking is turned off? The following code will compile and run without any problem:

```
'*** works with Option Strict Off
Dim SimonsLunch As New Burger(2)
```

The `Integer` value of 2 is implicitly converted to the enumeration value that maps to that number. In general, it's a bad habit to convert between named values and their internal `Integer` representations. After all, the main advantage to using enumerations is that they abstract away the internal numeric representations of named values. Furthermore, converting between an `Integer` and an enumeration type opens up the possibility of converting to an invalid enumeration value. This problem will arise, for example, when a programmer implicitly converts an `Integer` value that doesn't map to an enumeration value:

```
Dim SigmondsLunch As New Burger(5) '*** invalid enumeration value
```

When you turn on strict type checking, matters improve a little bit. Although you cannot implicitly convert between an `Integer` value and an enumeration value, the Visual Basic .NET compiler still allows you to write bad code because you can explicitly convert between an `Integer` value and an enumeration value:

```
'*** works with Option Strict On
Dim val As BurgerTypeEnum = CType(5, BurgerTypeEnum)
Dim TedsLunch As New Burger(val) '*** invalid enumeration value
```

The point being made here is that the use of an enumeration doesn't provide any real guarantees with respect to whether its values will be valid. Enumerations are best viewed as a programmer convenience rather than as a policing mechanism. If you want to write robust code, you should inspect enumeration values to verify that they contain valid values. You can do so by calling a shared method in the `System.Enum` class named `IsDefined`:

```
Class Burger
  Sub New(ByVal BurgerType As BurgerTypeEnum)

    '*** check whether enumeration value is valid
    If (Not [Enum].IsDefined(GetType(BurgerTypeEnum), BurgerType)) Then
      Throw New System.ArgumentException("Invalid burger type")
    End If

    '*** initialize burger

  End Sub
End Class
```

In the preceding code, the constructor of the `Burger` class has been rewritten to verify that the incoming `BurgerType` parameter contains a valid value. It does so by calling the `IsDefined` method and passing two parameters. The first parameter, a `Type` object created from the `BurgerTypeEnum` type, can be created with the following code:

```
GetType(BurgerTypeEnum)
```

The second parameter passed to `IsDefined` is the enumeration value being verified. If the `IsDefined` method returns `True`, the parameter contains a valid enumeration value. If IsDefined returns False, the parameter value is invalid. The constructor of the Burger class deals with such an invalid parameter value by throwing an ArgumentException back to its caller.

Creating an Enumeration to Act as a Flag

Sometimes it's helpful to create an enumeration that contains named values that are not mutually exclusive. Consider the case when the design of an enumeration contains named values that can be combined into a single value. Such an enumeration is often called a *flag*.

Let's look at an example of an enumeration that has been designed as a flag. Imagine you are designing the Hotdog class and you want to provide a constructor that allows the creator to specify a particular set of toppings. You could start by defining the HotdogGarnishFlags enumeration to serve as a parameter type in the constructor, as shown in Listing 10.1.

LISTING 10.1: An enumeration designed to be a flag

```
<System.Flags()> _
Enum HotdogGarnishFlags
  Chili = 1
  Mustard = 2
  Onions = 4
End Enum
```

When you create an enumeration definition for a flag, you must explicitly assign the values of named constants. You should start with a value of 1, and each number after that value should then be to the next power of 2. For example, you should number the constant values for a flag as 1, 2, 4, 8, 16, 32, 64, ... By following the scheme of using sequential powers of 2, you assign each named constant to a specific bit within the internal integer value.

When you create an enumeration to be a flag, you should also apply the System.Flags attribute as shown in Listing 10.1. The reason that this attribute is important has to do with code that is defined within the System.Enum class. The behavior of some methods, such as ToString and IsDefined, changes depending on whether an enumeration has been defined with or without the Flags attribute. By defining enumerations with the Flags attribute when appropriate, you will ensure that certain methods supplied by the Enum class will work as expected.

The advantage to using an enumeration flag in this design is that a new `Hotdog` object can be created with any combination of toppings. Consider the following class definition, which contains a constructor that uses `HotdogGarnishFlags` as a parameter type:

```
Class Hotdog
   Sub New(ByVal toppings As HotdogGarnishFlags)
      '*** initialize burger
   End Sub
End Class
```

In this code, matters are somewhat different than when the values of the `BurgerTypeEnum` were mutually exclusive. Now the values of the `HotdogGarnishFlags` enumeration can be combined. When you want to combine multiple flags into a single value, you should use the `Or` operator, as shown in Listing 10.2. Note that you combine flags using the `Or` operator, rather than the `And` operator. This distinction can be a little tricky for programmers who are working with bitwise operators for the first time.

LISTING 10.2: Combining flags into a single value using the `Or` operator

```
Dim JoesLunch As New Hotdog(HotdogGarnishFlags.Mustard)

Dim TedsLunch As New Hotdog(HotdogGarnishFlags.Mustard Or _
                    HotdogGarnishFlags.Onions)

Dim BriansLunch As New Hotdog(HotdogGarnishFlags.Chili Or _
                    HotdogGarnishFlags.Mustard Or _
                    HotdogGarnishFlags.Onions)
```

Whereas you use the `Or` operator to combine enumeration flags into a single value, you use the `And` operator to inspect an enumeration value to determine whether a particular flag has been set. Suppose you need to inspect a `HotdogGarnishFlags` value to see which flags have been set. Listing 10.3 shows a constructor that takes the parameter named `toppings` defined in terms of the `HotdogGarnishFlags` enumeration and conducts its initialization work depending on which flags have been set.

LISTING 10.3: Inspecting flags within an enumeration value using the bitwise And operator

```
Sub New(ByVal toppings As HotdogGarnishFlags)

  If ((toppings And HotdogGarnishFlags.Chili) <> 0) Then
    '*** code to add chili
  End If

  If ((toppings And HotdogGarnishFlags.Mustard) <> 0) Then
    '*** code to add mustard
  End If

  If ((toppings And HotdogGarnishFlags.Onions) <> 0) Then
    '*** code to add onions
  End If

End Sub
```

The constructor definition in Listing 10.3 conducts a bitwise comparison between the `toppings` parameter and each of the named values within the `HotdogGarnishFlags` enumeration. You can determine whether a particular flag has been set by conducting a bitwise comparison between the `toppings` parameter and the flag using the `And` operator. If this comparison yields a number other than 0, you know that the particular flag has been set.

Creating Structures

When you want to create a new structure, you create a new type definition using the `Structure` construct supplied by Visual Basic .NET. On the surface, a structure definition seems very similar to a class definition:

```
Structure BankAccount
  Public AccountNumber As Integer
  Public Balance As Decimal
End Structure
```

The Visual Basic .NET compiler treats structure definitions in a similar fashion as it does enumeration definitions. For example, the preceding structure definition is compiled into a sealed type that inherits from `System.ValueType`. It is as if you had written the following code:

```
NotInheritable Class BankAccount
             Inherits System.ValueType
  Public AccountNumber As Integer
  Public Balance As Decimal
End Class
```

Once again, this code will not compile; it simply gives a theoretical view of what your code would look like if the Visual Basic .NET compiler did not perform the translation automatically. In reality, the Visual Basic .NET compiler prohibits you from creating types that explicitly inherit from `System.ValueType`. When you want to create a user-defined value type, you must use either the `Enum` construct or the `Structure` construct.

Earlier versions of Visual Basic supported user-defined types (UDTs). Indeed, UDTs from previous versions of Visual Basic and structures in Visual Basic .NET have some similar characteristics. Nevertheless, you should recognize that structures in the new version of Visual Basic are far more capable than UDTs in the old Visual Basic. For example, you can create a structure that exposes public methods and properties as shown in Listing 10.4. You can also create a structure definition that contains a parameterized constructor for initialization. You can even write a structure to implement an interface.

LISTING 10.4: A structure definition can contain fields, methods, and properties.

```
Structure BankAccount

  Public AccountNumber As Integer
  Public Balance As Decimal

  Public Function GetAccountInformation() As String
    Return "Account #" & AccountNumber & _
          " has a balance of " & Balance
  End Function

  Public ReadOnly Property FormattedBalance() As String
    Get
      Return Balance.ToString("$#,###.00")
    End Get
  End Property

End Structure
```

Recall that a structure differs from a class in that it yields instances that are values instead of objects. However, the design capabilities of a structure are almost the same as those of a class, with a few noteworthy exceptions. As mentioned previously, a structure does not support inheritance. The design of a structure is also limited by the fact that its definition cannot contain a default constructor. That restriction arises because the CLR automatically provides a nonreplaceable implementation for the default constructor of every structure.

You can assume that a structure's built-in default constructor will initialize every field to its default value. For example, all fields based on numeric value types are initialized to a value of zero. All fields based on reference types are initialized to a value of `Nothing`.

While you are not allowed to add a default constructor to a structure definition, you can add one or more parameterized constructors. Listing 10.5 shows an example of a structure definition with a parameterized constructor. Clearly, this parameterized constructor makes it more convenient to initialize values created from the structure.

LISTING 10.5: A structure can contain a parameterized constructor.

```
Structure BankAccount
  Private AccountNumber As Integer
  Private Balance As Decimal
  '*** parameterized constructor
  Sub New(ByVal AccountNumber As Integer, ByVal Balance As Decimal)
    Me.AccountNumber = AccountNumber
    Me.Balance = Balance
  End Sub
End Structure

Class MyApp
  Shared Sub Main()
    '*** create structure instances on stack using New operator
    Dim act1 As New BankAccount(1024, 342.32D)
    Dim act2 As BankAccount = New BankAccount(3292, 988.72D)
  End Sub
End Class
```

To access the parameterized constructor of a structure, you can use the `New` operator as shown in Listing 10.5. You call a parameterized constructor of a structure using exactly the same syntax you use to call the parameterized constructor of a class:

```
Dim act1 As New BankAccount(1024, 342.32D)
Dim act2 As BankAccount = New BankAccount(3292, 988.72D)
```

It is somewhat peculiar that structures support value instantiation through use of the `New` operator. This point catches some programmers off guard because their intuition tells them that the New operator should only be used to create objects on the managed heap. This is not the case when using the New operator to initialize a value with a local variable, however. For example, the memory for the values created in the Main method of Listing 10.5 is allocated on the call stack.

The designers of the Visual Basic .NET language added support for using the New operator on structures so as to provide access to parameterized constructors. The use of the New operator has no effect on how the CLR allocates memory for a value. Structures are always treated as value types, and classes are always treated as reference types.

The Differences between Structures and Classes

When you are designing and writing code with Visual Basic .NET, you must sometimes decide between creating a new class and creating a new structure. You should make this decision according to whether your new type should behave with reference type semantics or value type semantics. How should the CLR manage memory for instances of your new type? Choosing between a class and a structure affects how instances of the type are created and duplicated, as well as how parameter values are passed during method invocation.

An example will put things into perspective. Imagine you have created a structure named BankAccountStructure and a class named BankAccountClass with the following definitions:

```
Public Structure BankAccountStructure
   Public AccountNumber As Integer
   Public Balance As Decimal
End Structure

Public Class BankAccountClass
   Public AccountNumber As Integer
   Public Balance As Decimal
End Class
```

What happens when you create instances from these two types and assign them to other variables? Let's start our examination by assigning one value created from BankAccountStructure to another such structure:

```
Dim val1 As BankAccountStructure
val1.AccountNumber = 1001
val1.Balance = 150.00D
Dim val2 As BankAccountStructure = val1
```

Recall that a variable defined in terms of a structure holds a value. When you assign `val1` to `val2`, you get a duplicate value as shown in the diagram on the left in Figure 10.2. In other words, structures automatically support *copy-on-assignment*.

Objects, by contrast, do not support copy-on-assignment. The diagram on the right in Figure 10.2 illustrates how things change when you write the same code but replace the structure definition with a class definition:

```
Dim rel1 As New BankAccountClass
ref1.AccountNumber = 1002
ref1.Balance = 225.00D
Dim ref2 As BankAccountClass = ref1
```

A variable defined in terms of a class holds a reference. When `ref1` is assigned to `ref2`, the reference is duplicated—not the object. This example includes only one instance of `BankAccountClass`. Classes are not like structures because they do not automatically support duplication. Copying an actual object requires more work and will be discussed later this chapter in the "Object Cloning" section.

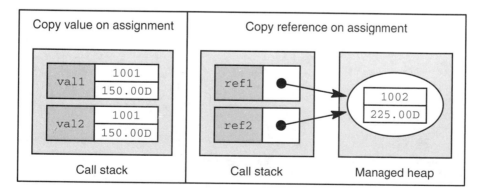

FIGURE 10.2: Values support copy-on-assignment; objects do not.

Passing Values and References as Parameters

How do a structure and a class differ with respect to how parameter values are passed back and forth during method invocation? To answer this question, imagine you are designing a method that accepts a single parameter. First, you must decide whether the parameter will be based on a value type or a reference type. Next, you must decide whether the parameter should be defined with the ByVal keyword or the ByRef keyword. Thus, you have four different choices with respect to how the CLR treats a parameter during method invocation (i.e., four ways you can pass a parameter):

1. You can define the parameter using a value type and the ByVal keyword.

2. You can define the parameter using a reference type and the ByVal keyword.

3. You can define the parameter using a value type and the ByRef keyword.

4. You can define the parameter using a reference type and the ByRef keyword.

Let's step through each of these possibilities to see how they differ. Examine the following code:

```
Shared Sub Main()

    '*** create and initialize value
    Dim val1 As BankAccountStructure
    var1.AccountNumber = 1001
    var1.Balance = 150.00D

    '*** create and initialize object
    Dim ref1 As New BankAccountClass
    ref1.AccountNumber = 1002
    ref1.Balance = 225.00D

    Method1(val1) '*** pass value by value
    Method2(ref1) '*** pass reference by value
    Method3(val1) '*** pass value by reference
    Method4(ref1) '*** pass reference by reference

End Sub
```

This code example demonstrates each of the four ways in which you can pass a parameter while invoking a method. Figure 10.3 shows how each technique differs from the other three with respect to how things are laid out on the call stack and on the managed heap.

What happens when you pass values and references using the ByVal keyword? To answer this question, let's first discuss the call to Method1. This method defines a ByVal parameter based on a value type. In this case, you are passing a value with by-value semantics:

```
Sub Method1(ByVal param1 As BankAccountStructure)
   '*** this method gets a copy of the caller's value
   '*** this method cannot modify the caller's variable
End Sub
```

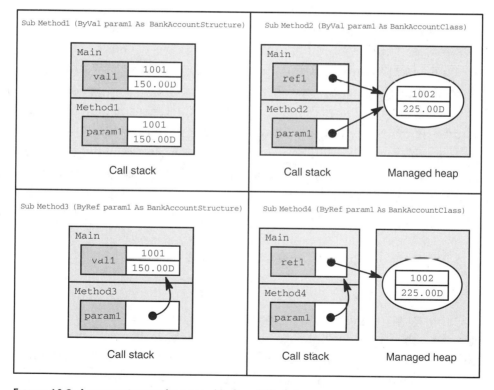

FIGURE 10.3: A parameter can be passed in four different ways.

When a caller invokes Method1, the CLR makes a copy of the value on the call stack, so Method1 gets its own private copy of the value. As you would expect, Method1 cannot modify the caller's variable.

Now let's see how things change when you declare a ByVal parameter using a reference type instead of a value type:

```
Sub Method2(ByVal param1 As BankAccountClass)
   '*** this method gets a copy of the caller's reference
   '*** this method can modify the caller's object
   param1.Balance = 500D
End Sub
```

How does changing the parameter to a reference type affect what happens at runtime? Your intuition might tell you that you are passing a copy of the object by value because you have used the ByVal keyword. In reality, this is not what happens when you call Method2. The CLR creates a copy of the reference, not the object. Both the caller and Method2 have their own private copies of references that point to the same object. Thus Method2 sees the same object as the caller, and this method can make modifications to the object that can be seen by the caller.

What happens when you pass values and references using parameters defined with the ByRef keyword? Once again, you must differentiate between the case of passing a value and passing a reference. Look at the definition for Method3, which contains a value type parameter defined using the ByRef keyword:

```
Sub Method3(ByRef param1 As BankAccountStructure)
   '*** this method has direct access to the caller's value
   '*** this method can modify the caller's value
   param1.Balance = 500D
End Sub
```

When a value is passed with by-reference semantics as in the case of Method3, the CLR does not copy the parameter value. Instead, Method3 is given direct access to the value in the caller's stack frame. The caller and Method3 see the same value, so Method3 can modify the caller's variable.

In the fourth and final case for parameter passing, the reference parameter is passed with by-reference semantics. Method4 demonstrates the use of a method that contains a reference type parameter defined using the ByRef keyword:

```
Sub Method4(ByRef param1 As BankAccountClass)
   '*** this method has direct access to the caller's reference
   '*** this method can reassign the caller's reference
   param1 = Nothing
End Sub
```

When `Method4` is called, the CLR does not make a copy of the caller's reference. Instead, `Method4` is given direct access to the caller's reference. As in the case of passing a reference type with the `ByVal` keyword, `Method4` can modify the object. Declaring a reference type parameter using the `ByRef` keyword does have one distinct advantage over using the `ByVal` keyword: `Method4` can assign the caller's reference variable value to another object or to a value of `Nothing`.

Deciding between Structures and Classes

You have just seen the mechanics of creating a user-defined structure. You have also seen some fundamental differences with respect to how the CLR treats values and objects. Now let's summarize the design issues to consider when trying to decide whether you should prefer a structure over a class in a given design.

Values can be more efficient than objects. A value can be created directly on the call stack, and it can be accessed directly without the need to go through a reference. Furthermore, the CLR doesn't have to manage the lifetime of a value in the same way that it manages the lifetime of an object on the managed heap. The bottom line: Values take up less memory and require less attention from the CLR. As a consequence, using structures is more efficient than using classes.

Also, structures automatically support the duplication of values. The CLR knows how to produce a copy of a value when you assign one structure variable to another and when you pass a value as a `ByVal` parameter. In contrast, classes do not automatically support the duplication of objects. Instead, the programmer must explicitly add support for object duplication, as described in the "Object Cloning" section later in this chapter.

While the use of structures can improve performance, you should keep in mind that structures have some noteworthy disadvantages when compared to classes. The first disadvantage relates to the lifetime of a value. Unlike an object, a value cannot live independently. A value is typically created on the call stack or embedded within an object on the managed heap, so its lifetime is directly controlled by the place in which it was created.

For example, when a value is created on the call stack as a result of a local variable declaration, its memory is released as soon as the current method finishes executing. When a value is embedded in an object as a result of an instance field declaration, its memory is released at the end of the object's lifetime. In contrast, an object can live independently and, therefore, provides more flexibility than a value.

A second disadvantage is that all structures are sealed and do not support inheritance. If you want to create a common base type from which other types can inherit, you must choose a class instead of a structure.

The final disadvantage of structures relates to polymorphism. While you can create a structure definition that implements an interface, it probably doesn't make sense to do so in most situations. When you assign a value created from a structure to an interface-based reference, boxing occurs. (Chapter 3 covered the details of how boxing works.) Achieving polymorphic behavior with a value therefore requires boxing, but boxing involves making a copy of the value and embedding it within an object on the managed heap. Thus a boxed value requires as much (or even more) overhead than a standard object. As a consequence, you lose the key performance advantages gained by using values. If you need to create a type that implements a specific interface, you should generally prefer a class over a structure.

Object Cloning

Structures and classes have some fundamental differences. One important difference is that structures support copy-on-assignment, whereas classes do not. Thus classes lack automatic support for making a copy of an object. You must decide whether you want to add explicit object cloning support on a class-by-class basis.

When you want to create a class that supports object cloning, you must provide a custom instance method that is responsible for producing a copy of the current object. By convention, this method should be named `Clone` and its containing class should explicitly implement the `ICloneable` interface to advertise the fact that its objects support cloning. Listing 10.6 shows an example of a class named `Dog` that supports object cloning in the conventional manner.

LISTING 10.6: Cloning involves creating a new object and copying field values.

```
Public Class Dog : Implements ICloneable

  '*** fields holding object state
  Public Name As String
  Public Age As Integer

  '*** custom method to add object cloning support
  Public Function Clone() As Object Implements ICloneable.Clone
    '*** create another instance
    Dim DogClone As New Dog()
    '*** copy field values to new instance
    DogClone.Name = Me.Name
    DogClone.Age = Me.Age
    '*** return clone reference to caller
    Return DogClone
  End Function

End Class
```

The `Clone` method has a return value defined in terms of the `Object` class. The generic nature of this return value reflects the fact that the `Clone` method must provide a standard return type for all classes that support object cloning. Thus, whenever strict type checking is enabled, a client must explicitly convert the return value when calling the `Clone` method. Here's the client-side code required to call the `Clone` method to copy a `Dog` object:

```
Dim dog1 As New Dog
dog1.Name = "Spot"
dog1.Age = 10
'*** copy instance by calling Clone
Dim dog2 As Dog = CType(dog1.Clone(), Dog)
```

Let's take a closer look at the implementation of the `Clone` method in the `Dog` class. The `Clone` method shown in Listing 10.6 creates a secondary object from the `Dog` class using the `New` operator. Next, it copies all the field values from the original object to the cloned secondary object. This implementation of the `Clone` method is fairly simple, using a *shallow copy*. That is, a cloned Dog object is an exact in-memory copy of the original Dog object. For this reason, a shallow copy can also be called a *bitwise copy* or a *memberwise copy*.

You've just seen one way to implement a Clone method that performs a shallow copy in Listing 10.6. You will be happy to know that the CLR offers an even easier technique for implementing a Clone method to produce a shallow copy. The System.Object class provides a protected method named MemberwiseClone that can do all the work for you. Because every class inherits from the Object class, you can always call the protected MemberwiseClone method inside the implementation of your Clone method. In Listing 10.7, the implementation of the Clone method for the Dog class is rewritten in a single line of code.

LISTING 10.7: The MemberwiseClone **method makes it easy to clone objects with a shallow copy.**

```
Public Class Dog : Implements ICloneable

  '*** fields holding object state
  Public Name As String
  Public Age As Integer

  '*** cloning support
  Public Function Clone() As Object Implements ICloneable.Clone
    Return Me.MemberwiseClone()
  End Function

End Class
```

A cloning technique involving a call to the MemberwiseClone method has the same effect as the technique involving the New operator and manual copying of field values from the original object to the cloned object. Both techniques result in the creation of a cloned object that represents a shallow copy. Most programmers prefer the call to MemberwiseClone because it is easier and eliminates the need to modify your implementation of Clone when you add or remove fields from your class definition.

These techniques for shallow-copy cloning are acceptable for some class definitions but unacceptable for others. In particular, shallow-copy cloning is usually acceptable only for a class whose fields are based on value types and/or the String type. In such a case, a shallow copy doesn't create any problems. The values of the value type fields are copied to the cloned object. With a field based on the `String` type, a reference is copied. This reference copying doesn't pose any problems because string objects are immutable in the CLR. That is, you cannot change the value of a string field in the cloned object and have that change be made visible to the original object. Therefore, the original object and the cloned object act as truly independent entities.

A `Clone` method that performs a shallow copy does not work, however, when a class contains one or more fields based on reference types other than the `String` type. Shallow-copy cloning does not copy the objects that are referenced by the fields of the object being cloned. An example will illustrate such a scenario in which a shallow copy is insufficient. Examine the following class named `Human`, which has two instance fields that contain references that point to other objects:

```
Public Class Human : Implements ICloneable
  Public Pet1 As New Dog
  Public Pet2 As New Dog
  Public Function Clone() As Object Implements ICloneable.Clone
    Return MemberwiseClone()
  End Function
End Class
```

When you create a new `Human` object, you are really creating an object graph of three objects, because a `Human` object holds references to two other `Dog` objects. What happens when an object created from the `Human` class is cloned with a shallow copy? For example, what happens when you execute the following code?

```
Dim human1, human2 As Human
'*** create first Human object
human1 = New Human
'*** clone second Human object
human2 = CType(human1.Clone(), Human)
```

With the current implementation of the `Clone` method, the fields `Pet1` and `Pet2` of the original object and the cloned object end up with references to the same `Dog` objects, as shown in Figure 10.4. A `Clone` method that performs a shallow copy copies only the target object. In this case, however, the implementation needs to clone every object in the object graph behind the target object.

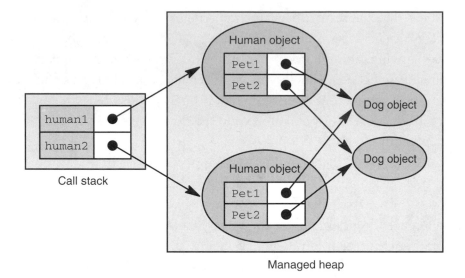

FIGURE 10.4: A shallow copy is insufficient for objects that hold references to other objects.

When shallow-copy cloning is insufficient, you must resort to a cloning technique that copies not only the target object but also the other objects referenced by the target object. That is, you need a *deep copy*. In Listing 10.8, the Human class has been rewritten to include a new implementation of the Clone method that performs a deep copy on an object graph containing three objects.

LISTING 10.8: A deep copy requires cloning objects that are referenced by fields.

```
Public Class Human : Implements ICloneable
  Public Pet1 As New Dog
  Public Pet2 As New Dog
  Public Function Clone() As Object Implements ICloneable.Clone
    Dim HumanClone As Human
    HumanClone = CType(Me.MemberwiseClone(), Human)
    HumanClone.Pet1 = CType(Pet1.Clone, Dog)
    HumanClone.Pet2 = CType(Pet2.Clone, Dog)
    Return HumanClone
  End Function
End Class
```

The new implementation of the Clone method clones the two Dog objects as well as the top-level Human object. Therefore, the cloning operation copies the entire object graph, as shown in Figure 10.5.

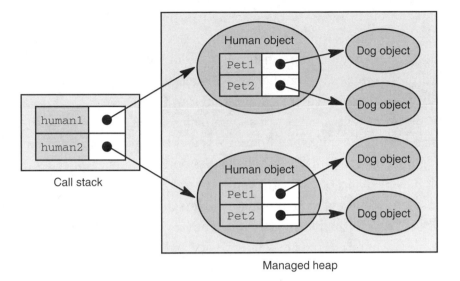

FIGURE 10.5: A deep-copy cloning operation duplicates every object in the object graph.

One last point about deep-copy cloning: It is much easier to implement a deep copy in the `Clone` method when every reference type used as a field also supports the `Clone` method. In Listing 10.8, for example, a `Human` object can simply call the `Clone` method on the `Dog` class to copy each of the two `Dog` objects. If the `Human` class contained a field based on a reference type that did not support the `Clone` method, it would be more difficult—even impossible—to implement a deep-copy clone correctly.

Garbage Collection and Object Lifetimes

The programming model of the CLR is based on the premise that the system is responsible for allocating and managing the memory for types, values, and objects. As a consequence, programmers using the .NET Framework do not have to worry about allocating and managing memory. In fact, when you are writing managed code that will run under normal conditions (i.e., safe mode), it is illegal to directly allocate memory or to directly access memory through the use of pointers.

The CLR's memory management scheme presents challenges for programmers who are making the transition from unmanaged languages such as C and C++. These programmers have been conditioned to use a very hands-on style of memory management in their code. That is, they are accustomed to allocating memory, using pointers, and explicitly releasing memory once they are done using it. Obviously, moving to a platform where programmers are neither responsible for nor allowed to manage memory directly will require a significant mind shift.

While the CLR's memory management scheme represents a drastic departure from those used by C and C++, it closely resembles the memory management scheme that Visual Basic has employed ever since its introduction more than a decade ago. The spirit of Visual Basic has always been to make programmers more productive. The scheme of shifting the responsibility of memory management away from programmers and giving it to the system was introduced in Visual Basic 1.0. Having the system manage memory behind the scenes makes it that much easier to write code—it's one less thing a programmer has to think about.

If you program in any version of Visual Basic, the underlying system is responsible for managing memory. However, the mechanisms for managing memory employed by the CLR do differ from the mechanisms used by previous versions of Visual Basic for this purpose. The CLR manages the lifetime of objects through the use of a *garbage collector*. Earlier versions of Visual Basic are based on COM and, consequently, manage object lifetimes through *reference counting*.

A simple example of a method that declares local variables to create a value and an object will illustrate one of the most important issues concerning memory management. In this example, we will use the `Integer` type to create a value and the `Dog` class to create an object. Assume the `Dog` class exposes a public method named `Bark`. Examine the following code:

```
Sub Method1()
  Dim val1 As Integer
  val1 = 10
  Dim ref1 As New Dog
  ref1.Bark()
End Sub
```

This code includes two local variables. When `Method1` completes, its stack frame is cleaned up and the memory for each variable is reclaimed. However, this example also involves the creation of an object on the heap. After the stack-based memory for the value in `val1` and the reference in ref1 have been reclaimed, a Dog object remains on the heap. This brings up two important questions:

- Who is responsible for reclaiming the memory for this object?
- When will the memory for this object be reclaimed?

The answers to these questions depend on which version of Visual Basic you are using.

Let's start the discussion of object lifetimes with a quick refresher on how things worked in earlier versions of Visual Basic. In older versions such as Visual Basic 6, the lifetimes of objects are managed by the COM runtime through reference counting. Every object is expected to keep track of how many clients have active references to it. Objects are also expected to remove themselves from memory when their reference count drops to zero.

Because earlier versions of Visual Basic rely on reference counting to manage object lifetimes, it has become an acknowledged best practice to explicitly release objects as soon as the program has finished using them. This goal is often accomplished by setting a local object reference equal to Nothing:

```
'*** code written in Visual Basic 6
Sub Method2()
  '*** create object
  Dim dog1 As New Dog
  '*** use object
  dog1.Bark()
  '*** release object
  Set dog1 = Nothing
End Sub
```

In the preceding code, the underlying runtime environment issues a Release call to the Dog object. The Dog object responds by decrementing its reference count and determining that the last reference has just been released. Next, the object executes any user-defined cleanup code. It then removes itself from memory.

If you wrote the Dog class in Visual Basic 6 and added an implementation of the Class_Terminate method, you would be guaranteed that this method would be called at a predictable time. In the preceding example, the execution of the line of code that sets the dog1 variable to Nothing will block this method's call until the cleanup code in the `Class_Terminate` method finishes executing.

The Garbage Collector

Now let's take a look at how things have changed in Visual Basic .NET. The biggest difference is that the CLR does not manage object lifetimes through reference counting. Instead, it employs a garbage collector to reclaim the memory for objects.

The garbage collector employs an algorithm to determine whether objects on the heap are reachable by the application. For an object to be reachable, the application must possess one or more references that make that object accessible. For example, if the garbage collector sees that a shared field or a local variable currently references an object, the object is considered reachable. Furthermore, any objects referenced by this object are also considered reachable.

If the garbage collector determines that an application does not possess any references that would make it possible to access an object, that object is considered to be unreachable. The garbage collector assumes that the memory occupied by unreachable objects is available for reclamation.

The garbage collector is typically triggered when an application goes beyond a certain memory usage threshold. When the garbage collector decides that it must determine which memory it can reclaim, it freezes program execution and builds a large object graph containing all reachable objects in the application. The next time that the CLR must create a new object, it assumes that it can reuse any memory that is not associated with a reachable object.

During a garbage collection cycle, the garbage collector may decide to compact the heap by moving all reachable objects into one contiguous section of memory located at the beginning of the heap. The act of compacting the heap helps to defragment memory, which in turn allows the CLR to create new objects more efficiently. Of course, the garbage collector must do more than simply move objects when compacting the heap. It must also ensure that all of the application's references that point to objects that have been moved are updated accordingly.

The details of how the garbage collector of the CLR performs its work are fascinating, but fairly complicated. If you are interested in learning more about the garbage collector's inner workings, you can read about them in *Applied Microsoft .NET Framework Programming in Microsoft Visual Basic .NET* by Jeffrey Richter and Francesco Balena. This book provides excellent coverage of what goes on behind the scenes and describes how Microsoft engineers designed their garbage collector to provide very high levels of performance.

Knowing the details of the garbage collector's operation is nice, but it's definitely not a requirement for writing efficient code with Visual Basic .NET. It is critical, however, that you understand the programming disciplines that should be used when writing code for a garbage-collected environment. The remainder of this chapter will focus on this important topic.

Garbage Collection versus Reference Counting

A memory management scheme that uses garbage collection is quite different from one that uses reference counting. The former scheme enjoys two advantages over reference counting but has one major disadvantage:

- A garbage collector can offer better performance than reference counting. *Advantage: garbage collection.*
- A garbage collector provides a far more elegant solution for dealing with circular references. *Advantage: garbage collection.*
- A garbage collector requires a more complicated structuring of cleanup code than reference counting. *Advantage: reference counting.*

Let's look at these points in more detail.

First, a garbage collection scheme can offer better performance. This benefit is especially noticeable with a server-side application in which objects are being continuously created and released within the scope of a single client request. Reference counting is significantly more expensive due to the extra interaction required between an object and its clients. That is, clients continually make calls to the object to increment and decrement its reference count.

Second, garbage collection can easily manage sets of objects that contain circular references. In contrast, a memory management scheme based on reference counting is vulnerable to memory leaks when a pair of objects acquire references to one another. If neither object lets go of the other, the two objects will never decrement their reference counts to zero. Even after the program has finished using these objects, they will remain in memory until the program ends. This situation is an example of a classic memory leak in COM.

When designing classes that will be used in an environment that uses reference counting, the developer must either avoid circular references or use well-known programming techniques that are explicitly designed to break down any object graphs that contain circular references. In an environment that uses garbage collection, circular references do not create the same problem. If two objects are unreachable, it doesn't matter whether they hold references to each other. The garbage collector can free their memory because it can determine that the program no longer uses them.

The third major difference between the use of reference counting and the use of garbage collection relates to how you write the code to clean up after your objects—and it places garbage collection at a distinct disadvantage. An example will illustrate why. Imagine you have created the Dog class in Visual Basic .NET. As you know, the CLR will manage the lifetime of every Dog object through garbage collection. Now imagine that someone has written the following code to create and use objects from the Dog class:

```
Sub Method3()

  '*** create two objects
  Dim dog1 As New Dog
  Dim dog2 As New Dog

  '*** use the object
  dog1.Bark()
  dog2.Bark()

  '*** release the first object
  dog1 = Nothing

End Sub
```

The important question you must ask yourself is, When are these two Dog objects destroyed? The answer: You really don't know. The Dog object referenced by the dog1 variable becomes unreachable once the variable is set to a value of Nothing. The Dog object referenced by the dog2 variable becomes unreachable once the method completes and the dog2 variable goes out of scope. However, an indeterminate length of time separates when these two objects become unreachable and when they are actually destroyed by the garbage collector. This indeterminate length of time makes writing cleanup code in Visual Basic .NET more complicated than it has been in previous versions of Visual Basic.

If you were creating the Dog class in Visual Basic 6, you would simply add your cleanup code to the Class_Terminate method. You would also be able to make the assumption that your cleanup code would be called in a timely fashion when the client released its last reference to the object. Because Visual Basic .NET does not support the Class_Terminate method, you must find another place to add your code to clean up various resources at the end of a Dog object's lifetime.

The remainder of this chapter focuses on two techniques to run cleanup code at the end of an object's lifetime: use of a Finalize method and use of a Dispose method. Both of these new techniques work very differently than use of a Class_Terminate method in Visual Basic 6.

Object Finalization

The CLR provides support for object finalization. With object finalization, a managed object can request that the CLR send it a notification before the garbage collector reclaims its memory. To request that your objects receive finalization notifications, you include an instance method named Finalize in the class definition. Listing 10.9 shows the starting point for adding a Finalize method to the Dog class.

In addition to your custom cleanup code, an implementation of Finalize should call the Finalize method supplied by its base class. Calling the base class Finalize should be done last. If your cleanup code in the derived class is vulnerable to a runtime exception, you should place that code inside a Try block with a corresponding Finally block that calls MyBase.Finalize, as shown in Listing 10.9.

LISTING 10.9: The CLR executes an object's `Finalize` method at the end of its lifetime.

```
Public Class Dog

  Protected Overrides Sub Finalize()
    Try
      '*** add your cleanup code here
    Finally
      MyBase.Finalize()
    End Try
  End Sub

  '*** other Dog class members omitted for clarity

End Class
```

Once you add a `Finalize` method, the CLR knows that objects created from your class require a finalization notification. When a client creates an object, the CLR adds a reference to an internal list of objects that require finalization. As a consequence, objects with a `Finalize` method take longer to create, and objects that lack a `Finalize` method have a measurable performance advantage over objects that include a `Finalize` method.

What happens at the end of an object's lifetime when it requires finalization? When the garbage collector determines that an object requiring finalization is no longer reachable by the application, it removes the object's reference from the first internal list and adds a reference to a second internal list. While the first internal list is for *objects that require finalization*, the second list is for *objects that are ready for finalization*. Note that objects that are referenced in this second internal list are reachable by the CLR, even though they are no longer reachable by the application. This ensures that objects requiring finalization are not collected before their `Finalize` methods have been called.

The CLR uses a dedicated background thread to monitor the internal list of objects that are ready for finalization. This background finalization thread calls the `Finalize` method of objects as they are added to the list. If several objects are added to this list at the same time, the background thread moves through the list in a serialized fashion, executing `Finalize` methods one after another. Once the background finalization thread has called an object's `Finalize` method, the object is removed from the second list and it becomes just like any other unreachable object. At this point, the CLR can reclaim its memory.

What would happen if an object's `Finalize` method throws an exception? Such a result isn't a big deal for the garbage collector. The CLR's finalization thread simply swallows such exceptions and moves on to the next object that is ready for finalization.

Object Design Issues Related to Finalization

Now that you have a basic understanding of the mechanics behind the `Finalize` method, let's reexamine things from a design perspective. While you might be tempted to use the `Finalize` method in the same manner in which you have used `Class_Terminate` in the past, that would be a mistake. Several design issues make writing code in the `Finalize` method much different than writing code in the `Class_Terminate` method.

How do the differences between the `Finalize` method and `Class_Terminate` affect application design? The first and foremost design issue is that there are no guarantees about exactly when the `Finalize` method will be called. For this reason, many developers use the term *nondeterministic finalization* when talking about a class with a `Finalize` method. Clearly, the `Finalize` method is not an ideal place to release time-sensitive resources such as a database connection or a file handle.

A second design issue is that the CLR provides no guarantees about the order in which it will call `Finalize` methods when a set of objects is ready for finalization. An example will illustrate why this point is important. Imagine you have designed the `Dog` class that contains an instance field based on the `Flea` class. Both of these classes contain a `Finalize` method. You might be tempted to write code in the `Finalize` method of the `Dog` class that accesses the `Flea` object. Unfortunately, such code will not work reliably. Problems will likely arise if the `Flea` object's `Finalize` method executes before the `Dog` object's `Finalize` method.

Because you cannot determine which `Finalize` method will run first, the `Finalize` method of the `Dog` class should not be written to access the `Flea` object. Use the following rule of thumb: When you write a `Finalize` method, do not attempt to access any other object that could also be in the process of undergoing finalization.

A third design issue is that the `Finalize` method always executes on a different thread. While this separation doesn't create a problem for most designs, you must exercise caution when using any programming technique that creates thread dependencies, such as the use of thread local storage. You might also be responsible for writing synchronization code if the finalization thread concurrently accesses the same objects as other application threads.

A fourth design issue is that an object with a poorly written `Finalize` method can block the background finalization thread indefinitely. If an object's `Finalize` method enters an infinite loop or encounters a synchronization lock with an infinite timeout, the finalization thread will never be able to call the `Finalize` method of any other object. In this way, a poorly written `Finalize` method can stop the garbage collector from functioning properly.

A fifth design issue is that the garbage collector calls `Finalize` on any object that experienced an exception during construction. Think about the following scenario: A client calls `New` on a class and the constructor throws an exception. What happens? The exception is thrown back to the client, but the client never gets a reference to the partially constructed object.

You might not expect the garbage collector to call the `Finalize` method on an object that failed to properly construct itself, but it does. The CLR calls the `Finalize` method in the preceding scenario to give a partially constructed object a chance to release any resources it might have acquired before the exception occurred in the constructor. You should keep this point in mind whenever you write an implementation for a `Finalize` method.

Controlling the Garbage Collector Programmatically

The CLR allows a programmer to manually trigger a garbage collection, if necessary. Programmatic access to the garbage collector occurs through shared public members of the `System.GC` class. The code in Listing 10.10 illustrates how to trigger the garbage collector so as to synchronously execute the `Finalize` method for a `Dog` object that is no longer reachable by the application.

LISTING 10.10: The garbage collector can be controlled through shared methods of the `System.GC` class.

```
'*** create object
Dim spot As New Dog()

'*** use object
Spot.Bark()

'*** release reference to object
spot = Nothing

'*** force GC to call object's Finalize method
System.GC.Collect()
System.GC.WaitForPendingFinalizers()
```

Why would you ever trigger a garbage collection programmatically? This technique can prove handy when you are testing and debugging the code in a `Finalize` method. In a production application, however, explicitly triggering a garbage collection is usually an unacceptable practice. It is especially undesirable for server-side applications that experience concurrent calls from multiple client applications. In such a scenario, it would be a very big mistake to trigger a garbage collection every time a client application submitted a request.

The CLR's garbage collector has been designed to automatically trigger collections when the application's memory usage exceeds predefined thresholds. The garbage collector can optimize different applications in different ways depending on how it sees an application using memory. It is naive to think that you know more than the garbage collector about when it should do its work. Triggering a garbage collection programmatically in a production application is almost guaranteed to have the opposite effect of what you're hoping for.

Disposable Objects

Now that you have seen the details of object finalization and the implementation of a `Finalize` method, let's revisit our discussion of designing classes. Obviously, the `Finalize` method isn't the best place to add the cleanup code for an object, because `Finalize` isn't called when you really want it to be called. Therefore, you should not rely on code in this method to clean up resources that need to be released in a time-critical fashion.

Let's take a step back and ask a more fundamental question: Does every object really need to execute cleanup code at the end of its lifetime? The answer really depends on what kinds of resources the object is holding. If an object holds nothing other than memory (i.e., values and objects), you have no concerns. You don't need to provide any custom cleanup code because managing memory is the responsibility of the garbage collector. In fact, a large percentage of your class designs likely won't require any custom cleanup code.

You do need to supply custom cleanup code that executes at the end of an object's lifetime when the object holds a time-sensitive resource that is not managed by the CLR. Examples of such resources include database connections and file handles.

Class authors who need to execute custom cleanup code at the end of an object's lifetime use the following .NET programming convention: They expose a public method named `Dispose`. When you add a public `Dispose` method to your code, it is recommended that you also implement the `IDisposable` interface to advertise the fact that the object contains a `Dispose` method. Listing 10.11 shows an example of how this convention works when supplying custom cleanup code to the `Dog` class.

LISTING 10.11: A class with a `Dispose` method allows objects to run cleanup code in a timely fashion.

```
Public Class Dog : Implements IDisposable

  Public Sub Dispose() Implements IDisposable.Dispose
    '*** your cleanup code goes here
  End Sub

  '*** other Dog class members omitted for clarity

End Class
```

This convention for executing cleanup code in a timely fashion requires participation from the client as well as the object. The client is responsible for calling the `Dispose` method of a disposable object once the program has finished with that object:

```
'*** create object
Dim spot As New Dog()
```

```
'*** use object
spot.Bark()
'*** call Dispose on object when done
spot.Dispose()
```

As shown in the preceding code, a call to `Dispose` allows an object to execute its cleanup code in a timely and predictable manner. Keep in mind that a disposable object puts additional burdens on the client-side code. That is, a client has to call `Dispose` at the right time. Furthermore, a client cannot make additional calls to an object after calling `Dispose`. As you can imagine, this burden becomes harder to manage in designs where multiple clients have access to the same disposable object.

A class author can implement the `Dispose` method without having to worry about all the issues surrounding the `Finalize` method that were discussed earlier in this chapter. When implementing `Dispose`, you should assume that the client will call `Dispose` in a timely fashion. Furthermore, when the `Dispose` method is executing, the object and all of the objects that it references remain reachable. As a result, an object can make calls to objects that it references in the `Dispose` method. Such is not the case with the `Finalize` method.

Once the application has disposed of an object, that object should be considered off limits. By convention, a disposable object should throw an exception if any method is called on it after the `Dispose` method executes. An exception type named `ObjectDisposedException` in the `System` namespace was built into the FCL for this exact purpose. The `Dog` class in Listing 10.12 shows one possible design in which a method confirms that an object hasn't been disposed of before servicing a method call.

LISTING 10.12: A disposable object should throw an `ObjectDisposedException` **whenever appropriate.**

```
Class Dog : Implements IDisposable

  Private ObjectDisposed As Boolean = False

  Public Sub Dispose() Implements System.IDisposable.Dispose
    Me.ObjectDisposed = True
    '*** add cleanup code here
  End Sub
```

continues

```
'*** user-defined method
Sub Bark()

  '*** make sure object hasn't already been disposed
  If ObjectDisposed Then
    Dim ObjectName As String = "Dog"
    Dim Message As String = "Object has been disposed"
    Throw New ObjectDisposedException(ObjectName, Message)
  End If

  '*** perform operation

End Sub

End Class
```

Using the `Dispose` and `Finalize` Methods in Combination

At this point you have seen how the `Finalize` method and the `Dispose` method work. Now let's ask another question: Would you ever want to include both methods in the same class definition? You might decide to do so if you're worried what will happen to a disposable object if the client forgets to call `Dispose`. This decision brings up a design issue that can trigger somewhat of a philosophical debate.

Should you add a `Finalize` method to deal with situations in which the client-side code did not live up to its responsibilities? Adding a `Finalize` method in conjunction with a `Dispose` method gives you a fallback in such cases. Nevertheless, you must consider a few important tradeoffs related to performance degradation and design complexity when you include both a `Finalize` method and a `Dispose` method.

Adding a `Finalize` method always affects performance, because the CLR must update the two internal finalization lists as each object goes through its life cycle. The CLR updates the first list during object construction, which slows down the creation of objects with the `New` operator. Objects that require finalization also increase the workload of the background finalization thread, which takes processing cycles away from the threads that are running the application code.

The performance hit for object finalization is most noticeable in server-side applications in which objects are frequently created and released within the scope of a single client request. When you are writing code for this type of server-side application, you should consider avoiding objects that require finalization in your design. For other kinds of applications, the overhead associated with finalization is often far less noticeable. For example, if you are designing a class for a long-lived object that will run in a desktop application, the finalization-related overhead will not be much of a concern.

Apart from the performance implications, a second problem arises when you create a class that contains both a `Finalize` method and a `Dispose` method: This approach complicates the design of the class. The `Dispose` method contains the cleanup code that you hope will run. The `Finalize` method contains the backup cleanup code that you want to run in cases where the client did not call `Dispose`.

While both `Dispose` and `Finalize` are written to contain cleanup code, they usually must be written differently. The code in a `Finalize` method is subject to several restrictions that are not an issue when writing a `Dispose` method, as discussed earlier in this chapter. The restriction that commonly requires your attention is the fact that code in the `Dispose` method can make calls to other objects that have a `Finalize` method, whereas code in a `Finalize` method cannot.

If you create a class that contains both a `Dispose` method and a `Finalize` method, you must ensure that the same cleanup code doesn't run more than once. In other words, you must structure your design so that the cleanup code in `Finalize` runs only when the `Dispose` method was not called. This goal can be accomplished by adding a call to a method named `SuppressFinalize` in your `Dispose` method, as shown in Listing 10.13.

LISTING 10.13: The `Dispose` method can call `SuppressFinalize` to disable finalization notification.

```
Class Dog : Implements IDisposable

  Public Sub Dispose() Implements IDisposable.Dispose

    '*** disable finalization notification
    System.GC.SuppressFinalize(Me)

    '*** add cleanup without finalization restrictions

  End Sub
```

continues

```
Protected Overrides Sub Finalize()
  Try
    '*** add cleanup with finalization restrictions
  Finally
    MyBase.Finalize()
  End Try
End Sub

End Class
```

SuppressFinalize is a shared method supplied by the System.GC class. A call to this method tells the CLR to remove the object's reference from the internal list of objects requiring finalization. When you call SuppressFinalize from the Dispose method, you are effectively telling the CLR that the current object no longer requires a finalization notification. Therefore, a call to Dispose ensures that the CLR does not call the Finalize method. However, in the case where the Dispose method was never called, the CLR still calls the Finalize method at the end of an object's lifetime.

As you can see, adding support for both the Dispose method and the Finalize method can be tricky. It can become even more complicated when the design uses inheritance. As an example, imagine you are designing a base class from which you want other programmers to inherit. What would you do if you wanted to add cleanup code in both the Dispose method and the Finalize method and you also wanted to allow programmers of derived classes to extend this cleanup code if necessary?

Although you could create a base class with this kind of design in several different ways, let's investigate one technique that's commonly used by Microsoft's engineers in FCL. Several disposable base classes, such as the Component class defined within the System.ComponentModel namespace, use the same design pattern. This design pattern allows you to easily create derived classes that extend the cleanup code within a base class that contains both a Dispose method and a Finalize method. Listing 10.14 shows an example of a base class that follows this design pattern.

LISTING 10.14: The Dog class provides cleanup code that is easily extendable in derived classes.

```
Public Class Dog : Implements IDisposable

  Public Sub Dispose() Implements IDisposable.Dispose
    System.GC.SuppressFinalize(Me)
    Dispose(True)
  End Sub

  Protected Overrides Sub Finalize()
    Try
      Dispose(False)
    Finally
      MyBase.Finalize()
    End Try
  End Sub

  Protected Overridable Sub Dispose(ByVal disposing As Boolean)
    If disposing Then
      '*** add cleanup code without finalization restrictions
    Else
      '*** add cleanup code with finalization restrictions
    End If
  End Sub

End Class
```

The Dog class in Listing 10.14 provides a public Dispose method and a protected Finalize method. Neither of these methods contains any cleanup code. Instead, both forward the caller to a third method that contains all of the cleanup code. In this design pattern, the third method that contains the actual cleanup code is a protected method that is also named Dispose. This implementation of Dispose, however, is an overloaded version that accepts a Boolean parameter named disposing.

When a client calls the public Dispose method, it forwards the call to the protected Dispose method and passes a value of True for the disposing parameter. When the CLR calls the Finalize method during finalization, it forwards the call to the parameterized Dispose method and passes a value of False for the disposing parameter. A key advantage of this design pattern is that all of the cleanup code for the class can be maintained in the definition of the protected Dispose method. You can query the dis-posing parameter to write conditional logic so that certain pieces of code don't run when the object is undergoing finalization.

Now that you've seen how to write a base class that follows this design pattern, you can appreciate how much easier it is to write a class that inherits from it. If you create a class that inherits from the Dog class, you don't have to worry about implementing either the public Dispose method or the protected Finalize method, because both of these methods are auto-matically inherited. You merely have to override the protected Dispose method that accepts the disposing parameter. This approach allows you to extend the cleanup code supplied by the base class. Listing 10.15 shows an example of the Beagle class that inherits from the Dog class and extends the cleanup code with more of its own code.

LISTING 10.15: The Dispose method is called on the base class after executing extended cleanup code.

```
Class Beagle : Inherits Dog
  Protected Overloads Overrides Sub Dispose(ByVal disposing As Boolean)

    '*** custom cleanup code for Beagle class
    If disposing Then
      '*** add clean up without finalization restrictions
    Else
      '*** add cleanup code with finalization restrictions
    End If

    '*** execute cleanup code from base class
    MyBase.Dispose(disposing)

  End Sub
End Class
```

In the Beagle class definition shown in Listing 10.15, the overriding implementation of the Dispose method chains a call back to the overridden implementation of Dispose from its base class. This chained call ensures that the cleanup code from both classes is run. Also, note the use of the Overloads keyword in the signature of the protected Dispose method. The Overloads keyword is required so that the Visual Basic .NET compiler will not hide the public Dispose method that takes no parameters.

SUMMARY

The CLR treats values as simple formatted chunks of memory. Even so, a value created from a structure can provide its own unique behavior in the form of methods and properties. The use of values can be more efficient than the use of objects, because a value can be created directly on the call stack and accessed without the use of a reference. A value is also more efficient than an object, because it doesn't require the attention of the garbage collector.

While objects require more overhead than values, they also provide greater capabilities. Objects can live independently, whereas values cannot. Because objects provide more flexibility than values, their design can become more complicated as well. Objects do not support the ability to copy themselves automatically. You can add explicit cloning support to a class when it's necessary to make a copy of an object. The CLR's reliance on garbage collection can complicate the structure of cleanup code that must run at the end of an object's lifetime. In some cases, an object might require a `Finalize` method and/or a `Dispose` method.

■ 11 ■

Assemblies

A N ASSEMBLY IS the fundamental unit in which managed code is compiled, distributed, and reused. Assemblies serve as the building blocks with which you build and deploy applications. As a .NET developer, you will be constantly producing your own assemblies and consuming assemblies that have been produced by others.

Chapter 1 introduced the basic concepts associated with assemblies. This chapter examines how assemblies are built and deployed in much greater depth. We begin by looking at problems that developers and administrators experienced in the past while trying to deploy and maintain applications and DLLs in a production environment. This background information will give you valuable insight into important design decisions that were made by the architects of the .NET Framework with respect to how the CLR locates assemblies and loads them into a running application.

Before we delve into the details of how assemblies are deployed, we will spend a few pages exploring the configuration process for a .NET application. Configuration is done through XML-based configuration files. Your understanding of how applications are configured will prove critical when you need to deploy an application and its dependent assemblies, because you often need to configure an application so that the CLR knows which version of an assembly DLL to load and where to look for it.

This chapter also describes the naming and identification of assemblies, as well as the mechanics employed to build an assembly with the exact name you want. It then discusses the various options for deploying assemblies on a target machine and explains how the CLR locates and loads assemblies at runtime.

The chapter ends with a discussion of versioning of assembly DLLs. Versioning of assemblies represents one of the tougher and more complex areas when it comes to developing, distributing, and deploying managed code. Once you understand the essential details of this process, you will be able to create an effective strategy for evolving a DLL after it has already been distributed and deployed in a production environment.

Learning from the Past

History is a fabulous teacher to those who are willing to learn from it. The history of the Windows operating system is filled with important lessons about what works and what doesn't work with respect to deploying and maintaining application code. Fortunately, the architects of the .NET Framework took many of these lessons to heart and used them in the design of the CLR.

History has taught us that the Windows Registry is often a source of problems. When an application relies on settings in the Windows Registry, it increases the complexity and the cost of that application's deployment and maintenance. This is especially true when production machines are being managed from across the network. Depending on what kind of network management software a company has at its disposal, writing to the Windows Registry from across the network is more costly at best and impossible at worst. The designers of the .NET Framework knew it was critical to devise a scheme for application and assembly deployment that did not depend on the Windows Registry.

History has also taught us that distributing code in terms of DLLs poses some very tough problems. Prior to the introduction of the .NET Framework, there were two commonly used styles of DLLs: *standard Windows DLLs* and *COM DLLs*. Standard Windows DLLs are reusable libraries of global functions that are typically written in the C programming language. COM DLLs are reusable libraries of creatable COM classes that are typically written in Visual Basic or C++. It's fair to say that both kinds of DLLs have experienced their share of deployment problems.

Because most standard Windows DLLs are stored in the `\Windows\System32` directory, they are vulnerable to naming conflicts. Problems often crop up when two companies each create DLLs that have the same file name. The history of the Windows operating system is replete with many installation programs that overwrite one company's DLL with a DLL produced by another company. When this happens, it breaks any applications that relied on the now-overwritten DLL.

COM DLLs pose an obvious deployment problem. Installing a COM DLL requires more than just copying it to the hard drive of the target machine. That is, to properly install a COM DLL, you must register the library so it can write configuration data to the Windows Registry, such as the physical path pointing to its location. The registration requirement makes it much more difficult (and sometimes impossible) to deploy COM DLLs from across the network. The configuration data in the Windows Registry are also quite brittle. You cannot relocate a COM DLL on a production machine without re-registering it—for this reason, COM has a reputation for fragile deployment.

Standard DLLs and COM DLLs also pose a noteworthy security risk. Several successful "hacker" attacks over the last few years have involved DLL replacement. If an attacker can access your hard drive and overwrite a DLL with an evil twin, he or she can change the behavior of your applications and the behavior of the operating system as a whole. Even though this sort of attack can be devastating, the scheme for loading standard Windows DLLs and COM DLLs does nothing to defend against it.

Of all the complaints that Microsoft has received from customers who were experiencing problems with standard Windows DLLs and COM DLLs, the vast majority have involved some kind of versioning problem. Nothing in Windows development has proven as problematic as versioning and redeploying a DLL over time. Installing a new version of a DLL often means breaking existing applications or introducing some mysterious and undesirable behavior.

Most of the problems related to versioning DLLs revolve around one simple fact: There is no reliable scheme for installing multiple versions of a DLL on a target machine at the same time. This issue becomes a problem when an older application has been built and tested using the original version of a DLL and a newer application has been built and tested using an updated version of the same DLL. To run both applications on the same machine in side-by-side fashion, the older application is forced to load and run with the newer version of the DLL.

The first issue with the updated version of the DLL is the most obvious: What happens if the updated version does not expose the same programming contract as the original version? For example, what happens if the original version of the DLL exposes a few public methods that are not supported by the updated version? Clearly, this situation is a recipe for disaster, because the updated version of the DLL is not compatible with the older application. It means you will break the older application when you install the updated DLL.

In theory, the older application should work correctly as long as the DLL producer has created the updated version of the DLL following the rules of *backward compatibility*. The most obvious requirement for achieving backward compatibility is that the updated version of the DLL must continue to support the same programming contract as the original version. For example, the producer of the DLL must not remove any public methods or modify their calling signatures.

In practice, achieving true backward compatibility has proved to be a very elusive goal, because it requires more than just holding the programming contract constant from one version of a DLL to the next. It's quite possible to break backward compatibility by changing private implementation details. In other words, you have to honor semantic contracts as well as syntactic contracts.

True backward compatibility requires that the code in an updated version of a DLL not introduce any new behavior or requirements that would adversely affect or break older applications that relied on an earlier version. Even fixing a bug in a new revision of a DLL can break existing applications when those applications have been written with workarounds for the bug. Likewise, modifying just a single line of code in a private method can lead to incompatibility between DLLs.

When the producer of a DLL advertises that a new version is backward compatible with earlier releases, this claim is really more of a guess than a guarantee. The only way to establish beyond doubt that an updated version is backward compatible is to perform regression testing on all applications that were compiled against earlier versions. In practice, performing regression testing on every application that was built against an earlier version of a DLL is never really possible.

In the end, only one deployment scenario is highly predictable—the case where an application is deployed with the exact version of the DLL that was present during the testing and debugging phases of application development. Of course, the fact that only one version of a DLL can be installed at any time makes this predictable deployment scenario impossible to achieve in the case when two or more applications have been built and tested using different versions of the same DLL. This is arguably the greatest flaw in the versioning support provided for standard Windows DLLs and COM DLLs.

This whirlwind tour has revealed some of the most notable problems related to deploying and maintaining application code on the Windows operating system. Finding solutions to these problems emerged as an important design goal for the architects of the .NET Framework and the CLR. In summary, the most significant problems of the past were as follows:

- Storing configuration data for applications and COM DLLs in the Windows Registry makes it more difficult to deploy and maintain applications.
- DLLs are vulnerable to file name conflicts.
- DLL replacement and tampering creates a dangerous security hole.
- The operating system provides no intrinsic support for installing different versions of the same DLL on the same machine. Installing a new version of a DLL effectively replaces any earlier version.
- A newer version of a DLL may break older applications when it is not backward compatible.
- DLLs said to be "backward compatible" don't always work as advertised. A DLL cannot really be guaranteed to be backward compatible unless it is put through regression testing with every application that uses it.

- The most predictable deployment scenario is to run an application that loads the exact version of a DLL that was present during the application's original testing and debugging.

The architects of the CLR designed assemblies to address all of these unresolved DLL issues. The remainder of this chapter is dedicated to explaining how assemblies are named, deployed, configured, and versioned in the .NET Framework. Along the way, you will see that the CLR has been designed to locate, identify, and load assemblies in a manner that addresses all of the problems on the preceding list. All in all, the CLR includes several valuable advancements and innovations that make it less costly and more predictable to deploy applications and DLLs in a production environment.

Microsoft marketing messages often claim that the .NET Framework and the CLR have put an end to the world of *DLL hell*. While certainly the CLR does make things significantly better, it does not make building, deploying, and versioning DLLs any less complex. In fact, it has quite the opposite effect: The rules for properly building, deploying, and versioning DLLs are more complicated than ever before. The authors and many of the instructors at DevelopMentor have become fond of telling the following joke:

Question: How did Microsoft put an end to DLL hell?

Answer: It stopped calling component libraries "DLLs" and started calling them "assemblies." Now instead of DLL hell, we have assembly purgatory.

This joke makes a serious point. The bar has definitely been raised in terms of what you need to know before you can build, deploy, configure, and version your code. All of the new bells and whistles won't have any value if you don't learn to use them properly. Programmers who ignore these details will be stuck in assembly purgatory for all of eternity. It's time to begin your journey out of assembly purgatory by examining how applications are configured for the CLR.

Configuring Applications

Back in the early days of 16-bit Windows, applications were commonly configured through the use of INI files. An INI file is a text-based configuration file with an `.INI` extension. Its structure typically contains named sections that hold configuration data in name-value pairs.

Application configuration that relied on INI files fell out of style when Microsoft introduced its 32-bit versions of Windows. When the company launched operating systems such as Windows NT and Windows 95, it encouraged developers to store their configuration information in the Windows Registry instead of INI files. As a result, the Windows Registry has evolved into a very important repository for all kinds of configuration data both for applications and for the Windows operating system itself.

For the reasons discussed in the previous section, it's more difficult to deploy and maintain applications in a network environment when they rely on configuration data in the Windows Registry. Recognizing this fact, the designers of the .NET Framework decided to avoid the Windows Registry and to return to a scheme based on configuration files that is more similar to INI files. In this sense, configuring Windows applications has come full circle, back to the way it was in the beginning.

Configuration Files in the .NET Framework

In the .NET Framework, desktop applications are configured using XML-based configuration files. If you choose to use a configuration file, the CLR requires this file to be deployed in the `AppBase` directory alongside the assembly EXE file of the target application. The CLR also requires configuration files to follow a specific naming convention. A configuration file must have the same name as the assembly EXE file of the target application with an additional extension of `.config`.

Suppose you want to create a configuration file to customize the behavior of the application `MyApp.exe`. You can do so by creating a simple text file named `MyApp.exe.config` in the same directory as `MyApp.exe`. You must then add the appropriate XML content to this configuration file to properly configure the application.

> To configure an ASP.NET application, you must use a special file named web.config. Read *Essential ASP.NET* by Fritz Onion to get the complete story on configuring ASP.NET applications.

The XML vocabulary for .NET configuration files is based on an XML schema that was created especially for the .NET Framework. This chapter will include several examples of the XML elements and attributes that go into a configuration file. It is recommended that you also become familiar with the reference section in the .NET Framework SDK documentation that lists the various XML elements and attributes you can use within a configuration file. To find this reference section, search for *Configuration File Schema*.

The following types of information can be stored in an application configuration file:

- Configuration information that indicates that the application must be loaded into a particular version of the CLR, such as version 1.0 or 1.1
- Configuration information that contains application-specific data for values that change over time, such as a database connection string or a URL for an address somewhere on the Internet
- Configuration information about one of the application's dependent assemblies that informs the CLR which version to load and where to locate the physical assembly file at runtime

Let's look at the skeleton of a typical configuration file. To create a configuration file for the application MyApp.exe, you could start by creating a text file named MyApp.exe.config and adding the XML shown in Listing 11.1.

LISTING 11.1: Application configuration files contain XML-based configuration settings.

```
<!- MyApp.exe.config ->
<configuration>

  <startup>
    <!- application start-up settings go here ->
  </startup>

  <appSettings>
```

```
    <!- custom appSettings go here ->
  </appSettings>

  <runtime>
    <!- custom assembly settings go here ->
  </runtime>

</configuration>
```

Configuration files must have a top-level element named `<configuration>`. Within the `<configuration>` element, you can add other elements that are predefined by the .NET Configuration File Schema such as `<startup>`, `<appSettings>`, and `<runtime>`. When you add XML content to these elements, it affects the behavior of the application. Different elements and attribute settings affect an application in different ways, however.

When the CLR initializes an application such as `MyApp.exe`, it searches the `AppBase` directory to see whether it contains an associated configuration file. If the CLR finds a configuration file, it loads the file and reads its settings. If the CLR doesn't find an associated configuration file, it loads and runs the application using the default machine-wide settings.

A sticky issue arises with respect to authoring and testing configuration files. That is, the CLR will fail to load a configuration file that contains invalid XML or whose content is not considered valid with respect to the .NET Configuration File Schema. However, the CLR doesn't inform the user (or the developer) when it fails to load a configuration file; it simply proceeds as if the configuration file does not exist.

This behavior can lead to frustration when you are authoring and testing configuration files for the very first time. For example, some developers don't realize that XML is case sensitive. If you write a configuration file and add a top-level element named `<Configuration>` instead of `<configuration>`, a problem will occur. The configuration file is considered invalid, so none of its content will have any effect on the application's behavior. Instead, the application runs with the default machine-wide settings. Things would be less frustrating during testing if the CLR gave some indication that it failed while attempting to load the configuration file—but that's not how things work.

The Visual Studio .NET IDE provides some features that do make it more convenient to author and test configuration files. First, it supplies a special XML code editor that provides color coding and element completion when you are working on a file with an extension of `.xml` or `.config`. This feature makes Visual Studio .NET a more agreeable environment than a simple text editor such as `NOTEPAD.EXE` in which to modify the XML in a configuration file.

Visual Studio .NET also assists you in creating and maintaining a configuration file for a Windows application project or a console application project. You can create a new configuration file for an EXE-based application project by executing the `Add New Item...` command from the `Project` menu. It brings up a dialog box that allows you to choose from many different kinds of items. Scrolling down a bit, you will see that `Application Configuration File` is one of the options. When you choose to add an `Application Configuration File` to your project, Visual Studio .NET adds a configuration file named `app.config`. You use this file to edit and store the XML content that holds the configuration settings for your application.

When you build an application project that contains an `app.config` file, Visual Studio .NET knows what to do. After it builds the assembly file for the EXE, it copies the `app.config` file to the same directory. Visual Studio .NET also knows that it must rename the configuration file. If the file name for output assembly is `MyApp.exe`, for instance, it knows to rename the configuration file to `MyApp.exe.config`. This feature is very convenient because it allows you to modify a configuration file and then quickly test the effects of the modification within the Visual Studio .NET debugger.

Application Settings

A common motivation for working with configuration files is to maintain *application settings*. Application settings are valuable for storing data such as URLs, database connection strings, or other values that might change after an application has gone into production. You don't want to hard-code a value that might change later into your application. The main idea behind application settings is a practical one: It is much easier to change a value in a configuration file than to change a value that has been compiled into an assembly.

Application settings are stored within a configuration file in an `<appSettings>` element that must be placed directly within the top-level `<configuration>` element. Each application setting is created by using an `<add>` element containing a `key` attribute and a `value` attribute, as shown in the following code:

```
<configuration>
  <appSettings>
    <add key="MyUrl" value="http://www.AcmeCorp.com/MyData.xml" />
  </appSettings>
</configuration>
```

Once an application has been initialized, it can query for application settings by using the system-defined class `ConfigurationSettings`, which is defined inside the `System.Configuration` namespace. The `ConfigurationSettings` class exposes a shared property named `AppSettings`, which in turn exposes a default property that accepts a string parameter. When you access the default property of `AppSettings`, you should pass a string parameter containing the `key` name of the desired application setting. Note that the string parameter for the `key` name is not case sensitive. Here's an example of how to write your code:

```
Imports System.Configuration

Class MyApp
  Shared Sub Main()
    Dim UrlToData As String
    UrlToData = ConfigurationSettings.AppSettings("MyUrl")
    '*** now use URL to download and parse XML file
  End Sub
End Class
```

There are a few interesting things to note about using this technique to query for application settings. For example, what happens when you query for the `key` name of an application setting that has not been defined? The default property for `AppSettings` does not throw an exception, but rather returns a value of `Nothing`. This outcome will occur when the application configuration file doesn't contain that particular key-value pair as well as when the application doesn't have any associated application configuration file.

What happens when the application configuration file has invalid XML or does not conform to the .NET Configuration File Schema? Recall that the CLR simply ignores an invalid configuration file when it initializes an application. Matters are much different when you query for an application setting, however. If the application has an invalid configuration file, an attempt to access the default property of `AppSettings` will throw a `ConfigurationException`. Don't let this behavior catch you off guard. Consider structuring code that accesses application settings within a `Try` statement with a `Catch` block to handle the occasion when someone has modified the configuration file and left it in an invalid state.

The `machine.config` File

In addition to application-specific configuration settings, the .NET Framework maintains a set of machine-wide configuration settings in a file called `machine.config`. This file is located in a special directory of configuration files that is specific to a particular version of the CLR. Thus a machine that has the CLR version 1.0 and the CLR version 1.1 will have two different `machine.config` files. The actual path to the `machine.config` file for version 1.1 of the CLR on Windows Server 2003 will look something like this:

```
C:\WINDOWS\Microsoft.NET\Framework\v1.1.4322\CONFIG\machine.config
```

The `machine.config` file controls the overall behavior of the CLR as well as many of the other Microsoft frameworks that are built on top of the CLR, such as Windows Forms, ASP.NET, and .NET Remoting. The purpose of this file is to give the system administrator the ability to modify the behavior of all applications as well as the behavior of CLR and its many subsystems. Listing 11.2 shows a skeleton of a typical `machine.config` file.

LISTING 11.2: The `machine.config` file contains machine-wide configuration settings.

```
<configuration>

  <configSections>
    <!-- machine-wide configuration settings -->
  </configSections>

  <appSettings>
    <!-- machine-wide application settings -->
  </appSettings>
```

```
<system.diagnostics>
  <!- machine-wide diagnostic settings ->
</system.diagnostics>

<system.net>
  <!- machine-wide client-side HTTP settings ->
</system.net>

<system.web>
  <!- machine-wide ASP.NET settings ->
</system.web>

<system.runtime.remoting>
  <!- machine-wide .NET Remoting settings ->
</system.runtime.remoting>

<system.windows.forms jitDebugging="false">
  <!- machine-wide settings for Windows Forms framework ->
</system.windows.forms>

</configuration>
```

You can add application settings to the `machine.config` file if you like. Thus you can maintain application settings on a machine-wide basis, enabling them to be shared across applications. This flexibility can facilitate maintenance in a scenario where several applications all rely on the same database connection string.

There is one important thing to keep in mind when you are configuring application settings on a machine-wide basis. If you place an `<appSettings>` element in a `machine.config` file, you are required to place it after an element named `<configSections>`. If you place an `<appSettings>` element before the `<configSections>` element, the entire `machine.config` file becomes invalid.

What happens if an `<appSettings>` value has the same `key` name in an application configuration file and in the `machine.config` file? The CLR always inspects the application configuration file before looking in `machine.config`. If it finds the `key` name in the application configuration file, it stops searching. That means an `<appSettings>` value in an application configuration file will always override an `<appSettings>` value with an identical `key` name in `machine.config`.

The `machine.config` file is an important resource that must be locked down. Someone with evil intentions could really cause problems on your machine if he or she were able to freely edit the contents of your `machine.config` file. By default, only Windows users who are members of the `Administrators` group and the `Power Users` group are able to modify the `machine.config` file.

Building Assemblies

Before you can learn about assembly deployment, configuration, and versioning, you must understand how assemblies are named. Let's first look at the different parts that make up an assembly name and see how you control each aspect of an assembly name during the build process. Next, we'll consider how building an assembly with a public key and a digital signature can help to identify the assembly's producer and to detect traces of assembly tampering.

Assembly Naming

Each assembly has a name consisting of four parts:

- Friendly name
- Version number
- Culture setting
- Public key (or public key token)

Friendly Name

The *friendly name* of an assembly file is simply the file name without the extension. For example, the friendly name of an assembly with a file name of `MyLibrary.dll` is `MyLibrary`. The friendly name for a system-supplied assembly file such as `System.Data.dll` is `System.Data`.

Version Number

The *version number* consists of a string with four dot-delimited numbers in the form of `1.0.24.0`. These four numbers represent the major number, the minor number, the build number, and the revision number, respectively. We'll discuss what each of these parts signifies when we discuss assembly versioning later in this chapter.

You can build an assembly with a specific version number by adding the following code to the top of one of the source files in your project:

```
Imports System.Reflection

<Assembly: AssemblyVersion("1.0.24.0")>

'*** type definitions go here
```

This example demonstrates how to apply an assembly-level attribute named AssemblyVersion. Note that it imports the System.Reflection namespace because that's where the AssemblyVersion attribute is defined. When you apply an assembly-level attribute, it must be defined in a source file after any Imports statements but before any type definitions.

You should apply the AssemblyVersion attribute in one—and only one—source file for a project. If you apply this attribute more than once within a single project, the compiler will generate an error. Visual Studio .NET uses a convention in which all assembly-level attributes are added to a common file named AssemblyInfo.vb. It creates an AssemblyInfo.vb file whenever you create a new project. This file is a good place to maintain all of your assembly-level attributes, such as the AssemblyVersion attribute.

Every assembly has a version number. This is true even when you compile an assembly without explicitly assigning a version number to it. For example, what happens when you compile an assembly without using the AssemblyVersion attribute? The Visual Basic .NET compiler automatically assigns the assembly a version number of 0.0.0.0.

Culture Setting

A *culture setting* can contain a two-letter code indicating that an assembly has been localized for a particular spoken language. The two-letter code for English, for example, is en. A culture setting can also carry an optional country code. For example, a culture setting of en-US indicates that an assembly has been localized for English in the United States.

Most of the assemblies that you will produce and consume will not have a culture setting. Instead, an assembly that contains executable code typically has a culture setting of `neutral`.

The majority of assemblies that are localized for a particular spoken language are resource-only assemblies that do not contain executable code. Such an assembly is known as a *satellite assembly*. This book does not provide in-depth coverage of how to build, reuse, and deploy satellite assemblies. If you plan to localize applications using these kinds of assemblies, read *Windows Forms Programming in Visual Basic .NET* by Chris Sells. From this point on, this chapter will exclusively focus on culture-neutral assemblies.

Public Key

A *public key* is a unique value that identifies a particular company or developer. No two companies should ever use the same public key. Therefore, an assembly with a public key should be distinguishable from any other assembly produced by another company. This is true even in the case where an assembly produced by another company has an identical friendly name, version number, and culture setting.

As an example, imagine that two companies produced different assemblies named `MyLibrary.dll` and that both assemblies are culture-neutral and have the same version number. The CLR can still tell them apart as long as each company has compiled its build of `MyLibrary.dll` with a different public key.

A public key is a large value that occupies 128 bytes. This value is often stored in a compact binary format in a key file. Alternatively, it can be stored or written using a text-based hexadecimal format that looks like this:

```
00 24 00 00 04 80 00 00 94 00 00 00 06 02 00 00
00 24 00 00 52 53 41 31 00 04 00 00 01 00 01 00
AD 6A 11 52 AA AD FE 79 3F 6C 54 6F D1 7F F8 CB
C8 D8 34 40 B0 4C E8 03 0A F0 B2 E8 39 52 4D E2
69 1D A6 B8 18 11 33 A9 68 EA A6 7B BB B1 BD 5C
7E 97 47 90 62 F3 9B 15 6E 17 05 79 F5 53 DB 16
E7 7F 4B E6 A9 C0 DB 21 A4 78 28 5D 77 1F 19 3C
7B E1 D7 89 30 12 E3 3A 33 4A 3E A3 1F 07 38 AB
60 5A D7 38 A2 59 5E 6F 96 CF 9E FF D4 AD AF 66
2A 0F 8F FC AE E0 26 D8 C1 EA 0F 0E 6E 99 6F A5
```

Because a public key value is so large, a smaller 8-byte value known as the *public key token* is often used in its place. The public key token is often represented by a 16-character hexadecimal string value that looks like this:

```
29989D7A39ACF230
```

The CLR creates public key tokens from public key values using a special internal function. You should assume that a one-to-one correspondence exists between a public key value and a public key token. That is, for a specific public key value, there is exactly one corresponding public key token. Conversely, for a specific public key token, there is exactly one corresponding public key value. This relationship is very important because it allows a public key token to identify a public key value, which in turn allows a public key token to identify the company that has produced an assembly containing a particular public key value.

Lies, Damned Lies, and Statistics

The authors are lying to you when they say there is a one-to-one correspondence between a public key value and a public key token. The CLR cannot really provide the guarantee that it will never generate the same 8-byte public key token for two different 128-byte public key values. Instead, the CLR relies on the fact that it is highly unlikely that this duplication will ever occur.

For any two 128-byte public key values, there is a 1 in 18,446,744,073,709,600,000 chance that the CLR will generate the same 8-byte public key token. Therefore, it is reasonable to assume that two 128-byte public key values will never collide into the same 8-byte public key token. Statistically speaking, you have a better chance of meeting Bill Gates in a bar and being written into his will.

While humans would be hard-pressed to read and write 128-byte public key values, it's obviously much easier to read and write public key tokens. Public key tokens also conserve space. For this reason, the compiler uses the public key token instead of the public key value when adding a reference to track a dependent assembly.

Assembly Format Strings

You might find yourself writing a configuration file or writing code in which you must fully qualify an assembly by name. You can specify all four parts of an assembly name with an assembly *format string*. Here's an example of a format string with a fully qualified assembly name:

```
MyLibrary,
Version=1.0.24.0,
Culture=neutral,
PublicKeyToken=29989D7A39ACF230
```

This example uses line breaks to make the format string more readable. In reality, a format string should be placed in a single line. This point is important to remember when you are adding a format string to a configuration file or passing it as a parameter to a function or a command-line utility.

The first part of a format string holds the assembly's friendly name. The other three parts of the assembly name are then stored as name-value pairs delimited by commas. The preceding example of a format string involves an explicit setting for a friendly name, a version number, and a public key token. The culture setting in this assembly name has been explicitly qualified as `neutral`.

What should you do when you want to create a format string for an assembly that does not have a public key value? You create a format string that explicitly states that the public key token has a value of `null`. This would change the fully qualified format string in the preceding example to look like this:

```
MyLibrary, Version=1.0.24.0, Culture=neutral, PublicKeyToken=null
```

It's rarely necessary to generate a format string by hand. If you have access to an assembly file, you can generate the format string with a program that looks like this:

```
Imports System.Reflection

Class MyApp
  Shared Sub Main()
    Dim AssemblyPath As String = "C:\Apps\bin\MyLibrary.dll"
    Dim asm As [Assembly] = [Assembly].LoadFrom(AssemblyPath)
    System.Console.WriteLine(asm.FullName)
  End Sub
End Class
```

Strong Names

While a public key gives your assembly a unique name, its purpose goes much further than that. The CLR relies on public key technology to verify the identity of the company that produced the assembly and to prevent assembly tampering. Verification of the assembly producer's identity and protection against tampering is achieved by complementing the public key with a digital signature. An assembly that has both a public key and a digital signature is said to have a *strong name*.

To build an assembly with a strong name, you must first acquire a pair of keys:

- A public key whose value will be written into the physical image of assembly files
- A private key that will be used to generate digital signatures

The act of using the private key to write a digital signature to the image of an assembly file is known as *assembly signing*.

Let's step through the process of generating a public/private key pair and building an assembly with a strong name. This discussion will follow along the actual steps required in the build process. After you have seen the build mechanics, we will explore the theory behind how the strong name helps to identify the developer and to prevent tampering.

You cannot generate a key pair using Visual Studio .NET. Instead, you must step outside of Visual Studio .NET and use SN.EXE. SN.EXE—the .NET Framework Strong Name Utility—is a command-line utility that is supplied by the .NET Framework SDK. It allows you to create and manage the key pairs required to build strongly named assemblies. When you use SN.EXE, you pass command-line switches to it that perform various tasks. Note that the switches used by SN.EXE are case sensitive. To see a list of the supported switches, run SN.EXE and pass a question mark as a switch:

```
SN.EXE -?
```

> You must launch the Visual Studio .NET Command Prompt when you want to run SN.EXE. The Visual Studio .NET Command Prompt has been configured to include the path to this utility's location on your hard disk.

To create a key file that contains a new public/private key pair, you should call SN.EXE from the command line, passing the -k switch and the name of the target key file as parameters. For example, if you wanted to generate a key file named AcmeCorp.snk, you could issue the following instruction from the command line:

```
SN.EXE -k AcmeCorp.snk
```

While it's possible to generate a new public/private key pair for each assembly project, it's common practice to use a single public/private key pair for several different assembly projects. A company might use the same public/private key pair on a company-wide or department-wide basis, for example. Just make sure that each assembly you build using the same public/private key pair has a unique friendly name.

Once you've generated (or acquired) a key file with a public/private key pair, you are ready to build an assembly with a strong name. First, make sure you have placed the key file in your project directory. Next, add the following code to the top of one of the source files in your project such as AssemblyInfo.vb:

```
Imports System.Reflection

<Assembly: AssemblyVersion("1.0.24.0")>
<Assembly: AssemblyKeyFile("..\..\AcmeCorp.snk")>

'*** type definitions go here
```

This example demonstrates how to apply the assembly-level attribute named AssemblyKeyFile. This attribute is similar to the AssemblyVersion attribute in the sense that it is defined in the System.Reflection namespace.

Notice that the path to the key file in this example starts with two dots and a backslash followed by two more dots and another backslash:

```
..\..\AcmeCorp.snk
```

You should typically use this path when you have placed a key file such as AcmeCorp.snk in the project directory that holds other projects files such as the .vbproj file and your .vb source files. You need the dots and backslashes because this path is relative to the place where the Visual Basic .NET compiler is initially building the assembly. By default, Visual Studio .NET configures a new Visual Basic .NET project to use a subdirectory of the project directory, such as `\obj\Debug` or `\obj\Release`. Using the path `..\..\AcmeCorp.snk` simply tells the Visual Basic .NET compiler to move up two directories so that it can locate the key file during compilation.

When you build a project that contains the `AssemblyKeyFile` attribute, the Visual Basic .NET compiler builds the output assembly with a strong name. To do so, it must be able to read the values for the public key and the private key from the key file during compilation. The compiler records the full 128-byte public key value into the manifest of the output assembly file. It uses the private key to generate a digital signature that is appended to the end of the output assembly file. Figure 11.1 shows the resulting layout of the assembly file. If you open up a strongly named assembly using `ILDASM.EXE` and inspect the assembly manifest, you will be able to see its public key.

Assembly Signing and Tampering Protection

Now that you have seen the steps for building an assembly with a strong name, let's take a more in-depth look at the .NET Framework scheme to protect against tampering. Let's start by discussing digital signatures.

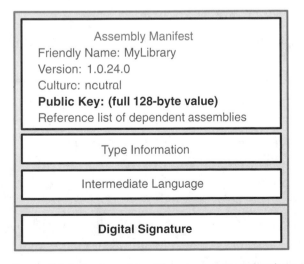

FIGURE 11.1: An assembly with a strong name contains a public key and a digital signature.

Generating Digital Signatures

A digital signature is generated using an advanced type of mathematics known as *cryptography*. In particular, the .NET Framework relies on two industry-standard forms of cryptography: one-way hash functions and asymmetric encryption.

A *one-way hash function* (also known as a hash function) allows you to create a digital fingerprint for a large digital object. With this type of cryptography, you feed a large digital object such as a public key or a file image to a hash function; the hash function, in turn, generates a much smaller piece of data known as a *hash value*. The cryptography involved does two important things:

- The hash function always produces an identical hash value for any given digital object.
- The hash function is very unlikely to generate an identical hash value for two different digital objects, even when two really large digital objects differ by even a single bit of information.

Recall that the CLR uses a special internal function to generate an 8-byte public key token from a 128-byte public key value. This special internal function calls a hash function to do its work. In this way, the CLR and compilers are able to produce identical public key tokens whenever they hash the same public key value. This scheme is also how the CLR ensures (for all practical purposes) that no two public key values will ever hash to the same public key token.

Apart from helping to create public key tokens, a hash function plays an important role in generating a digital signature for an assembly with a strong name. It does not generate a hash value from a public key value in this case, but rather creates a hash value from the physical image of the assembly file itself.

The hash value of an assembly file serves as its digital fingerprint for a particular build. The idea is that you can send two different assembly files to the same hash function to determine whether their physical layouts are identical. If both assembly files generate hash values that are equal, then one assembly file must be an exact copy of the other.

There's one more step to generating a digital signature from the hash value of an assembly file—asymmetric encryption. *Asymmetric encryption* is a type of cryptography in which data is encrypted and decrypted using public/private key pairs. The public key and the private key complement each other: One key is used to encrypt data and the other is used to decrypt data. In the case of signing an assembly, the private key generates the digital signature by encrypting the hash value of an assembly file. At some later time, the public key can be used to decrypt the digital signature and retrieve the hash value of that assembly file.

Now that you understand how the various cryptography pieces fit together, let's walk through the sequence of events that occurs during compilation. The compiler makes two passes to build an assembly with a strong name.

In the first pass, the compiler generates the image for the assembly file containing the friendly name, the version number, the culture setting, the public key value, the type information, and the executable code in the form of IL. The compiler cannot generate the digital signature during this first pass, so it just leaves some blank space at the end of the assembly file to act as a placeholder.

In the second pass, the compiler generates a hash value from the physical image of the assembly file that was built during the first pass. It then encrypts this hash value with the private key to generate the digital signature. As a final step, the compiler writes the digital signature into the placeholder at the end of the assembly file, as shown in Figure 11.1.

Strong Name Verification

To verify the authenticity of an assembly's digital signature after the assembly has been distributed by the company that produced it, the CLR uses a process known as *strong name verification*. The CLR uses the public key value within the assembly manifest to decrypt the digital signature and retrieve the hash value of the assembly image that was present during assembly signing. It then uses the same hash function to generate a hash value from the physical image of the current assembly file. At this point, the CLR has generated two different hash values with which it can conduct an important comparison.

When the CLR compares the two hash values, if they are equal, the CLR considers the verification test to be a success because it is sure of two things:

- The digital signature was generated by someone in possession of the private key.
- The physical image of the assembly file that is present during verification is an exact match of the physical image of the assembly file that was present during signing.

If the CLR determines that the two hash values are not equal, it considers the verification test to be a failure. In this case, the CLR knows that either the producer of the assembly did not possess the correct private key or the assembly's image was modified after it was signed.

To get a better sense of how the CLR uses strong name verification at runtime to prevent tampering with assemblies, let's walk through a typical scenario using `MyApp.exe` and `MyLibrary.dll`. Imagine you have built `MyLibrary.dll` with a strong name, then compiled `MyApp.exe` with a reference to `MyLibrary.dll`. Someone who lacks your private key would now find it far more difficult to change the behavior of the application on a production machine by replacing the real version of `MyLibrary.dll` with an adulterated version.

The assembly manifest for `MyApp.exe` contains a reference with the public key token associated with the public key value that's been compiled into `MyLibrary.dll`. Therefore, you have the guarantee that the CLR will only load a version of `MyLibrary.dll` that meets two important criteria:

- The assembly file for `MyLibrary.dll` must contain a public key value that matches the public key token in the assembly manifest of `MyApp.exe`.
- The version of `MyLibrary.dll` must have been signed by someone in possession of your private key.

Consider what happens when a user runs `MyApp.exe` and this application executes code that makes the first call to code in `MyLibrary.dll`. At this point, the CLR will attempt to load `MyLibrary.dll`. Because the CLR knows that `MyLibrary.dll` has a strong name, it runs a verification check as the first part of the loading process. The strong name verification check allows the CLR to detect whenever someone without access to the private key has made changes to the physical image of the assembly file.

Imagine that a bad guy wants to tamper with `MyLibrary.dll`. Perhaps he wants to change the behavior of one or more methods by modifying the IL within the assembly file. Ultimately, this bad guy plans to replace your build version of `MyLibrary.dll` on a production machine with an altered version so that he can change the behavior of the application `MyApp.exe` when it runs.

But the strong name verification scheme thwarts the bad guy. For any specific physical layout for the assembly file `MyLibrary.dll`, only one digital signature can possibly be valid. Therefore, any changes made to an assembly's physical image after it has been signed will render the existing digital signature invalid. If the bad guy adds, removes, or changes even a single bit of information from the physical image of `MyLibrary.dll` after it has been signed, the CLR can detect this tampering. A change to the physical image of the assembly requires re-signing the assembly file, but the bad guy cannot re-sign the assembly because he does not have the private key.

Note that the strong name verification scheme doesn't really prevent assembly tampering. It only prevents a tampering attempt from going undetected. When the CLR attempts to load a strongly named assembly with a digital signature that doesn't match the physical layout of the assembly file, the load attempt fails and the CLR throws a `System.IO.FileLoadException` with a message indicating that strong name verification has failed. In most cases, the hosting application will not be able to do its work. Nevertheless, this scenario is preferable to running the application with evil code that's been altered by the bad guy.

A critical point about tampering detection is that the entire scheme is based on the premise that the private key hasn't fallen into the wrong hands. Any individual who acquires your private key can build an assembly with your public key value and a valid digital signature. In this way, the bad guys can defeat the verification checks used by the CLR. If your company plans to distribute strongly named assemblies, you must carefully plan how to manage your private keys so they do not become compromised.

Referencing Assemblies without Strong Names

One important restriction applies when you are building an assembly project that has a strong name: You can only reference other assemblies that also have strong names. If you attempt to build an assembly project with a strong name while referencing an assembly without a strong name, you will receive a compile-time error.

Why does this restriction exist? It affects the reliability of the tampering protection. When you reference a strongly named assembly, the CLR prevents tampering from going undetected by running verification checks against the dependent assembly's digital signature. This scheme would be less reliable if your application depended on a strongly named assembly, which in turn depended on another assembly that did not have a strong name. A bad guy could replace the assembly that did not have the strong name, and the CLR could not detect this change. The CLR enforces this restriction so you are guaranteed that a strongly named assembly depends on only other strongly named assemblies.

Digital Signatures versus Digital Certificates

A digital signature associated with a strong name differs significantly from the *digital certificate* that is used in other security schemes, such as code signing with Authenticode or Secure Sockets Layer (SSL). It is important that you distinguish between the two, because a digital signature doesn't carry as much information as a digital certificate.

A digital certificate contains descriptive information about its owner. For example, it often contains a company name and contact information. When a vendor has used Authenticode to sign a piece of code such as a DLL, someone can inspect the digital certificate and determine the name of the company that produced the code.

Now compare the information stored within a digital certificate to the information stored within the public key value and a digital signature in the case of an assembly with a strong name. Neither the public key value nor the digital signature contains any descriptive information about who actually produced the assembly. Therefore, a strong name is not as powerful as a digital certificate when it comes to identifying the producer of an assembly.

How much assistance does a public key value and a digital signature really give you when it comes to identifying the producer of a particular assembly? A strong name can help to identify the producer of an assembly only if the public key value or token is known ahead of time.

Building an assembly with a strong name offers you the following guarantee: The DLL that is loaded and used by an application at runtime on a production machine has been produced by the same company as the DLL that was present on the development workstation at compile time. This guarantee is made possible because of the way references are recorded during compilation on a development workstation. Each reference tracks the identity of a dependent assembly's producer in the form of a public key token.

The .NET Framework does support signing an assembly with a digital certificate, which means that an assembly can carry descriptive information about its producer. Nevertheless, you will encounter assemblies with strong names and digital signatures far more often than you see assemblies with digital certificates.

Delay Signing

As described in the last section, the CLR verification scheme for strongly named assemblies breaks down whenever a private key falls into the wrong hands. You should take precautions to prevent this kind of problem from happening. After all, you don't want developers who are lackadaisical about security exposing your company's private key in a directory on their hard disk. You also don't want disgruntled employees or ex-employees who have been hired away by the competition leaving the company in possession of the private key.

How can a company protect itself from these possibilities? One highly recommended practice is to restrict private key access to only a few individuals. This tactic is especially beneficial in a large company with many developers. You can lower the risk of having the private key become compromised by storing it in a highly secure location and making it accessible to only a small group of trusted individuals.

While you can restrict access to the private key, sometimes every developer needs the ability to build an assembly containing your company's public key value. For example, developers may need to build an assembly that contains the proper public key value so that they can perform testing and debugging and so that they can compile other assemblies against it. For this reason, the CLR supports a scheme known as *delay signing*. Delay signing allows developers to build an assembly that contains a public key value without accessing the private key.

To use delay signing, start with SN.EXE. SN.EXE allows you to take a key file with a private/public key pair and use it to generate a second key file that contains only the public key. For example, you can take a key file that contains a public/private key pair such as AcmeCorp.snk and generate another key file with just the public key by calling SN.EXE with the following command-line instruction:

```
SN.EXE -p AcmeCorp.snk AcmeCorpPublicKey.snk
```

When you issue this command, SN.EXE reads the public key value from AcmeCorp.snk and writes it into a new key file named AcmeCorpPublicKey.snk. You can now distribute AcmeCorpPublicKey.snk to all the developers in your company without giving any of them access to the private key. The developers can, in turn, use the delay signing technique to build assemblies that contain the proper public key value by complementing the AssemblyKeyFile attribute with the AssemblyDelaySign attribute:

```
Imports System.Reflection

<Assembly: AssemblyVersion("1.0.24.0")>
<Assembly: AssemblyKeyFile("..\..\AcmeCorpPublicKey.snk")>
<Assembly: AssemblyDelaySign(True)>
```

When you build an assembly with delay signing, the compiler generates the assembly as usual, with one exception: It leaves out the digital signature. However, the compiler does reserve blank space for the digital signature in the physical layout of the assembly file. As a result, someone with the private key can sign the assembly at a later time.

Let's revisit our earlier example to put this idea into perspective. Imagine you built MyLibrary.dll using delay signing. Next, you compiled MyApp.exe against MyLibrary.dll. As part of the compilation process, MyApp.exe picked up the correct public key token for the public key value that is compiled inside MyLibrary.dll. You can now test and debug both assemblies on your development workstation without accessing the private key.

An assembly that has been compiled using delay signing cannot be verified by the CLR until it has been signed with the private key. This constraint creates a problem on a development workstation, because you often need to run and test the assembly before it has been signed. When you try to run `MyApp.exe` and test `MyLibrary.dll`, the CLR will fail to load the DLL because the DLL fails the strong name verification check.

To solve this problem `SN.EXE` provides the ability to disable these verification checks for a specific assembly on a machine-wide basis. To disable verification checks for `MyLibrary.dll`, you can call `SN.EXE` and pass the `-Vr` switch:

```
SN.EXE -Vr MyLibrary.dll
```

Calling `SN.EXE` in this manner adds an entry to the Windows Registry that instructs the CLR to skip strong name verification checks for any version of `MyLibrary.dll` that contains the same public key value. Note that `SN.EXE` also supports a `-Vu` switch to re-enable verification checks for an assembly and a `-Vl` switch to list the assemblies for which verification checks are currently disabled.

Of course, the ability to disable verification checks poses a potential security problem. A bad guy who disables security checks for an assembly can replace that assembly with one of his own without being detected by the CLR. For this reason, only Windows users in the `Administrators` group or the `Power Users` group are assigned permissions to disable verification checks for an assembly using `SN.EXE`.

What happens when it's time to distribute an assembly such as `MyLibrary.dll` that has been built with delay signing? After the testing and debugging are complete, the assembly must be signed prior to distribution. Of course, assembly signing can be done only by someone with access to the private key. Someone with the private key can use `SN.EXE` and the `-R` switch to sign the assembly by issuing the following command-line instruction:

```
SN.EXE -R MyLibrary.dll AcmeCorp.snk
```

When you call `SN.EXE` using the `-R` switch, it generates the digital signature in the same fashion as the compiler uses the private key to generate a hash value from the physical layout of the assembly file `MyLibrary.dll`. Once `SN.EXE` has generated the digital signature, it writes it into the space that was reserved earlier by the compiler. At this point, `MyLibrary.dll` is ready for distribution.

Deploying Assemblies

So far, you have learned about the four parts that make up an assembly name as well as the mechanics for building an assembly with a version number and a strong name. Now let's move on to your options for deploying assembly DLLs on a developer workstation or a production machine.

The four-part name of an assembly is *location independent*. That is, no part of the name of an assembly DLL tells the CLR or a hosting application anything about the location of the actual assembly file. This location independence provides a valuable degree of flexibility, because a single assembly DLL can be deployed in several different ways and in many different places. It also means that the CLR must use something other than the assembly name to locate the assembly file at runtime.

Deploying an assembly DLL is different than deploying a COM DLL, largely because COM DLLs require entries in the Windows Registry containing their physical path so that the COM runtime can locate them when needed. In contrast, assembly DLL deployment doesn't involve adding entries to the Windows Registry. As a consequence, the CLR must use some other means to locate an assembly DLL at runtime.

There are three primary ways to deploy an assembly DLL on a target machine:

- A DLL can be deployed as a private assembly by locating it in the AppBase directory.
- A DLL can be installed in a machine-wide repository called the Global Assembly Cache (GAC).
- An assembly DLL can be configured with a `<codeBase>` element, which allows the CLR to download the DLL on demand from across the network the first time it's used by a hosting application.

Each technique has advantages and disadvantages. Let's examine each one in greater detail.

Deploying Private Assemblies

Deploying a DLL as a private assembly involves the least amount of complexity. You simply deploy the DLL inside the `AppBase` directory of the hosting application or inside a subdirectory of the `AppBase` directory. It most cases, it's really that easy.

One of the biggest advantages of private assembly deployment is that it allows for *XCOPY deployment*. An application, its configuration file, and all its private assemblies are contained within a single directory structure. Once your application and its private assemblies have been thoroughly tested, you can deploy the application as a whole by copying the `AppBase` directory structure to the target machine via a utility such as `XCOPY.EXE` or a network transfer protocol such as FTP. You can even deploy an application by using drag-and-drop in Windows Explorer. Once you have copied the `AppBase` directory structure, the application is ready for use.

A private assembly can never be deployed outside the `AppBase` directory; it must be deployed inside the `AppBase` directory or in one of its subdirectories. This constraint represents a noteworthy limitation of private assembly deployment. You cannot share a private assembly across two or more applications that are deployed in separate directories. Of course, that's why they are called private assemblies: A private assembly is private to one particular application.

Private assemblies offer definite benefits when you need to deploy multiple versions of the same assembly DLL on the same machine. Two different applications can each be deployed with a different version of the same assembly DLL. Unlike the way deployment has worked in the past with standard Windows DLLs and COM DLLs, every managed application can be deployed along with the version of an assembly DLL against which it was built and tested. As a result, you don't have to worry about an installation program for one application overwriting an earlier version of an assembly DLL that's being used by another application.

Loading a Private Assembly

The CLR discovers the physical path to a private assembly at runtime through a searching process known as *probing*. When CLR starts probing for a private assembly, it determines the file name of the assembly by taking its friendly name and adding an extension of .dll.

Once the CLR determines the name of the target assembly file, it searches inside the AppBase directory in an attempt to find it. If the CLR finds the assembly file, probing stops and the CLR loads the assembly into memory. If the CLR cannot locate the assembly file, it continues the probing process by looking in a subdirectory of the AppBase directory that has the same name as the assembly itself. For example, if the CLR was probing for an assembly named MyLibrary, it would look for a subdirectory named MyLibrary in the AppBase directory that contained the assembly file MyLibrary.dll.

If the CLR finds the assembly file in this subdirectory, probing stops and the CLR loads the assembly into memory. If the CLR cannot locate the assembly file in this subdirectory, it continues the probing process by looking in the same two directories for an assembly file with an .exe extension instead of a .dll extension.

As you see, the CLR automatically looks at four different paths while probing for a private assembly. For example, if an application had an App-Base directory with a path of C:\MyApp, the CLR would probe for the assembly file using these four file paths:

```
c:\MyApp\MyLibrary.dll
c:\MyApp\MyLibrary\MyLibrary.dll
c:\MyApp\MyLibrary.exe
c:\MyApp\MyLibrary\MyLibrary.exe
```

The CLR will automatically inspect these four file paths when probing for a culture-neutral assembly. When it is probing for a satellite assembly with a cultural identifier, the CLR will also look in subdirectories that have the same name as the cultural identifier itself. This extra support makes it easier to deploy multiple resource-only assemblies that have been localized for different spoken languages.

A private assembly can be deployed in any subdirectory inside the App-Base directory. If you choose a subdirectory with a name other than the ones outlined above, the CLR requires extra configuration information to assist it during the probing process. Namely, you must add a special <probing> element to the application configuration file to give the CLR a probing hint.

Suppose you wanted to create a subdirectory named `MyAssemblies` inside the `AppBase` directory and then deploy some of your dependent assemblies inside of this subdirectory. The application would not be able to load these private assemblies until you modified your application configuration file to look like this:

```
<configuration>
  <runtime>
    <assemblyBinding xmlns="urn:schemas-microsoft-com:asm.v1">
      <probing privatePath="MyAssemblies"/>
    </assemblyBinding>
  </runtime>
</configuration>
```

The `<probing>` element contains a `privatePath` attribute that tells the CLR where to look. If you want to add multiple subdirectories to the private path, you can concatenate them together using a semicolon-delimited string.

Notice that the `<probing>` element in the preceding file has been placed inside another element named `<assemblyBinding>`. The `<assembly-Binding>` element includes an attribute named `xmlns` whose value contains an XML namespace specific to .NET configuration files. If you type this XML content by hand, make sure you don't introduce any typographical errors. Missing even a single character will drop you right into the middle of assembly purgatory.

As noted earlier, the CLR looks through a predetermined sequence of directories during probing. Given a `privatePath` value of `MyAssemblies`, the CLR will now probe for an assembly named `MyLibrary` in the following order:

```
C:/Apps/MyLibrary.DLL
C:/Apps/MyLibrary/MyLibrary.DLL
C:/Apps/MyAssemblies/MyLibrary.DLL
C:/Apps/MyAssemblies/MyLibrary/MyLibrary.DLL
C:/Apps/MyLibrary.EXE.
C:/Apps/MyLibrary/MyLibrary.EXE.
C:/Apps/MyAssemblies/MyLibrary.EXE.
C:/Apps/MyAssemblies/MyLibrary/MyLibrary.EXE
```

The sequence of file paths in which the CLR probes for an assembly file is important because the probing process stops once the CLR locates an assembly file with the correct file name. If you deploy an application along with one version of `MyLibrary.dll` in the `AppBase` directory and a second version in the subdirectory `MyAssemblies`, which DLL file will the CLR load? The CLR will load the DLL in the `AppBase` directory, because it is always the first directory searched during the probing process.

You can deploy an assembly as a private assembly whether or not it has a strong name. The presence of a strong name, however, forces the CLR to do a little extra work while it is loading a private assembly.

First, the CLR always runs a strong name verification check at load time to ensure that the assembly has a valid digital signature. This process was described earlier in this chapter. The CLR then runs a second check to ensure that the assembly being loaded has the proper version number. We will defer the discussion of how the CLR determines the proper version number until later in this chapter. For now, just note that these extra checks occur only when you load a private assembly with a strong name. No such checks are performed when you load a private assembly without a strong name.

The .NET Framework Configuration Administrative Tool

When you are configuring applications and their dependent assemblies, the .NET Framework provides a convenient GUI-based tool for this purpose named *Microsoft .NET Framework Configuration Administrative Tool* (`MSCOR-CFG.MSC`). This administrative tool is a Microsoft Management Console (MMC) snap-in that can be launched from a shortcut in the `Administrative Tools` group (found under the Windows `Start` menu). Figure 11.2 shows this utility's user interface.

The Microsoft .NET Framework Configuration Administrative Tool can do most of the work of creating an application configuration file automatically. Using it, you can configure an application by interacting with standard Windows controls such as text boxes, radio buttons, and check boxes. When you configure an application in this manner, the Microsoft .NET Framework Configuration Administrative Tool does the grunt work of creating the appropriate XML content and adding it to the application configuration file.

Deploying Assemblies in the Global Assembly Cache

Private assemblies are more useful in some deployment scenarios and less useful in others. One potential problem with a private assembly is that it is private to a single application. You should not use private assembly

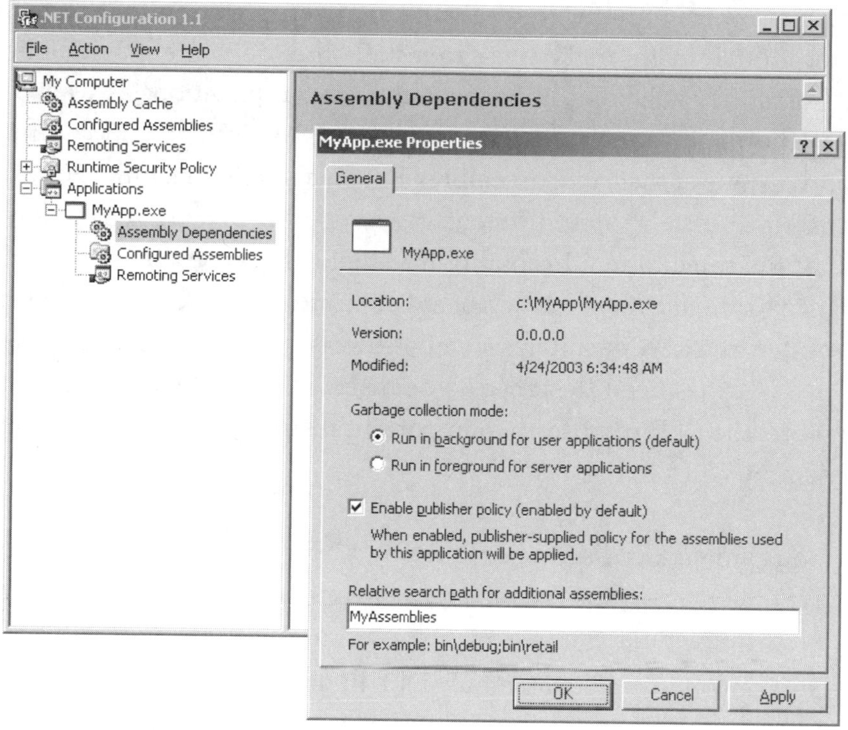

FIGURE 11.2: The .NET Framework Configuration Administrative Tool facilitates application configuration.

deployment when you would like to share an assembly DLL across several applications on the same machine. The best way share an assembly DLL in this way is to install it into a machine-wide repository named the *Global Assembly Cache (GAC)*. Once you install an assembly DLL into the GAC, that assembly is available to any application on that machine.

Benefits and Drawbacks of Using the GAC

Installing an assembly DLL in the GAC eliminates path dependency problems between an application and a dependent DLL. That is, it no longer matters where the `AppBase` directory for an application is located. The CLR can always find and load an assembly DLL when it has been installed in the GAC. As a result, you don't have to worry about deploying the DLL in the `AppBase` directory as you do with private assembly deployment.

Microsoft deploys its own assemblies, such as `mscorlib.dll`, `System.dll`, and `System.Data.dll`, in the GAC, so these system-provided assemblies are automatically available to any application that runs from any location. It might make sense to install other dependent assemblies in the GAC if they will be used by many different applications as well.

Another significant benefit to using the GAC is that you can install many versions of the same assembly DLL on a single machine. For example, you can install three different versions of `MyLibrary.dll` into the GAC at the same time. This ability is valuable because different applications can load whichever version of `MyLibrary.dll` makes the most sense. As you see, the GAC facilitates side-by-side assembly deployment.

The GAC has been designed to be a secure repository of assemblies. Therefore, the CLR imposes two important restrictions on the installation of assembly DLLs in the GAC:

- You cannot add assemblies to the GAC or remove them unless you are a member of the Administrators group or the Power Users group on the target machine.
- You cannot install an assembly DLL in the GAC unless it contains a strong name, because the CLR performs a strong name verification check on the assembly's digital signature whenever you install an assembly DLL in the GAC. This check provides the guarantee that the GAC contains only assemblies that have been signed by someone in possession of the proper private key.

You will experience problems if you try to install assemblies that have been built with delay signing into the GAC. Such an assembly cannot pass the strong name verification check conducted by the CLR when you attempt to install it into the GAC. To install an assembly built with delay signing into the GAC, you must disable strong name verification checks for the assembly using `SN.EXE` as described earlier this chapter.

Interestingly, the CLR does not perform strong name verification checks on assemblies in the GAC when it loads them into applications at runtime. Instead, the CLR assumes that assemblies in the GAC are trusted. Assembly deployment in the GAC therefore provides a small optimization benefit. It is the only place from which you can load a strongly named assembly without paying the price of running a strong name verification check on the assembly's digital signature at runtime.

Assembly deployment in the GAC does increase the cost of deployment, because the GAC does not allow for the possibility of XCOPY deployment from across the network. Instead, GAC deployment requires someone with a privileged Windows account to install an assembly locally on the target machine. A more sophisticated approach for installing assemblies into the GAC on target machines from across the network requires packaging them inside MSI files and distributing them with a complex and more costly network management tool such as Active Directory or Systems Management Server (SMS).

Assembly Management within the GAC

The CLR contains a system component named the *assembly manager* that takes on the responsibilities of storing assembly files in the GAC and loading them at runtime when they are first used by an application. The assembly manager is loaded from the system component FUSION.DLL.

The manner in which the assembly manager stores and retrieves assembly files on a target machine should be considered a private implementation detail of the CLR. This section describes some of these details simply to give you a better sense of how the GAC works. In the real world, you should never design applications or use deployment techniques that rely on these private details because they are likely to change in future versions of the CLR.

The assembly manager stores assembly files in the GAC using a special directory structure in the Windows file system. This directory structure is created as a subdirectory in the Windows directory with the following path:

```
C:\Windows\assembly\GAC
```

When you install assemblies into the GAC, the assembly manager creates new directories in which to store them. In fact, the assembly manager will create a unique directory for each assembly that is stored in the GAC. The reason for this practice is that the GAC must be able to accommodate two assemblies whose names differ only by their public key value or their version number. After all, many different assemblies could have the file name MyLibrary.dll. Recognizing this possibility, the assembly manager creates a unique directory for each assembly using all four parts of the assembly name. For example, imagine you install version `1.0.24.0` of `MyLibrary.dll` in the GAC and this assembly has a public key token of `29989d7a39acf230`. The assembly manager creates a new directory with the following path:

```
C:\WINDOWS\assembly\GAC\MyLibrary\1.0.24.0__29989d7a39acf230
```

As you can see, the assembly manager uses its own internal naming scheme for directories when it stores an assembly in the GAC. When the assembly manager needs to load an assembly with a specific four-part name, it knows where to locate the assembly because it follows the same naming scheme.

When you want to install an assembly in the GAC, you are not required to interact directly with `FUSION.DLL`. Instead, you use a utility that interacts with `FUSION.DLL` on your behalf. To install an assembly into the GAC on a development workstation for testing, you can use a command-line utility named `GACUTIL.EXE` that ships with the .NET Framework SDK. This utility provides an `-i` switch that allows you to install an assembly with the following command-line instruction:

```
GACUTIL.EXE -i MyLibrary.dll
```

To install an assembly in the GAC using this technique, you must have access to the assembly file. Note that the assembly manager makes a copy of the assembly file when it's installed in the GAC. After installation, the assembly manager is only concerned with this copy. You can therefore delete the original assembly file after it has been installed in the GAC. If you installed the assembly file from a CD, for example, you can remove the CD without any problems. If you installed the assembly file from a network share, you can disconnect from the network without any problems.

The `GACUTIL.EXE` utility also provides a means of removing an assembly from the GAC—namely, the `-u` switch. However, this brings up an interesting point about using the `GACUTIL.EXE` utility. You have just seen that you pass the name of the assembly file when you want to install an assembly in the GAC. When you want to remove an assembly, however, you do not pass a file name. You pass the friendly name instead:

```
GACUTIL.EXE -u MyLibrary
```

This instruction will remove any assembly from the GAC whose friendly name is `MyLibrary`. It can therefore be used to remove several different versions of `MyLibrary` simultaneously. If you want to remove only one specific version, you can qualify the friendly name using a more-specific format string:

```
GACUTIL.EXE -u MyLibrary, Version=1.0.24.0
```

In some situations, you might want to qualify the public key token and the culture setting as well. To fully qualify the assembly name that you want to remove, you can use all four parts of the assembly name in a format string (see the section "Assembly Format Strings" earlier in this chapter).

You can also examine and manage the assemblies in the GAC using a GUI-based utility called the *Assembly Cache Viewer*. The Assembly Cache Viewer is an administrative utility that runs within Windows Explorer as a Windows shell extension named `SHFUSION.DLL`. To access the Assembly Cache Viewer, you launch Windows Explorer and navigate to the `\Windows\assembly` directory, as shown in Figure 11.3.

The view supplied by the Assembly Cache Viewer does not show the actual physical layout of the directory structure maintained by the GAC. Instead, it provides a prettier, flattened-out picture where all the assemblies can be seen within a single scrollable view. Every assembly is displayed with its friendly name, version number, culture setting, and public key token.

The Assembly Cache Viewer is available on production machines with the CLR as well as on development workstations. It provides administrators and developers alike with a simple means for installing and removing assemblies from the GAC. To install an assembly DLL, you can drag an assembly file from Windows Explorer and drop it on top of the view provided by the Assembly Cache Viewer. To remove an assembly from the GAC, you can select it in the Assembly Cache Viewer and press the Delete key on your keyboard.

`FUSION.DLL` is the only component that's allowed to read and write files into the GAC. When you manage assemblies using the Assembly Cache Viewer, the Windows shell extension `SHFUSION.DLL` interacts with `FUSION.DLL` behind the scenes to carry out your commands. You must be a

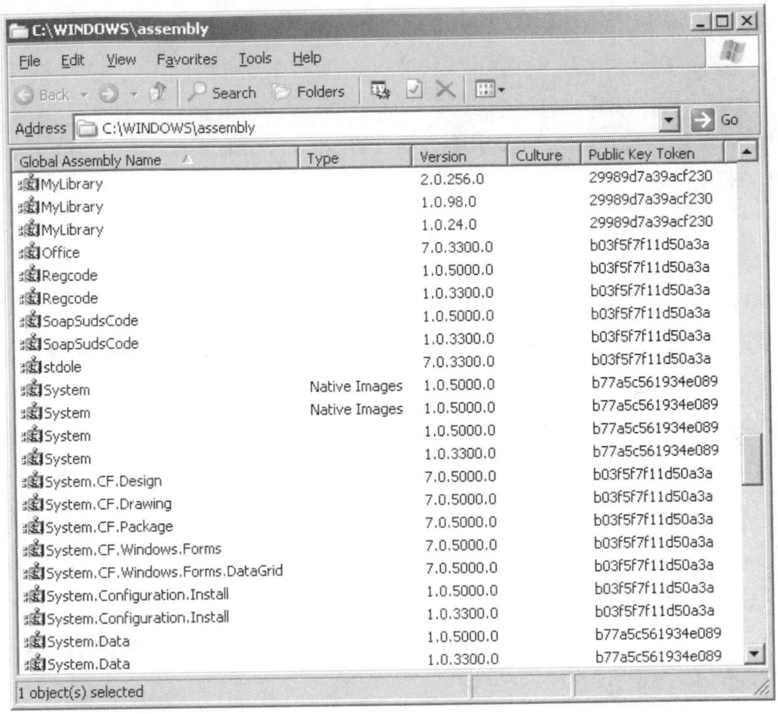

FIGURE 11.3: The Assembly Cache Viewer allows you to examine and manage assemblies in the GAC.

member of the Administrators group or the Power Users group on the target machine to install or remove assemblies with the Assembly Cache Viewer.

The most polished way to deploy assembly DLLs that are installed in the GAC in a production environment is to use Microsoft Installer technology. It requires that you (or someone in your company) learn how to build MSI files to distribute your assembly files. You can then create an MSI file that automates the installation of an assembly DLL in the GAC. The installation program within an MSI file can also be written to associate an assembly DLL with a specific Windows application. With this approach, the Windows operating system can automatically remove the assembly DLL from the GAC if the Windows application is ever uninstalled.

If you are interested in creating MSI files for distributing your applications and assembly DLLs, you will be glad to know that Visual Studio .NET can help. You can create a new project and choose the Setup Wizard under the `Setup and Deployment` projects folder. This type of project can be used to create an MSI file. Furthermore, Visual Studio .NET supplies a handy designer that makes it easier to add assemblies, extra content, Windows shortcuts, and custom instructions into the installation program that is built into the output MSI file.

Deploying Assemblies with a `<codeBase>` Element

The third option for deploying a dependent assembly on a target machine is to configure it using a `<codeBase>` element. A configured `<codeBase>` element is powerful because it makes it possible to download an assembly DLL from across the network. As a result, the CLR can download an assembly DLL to a target machine on demand the first time it is used by an application.

While you can configure a dependent assembly without a strong name using a `<codeBase>` element, that assembly must then be deployed with many of the same restrictions as a private assembly. A `<codeBase>` element is far more flexible when you are configuring a dependent assembly with a strong name, because an assembly with a strong name can be deployed outside of the `AppBase` directory.

For example, you can use a `<codeBase>` element to deploy a strongly named assembly in any directory on the target machine. You can even deploy a strongly named assembly on a file server or a Web server. You can then use a `<codeBase>` element to configure an application on a target machine to download that strongly named assembly on demand from across the network. If you plan to deploy your assemblies using `<code-Base>` elements, you should consider building them with strong names to take advantage of this extra flexibility.

Configuring a `<codeBase>` Element

You can add a `<codeBase>` element to an application configuration file to supply the CLR with custom configuration information about a dependent assembly. Listing 11.3 shows an example of such an application-specific `<codeBase>` element. Alternatively, you can add a `<codeBase>` element to the `machine.config` file to configure a dependent assembly on a machine-wide basis.

LISTING 11.3: A `<codeBase>` **element can configure a dependent assembly for download-on-demand.**

```
<!- MyApp.exe.config ->
<configuration>
  <runtime>
    <assemblyBinding xmlns="urn:schemas-microsoft-com:asm.v1">
      <dependentAssembly>
        <assemblyIdentity
          name="MyLibrary" publicKeyToken="29989D7A39ACF230" />
        <codeBase
          version="1.0.24.0"
          href="http://www.AcmeCorp.com/Downloads/MyLibrary.dll"/>
      </dependentAssembly>
    </assemblyBinding>
  </runtime>
</configuration>
```

Examine the `<codeBase>` element shown in Listing 11.3. As you can see, a `<codeBase>` element must be placed inside a `<dependentAssembly>` element. The `<dependentAssembly>` element in this example also has an inner `<assemblyIdentity>` element, which in turn has attributes to identify the friendly name and the public key token of the dependent assembly being configured. If you do not include information about the assembly's culture setting, the CLR assumes it has a culture setting of `neutral`.

While a `<dependentAssembly>` element contains only one `<assemblyIdentity>` element, it can have many inner `<codeBase>` elements. In fact, each separate version of an assembly needs a separate `<codeBase>` element. While the `<dependentAssembly>` element in Listing 11.3 contains only a single `<codeBase>` element for version `1.0.24.0`, it would be possible to add more `<codeBase>` elements for other versions of this assembly as well.

The `<codeBase>` element contains an `href` attribute in addition to the `version` attribute. The `href` attribute provides the CLR with a *uniform resource identifier (URI)* that allows it to determine the location of the assembly file. If you want to configure a dependent assembly on the local file system using a `<codeBase>` element, you should configure the `href` attribute with a URI that looks like this:

```
href="file:///c:\AcmeCorpSharedAssemblies\MyLibrary.dll"
```

If you want to configure a dependent assembly for download from a file server using a UNC path name, you should configure the `href` attribute with a URI that looks like this:

```
href="file://AcmeCorpFileServer1\Downloads\MyLibrary.dll"
```

If you want to configure a dependent assembly for download from a Web server using HTTP, you should configure the `href` attribute with a URI that looks like this:

```
href="http://AcmeCorp.com/Downloads/MyLibrary.dll"
```

You can also configure a `<codeBase>` element for a dependent assembly using the .NET Framework Configuration Administrative Tool. This approach eliminates the need to deal directly with the XML that goes into an application configuration file or into the `machine.config` file. Figure 11.4 shows a tabbed dialog box that allows you to enter a version number and a URI. When you type this information into the tabbed dialog box and then

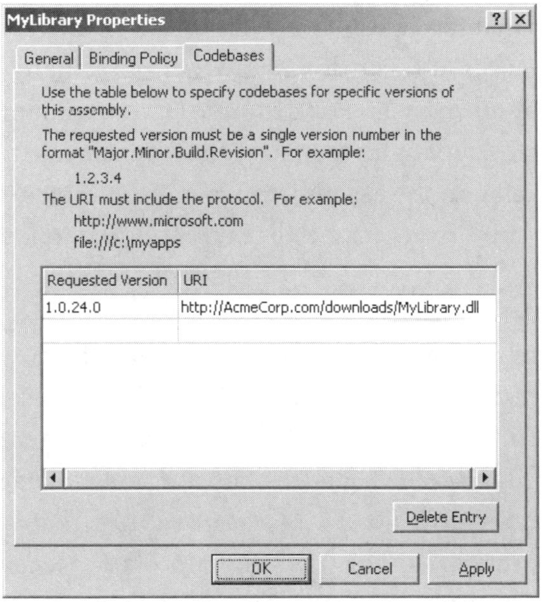

FIGURE 11.4: You can easily configure a `<codeBase>` element with the GUI-based administrative tool.

click OK or Apply, the .NET Framework Configuration Administrative Tool modifies your application configuration file by including the proper XML content for the <codeBase> element.

The Download Cache

What happens when the assembly manager of the CLR downloads a dependent assembly from across the network using a <codeBase> element? The assembly manager does not load the assembly file directly into memory within a running application. Instead, it downloads the assembly file and writes it to disk in a temporary storage area known as the *download cache*.

This caching scheme has one obvious advantage: It eliminates the need to copy the assembly file across the network more than once. The assembly file just needs to be downloaded by the assembly manager and persisted to disk the first time it's used by an application. The next time any application needs to load that assembly, the assembly manager can simply load the assembly file from the download cache on the local hard drive—it doesn't have to download the assembly from across the network again.

The download cache differs from the GAC in two important ways. The first difference is that the GAC is truly a machine-wide repository, whereas the download cache is not. The download cache is actually managed by the CLR on a user-by-user basis. For example, if a user named Bob runs an application that downloads an assembly file from across the network using a <codeBase> element, the assembly manager will store the assembly file within a private subdirectory for this user under the following path:

```
C:\Documents And Settings\Bob\Local Settings\Application Data\
```

The second big difference between the GAC and the download cache has to do with security and trust. The assembly manager treats the GAC as a secure and fully trusted repository of assemblies. The download cache is less secure and not fully trusted. Therefore, the assembly manager treats assemblies loaded from the download cache as *mobile code* that is subject to additional security restrictions. This point is important because the CLR runs mobile code in a restricted sandbox to protect the host machine from attacks.

The additional security restrictions placed on mobile code by the assembly manager are provided by a layer of the CLR known as *Code Access Secu-*

rity (CAS). The assembly manager uses CAS to collect certain forms of evidence about an assembly when it is loaded into memory. The assembly manager then uses this evidence together with preconfigured policy information to create a set of permissions for each assembly.

An assembly loaded from the GAC or any other place on the local hard drive is considered to be fully trusted by the assembly manager; the CLR places no security restrictions on such code. Because mobile code does not originate from the local hard drive, however, the assembly manager loads it with a much more restrictive set of permissions by default. For example, mobile code does not have unrestricted access to read and write files to the local hard disk by default.

If you plan to use mobile code in your deployment strategies, you must learn the concepts and administrative details associated with CAS. This book will not cover these details. You can find the necessary information by searching the .NET Framework SDK documentation for *Code Access Security*. If you want to understand how CAS works from the bottom up, read the chapter dedicated to Code Access Security in *Essential .NET* by Don Box.

The CLR's Assembly Loading Process

You have just seen three different options for deploying an assembly. Now it's time to discuss what happens at runtime when the assembly manager needs to load a dependent assembly into a running application. The assembly manager starts by generating a format string that contains the four-part name of the assembly being sought. It usually determines the format string by looking at a reference in the manifest of another assembly.

Let's walk through an example. Suppose you run `MyApp.exe`, whose first line of code requires the CLR to load `MyLibrary.dll`. The assembly manager looks inside the assembly manifest for `MyApp.exe` and discovers the four-part name of the assembly file for `MyLibrary.dll` that was present when `MyApp.exe` was compiled. If `MyLibrary.dll` has a strong name, the assembly manager generates a format string containing a public key token:

```
MyLibrary,
Version=1.0.24.0,
Culture=neutral,
PublicKeyToken=29989D7A39ACF230
```

If `MyLibrary.dll` does not have a strong name, the assembly manager generates a format string with a public key token that is equal to `null`:

```
MyLibrary,
Version=1.0.24.0,
Culture=neutral,
PublicKeyToken=null
```

At this point, the assembly manager has obtained the four-part name of the dependent assembly that was present during the compilation of `MyApp.exe`. Next, it looks for any configuration information that might redirect the application to use a different version number. Let's defer a discussion of version redirection until later in this chapter. For now, just assume that the version number is not redirected.

Now the assembly manager is ready to search for the assembly file. It conducts its search in three steps:

1. Search for the assembly in the GAC
2. Search for the assembly using configuration information in a `<code-Base>` element
3. Search for the assembly by probing within the AppBase directory

The assembly manager always looks in the GAC first. This has an important implication. Think about what would happen if you deployed three different copies of the same assembly DLL. For example, suppose you put one copy of the assembly DLL in the `AppBase` directory, deploy a second copy using a `<codeBase>` element, and install a third copy in the GAC. The assembly manager will always load the assembly DLL from the GAC. Once it finds an assembly in the GAC, it stops the search and doesn't look anywhere else.

Remember—the GAC is a secure repository that contains only strongly named assemblies. Therefore, the assembly manager doesn't bother looking in the GAC when it's searching for an assembly without a strong name. That would just be a waste of time.

If the assembly manager cannot find the assembly in the GAC, it then determines whether the assembly has a configured `<codeBase>` element. If it finds such a `<codeBase>` element, the assembly manager checks whether the URI points to a location on the local hard disk. If it does, the assembly manager loads the assembly file directly from that location.

If the URI in the `<codeBase>` element points to an assembly file on another machine, however, the assembly manager knows that it can only load a local copy of the assembly file from the download cache. Therefore, it checks the download cache to see whether the assembly file has already been downloaded. If the assembly file has not been downloaded, then the assembly manager copies it from across the network to the download cache. It then loads the assembly file from the download cache.

What happens if the assembly manager attempts to download a dependent assembly using the information in a `<codeBase>` element but the URI doesn't point to an accessible assembly file? This situation can arise if the URI points to an incorrect address for the assembly file, or if the network or the server machine holding the assembly file is not available. If the assembly manager cannot download the file, the load attempt will fail and the assembly manager will throw a `FileNotFoundException`. Note that the assembly manager does not continue searching in other places, such as the `AppBase` directory.

Also note that the assembly manager will inspect an assembly file that has been downloaded to the download cache from across the network. The assembly file must match with respect to its friendly name, version number, culture setting, and public key token. If a mismatch occurs, the assembly manager will fail the load attempt and throw an exception.

If the assembly manager cannot find an assembly file in the GAC and the assembly has no configured `<codeBase>` element, it resorts to probing the `AppBase` directory. The assembly manager conducts the probing process first by looking directly in the `AppBase` directory and then by looking in various subdirectories according to the rules outlined earlier this chapter in the "Loading a Private Assembly" section.

What happens if the assembly manager cannot find the assembly file while probing within the `AppBase` directory? It gives up and throws a `FileNotFoundException` to the line of code that triggered the assembly manager to begin looking for the assembly in the first place.

The assembly manager always inspects an assembly file that is being loaded as a result of its probing. This inspection is meant to ensure that the assembly has the expected culture setting and the expected public key token. When the assembly manager loads an assembly with a strong name, it also inspects the assembly file to ensure that the assembly has the expected version number. If the assembly manager finds an unexpected version number, culture setting, or public key token, it fails the load attempt and throws a `FileLoadException`.

The Assembly Binding Log Viewer

As you might suspect, many things can go wrong when you are trying to deploy an application along with dependent assembly DLLs. If you experience problems during testing, try using the handy utility known as the *Assembly Binding Log Viewer* (FUSLOGVW.EXE) that is distributed as part of the .NET Framework SDK. This utility allows you to trace the assembly manager's steps when an attempt to load a dependent assembly fails.

To use the Assembly Binding Log Viewer, you must first launch the executable file FUSLOGVW.EXE. You can then instruct the assembly manager to begin logging assembly load attempt failures by checking the `Log Failures` check box, as shown in Figure 11.5.

After you have enabled this check box, you should run the application and reproduce the problem where it fails while attempting to load a

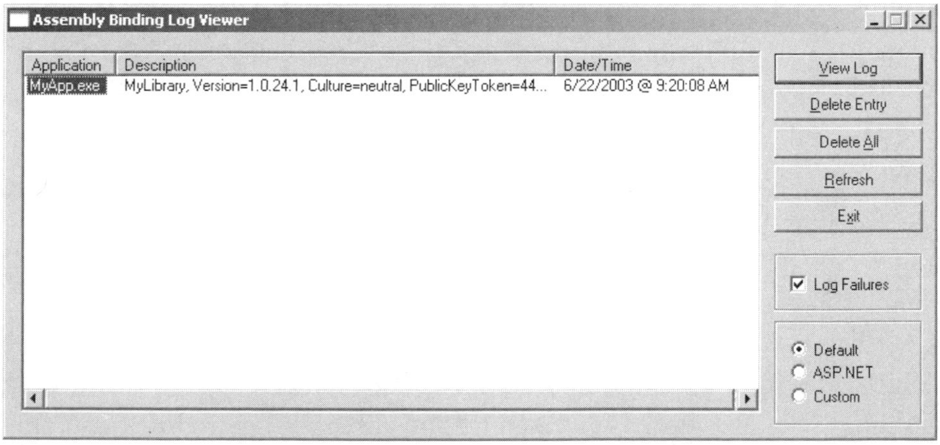

FIGURE 11.5: The Assembly Binding Log Viewer allows you to troubleshoot assembly loading problems.

dependent assembly. The assembly manager will provide an audit log with step-by-step information about the process it went through while attempting to load the assembly. When you click the `Refresh` button, an entry for the application should appear in `FUSLOGVW.EXE` as shown in Figure 11.5. If you select this entry and then click the `View Log` button, `FUSLOGVW.EXE` will display an HTML page in Internet Explorer with a wealth of information about the steps that the assembly manager went through as it attempted to locate and load the assembly file.

As a .NET developer, you should definitely become familiar with the Assembly Binding Log Viewer. This utility can also elucidate the assembly manager's steps taken during successful assembly load attempts. You are encouraged to read through the documentation for this utility supplied in the .NET Framework SDK.

The Native Image Cache

In Chapter 1, you learned that executable code within an assembly is distributed in the form of intermediate language (IL). In the typical case, the CLR uses a just-in-time (JIT) compiler to translate the IL into machine code while an application is running. The CLR performs JIT compilation on a method-by-method basis, which means that it compiles the IL for each method the first time it is called and stores the resulting machine code in memory. This machine code for a method can then be reused whenever that method is executed throughout the lifetime of the application.

One downside to this scheme is that the machine code generated by the JIT compiler is retained in memory. The machine code is therefore discarded when an application is unloaded. As a result, the JIT compilation process must start from scratch every time an application is run.

The CLR provides a potential optimization through a feature known as *precompiling*. In precompiling, the IL for method definitions is compiled into machine code when an assembly is installed on a target machine. This approach can improve the performance of certain applications because the machine code is already stored on the local hard disk. There is no need to waste processing cycles with JIT compilation while an application is running.

Some people use the term *preJITing* when they are talking about precompiling. The authors generally avoid this term because it's a bit of an oxymoron. Just be aware that precompiling and preJITing are sometimes used to mean the same thing.

Once you have installed an assembly in the GAC or deployed it as a private assembly, you can precompile its IL by using the *CLR Native Image Generator* (NGEN.EXE). NGEN.EXE is a command-line utility that ships with the CLR and with the .NET Framework SDK. You can precompile an assembly with this utility by calling it from the command line and passing either an assembly file path or an assembly name:

```
NGEN.EXE MyLibrary.dll
```

Note that precompilation is not limited to assembly DLLs. You can also use NGEN.EXE to precompile the IL within an EXE-based application:

```
NGEN.EXE MyApp.exe
```

When you use NGEN.EXE to precompile the IL within an assembly, it produces a special file known as a *native image*. The CLR stores native image files in a dedicated directory structure called the *native image cache*. The native image cache is located next to the directory structure for the GAC.

A native image file contains the compiled machine code for the assembly's methods and a minimal amount of metadata. It does not contain all the type information for the original assembly file. Therefore, the CLR still needs the original assembly file in addition to the native image file before it can load and run its code. Don't be fooled into thinking you can delete the original assembly file from the hard drive of a target machine once you have generated a native image for it.

When the CLR loads an assembly, it checks whether that assembly has an associated native image available in the native image cache. If one exists, the CLR loads the entire set of the machine code from the native image into the application. If a native image for the assembly isn't available, then the CLR JIT compiles methods from the assembly's IL into machine code on a method-by-method basis.

Precompiling an assembly is not always the right choice, because an important tradeoff must be made between saving processing cycles and wasting memory. When the CLR loads an assembly with an associated native image, it always loads the machine code for every method into memory—whether or not the application actually uses that method. The CLR must also load the original IL-based assembly into memory to read the assembly's type information. Thus the CLR must load two files into memory when you have precompiled an assembly. While precompiling can save time by avoiding JIT compilation at runtime, it can also use more memory than is strictly necessary.

A simple example will clarify this tradeoff. Imagine you have a assembly DLL that contains 1000 methods. This assembly DLL is used by an application that calls only 20 of these methods. What happens when you precompile this assembly and then run the application? The CLR loads the machine code for all 1000 methods, even though the application will never use 980 of them. In this scenario, the disadvantages of using memory unnecessarily will likely outweigh the benefits of precompiling the IL for 20 methods.

Precompilation is most often beneficial when it is used with assemblies associated with GUI-based applications that run on the desktop. In this scenario, precompilation allows a large application with complex initialization routines to start up much faster. The user of the application doesn't have to wait for the CLR to JIT compile hundreds or possibly thousands of methods at start-up. It is interesting to note that one of the few FCL assemblies that Microsoft ships with a precompiled native image is `System.Windows.Forms.dll`.

Precompilation is typically not as beneficial for assemblies associated with server-side applications. The cost of JIT compilation isn't especially expensive when you consider that a single method is used many times once it has been JIT compiled. Conversely, precompilation can be overly expensive when an application uses only a small percentage of the methods within a large assembly. Microsoft distributes the majority of FCL assemblies without associated native images.

If you are wondering whether you should precompile an assembly as part of your deployment strategy, you should conduct performance testing. Test the performance of the application and its dependent assemblies first using JIT compilation and then using precompilation. Only by monitoring application characteristics such as start-up time, responsiveness, and memory usage will you be able to determine whether precompilation offers any benefits.

Versioning Assemblies

The first section in this chapter discussed DLL versioning problems that have long perplexed Windows developers. When you are versioning a standard Windows DLL or a COM DLL, backward compatibility is critical, because installing a new version of a DLL on a target machine effectively overwrites any earlier versions. When you author a new version of a DLL that fails to meet all the requirements of backward compatibility, bad things often happen. When older applications are forced to use a newer, incompatible version of a DLL, they either break or start behaving in a strange and mysterious fashion.

The .NET Framework greatly improves this situation, because backward compatibility between versions of an assembly DLL is not so critical. The CLR allows for side-by-side deployment, in which several applications can each load a different version of the same assembly. This one factor by itself gives the .NET Framework an immeasurable advantage over what came before with respect to keeping applications alive and healthy on a target machine.

With the .NET Framework, you can revise an assembly DLL in a fashion that is not backward compatible and feel good about deploying it on a production machine. Older applications that rely on an earlier version of your assembly DLL are not forced to use the new version. That is, they can continue to run using the earlier version that was present during testing and debugging.

Of course, that is not to say that designing a new version to be backward compatible isn't valuable. Backward compatibility allows you to seamlessly update the behavior of older applications by redirecting them to use a newer version of a dependent assembly DLL. This principle is one of the ideas that make component-based software designs so powerful. Just recognize that the CLR doesn't force you to make a new version of an assembly DLL backward compatible if such compatibility doesn't make sense.

The Requirements of Backward Compatibility

When it's time to design and implement a new version of an assembly DLL, you get to decide whether you will make it backward compatible with earlier versions. On the positive side, designing and implementing a new version of an assembly to be backward compatible means you can seamlessly update preexisting applications with your new code. It allows you to introduce bug fixes and security patches. It also allows you to update older applications with an improved implementation that is superior to earlier versions with respect to performance, efficiency, and/or robustness.

On the negative side, designing and implementing a new version to be backward compatible introduces a strict set of requirements that can prevent you from creating exactly the design and/or implementation you really want. You certainly have less freedom than in the case where you are designing and implementing a new version that is not intended to be backward compatible.

Let's walk through an example to illustrate what is involved in designing a new version of an assembly that is backward compatible. Imagine you are given the task of revising `MyLibrary.dll` so that it's backward compatible with an earlier version. What requirements must you meet?

First, the new version of `MyLibrary.dll` must continue to support the same programming contract that is exposed by the earlier version. That is, the new version must continue to supply the same public types with the same public members. Furthermore, you cannot change the parameter types of public methods or public properties. You cannot change the type of any public field.

Chapter 4 discussed a few other subtle design issues that can lead you to breaking backward compatibility unintentionally. For example, you will break backward compatibility in the following scenarios:

- You change the value of a public `Const` field in a public class.
- You change the default value of a parameter defined using the `Optional` keyword in a public method of a public class.
- You add an `Optional` parameter to public method in a public class.

If this isn't clear to you, reread the "Method Overloading versus Optional Parameters" section in Chapter 4, which discussed why you are better off avoiding the Optional keyword and using method overloading to simulate optional parameters.

What if the earlier version of your assembly exposes public classes that support inheritance? For example, what if preexisting applications have created derived classes from a public base class within the assembly that you are revising? Now your versioning concerns become even more complex. You must worry about protected members in addition to public members, because modifications to protected members can introduce breaking changes to derived classes. You can simplify your version-related concerns by disallowing inheritance across assembly boundaries. Chapter 5 described one technique to prohibit cross-assembly inheritance involving Friend constructors.

Keeping the public programming contract intact from one version to the next is not all that's required to ensure backward compatibility. You must also avoid introducing any new requirements to the hosting application that uses MyLibrary.dll. A few examples will demonstrate the potential problems.

Imagine that the earlier version of MyLibrary.dll reads interest rates from a local application configuration file, but does not require network connectivity. In the new version, you plan to improve MyLibrary.dll by obtaining interest rates dynamically from a central location. To do so, you will modify a private method so that it downloads an XML file from your company's Web server. Can this change create a problem with backward compatibility?

Of course it can. Suppose the client application and MyLibrary.dll run on a computer that has no network connectivity. The application runs correctly with the earlier version of MyLibrary.dll, but it breaks when you redirect it to use the new version—it can't download the XML file from across the network.

It's your job to think through as many scenarios as possible and determine how changes to the assembly's implementation will affect backward compatibility. Does the new version of MyLibrary.dll introduce new references to third-party assemblies? Does the new version of MyLibrary.dll introduce dependencies on functionality from the FCL that isn't available under older versions of Windows, such as Windows 98 and Windows NT? The number of scenarios is infinite, of course, and you can never really think through all of them. That's why backward compatibility has proved to be such an elusive concept.

Say Goodbye to the Visual Basic 6 Compatibility Checker

If you have worked with Visual Basic 6, you are probably familiar with Visual Studio's compatibility checker, which runs whenever you rebuild an ActiveX DLL project in Binary Compatibility mode. With this wonderful feature, the compiler automatically confirms that you haven't changed the programming contract between an earlier version of a COM DLL and the new version that's being built.

Unfortunately, Visual Studio .NET does not provide any equivalent feature. In fact, the IDE lacks any built-in tool to help you maintain backward compatibility. You must rely on your eyes and your attention to detail to make sure you have not changed the programming contract between versions.

Version Numbers

Earlier this chapter you saw how to assign an explicit version number to an assembly during compile time by using the `AssemblyVersion` attribute. Refresh your memory by reviewing this attribute:

```
'*** AssemblyInfo.vb

Imports System.Reflection

<Assembly: AssemblyVersion("1.0.24.0")>
```

A version number is broken up into four smaller numbers delimited by dots. These inner numbers that make up the version number are (from left to right) the *major number*, the *minor number*, the *build number*, and the *revision number*. The version number as a whole is used to differentiate different builds from one another. The different parts of a version number tell the consumers of an assembly how one build relates to another.

The producer of an assembly DLL should use the major number and the minor number to indicate whether two different builds are backward compatible with each other. For example, the producer of an assembly DLL should keep the major number and the minor number constant when distributing a new version that is backward compatible with an earlier version. The producer of an assembly DLL should increment either the major number or the minor number when distributing a new version that was not designed to be backward compatible with earlier versions.

The producer of an assembly DLL should increment the build number with each release. A development team often produces a new build every day or every few days. Each build can be sent to another team for testing purposes. The build number enables the team to track which build of the assembly was used during a specific test.

A higher build number often signals that the new version has an improved implementation and possibly new functionality. If the build number changes but the major and minor numbers remain constant, then the producer of the assembly DLL is advertising that the new version is backward compatible.

The revision number indicates that the current build contains nothing more than bug fixes and security patches for a previous release with the same build number. Suppose you have just released version 1.0.24.0 and you discover it has a bug. You can fix the bug and create a new build with the version number 1.0.24.1 to indicate that it contains nothing new other than a bug fix.

> The four parts of a version number have meaning to the humans who are producing and consuming assemblies, but they have no meaning to the CLR. When the CLR compares two version numbers, it does not see shades of gray. Instead, the CLR sees the two version numbers as either an exact match or different numbers.

Best practice calls for managing all four parts of a version number yourself. You do so by explicitly assigning these numbers when you apply the

`AssemblyVersion` attribute. Alternatively, the Visual Basic .NET compiler can automatically generate a revision number and a build number for you. Examine the following code:

```
<Assembly: AssemblyVersion("1.0.*")>
```

When you use an asterisk at the end of the version number in place of an explicit build number and revision number, the compiler automatically generates these numbers for you. It generates the build number from the number of days since January 1, 2000. It generates the revision number from an internal algorithm that uses the computer's internal clock. When you allow the compiler to generate your build number and revision number in this fashion, your version number will look something like this:

```
1.0.1273.12750
```

It isn't recommended that you allow the compiler to generate any part of your version number. For this reason, you should avoid using an asterisk in your assembly version number. This advice is inconsistent with Visual Studio .NET, which creates an `AssemblyInfo.vb` file for each new project that contains an `AssemblyVersion` attribute with an asterisk. You will have more control over managing your version numbers if you eliminate the asterisk in the version number and replace it with an explicit build number and an explicit revision number.

The CLR and Versioning Policy

The CLR enforces an important set of rules with respect to versioning policy, as part of its attempt to ensure that a running application loads the most appropriate version of a dependent assembly. If the CLR determines that versioning policy rules have been broken while it is attempting to load an assembly, the load attempt will fail and the CLR will throw an exception to the hosting application.

Versioning policy is not enforced for all assemblies, however. In particular, the CLR enforces versioning policy only for assemblies that have a strong name. It never checks version numbers when it loads an assembly without a strong name. Thus the rules described in this section apply only when you have compiled an application or an assembly DLL against another assembly with a strong name.

Recall that the version number of a dependent assembly is recorded in the manifest of the assembly that references it at compile time. For example, if you compile MyApp.exe against version 1.0.24.0 of MyLibrary.dll, then that version number is recorded in the assembly manifest of MyApp.exe. It allows the CLR to discover which version of MyLibrary.dll was present when MyApp.exe was compiled.

The CLR employs a default versioning policy that is very conservative: It requires that all four parts of the compile-time version number match all four parts of the version number of the assembly that is loaded at runtime. For example, if MyApp.exe was compiled against version 1.0.24.0 of MyLibrary.dll, then the CLR will load only a build of MyLibrary.dll that has the exact same version number.

Let's walk through a few examples so you can see how this default versioning policy affects an application. Imagine you build version 1.0.24.0 of MyLibrary.dll and then build MyApp.exe against it. The application has no problem loading and running with version 1.0.24.0 of MyLibrary.dll because that version was present when MyApp.exe was compiled.

Now suppose you make a bug fix in MyLibrary.dll and rebuild the dependent assembly with a version number of 1.0.24.1. What happens if you install version 1.0.24.0 and version 1.0.24.1 in the GAC? Which version will the CLR load when you run MyApp.exe? By default, it loads version 1.0.24.0 because that version was present when MyApp.exe was built. The CLR does not automatically redirect the application to use a different version number, even when the GAC contains an alternative assembly with an incremented revision number.

Now let's look at a similar example with a less fortunate outcome. Suppose you did not install any version of MyLibrary.dll in the GAC. Instead, you initially deployed MyApp.exe along with version 1.0.24.0 of MyLibrary.dll as a private assembly in the AppBase directory. Things work properly at first because the CLR can locate MyLibrary.dll through probing and it sees that this build of MyLibrary.dll has the same version number that was present when MyApp.exe was compiled.

Now you decide to update the application by replacing version 1.0.24.0 of MyLibrary.dll with version 1.0.24.1. You perform the update by simply overwriting the old DLL file with the new one in the App-

`Base` directory. You soon discover that the application no longer works. The CLR detects a version mismatch between the version of `MyLibrary.dll` that was present at compile time and the version that it is attempting to load at runtime. The line of code in `MyApp.exe` that triggers the CLR to load `MyLibrary.dll` is thrown a `FileLoadException` exception due to a violation of versioning policy.

Your initial reaction might be to fault the CLR for having an overly conservative versioning policy. After all, the CLR will not even load an assembly with a bug fix whose version number differs only in terms of the revision number; it requires that the version number match exactly with all four parts. In fact, the versioning policy of the CLR is based on the premise that only one highly predictable deployment scenario exists—the scenario where an application runs using the exact versions of dependent assemblies that were present during testing and debugging.

Redirecting to a Different Version Number

It is possible (and common practice) for an application to load a different version of a dependent assembly than was present at compile time. This approach, known as *version redirection*, requires explicit configuration information. By adding custom information to a configuration file, you can instruct the CLR to load a newer and better version. Of course, you should only redirect a version number when you know that the new version is backward compatible with the compile-time version.

To see how version redirection works, let's revisit the example in which a bug fix was applied in version `1.0.24.1` of `MyLibrary.dll`. By default, `MyApp.exe` cannot use this newer build because it was compiled against version `1.0.24.0`. You can, however, instruct the CLR to redirect the application so that it loads the new version of `MyLibrary.dll` by creating an application configuration file with the XML content shown in Listing 11.4.

Earlier this chapter, you encountered a `<dependentAssembly>` element that contains an `<assemblyIdentity>` element. This new configuration option simply adds a `<bindingRedirect>` element within a `<dependent-Assembly>` element. The `<bindingRedirect>` element contains an `old-Version` attribute and a `newVersion` attribute. These two attributes instruct the CLR to redirect an application that was compiled against the

LISTING 11.4: You can redirect an application to a different version of a dependent assembly by using a `<bindingRedirect>` **element.**

```
<configuration>
  <runtime>
    <assemblyBinding xmlns="urn:schemas-microsoft-com:asm.v1">
      <dependentAssembly>
        <assemblyIdentity
          name="MyLibrary"
          publicKeyToken="29989D7A39ACF230" />
        <bindingRedirect
          oldVersion="1.0.24.0"
          newVersion="1.0.24.1" />
      </dependentAssembly>
    </assemblyBinding>
  </runtime>
</configuration>
```

old version number of `1.0.24.0` so that it loads the new version number `1.0.24.1` instead. Once this application configuration file is in place, `MyApp.exe` can successfully load and run with the new version of `MyLibrary.dll` containing the bug fix.

In addition to redirecting an application to use an incremented revision number, the `<bindingRedirect>` element can be used to redirect an application to use a later build number that is known to be backward compatible. For example, imagine you produced a new version of `MyLibrary.dll` that contained an improved implementation. If you designed this new version to be backward compatible, you could configure an older application such as `MyApp.exe` to be redirected to use this new version with the following configuration information:

```
<bindingRedirect
  oldVersion="1.0.24.0"
  newVersion="1.0.98.0" />
```

The `oldVersion` attribute of a `<bindingRedirect>` element can also be configured with a range of version numbers as opposed to a specific version number. To create this range, you include two version numbers separated by a hyphen. For example, suppose you wanted to redirect all previous build numbers and revision numbers with the same major number and minor number to a new build with a version number of `1.0.98.0`. You can configure the `<bindingRedirect>` element to look like this:

```
<bindingRedirect
  oldVersion="1.0.0.0-1.0.98.0"
  newVersion="1.0.98.0" />
```

Alternatively, you can configure a `<bindingRedirect>` element for a dependent assembly using the .NET Framework Configuration Administrative Tool. This utility eliminates the need to deal directly with the XML that goes into an application configuration file. Figure 11.6 shows a tabbed dialog box in which you can enter the old version number and the new version number. When you type in this information and then click `OK` or `Apply`, the .NET Framework Configuration Administrative Tool modifies the application configuration file so that it has the proper XML content for the `<bindingRedirect>` element.

In the preceding example, a version number at the application level was redirected using an application configuration file. That's not the only level

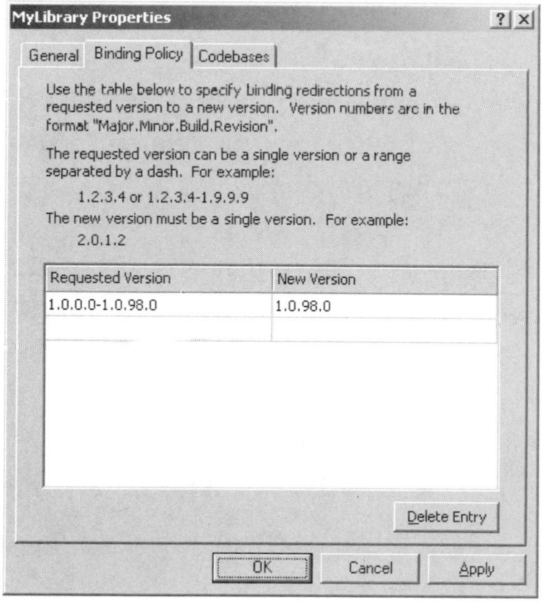

FIGURE 11.6: You can redirect a range of version numbers to a new version number.

at which you can redirect the version number of a dependent assembly. In fact, CLR supports redirection of a version number of a dependent assembly at three different levels (listed here in the order in which the CLR inspects them):

- Application level (application configuration file)
- Assembly level (publisher policy file)
- Machine level (`machine.config`)

At the assembly level, an assembly can be distributed along with its own configuration information. To do so, you create a *publisher policy file*. The next section explains what publisher policy files are as well as how to build and deploy them.

At the machine level, you can redirect a version number by adding a `<bindingRedirect>` element to the `machine.config` file. Redirecting a version number in the `machine.config` file allows the system administrator to redirect all applications on a target machine so that they load a specific version of a particular assembly. The .NET Framework Configuration Administrative Tool can configure an assembly on a machine-wide basis so that an administrator doesn't have to modify the `machine.config` file by hand.

Now that you have seen the three possible levels of version redirection, let's review what happens when the CLR determines that it must load an assembly into a running application:

1. The CLR creates an assembly format string from an assembly reference that contains the compile-time version number.
2. The CLR searches each of the three levels for any configuration information related to version redirection.
3. If the CLR finds redirection information at a particular level, it modifies the version number in the assembly format string.
4. The CLR uses the resulting assembly format string to search for the assembly file.

The order in which the CLR applies redirection information is important. First, the CLR looks for redirection information in the application configuration file. Next, it determines whether the target assembly has an associated publisher policy file containing redirection information. Finally, the CLR looks in the `machine.config` file. An important implication of this predefined order is that the system administrator always gets the last say with respect to which version is actually loaded.

Another subtle point about version redirection deserves some attention—namely, what happens when the CLR finds configuration information at more than one level? The CLR performs version redirection in a later level based on the output of the previous level. For example, the `newVersion` attribute in a `<bindingRedirect>` element in the application configuration file will map to the `oldVersion` attribute in a `<bindingRedirect>` element in `machine.config`. This relationship can be a little tricky to grasp at first, but an example will clarify matters.

Suppose that `MyApp.exe` was compiled against version `1.0.24.0` of `MyLibrary.dll`. Also suppose that three versions of `MyLibrary.dll` are currently installed in the GAC with version numbers of `1.0.24.0`, `1.0.24.1`, and `1.0.98.0`, respectively. Now you add a `<bindingRedirect>` element in `MyApp.exe.config` and a second `<bindingRedirect>` element in `machine.config`. The configuration information in `MyApp.exe.config` redirects version `1.0.24.0` to version `1.0.24.1`. The configuration information in `machine.config` redirects version `1.0.24.0` to version `1.0.98.0`. Which version of `MyLibrary.dll` is loaded at runtime?

In this example, the CLR will load version `1.0.24.1` instead of version `1.0.98.0`, because the CLR redirects the version number at the application level from `1.0.24.0` to `1.0.24.1`. When the CLR examines `machine.config` for redirection information, it looks for an `oldVersion` of `1.0.24.1` instead of `1.0.24.0`. Because `machine.config` did not include any configuration information instructing the CLR to redirect version `1.0.24.1`, the redirection information in `machine.config` has no effect.

You should draw an important conclusion from this example: Version redirection at a prior level can affect version redirection at a later level. As the preceding example amply demonstrates, you can get into trouble if you don't understand how things work.

You could also configure the `oldVersion` attribute in the `machine.config` file with a range of version numbers instead of a specific version number to avoid potential problems. Things would have been different in the example scenario if the `oldVersion` attribute in the `<bindingRedirect>` element of the `machine.config` file had been configured to redirect from a range of `1.0.0.0 - 1.0.98.0`. Namely, the version redirection at the machine level would have worked as it was intended.

Publisher Policy Files

A publisher policy file contains configuration information. In this sense, it is similar to an application configuration file or the `machine.config` file. A publisher policy file differs from these other kinds of configuration files, however, in that it contains configuration information for only one specific assembly.

Publisher policy files provide a means for companies that produce reusable libraries to distribute custom configuration information along with their assemblies. Such a file usually contains one or more `<bindingRedirect>` elements to redirect applications from an older version of an assembly to a newer version. In this way, publisher policy files remove the burden of configuring version redirection from those who are responsible for maintaining application configuration files and the `machine.config` file.

A publisher policy file can also contain `<codeBase>` elements to facilitate downloading different versions of an assembly on demand from across the network. As a result, it can redirect an application to a later version and then instruct the CLR about how to download the assembly file for that version from across the network.

Unlike the other kinds of configuration files, a publisher policy file is not a text-based file. Instead, it is a compiled assembly with a strong name. It must also follow a strict naming convention defined by the CLR. Furthermore, a publisher policy file has no effect on the assembly manager until you install it into the GAC on the target machine. Let's walk through the steps of building and deploying a publisher policy file for `MyLibrary.dll` so you can see how one is used.

Building Publisher Policy Files

When you want to build a publisher policy file, you start by adding configuration information to a text file. For example, you might add the XML content shown in Listing 11.4 to a text file named `MyLibrary.dll.config`. Next, you make a copy of the public/private key file `AcmeCorp.snk` that was used to build `MyLibrary.dll` and place it in the same directory that contains `MyLibrary.dll.config`. Now you are ready to create the actual publisher policy file.

The easiest way to build a publisher policy file is to use the .NET Framework SDK utility called the *Assembly Linker* (`AL.EXE`). You can run `AL.EXE` to build a publisher policy file by issuing the following instruction from the command line:

```
AL.EXE /link:MyLibrary.dll.config
       /out:policy.1.0.MyLibrary.dll
       /keyf:AcmeCorp.snk
       /v:1.0.0.0
```

When you call `AL.EXE`, you must pass parameterized information to it using four important switches. The preceding code included line breaks to make it easier to see how the parameterized information is passed with each switch. In the real world, when you call `AL.EXE` from the command line or from a batch file, you should separate the switches with spaces instead of line breaks.

The first switch, `/link`, informs `AL.EXE` to compile the XML content from `MyLibrary.dll.config` into the output assembly file. It forces `AL.EXE` to add your configuration information to the image of the output assembly file.

The second switch, `/out`, allows you to specify the name of the output assembly. It is important that you follow the CLR naming convention for publisher policy files. The name of a publisher policy file always starts with the word `policy`. Next, you include the major number, the minor number, and the name of the target assembly associated with the publisher policy file. Thus, in the preceding example, the publisher policy file is named `policy.1.0.MyLibrary.dll`.

The publisher policy file named `policy.1.0.MyLibrary.dll` is intended to supply configuration information only for builds of `MyLibrary.dll` with a major number of `1` and a minor number of `0`. In other words, you need a separate publisher policy file each time you increment either the major number or the minor number. The idea behind this scheme is that you should be redirecting only between backward-compatible version numbers that share the same major and minor numbers.

The third switch, /keyf, allows you to specify a key file containing a public/private pair. This key file enables AL.EXE to build the output publisher policy file with a strong name. Note that the CLR requires you to build a publisher policy file using the same public/private key pair that was used to build the assembly associated with the publisher policy file.

The fourth switch, /v, allows you to specify a version number for the publisher policy file. Note that the version number for the publisher policy file is totally unrelated to the version number for the target assembly. In the preceding example, the publisher policy file was given a version number of 1.0.0.0. If the CLR finds multiple versions of the publisher policy file, it uses the one with the highest version number.

Deploying Publisher Policy Files

You deploy a publisher policy file by installing it in the GAC. That's all there is to it.

While publisher policy files can be used with private assembly deployment, it doesn't make much sense to pursue this course. Given the fact that publisher policy files must be installed in the GAC, it's clear that they cannot be used in an XCOPY deployment scheme. On the other hand, the ability to use XCOPY deployment is a major reason to use private assembly deployment. Thus, when you need to configure a private assembly, you should prefer using the application configuration file instead of a publisher policy file.

Publisher policy files are primarily used to configure assemblies that have been installed in the GAC. In the typical deployment scenario, the producer of an assembly packages a new version of that assembly along with a publisher policy file in an installation program such as an MSI file. When the user runs this installation program on a target machine, the new version of the assembly and the publisher policy file are both installed in the GAC at the same time. The publisher policy file can then effectively redirect every application on that target machine to use the new version without requiring modifications to the machine.config file or any application configuration file.

Disabling Version Redirection from Publisher Policy Files

Suppose a publisher policy file redirects an application to a new version of a dependent assembly that has been advertised as being backward compatible. What should you do if the new version breaks the application or makes it behave in an undesirable fashion? The CLR provides a solution to this problem. An application configuration file can instruct the CLR to ignore configuration information from a publisher policy file.

Examine the application configuration file shown in Listing 11.5. It contains a `<publisherPolicy>` element that has an `apply` attribute with a value of `no`. This configuration information allows the application to ignore the publisher policy file. As a result, the application can load and run with the same version of the assembly that was present during compilation and testing. Thus, the CLR allows the application to return to a state that is known to be reliable.

LISTING 11.5: An application configuration file can disable a publisher policy file for a dependent assembly.

```
<configuration>
  <runtime>
    <assemblyBinding xmlns="urn:schemas-microsoft-com:asm.v1">
      <dependentAssembly>
        <assemblyIdentity
          name="MyLibrary"
          publicKeyToken="29989D7A39ACF230" />
        <publisherPolicy apply="no"/>
      </dependentAssembly>
    </assemblyBinding>
  </runtime>
</configuration>
```

You can also place a `<publisherPolicy>` element inside an `<assemblyBinding>` element instead of inside a `<dependentAssembly>` element, as shown in Listing 11.6. In this case, the CLR ignores the publisher policy files for every dependent assembly. The application can then load the exact version of each dependent assembly that was present when the application was compiled.

LISTING 11.6: An application configuration file can disable a publisher policy file for all dependent assemblies.

```
<configuration>
  <runtime>
    <assemblyBinding xmlns="urn:schemas-microsoft-com:asm.v1">
      <publisherPolicy apply="no"/>
    </assemblyBinding>
  </runtime>
</configuration>
```

A `<publisherPolicy>` element only affects whether the CLR uses configuration information from publisher policy files; it never disables the configuration information in the `machine.config` file. A `<bindingRedirect>` element in the `machine.config` file can always be used to override any other configuration information with respect to version redirection. The result—the system administrator always gets the last word with respect to which version of an assembly DLL is actually loaded.

SUMMARY

This chapter provided essential details on naming, building, deploying, and revising assemblies. There is a wealth of information that you need to learn to properly build and distribute the software that you write with Visual Basic .NET. Consequently, your journey out of assembly purgatory has become longer than you might have initially expected.

Every assembly has a four-part name consisting of a friendly name, a version number, a culture setting, and a public key token. This four-part name gives every assembly a unique identity from the CLR's perspective. You can also control the name of an output assembly during the build process by applying the `AssemblyVersion` attribute and the `Assembly-KeyFile` attribute.

Strong names help to make assembly names unique across companies. They also provide a degree of authentication and verification, which enables the CLR to identify the assembly producer and detect traces of assembly tampering.

Assemblies can be deployed in three ways on a target machine. First, you can deploy a dependent assembly as a private assembly to take advantage of XCOPY and to lower the cost of distributing an application in a network environment. Second, you can deploy a dependent assembly in the GAC to share it across several applications. Third, you can configure a dependent assembly with a `<codeBase>` element so that the CLR will download it on demand from across the network.

Thanks to the advances of the .NET Framework, many versioning problems from the past have disappeared. The CLR allows multiple versions of the same dependent assembly to be loaded into different applications on the same machine at the same time. Designing and implementing a new version of an assembly DLL to be backward compatible with an earlier version is not as critical as it is when revising DLLs created with unmanaged code.

The CLR makes it possible to redirect older applications to load and run with an updated version of a dependent assembly. Unfortunately, the rules for configuring version redirection are fairly complicated. The CLR will never redirect an application to use a different version of a dependent assembly unless someone has provided explicit configuration information telling it to do so. Your first responsibility, then, is to design and implement a new version that is backward compatible. Your second responsibility is to tell the CLR to use the new version instead of older versions.

The CLR supports the use of configuration information for version redirection at three different levels. As a result, the person configuring the application, the assembly producer, and the system administrator all have a say in which version of a dependent assembly is ultimately loaded. The CLR also allows an application to return to a more predictable state by ignoring the configuration information contained in a publisher policy file.

12

COM Interoperability

M ANY SOFTWARE DEVELOPERS (the authors included) spent a good deal of time in the 1990s learning how to produce and consume component library DLLs written for the Component Object Model (COM). As a result, a wealth of code exists today in COM DLLs. If we lived in a perfect world, we could instantly dispose of these COM DLLs and rewrite them using a managed language such as Visual Basic .NET or C#. Unfortunately, we do not live in such a world.

Instead, we live in a practical world where migrating unmanaged code to a managed language doesn't always make sense. For example, porting Visual Basic 6 code to the Visual Basic .NET language can be tedious and expensive. Doing it properly involves far more than just running a wizard. It requires redesigning classes and rewriting existing code to use managed libraries instead of unmanaged libraries. Furthermore, you have to worry about finding and fixing any new bugs that crept into your code during the migration process.

Porting a Visual Basic 6 project can make you feel like you're spending money and time trying to fix something that isn't broken. It's often a reasonable choice to leave a project in Visual Basic 6 and to interoperate with it using the new code you write in Visual Basic .NET. Fortunately, it's relatively easy to program against a Visual Basic 6 DLL from Visual Basic .NET, because the CLR provides a built-in layer for COM interoperability.

This chapter will teach you how to work with the COM interoperability layer. It starts with a brief primer on COM for those who need that background. Next, it delves into the details of programming against a COM DLL from Visual Basic .NET. Along the way, you will learn the requirements for deploying a managed application that depends on a COM DLL.

The COM interoperability layer provides flexibility because it allows you to work in two directions. After you have learned how to program against a COM DLL from managed code, this chapter describes how to create and deploy a managed assembly DLL that can be used by a COM-based client application. Armed with a few essential techniques and concepts, you will be able to produce Visual Basic .NET DLLs that can be used to extend the behavior of a Visual Basic 6 application or an ASP page written in JavaScript or VBScript.

A Brief History of COM

To learn the details of COM interoperability within the CLR, you must first understand the fundamentals of COM. This section provides a quick primer on COM for those readers who never learned about it or who might have forgotten some of the details. If the details of COM's inner workings are still fresh in your memory, feel free to skip ahead to the next section.

A COM DLL serves up objects through creatable classes known as *coclasses*. A client application creates an object from a COM DLL through a process known as *activation*. A client application must activate a COM object from a coclass before it can begin to execute the object's methods.

COM does not allow a coclass to expose public methods. Instead, a coclass can expose functionality only by implementing *COM interfaces*. When a client application activates a COM object, it must establish a connection to the object based on a specific COM interface. The act of establishing an interface-based connection is called *binding*. Once the client application is bound to a COM object through an interface reference, it can call any method defined within that interface.

Creating COM DLLs

Unmanaged versions of Visual Basic such as Visual Basic 6 make it possible (and easy) to produce and consume COM DLLs. Visual Basic has always been very good at hiding details associated with COM programming that are complex or tedious. For example, you don't have to worry about programming in terms of interfaces when you produce or consume COM DLLs using Visual Basic 6.

When you want to create a COM DLL with Visual Basic 6, you create a new *ActiveX DLL project*. Within the ActiveX DLL project, you create a new *MultiUse class* for each COM coclass that you want to expose from the DLL. You don't have to worry about defining and explicitly implementing COM interfaces, however—you just add public methods to a MultiUse class and let the Visual Basic 6 compiler to do the rest of the work behind the scenes.

This chapter will introduce the concepts of COM interoperability using an example COM DLL named `PetsLibrary.dll`. Figure 12.1 shows the Visual Basic 6 project used to create this COM DLL. It contains a single MultiUse class named `Dog`. Within the `Dog` class, there are two public methods named `Bark` and `RollOver`.

When you build an ActiveX DLL project, the Visual Basic 6 compiler does a good deal of extra work to transform a MultiUse class into a COM

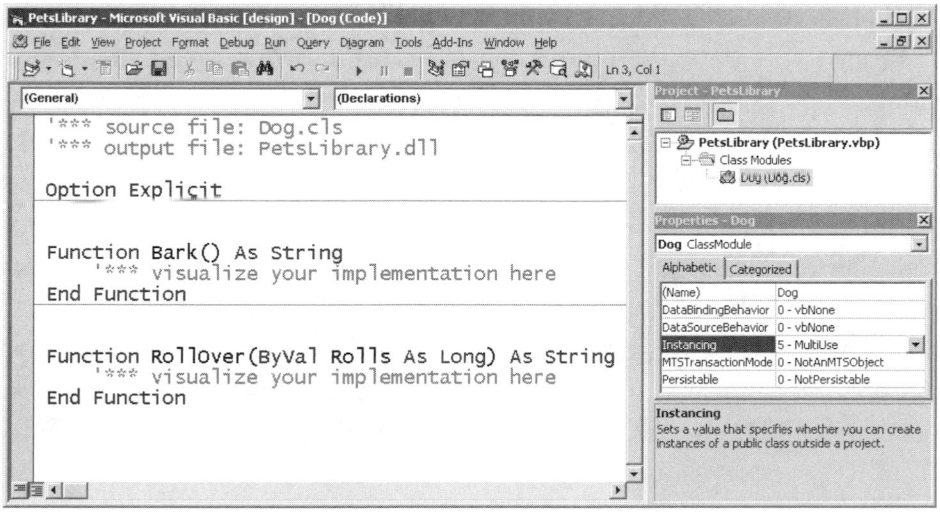

FIGURE 12.1: You can create a COM DLL with Visual Basic 6 by creating an ActiveX DLL project.

interface and a coclass to meet the requirements of the COM programming model. When you build the project shown in Figure 12.1, the compiler generates a COM interface named _Dog that contains the same two methods as the MultiUse class Dog. The compiler also generates a coclass named Dog, which is defined with the _Dog interface as its *default interface*. It is now possible for a client application to activate a COM object using the Dog coclass and to bind to this object using the _Dog interface.

Comparing the Programming Models of COM and the CLR

While COM requires programming in terms of interfaces, the CLR does not. This difference represents a significant departure between the older programming model of COM and the newer programming model of the CLR. While the CLR *allows* you to design and program in terms of interfaces, it doesn't *force* you to do so when that approach doesn't makes sense. Instead, you can design creatable classes in Visual Basic .NET that expose public methods. Public creatable classes that expose public methods make the use of interfaces unnecessary.

Type Libraries

Certain aspects of COM programming require the discovery of type information, such as the definitions for coclasses and interfaces. COM type information is stored in a binary repository called a *type library*. Type libraries are sometimes produced as stand-alone files with an extension such as .TLB. The type library that describes the coclasses and interfaces within a COM DLL, however, is usually bundled directly inside the binary image of the DLL itself. In this way, the type information for a COM DLL is always distributed along with the code it's used to describe.

COM does not use namespaces or strong names, so it must rely on another technique to uniquely identify entities such as type libraries, coclasses, and interfaces. COM uses *globally unique IDs (GUIDs)* for identification purposes. A GUID is a 128-bit integer that is guaranteed to be unique across time and space. When a GUID is added to the Windows Registry, a source file, or a configuration file, it is stored in a 32-character hexadecimal format, as in the following example:

```
A1F59DF9-7C29-47FB-BF73-05000DA84A0B
```

Certain types of GUIDs have special names:

- A GUID that's used to identify a type library is called a *LibID*.
- A GUID that's used to identify a coclass is called a *CLSID*.
- A GUID that's used to identify a COM interface is called an *IID*.

The Windows operating system contains a built-in component that can generate new GUIDs on demand. As a developer, you can generate new GUIDs using a development utility such as GUIDGEN.EXE. In reality, most Visual Basic programmers who create and use COM DLLs have never had to deal with GUIDs directly. Instead, the Visual Basic compiler has always been able to generate and track GUIDs behind the scenes.

The first time you build an ActiveX DLL project, the Visual Basic 6 compiler generates a new GUID to serve as the LibID for the DLL project's type library. The compiler also generates a pair of GUIDs for each MultiUse class to serve as the CLSID for a coclass and the IID of its default interface.

Comparing COM Type Information and CLR Type Information

A COM type library contains only a fraction of the type information that's required inside a managed assembly that targets the CLR. Unlike a type library, a managed assembly contains metadata and type information describing its private implementation details. Because a COM type library contains only type information pertaining to its public programming contract, its contents are generally limited to public type definitions for coclasses, interfaces, structures, and enumerations.

Interface Definition Language

There is an elderly language available for building COM type libraries called *interface definition language (IDL)*. Listing 12.1 shows an example of an

IDL source file that contains a text-readable type definition for a COM interface and a coclass. The definition of a COM interface consists of the names and calling signatures for a set of methods. The definition of a coclass contains a list of one or more implemented interfaces and a designation of which interface will serve as the default interface.

LISTING 12.1: IDL is used to define coclasses and COM interfaces within a type library.

```
[ uuid(C097B3D8-EFF5-4868-A115-9C5C5DFEAE56) ]      // LibID
library PetsLibrary
{

  [ uuid(3ABDF116-166F-4452-8E01-F4E7316057C9) ]      // IID
  interface _Dog : IDispatch {
    HRESULT Bark([out, retval] BSTR* );
    HRESULT RollOver([in] int Rolls, [out, retval] BSTR*);
  };

  [ uuid(A1F59DF9-7C29-47FB-BF73-05000DA84A0B) ]      // CLSID
  coclass Dog {
    [default] interface _Dog;
  };

};
```

In the past, IDL has been used by C++ developers who needed a language to build type libraries for their COM DLLs. Visual Basic developers have rarely had to resort to programming in IDL because the Visual Basic 6 compiler knows how to build a type library directly from Visual Basic source code. However, it can still be insightful to examine method definitions that are written in IDL. In particular, you can easily reverse-engineer the contents of a type library into IDL using a COM developer's utility named OLEVIEW.EXE, as shown in Figure 12.2. By using OLEVIEW.EXE to transform a type library into IDL, you can see how the Visual Basic 6 compiler translated your Visual Basic 6 source code into COM type definitions.

Referencing a Type Library

When you create a new project in Visual Basic 6 and you want to program against a COM DLL such as PetsLibrary.dll, you must first add a reference via the Project References dialog. When you add a reference to PetsLibrary.dll, you are really supplying the Visual Basic 6 IDE with the

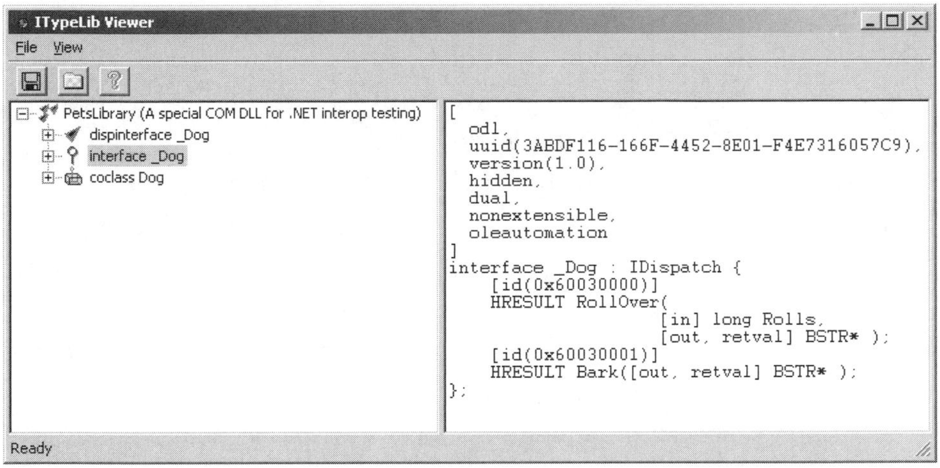

FIGURE 12.2: The `OLEVIEW.EXE` utility allows you to examine the contents of a COM type library.

information needed to locate the DLL's type library. Once the Visual Basic 6 IDE can read type definitions within the type library, it can supply you with IntelliSense when you are programming against types defined within `PetsLibrary.dll`.

The ability to read coclass and interface definitions from a type library is also very important to the Visual Basic 6 compiler. The compiler inspects the type library during compilation to acquire the CLSID for the `Dog` coclass and the IID for its default interface `_Dog`. It must also inspect the type library during compilation to read the method signatures defined within the `_Dog` interface.

By examining the method signatures defined within the type library, the Visual Basic 6 compiler is able to generate low-level binding code for calling methods on a COM object. In this style of binding, a COM object exposes an array of function pointers known as a *vtable*. When you write code to call methods on a COM object through a strongly typed reference variable, the compiler generates binding code to interact with the object through function pointers it obtains from the vtable.

When a client is bound to an object through a vtable, this style of binding is known as *early binding* (or *vtable binding*). Early binding is the preferred manner for communicating with a COM object because it provides the fastest way to invoke a method in COM. When you write code that uses early binding, you also gain the benefits of conveniences such as IntelliSense and compile-time type checking.

COM DLLs and the Windows Registry

Unlike the CLR, the COM runtime requires DLLs to have associated entries in the Windows Registry. For example, the COM runtime depends on a Registry entry to discover the physical path to a COM DLL during object activation. In particular, each CLSID must have an associated `Inproc-Server32` Registry key with a default value containing the physical path to its DLL file, as shown in Figure 12.3.

A CLSID can be complemented with a text-based alias known as a ProgID. A ProgID allows other programmers to activate COM objects using a human-readable class name. The Visual Basic 6 compiler generates a ProgID by appending the project name to the name of the MultiUse class. For example, the MultiUse class `Dog` in the project `PetsLibrary` is assigned a ProgID of `PetsLibrary.Dog`. Figure 12.3 shows how entries in the Windows Registry map this ProgID to its associated CLSID.

In addition to Registry entries for each CLSID and ProgID, the COM runtime and development tools such as Visual Basic 6 require Registry entries related to a type library and the interfaces defined inside it. A LibID requires a set of Registry entries that track the physical path to the file that contains the type library. Each IID requires a set of Registry entries that map it back to the LibID associated with the type library in which it is defined.

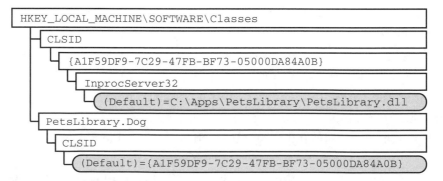

FIGURE 12.3: COM locates a DLL file by inspecting Windows Registry entries for the CLSID and ProgID.

When you deploy a COM DLL to a target machine, you must ensure that all of the appropriate entries are added to the Windows Registry. Fortunately, all COM DLLs built with Visual Basic are self-registering. The majority of COM DLLs built with C++ are self-registering, too. As a result, a COM DLL usually contains the necessary code for writing all its required entries to the Windows Registry. For example, the self-registration code for a Visual Basic 6 DLL is automatically added by the compiler when you build an ActiveX DLL project.

Once you have copied a COM DLL onto a target machine, you must tell it to run its self-registration code. To do so, you typically use the REGSVR32.EXE utility. You run this utility from the command line or from a batch file and tell it which DLL to register:

```
REGSVR32.EXE PetsLibrary.DLL
```

When you run REGSVR32.EXE in this way, this utility loads the DLL into memory and makes a call that tells the DLL to execute its self-registration code. After a COM DLL is registered with REGSVR32.EXE, it is ready to be used by an application.

Activating and Using a COM Object

Now that you have seen how a COM DLL is built and registered, let's consider how to program against it. When you want to write code that activates objects from a COM DLL such as PetsLibrary.dll, Visual Basic 6 makes things very easy. You use the Project References dialog to add a reference to the type library for PetsLibrary.dll, which allows the Visual Basic 6 IDE to discover the coclass Dog and the COM interface _Dog that are defined by the type library inside PetsLibrary.dll.

When you program against a COM DLL in Visual Basic 6, you don't need to program in terms of COM interfaces. The IntelliSense feature makes it seem as though each coclass and its default interface are a single unified type. It creates the illusion that a COM DLL contains creatable classes that expose public methods. In reality, the Visual Basic 6 compiler knows that it must generate compiled code that activates COM objects using coclasses and binds to these objects using COM interfaces. For example, consider the following code in a Visual Basic 6 application, which activates a Dog object from PetsLibrary.dll:

```
'*** activate object
Dim dog1 As PetsLibrary.Dog
Set dog1 = New PetsLibrary.Dog

'*** use object
dog1.Bark
dog1.RollOver 3

'*** release object
Set dog1 = Nothing
```

The Visual Basic 6 compiler translates the call to the `New` operator into a call to an internal COM function named `CoCreateInstanceEx`. The call to `CoCreateInstanceEx` passes the appropriate CLSID to activate a COM object from the coclass `Dog`. The Visual Basic 6 compiler also generates code to bind the reference variable `dog1` using the IID for the default COM interface `_Dog`. This allows the connection between the application and the object to be established using early binding.

When the Visual Basic 6 compiler builds this application, the CLSID and the default IID for the `Dog` coclass are compiled into the resulting EXE file. In other words, the application has a dependency on these two GUIDs. If you intend to use the application with an updated release of the DLL, then you must rebuild the DLL using Visual Basic's *binary compatibility mode*. Failure to do so will result in the default IID changing from build to build. The application will not work properly with a new IID because it has a dependency on the old IID that was present during compilation.

Error Reporting in COM

When a COM object needs to report an error to its caller, it does so by following the rules dictated by the COM programming model. Error handling works quite differently in COM than in the programming model of the CLR, which uses structured exception handling. In particular, COM uses two error reporting mechanisms: HRESULT values and COM exceptions.

HRESULT *Values*

An HRESULT is a standard return type for COM methods based on a 32-bit integer. A COM method returns an HRESULT value to indicate whether it completed successfully. When a method returns an HRESULT indicating failure, this value represents a *COM error code* that signifies what went wrong.

In Listing 12.1, both the `Bark` method and the `RollOver` method have return values based on the `HRESULT` type. This might seem strange at first when you look at the method signatures as they exist in Visual Basic 6 source code. For example, the `RollOver` method is defined in Visual Basic 6 with a logical return value of type `String`:

```
Function RollOver(ByVal Rolls As Long) As String
```

The `RollOver` method definition in IDL that has been reverse-engineered from the type library reveals how the method is really defined and called in terms of COM:

```
HRESULT RollOver([in] int Rolls, [out, retval] BSTR*);
```

What a Visual Basic 6 programmer sees as the `RollOver` function's logical return value is defined as a special `[retval]` parameter when it is translated into COM type information. The Visual Basic 6 runtime does the work of calling COM methods and inspecting the returned `HRESULT` values for you. If an `HRESULT` value indicates that a COM method called failed, the runtime raises a trappable runtime error. As a consequence, a Visual Basic 6 programmer doesn't have to inspect `HRESULT` values directly. Instead, he or she deals with a failed COM method call by routing the flow of execution to an error handler and inspecting the error code that is passed in `Err.Number`.

COM Exceptions

An `HRESULT` value that indicates failure can be used to track a COM error code, but it cannot be used to track any text-based information, such as an error message. To fill this gap, COM extends the information passed in `HRESULT` values by using COM exceptions. A COM exception is an object that holds extra error information, such as an error message and error source. When a COM object needs to report an error condition, it interacts with the COM runtime to create a COM exception object. This object is passed up the call chain to propagate error information back to its caller.

Let's walk through an example of how this error-handling mechanism works. Imagine you want raise a COM exception from a COM DLL written in Visual Basic 6. Examine the definition of the `RollOver` method in Listing 12.2. This method illustrates how to raise a COM exception from a

Visual Basic 6 DLL using `Err.Raise` syntax. When you call `Error.Raise`, you should pass an error code, a error source, and an error message.

LISTING 12.2: A Visual Basic 6 DLL can raise a COM exception using the `Err.Raise` syntax.

```
'*** Visual Basic 6 code raising a COM exception

Function RollOver(ByVal Rolls As Long) As String

  If(Rolls > 10) Then
    '*** calculate HRESULT with error code
    Dim ErrorCode As Long
    ErrorCode = vbObjectError + 1024
    '*** raise COM exception
    Err.Raise ErrorCode, "PetsLibrary.dll", "Too many rolls!"
  End If

  '*** continue with request

End Function
```

Creating User-Defined Error Codes

An important aspect of raising errors in COM has to do with returning a failed HRESULT value that contains a COM error code. In Visual Basic 6, the typical scheme is to define an error code in terms of the built-in constant `vbObjectError`. The `vbObjectError` constant contains the value of a failed HRESULT, indicating that an error has been raised from a user-defined error source. A common convention in Visual Basic 6 is to create user-defined error codes in terms of the `vbObjectError` constant and then add a standard offset (e.g., 1024) to define a range of error codes that do not conflict with any of Microsoft's preexisting error codes. Here's an example of defining a set of error codes in a Visual Basic 6 DLL project:

```
Enum PetsLibraryErrors
  UnexpectedError = vbObjectError + 1024    '*** &H80040400
  PetUnableToPerformCommand                 '*** &H80040401
  PetUnwillingToPerformCommand              '*** &H80040402
End Enum
```

Once you have defined an enumeration like `PetsLibraryErrors`, the `Err.Raise` syntax becomes more readable:

```
Err.Raise PetUnwillingToPerformCommand, _
        "PetsLibrary.dll", _
        "Too many rolls!"
```

A Visual Basic 6 application that calls the `RollOver` method and experiences this exception can deal with it by using an error handler that inspects the error code in `Err.Number`:

```
Sub ExerciseDog(ByVal target As Dog)
  On Error GoTo ErrorHandler
  Dim Rolls As Long
  '*** assign a number to Rolls
  target.RollOver Rolls
  Exit Sub
ErrorHandler:
  Select Case Err.Number
    Case PetUnwillingToPerformCommand
      '*** error handler
      Dim ErrorMessage As String
      ErrorMessage = Err.Description
  End Select
End Sub
```

When the `ExerciseDog` method attempts to call the `RollOver` method, the target `Dog` object raises a COM exception and returns a failed `HRESULT` value. The Visual Basic 6 runtime sees that the object is reporting an error condition, so it populates `Err.Number` with the error code and `Err.Description` with the error message. The Visual Basic 6 runtime then raises a trappable runtime error that can be handled by the client application.

Managing Object Lifetimes in COM

Once a COM object has been activated, its lifetime is controlled through reference counting. Such an object is very different from an object whose lifetime is controlled by the garbage collector. Thus a COM object and a managed object differ significantly. The two models of lifetime management also lead to different programming styles.

The COM programming model dictates that every COM object be responsible for managing its own lifetime. As clients establish and drop connections to a COM object, the object must have some way to increment and decrement an internal reference count. For this reason, every COM object must implement a core COM interface named `IUnknown` that exposes

AddRef and Release methods. A client application is required to call AddRef on a COM object when it establishes a new connection; it is required to call Release just prior to dropping a connection. This approach allows a COM object to accurately track how many clients are connected. In addition, the object can readily determine when the last connection has been dropped. At that point in time, a COM object removes itself from memory.

Visual Basic 6 hides the details of dealing with the IUnknown interface from application developers. When you compile a MultiUse class, the Visual Basic 6 compiler automatically builds in support for reference counting, including an implementation of AddRef and Release. When the last call to Release is made on a Visual Basic 6 object, the object removes itself from memory.

When you write code against a COM object in Visual Basic 6, you are neither required nor allowed to make explicit calls to AddRef and Release. Instead, the Visual Basic runtime makes all of the necessary calls to these two methods behind the scenes. A quick example will illustrate this point:

```
'*** create COM object with Visual Basic 6
Dim dog1 As Dog
Set dog1 = New Dog   '*** AddRef called here

'*** use object
dog1.Bark

'*** release object
Set dog1 = Nothing   '*** Release called here
```

In the preceding code, the COM object's AddRef method is called as part of the activation sequence. This results in a COM object that has an outstanding reference count of 1. When the reference variable dog1 is assigned a value of Nothing, the Visual Basic runtime makes the final call to Release. Note that the runtime blocks the line of code that assigns a value of Nothing to dog1 while it makes the call to Release.

Imagine that the MultiUse class Dog has been defined with a Class_Terminate method. A Class_Terminate method is known as a *destructor* because it is automatically executed at the end of an object's lifetime. More specifically, a Visual Basic 6 object executes its Class_Terminate method during the final Release call just before it removes itself from memory. Because the `Class_Terminate` always executes at the end of an object's lifetime, it serves as a good place to add custom cleanup code.

A `Class_Terminate` method executes synchronously when the client application assigns the last reference variable a value of `Nothing`. As a result, this method fires at a predictable time. This behavior is very different from that of a managed object with a `Finalize` method. A `Finalize` method executes at a time that is not predictable. This difference in lifetime management creates a mismatch between the programming models of COM and of the CLR. We will revisit this important topic later in the chapter, when we discuss programming against COM objects from managed code.

Scripting Clients and Late Binding

Several scripting languages are capable of programming against a COM DLL. For instance, JavaScript and VBScript are frequently used to activate and program against COM objects, which makes it possible to use COM DLLs from the code written in ASP pages. The way in which a scripting language interacts with COM objects is very different from the behavior described so far in this chapter, however.

Code written in a scripting language is not compiled before it is executed, but rather fed to an execution engine known as a *script interpreter*. A script interpreter cannot take advantage of the coclass and COM interface definitions within a type library. Instead, a scripting language and its underlying script interpreter must provide an alternative means for activating and binding to a COM object that doesn't rely on type information from within a type library.

A scripting language makes it possible to activate a COM object without requiring a dependency on a CLSID. This is the primary reason why COM supports object activation through a ProgID. A ProgID allows the scripting language to activate a COM object in terms of a class name that is expressed as a human-readable string. The following example shows VBScript code in an ASP page that activates a `Dog` object created from `PetsLibrary.dll`:

```
Dim dog1
Set dog1 = Server.CreateObject("PetsLibrary.Dog")
```

Because a script interpreter cannot read interface definitions from a type library, it cannot be used to achieve early binding with a COM object. Instead, a scripting interpreter invokes methods on a COM object through *late binding*.

Late binding is a protocol for discovering and binding to COM methods at runtime. All COM objects that support late binding implement a standard COM interface named IDispatch. Visual Basic programmers don't have to worry about implementing IDispatch manually because the Visual Basic 6 compiler automatically adds support for it whenever you build a ActiveX DLL project with a MultiUse class.

An example will illustrate how late binding works. Examine the following VBScript code, which activates a Dog object and then invokes the Bark method and the RollOver method:

```
Dim dog1, result1, result2

'*** activate COM object using ProgID
Set dog1 = Server.CreateObject("PetsLibrary.Dog")

'*** call methods though late binding
result1 = dog1.Bark()
result2 = dog1.RollOver(3)

'*** release COM object
Set dog1 = Nothing
```

A scripting language such as VBScript does not allow you to specify a type when you declare a variable. Instead, VBScript is a loosely typed language in which all variables are implicitly declared using the VARIANT type. When you activate a COM object and assign it to a reference variable such as dog1, the script interpreter binds to the object by establishing a connection based on the IDispatch interface.

When executing the VBScript code that calls a COM method, the script interpreter must first bind to the target method. It does so by calling an IDispatch method named GetIDsOfNames. This method accepts an input string parameter containing the name of the target method. A successful call to GetIDsOfNames returns an integer known as a DispID that is used to identify the target method.

Once the scripting interpreter has acquired a `DispID`, it has become bound to the target method. It can then execute the method by calling another `IDispatch` method named `Invoke`. When the scripting interpreter calls `Invoke`, it passes the `DispID` of the target method and a `VARIANT` array containing the target method's input parameters. The COM object responds to this call to `Invoke` by executing the target method and using the `VARIANT` type to pass any output parameters and a return value back to the scripting interpreter.

There are several interesting things to note about late binding:

- Late binding is slower than early binding, partly because it takes extra time to bind to methods at runtime.

- Performance of late binding is also adversely affected by the requirement to convert parameter values into a `VARIANT` array in each call to `Invoke`.

- Although you can criticize code that relies on late binding for being slow, such code is far less fragile than code that relies on early binding. Late binding doesn't involve dependencies on GUIDs or type definitions compiled into type libraries, so you can rebuild an ActiveX DLL project using Visual Basic 6 without Binary Compatibility mode and not risk breaking code that's written in a scripting language.

This section has provided a fast and furious look at the inner workings of COM. Armed with this background information, you are now ready to explore how the COM interoperability layer of the CLR works. If you want to read more about the details of COM, you can download a free electronic version of Ted Pattison's book, *Programming Distributed Applications Using COM+ and Microsoft Visual Basic 6.0*, from http://Barracuda.net/Publications/ProgDist.chm.

Accessing COM from Visual Basic .NET

When you are writing managed code in Visual Basic .NET, you cannot program directly against a COM type definition within a type library such as a coclass or interface. Instead, you must first create or acquire a special shim

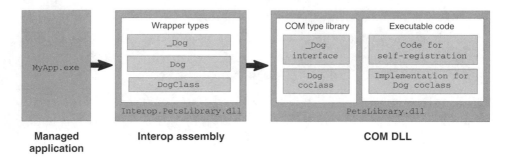

FIGURE 12.4: An interop assembly provides managed wrapper types for a COM DLL.

DLL called an *interop assembly*. An interop assembly contains COM type definitions that have been translated into managed types. It provides a gateway into a COM DLL because it contains a set of managed types that allow you to indirectly program against the types defined within the DLL's type library.

Figure 12.4 shows how the various pieces fit together. An interop assembly named `Interop.PetsLibrary.dll` has been generated to provide access to the COM types inside `PetsLibrary.dll`. It contains managed types to wrap the COM coclass `Dog` as well as the COM interface `_Dog`. Once you have referenced the interop assembly from within a Visual Basic .NET project, you can start programming against the wrapper types within it. This will, in turn, allow you to activate and use objects from the COM DLL.

Interop Assemblies

In many cases, your first step to interoperating with a COM DLL is to generate an interop assembly. The CLR contains a built-in component called the *type library importer* for generating an interop assembly from an existing type library. There are several different ways in which you can use the CLR's type library converter. Here we will demonstrate its use first with a command-line utility named `TLBIMP.EXE` and then with Visual Studio .NET.

Generating an Interop Assembly with `TLBIMP.EXE`

As just mentioned, the .NET Framework SDK utility provides a handy utility for generating interop assemblies named `TLBIMP.EXE`. This utility accepts the name of a type library file (or the name of a COM DLL file that contains a type library) as an input parameter and calls the type library importer to generate an interop assembly as output. `TLBIMP.EXE` accepts several command-line switches as parameters. Here's an example of a command-line instruction to build an interop assembly for `PetsLibrary.dll`:

```
TLBIMP.EXE PetsLibrary.dll
          /out:Interop.PetsLibrary.dll
          /namespace:PetsLibrary
          /keyfile:AcmeCorp.snk
```

In this example, line breaks are used between the parameterized switches to make the code more readable. In the real world, you cannot use line breaks between the parameterized switches when executing a command with `TLBIMP.EXE`. Instead, you must place all the parameterized switches on a single line.

The `TLBIMP.EXE` utility supports the `/out` switch, which allows you to specify the name of the interop assembly that is being built. By convention, you should name an interop assembly by using the same name as the target COM DLL with an additional prefix of `Interop`. For example, the interop assembly generated for the COM DLL `PetsLibrary.DLL` has been named `Interop.PetsLibrary.DLL`.

When you generate an interop assembly for a COM DLL, the type library importer generates managed wrapper types for each coclass and interface defined within the source type library. You can use `TLBIMP.EXE`'s `/namespace` switch to direct the type library importer to generate these wrapper types inside a specific namespace. In the preceding example, the `/namespace` switch was used to generate the wrapper types for `PetsLibrary.DLL` in a namespace named `PetsLibrary`.

The last thing you should notice about the previous example is that the call to `TLBIMP.EXE` contains a `/keyfile` parameter, which includes the name of a key file with a public/private key pair. It has the effect of generating an interop assembly with a strong name. Generating interop assemblies with strong names is a requirement if you want to use advanced deployment options such as installing the interop assembly in the GAC.

Now, think about what steps you need to take to deploy a managed application that depends on a COM DLL. First, you must install and register the COM DLL on the target machine. Second, you must deploy the managed application's EXE file and the interop assembly on the target machine.

The interop assembly can be deployed along with the EXE file as a private assembly in the `AppBase` directory. Alternatively, you can deploy the interop assembly in the GAC as a shared assembly. Remember—you must build your interop assemblies with strong names if you intend to deploy them in the GAC.

Generating an Interop Assembly with Visual Studio .NET

Visual Studio .NET provides an easier (but somewhat less flexible) way to generate an interop assembly. First, you open the project in which you want to program against a COM DLL. Next, you bring up the current project's `Add Reference` dialog and navigate to the COM tab, as shown in Figure 12.5.

This tab provides a scrollable view that displays all of the type libraries that have been registered on your developer workstation. When you select one of these type libraries and click OK, Visual Studio .NET calls the type library importer to generate an interop assembly in your project's output directory. By default, the output directory for a project is configured to be the `\bin` directory. Visual Studio .NET also adds a reference to this interop

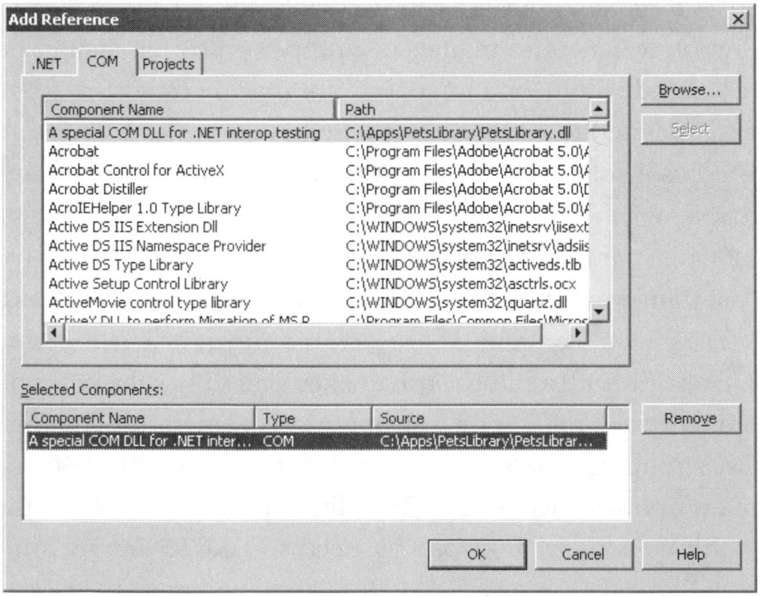

FIGURE 12.5: You can create an interop assembly using the COM tab of the `Add Reference` dialog.

assembly so that you can begin writing code in the application against the managed types within the newly generated interop assembly.

Visual Studio .NET creates interop assemblies following the naming convention discussed earlier. In other words, it will generate an interop assembly file named `Interop.PetsLibrary.dll` when you add a reference to the COM DLL named `PetsLibrary.dll`. In addition, Visual Studio .NET directs the type library importer to generate the managed types in a namespace named after the COM DLL. Thus the managed wrapper types for `PetsLibrary.DLL` are created in a namespace named `PetsLibrary`.

Note that Visual Studio .NET doesn't generate an interop assembly with a strong name when you add a reference to a Visual Basic .NET project with the `Add Reference` dialog. Instead, you must resort to using `TLBIMP.EXE` from the command line instead of Visual Studio .NET when you need to generate an interop assembly that will be installed in the GAC. The `TLBIMP.EXE` utility also provides several other options through command-line parameterized switches that are not available when you generate an interop assembly via Visual Studio .NET.

Primary Interop Assemblies

In certain situations, a company that produces COM DLLs might decide to distribute a COM DLL along with its own interop assembly. This practice allows the company to make its COM DLL accessible to managed applications as well as to COM applications. When a company produces an interop assembly for one of its COM DLLs, the assembly can be generated in a certain way so that it's recognized as a *primary interop assembly (PIA)*.

A PIA offers two major advantages over a standard interop assembly:

- The PIA is the only interop assembly that should ever be used to provide COM interoperability to its associated COM DLL. Therefore, the use of a PIA ensures that every managed assembly that uses a COM DLL references the same interop assembly with a uniform public key value.

- The PIA should be registered so that it's recognized by Visual Studio .NET. Once you have registered a PIA on a development workstation, Visual Studio .NET knows to use the preexisting PIA instead of generating a new interop assembly when you add a reference to the COM DLL with which it is associated.

PIAs are frequently created and distributed by groups within Microsoft. For instance, Microsoft Office is an application that is only programmable through COM. The Microsoft Office team uses PIAs so that developers using Visual Basic .NET and C# can program against products such as Word, Excel, and PowerPoint. If you look at the list of assemblies that have been installed in the GAC on a typical production machine, you will likely see PIAs produced by Microsoft and by other companies as well.

If you have produced a COM DLL and would like to build a PIA for it, you must recognize that this effort entails several requirements beyond building a standard interop assembly.

The first requirement is that you should be the actual producer of a COM DLL before you build a PIA for it. While this point is a convention rather than a hard-and-fast rule, it is an important guideline that everyone should follow. It will ensure that a COM DLL never has two associated PIAs that have different public key values.

The second requirement is that a PIA must be built with a strong name. Thus you must pass a public/private key file when you build a PIA with `TLBIMP.EXE`. If you don't supply a public/private key pair, `TLBIMP.EXE` will generate an error when you attempt to build a PIA.

The third requirement is that a PIA must contain a special attribute named `PrimaryInteropAssembly`. You can generate an interop assembly with this attribute by passing the `/primary` switch to `TLBIMP.EXE`.

The fourth requirement is that the PIA must contain explicit references to any external COM dependencies. For example, imagine you want to build a PIA for a COM DLL named `PetsLibrary.dll` that depends on another COM DLL named `Utils.dll`. To do so, you must first build and register a PIA for `Utils.dll`. Only then can you build a PIA for `PetsLibrary.dll` by passing the name of `Utils.dll` to `TLBIMP.EXE` using the `/reference` switch.

```
TLBIMP.EXE PetsLibrary.dll
           /primary
           /reference:AcmeCorp.Interop.Utils.dll
           /out:AcmeCorp.Interop.PetsLibrary.dll
           /namespace:AcmeCorp.PetsLibrary
           /keyfile:AcmeCorp.snk
```

Notice that the output file name of the PIA in the preceding code has been prefixed with the company name AcmeCorp. The namespace has been prefixed with AcmeCorp as well. This example illustrates two common naming conventions used with PIAs: You should add your company name to the beginning of a PIA file name and to the beginning of its primary namespace. Microsoft follows these naming conventions for its PIAs. You should follow them as well if you plan to create and distribute PIAs along with your COM DLLs.

Once you have generated a PIA with TLBIMP.EXE, you have the option of installing it in the GAC. You can accomplish this by using the GACUTIL.EXE utility:

```
GACUTIL.EXE -i AcmeCorp.Interop.PetsLibrary.dll
```

After you have installed the PIA in the GAC, you can register it on a development workstation by using a .NET Framework utility named REGASM.EXE. Here's an example of the command you can run from the command line:

```
REGASM.EXE AcmeCorp.Interop.PetsLibrary.dll
```

The act of registering a PIA with REGASM.EXE adds information to the type library's LibID within the Windows Registry to inform Visual Studio .NET that this particular COM type library has an associated PIA. The next time you add a reference to that type library from the COM tab of the Add Reference dialog, Visual Studio .NET knows not to build a new interop assembly but instead to use the PIA.

If you want to deploy the PIA without installing it in the GAC, then you must take one more step. When you register the assembly with REGASM.EXE, you must pass the /codebase switch:

```
REGASM.EXE AcmeCorp.Interop.PetsLibrary.dll /codebase
```

When you add this switch, REGASM.EXE adds the assembly file's physical path to the Windows Registry so that Visual Studio .NET can locate it when it is referenced within a project. Figure 12.6 shows the Registry keys and values associated with a registered PIA.

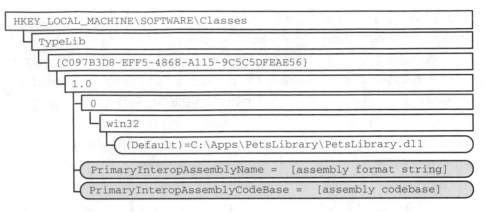

FIGURE 12.6: REGASM.EXE adds Windows Registry entries to map a type library to a primary interop assembly.

Programming against an Interop Assembly

Once you have generated (or otherwise acquired) an interop assembly, you can use it to write Visual Basic .NET code that activates and uses COM objects from a target COM DLL. Remember—you must first reference the interop assembly from within the current project before you can program against the wrapper types inside it.

Here we'll focus on the set of wrapper types that are generated by the type library importer for a coclass and its default interface. When you generate an interop assembly for PetsLibrary.dll that contains a coclass named Dog and a default interface named _Dog, the type library importer actually creates three managed wrapper types—not two—as shown in Figure 12.7.

In our example, the type library importer creates a managed wrapper interface named _Dog to wrap the COM interface named _Dog. The managed wrapper interface contains managed method definitions that match the methods defined in the COM interface. The managed wrapper interface is also defined with the GUID attribute, allowing it to track the IID of its associated COM interface.

Although the type library importer creates only one managed wrapper type for the COM interface _Dog, it creates two managed wrapper types for the coclass Dog:

- A managed class named DogClass
- A managed interface named Dog

FIGURE 12.7: The type library importer creates three wrapper types for a coclass and its default interface.

Let's explore how the type library importer creates each of these wrapper type definitions in a little more detail.

The DogClass wrapper type is a creatable class type that can be used to activate objects from the coclass Dog. When the type library importer creates the definition for DogClass, it uses the GUID attribute to track the CLSID of its associated coclass. In addition, the type library importer generates the class definition for DogClass with the same set of public methods that are defined in the default interface. As a consequence, the DogClass wrapper type can be used not only to activate a COM object but also to execute its public methods.

The Dog wrapper type is an interface that inherits from the other managed interface, _Dog. The fact that Dog inherits from _Dog means that both interfaces contain the same set of methods as the COM interface _Dog. When the type library importer defines the managed interface type Dog, it does so with the CoClass attribute to associate this interface type with the creatable type DogClass.

At first, you might think that this set of three managed wrapper types is fairly convoluted and confusing. In fact, there are several good reasons why the designers of the type library importer decided to create managed wrapper types in this fashion. The three wrapper types created for PetsLibrary.dll provide a good deal of flexibility when it comes to writing code to activate and use a Dog object. A few examples will illustrate this point.

Examine the code in Listing 12.3, which demonstrates four different techniques used to achieve the same results. Each of these techniques activates a COM object from the coclass Dog and then calls the Bark method through a reference variable that's bound to the object's default interface _Dog.

LISTING 12.3: Four coding techniques for using an interop assembly's wrapper classes

```
Imports PetsLibrary

Class MyApp
  Shared Sub Main()
      Dim result1, result2, result3, result4 As String

    '*** technique 1
    Dim dog1 As New DogClass
    result1 = dog1.Bark()

    '*** technique 2
    Dim dog2 As New Dog
    result2 = dog2.Bark()

    '*** technique 3
    Dim dog3 As _Dog = New Dog
    result3 = dog3.Bark()

    '*** technique 4
    Dim dog4 As _Dog = New DogClass
    result4 = dog4.Bark()

  End Sub
End Class
```

With technique 1, the code is written strictly in terms of the creatable wrapper type DogClass. Because it is a creatable type, you can use the New operator to create a new object. When you call New on the DogClass type, the COM interoperability layer interacts with the COM runtime by calling CoCreateInstanceEx. The COM interoperability layer passes the appropriate CLSID to activate a COM object from the Dog coclass. It also performs the task of binding to the COM object's default interface using the proper IID. This makes it possible to call the COM object's Bark method through the reference variable dog1.

With technique 2, the code is written strictly in terms of the managed wrapper interface Dog. Note that it's the same code as that created with technique 1, with one exception: The wrapper class `DogClass` has been replaced with the wrapper interface `Dog`. This code works thanks to some extra assistance supplied by the Visual Basic .NET compiler. The compiler usually doesn't allow you create an object by using the `New` operator with an interface type. It does allow you to use the `New` operator with the wrapper interface type `Dog`, however, because this interface has been defined with the `CoClass` attribute. The `CoClass` attribute redirects the compiler to use the `DogClass` type to instantiate the requested object. As in technique 1, the COM interoperability layer activates the object and then binds the `dog2` reference variable to its default interface, which makes it possible to execute the `Bark` method.

With techniques 3 and 4, the code is more in line with traditional COM programming. Both examples explicitly bind to the object through an interface type.

Why does the type library importer create a set of managed wrapper types that gives you so many different ways to accomplish the same thing? After all, technique 1 is almost identical to technique 2, and technique 3 is almost identical to technique 4. One reason is to provide you with more flexibility and convenience. A second reason is to make it easier to migrate Visual Basic 6 code to Visual Basic .NET.

When you port a project from Visual Basic 6, you may need to rely on functionality that is available only in a COM DLL. The type library importer does an excellent job of minimizing the work you must do when you seek to reuse code you originally wrote in Visual Basic 6 to call COM DLLs from Visual Basic .NET.

Runtime Callable Wrappers

When you activate a COM object from a managed application, your code does not obtain a direct reference to the COM object. Instead, the COM interoperability layer creates a special proxy and inserts it between the managed reference and the COM object, as shown in Figure 12.8. This proxy is a managed object known as a *runtime callable wrapper (RCW)*. The RCW is an essential piece of the COM interoperability layer because it manages the flow of execution as it transitions between managed and unmanaged code.

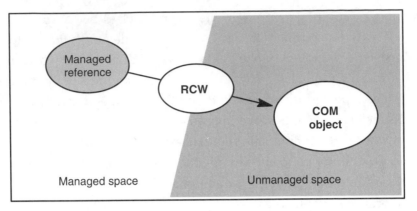

FIGURE 12.8: An RCW marshals method calls across the managed–unmanaged boundary crossing.

An RCW takes responsibility for forwarding method calls from a managed caller to a COM object. A large part of its duties involves translating parameters when their types have different in-memory representations in the managed world and the unmanaged world. The act of translating parameters during a method call is known as *marshaling*.

Let's look at an example of when marshaling occurs. Suppose you are passing a string value back and forth between managed and unmanaged code. In the managed world, a string is represented in memory using a heap-based object created from the System.String class. A COM object could not possibly deal with such a managed object. Therefore, an RCW must translate the string value into a form that a COM object can understand. In the world of COM, strings are most often represented using a COM type named BSTR.

When a managed caller passes a string value to a COM object, the RCW must translate a System.String object into a BSTR. Conversely, when a COM object returns a string value back to a managed caller in a return value, the RCW must translate a BSTR into System.String object. A string value is just one example. In fact, many other types of objects and values must be marshaled as they are passed back and forth across the RCW.

While the details of marshaling parameters can become quite complex, it is rarely a problem that concerns you as a programmer. The good news is that an RCW knows how to automatically convert back and forth between the types that are commonly used in COM and in the CLR. The bad news is that marshaling parameters requires extra processing and, therefore, has the potential to degrade the performance of your code.

Calls from managed code to COM DLLs can be quite expensive. While you will likely encounter situations where you must write Visual Basic .NET code that uses a COM DLL, you should do whatever you can to minimize the number of COM calls made from managed code. If you don't follow this guideline, you could degrade the performance of your application unnecessarily.

Imagine a scenario where you have created a Visual Basic 6 DLL project that contains custom data access code written against the ADO library. This DLL project contains methods that have been written to move through a large database table, one record at a time, by making calls to an ADO `Recordset` object. Each method within the DLL project could potentially call hundreds or even thousands of methods on a `Recordset` object each time it executes.

The ADO library is directly accessible through a COM DLL. No marshaling-related performance penalty is incurred in this scenario because Visual Basic 6 and ADO are both based on COM. Therefore, marshaling parameters is unnecessary when a Visual Basic 6 DLL calls methods on an ADO `Recordset` object. But what would happen if you decided to port your Visual Basic 6 code to Visual Basic .NET and you continued to use the ADO library? Now a potential performance problem emerges that requires your attention.

Method calls between Visual Basic .NET and an ADO `Recordset` object require marshaling. This constraint can have a significant effect on performance if you are making hundreds or thousands of COM calls across the RCW inside the scope of a single method. In most cases, the code ported to Visual Basic .NET will run noticeably more slowly than the Visual Basic 6 code.

So how do you fix this problem? The best way to solve marshaling-related performance problems is to remove dependencies on COM libraries such as ADO. This means you must rewrite your data access code using a managed library such as ADO.NET. While switching libraries will add to the cost of porting a project, it will also provide much better performance because it eliminates the need for marshaling.

An easier and less costly way to address this performance problem is to leave your data access code as is in Visual Basic 6. After all, nothing prevents you from writing new Visual Basic .NET applications that interoperate with your existing Visual Basic 6 DLL. This approach can significantly reduce the number of interop calls that are required per client request if you must continue to rely on the ADO library.

Dealing with COM Exceptions

The RCW also plays an important role when a COM object reports an error condition. Consider what happens when a managed caller invokes a method on a COM object and the method call fails. A COM object reports an error condition by returning an HRESULT indicating failure and by propagating a COM exception object back to its caller. Fortunately, a managed caller doesn't have to inspect the HRESULT or deal with the COM exception object directly. Instead, the RCW converts a failed HRESULT and a COM exception into a managed exception. In particular, the RCW interacts with the COM exception object and propagates the relevant error information back to the managed caller by throwing a managed exception object of type COMException.

The COMException class is defined in the System.Runtime.Interop-Services namespace. This specialized exception class has been designed to track COM-related error information, such as the error code (i.e., HRESULT), the error source, and the error message. When a COM object raises an error, you can handle it using a simple Try statement containing a Catch block based on the COMException type:

```
Dim dog1 As New Dog
Dim rolls As Integer
'*** assign some value to rolls
Try
  dog1.RollOver(rolls)
Catch ex As COMException
  '*** retrieve COM error information
  Dim HRESULT As Integer = ex.ErrorCode
  Dim source As String = ex.Source
  Dim msg As String = ex.Message
End Try
```

The way in which you handle error conditions differs depending on whether the error occurs in managed code or COM code. In managed code, you determine what kind of error condition occurred by inspecting the type of the exception object. In COM code, you determine what kind of error condition occurred by inspecting the value of the error code. When you write managed code to handle COM exceptions, it's a common practice to structure an error handler using a `Select Case` statement that inspects the `ErrorCode` property.

Recall that Visual Basic 6 programmers often define their error codes using custom enumerations. Things work out very conveniently in Visual Basic .NET when you build an interop assembly from a Visual Basic 6 DLL that defines a public enumeration such as `PetsLibraryErrors`:

```
Enum PetsLibraryErrors
    UnexpectedError = vbObjectError + 1024      '*** &H80040400
    PetUnableToPerformCommand                   '*** &H80040401
    PetUnwillingToPerformCommand                '*** &H80040402
End Enum
```

The type library importer converts the definition for a COM enumeration directly into a managed wrapper type. Once you have referenced the interop assembly that holds the wrapper type for a COM enumeration such as `PetsLibraryErrors`, you can then use its named values in your Visual Basic .NET source code. Listing 12.4 shows an example in which a `Select Case` statement is nested within a `Catch` block based on the `COMException` type. As this code amply demonstrates, the enumeration values can significantly improve the readability of your error-handling code.

LISTING 12.4: The RCW converts HRESULT **values and COM exceptions in a** COMException **object.**

```
'*** VB.NET client using PetsLibrary
Imports PetsLibrary
Imports System.Runtime.InteropServices

Class MyApp
  Shared Sub Main()
    Dim dog1 As New Dog
    Dim rolls As Integer
    '*** assign some value to rolls
```

continues

```
Try
     dog1.RollOver(rolls)
   Catch ex As COMException
     Select Case ex.ErrorCode
       Case PetsLibraryErrors.PetUnableToPerformCommand
         '*** error handler 1
       Case PetsLibraryErrors.PetUnwillingToPerformCommand
         '*** error handler 2
     End Select
   End Try
 End Sub
End Class
```

Releasing COM Objects

One tricky aspect of using the COM interoperability layer has to do with managing the lifetime of a COM object. COM and the CLR use different models to manage the lifetime of their objects. That is, COM uses reference counting, while the CLR uses garbage collection. When you create a COM object with Visual Basic .NET, you must follow the rules that apply to programming against reference-counted objects.

COM objects are written to be destroyed the instant that the hosting application finishes using them. For example, if you have written a Visual Basic 6 class that contains a `Class_Terminate` method, you expect that this method will be executed in a timely manner. This will be the case if a Visual Basic 6 programmer creates an object from the class and then sets the reference variable equal to `Nothing` after using an object:

```
'*** create COM object with Visual Basic 6
Dim dog1 As Dog
Set dog1 = New Dog

'*** use object
dog1.Bark

'*** release object
Set dog1 = Nothing  '*** Class_Terminate fires here
```

Assigning a value of `Nothing` to a reference variable in Visual Basic 6 has a dramatic effect. The Visual Basic 6 runtime issues a `Release` call to the COM object. When the object realizes that the last connection is being dropped, it executes it `Class_Terminate` method and then removes itself from memory. The object does all this work synchronously while the client application is blocked waiting for the line of code that set `dog1` equal to `Nothing` to return control.

Matters are much different with Visual Basic .NET. Recall that a managed reference does not hold on to a COM object directly, but rather holds on to an RCW. The RCW is a managed object whose lifetime is controlled by the garbage collector. Thus, when you assign a value of `Nothing` to the reference variable `dog1`, the COM object is not destroyed in a timely fashion as it was in the Visual Basic 6 example. The following code demonstrates the problem:

```
'*** create COM object with Visual Basic .NET
Dim dogProxy As New Dog

'*** use object
dogProxy.Bark()

'*** release proxy
dogProxy = Nothing
```

When you assign a value of `Nothing` to the reference variable `dog-Proxy`, you have in effect turned the RCW into an unreachable managed object. Nevertheless, the RCW and the COM object remain alive in memory. At some unpredictable point in the future, the garbage collector will determine that the RCW is unreachable and call its `Finalize` method. The RCW's `Finalize` method makes the final `Release` call on the COM object, which triggers the call to `Class_Terminate`. Because this call is made long after it should have occurred, this style of code is considered unacceptable.

When you are programming against COM objects from managed code, you must program in a style that is consistent with a programming model based on reference counting. In short, you must make an explicit call to release a COM object as soon as the hosting application is finished with it. To make this call, you use a class named `Marshal` that is defined within the `System.Runtime.InteropServices` namespace. The `Marshal` class exposes a shared public method named `ReleaseComObject`.

Listing 12.5 shows an example of the proper technique for explicitly releasing a COM object using this method. A call to `ReleaseComObject` forces the RCW to call `Release` on the COM object. Note that the call to

`ReleaseComObject` blocks the flow of execution while the RCW calls `Release`. As a result, such a call will not return until the COM object has executed its destructor and removed itself from memory.

LISTING 12.5: A call to `ReleaseComObject` synchronously triggers a COM object's cleanup code.

```
Imports PetsLibrary
Imports System.Runtime.InteropServices

Class MyApp
  Shared Sub Main()

    '*** create COM object
    Dim dog1 As New Dog

    '*** use COM object
    dog1.Bark()

    '*** release and destroy COM object
    Marshal.ReleaseComObject(dog1)        '*** Class_Terminate fires here

  End Sub
End Class
```

What you have just seen should lead you to an important conclusion: COM objects are designed and written under the assumption that they will be released in a timely fashion. As a consequence, you must program against COM objects in a style that is inconsistent with the programming model of the CLR. That is, you must get into the habit of calling `ReleaseComObject` whenever a managed application has finished using a COM object.

Accessing a COM Object through Late Binding

Most COM objects provide support for late binding. Recall that late binding allows developers using a scripting language such as JavaScript or VBScript to program against a COM object. In a handful of scenarios, it can also be useful to access a COM object with late binding from Visual Basic .NET.

Let's start by asking an obvious question: Why would you ever want to write code in Visual Basic .NET that programs against a COM object using late binding? After all, late binding is slower. It will degrade your performance, which is a definite disadvantage. At the same time, it offers a few noteworthy advantages.

When you use late binding from Visual Basic .NET, you eliminate the need to generate and deploy an interop assembly. That means you can activate and use a COM object directly without requiring any managed wrapper types. You also avoid dependencies on GUIDs, such as the CLSID and the default IID for a MultiUse class. This can be useful if you are working with several different versions of a Visual Basic 6 DLL that has been rebuilt without using the Binary Compatibility mode of Visual Basic 6. Code that uses late binding will work with different builds of a COM DLL even when the value for the default IID has changed.

When you plan to access a COM object using late binding in Visual Basic .NET, it usually makes sense to activate the object using a ProgID. To do so, you can use the `System.Activator`, as shown in Listing 12.6. First, you must create a `System.Type` object from the target ProgID by calling a shared method of the `Type` class named `GetTypeFromProgID`. Next, you pass this `Type` object in a call to a shared method of the `Activator` class named `CreateInstance`.

LISTING 12.6: Late binding to a COM object

```
Option Strict Off

Imports System
Imports System.Runtimc.InteropServices

Module MyApp
  Sub Main()

    '*** activate COM object from ProgID
    Dim DogComType As Type = Type.GetTypeFromProgID("PetsLibrary.Dog")
    Dim dog1 As Object = Activator.CreateInstance(DogComType)

    '*** call to COM object through late binding
    Dim result1 As String = dog1.Bark()
    Dim result2 As String = dog1.RollOver(3)

    '*** release COM object
    Marshal.ReleaseComObject(dog1)

  End Sub
End Module
```

The call to `CreateInstance` in Listing 12.6 activates a COM object from `PetsLibrary.dll` and binds it to the reference variable `dog1`. The connection is established using the `IDispatch` interface, leaving the object ready to support late binding.

When you want to use late binding in Visual Basic .NET, two important requirements must be met:

- You must disable `Option Strict`.
- You must program through a reference variable defined in terms of the `Object` type.

When you call methods such as `Bark` and `RollOver` through an `Object` variable, the Visual Basic .NET compiler emits extra code to call into the `Microsoft.VisualBasic` assembly to perform the work required in late binding. The `Microsoft.VisualBasic` assembly provides helper methods that facilitate calls to `IDispatch` methods such as `GetIDsOfNames` and `Invoke`.

Creating Visual Basic .NET DLLs for COM Clients

In the preceding section, you saw how to use the COM interoperability in one direction. This section looks at this issue from the opposite direction—that is, it describes how to build and register a managed assembly DLL so that it will be accessible to a COM-based application. This ability will allow you to use Visual Basic .NET DLLs to extend the behavior of unmanaged applications that are written in Visual Basic 6 or a scripting language such as JavaScript or VBScript.

When you design a Visual Basic .NET DLL for COM-based clients, you expose functionality through the use of public classes and interfaces. However, your design should take into consideration the fact that COM doesn't support many CTS programming features. For example, it doesn't support shared members, so you shouldn't design classes with public shared members. Likewise, COM doesn't support method overloading, so you shouldn't design classes or interfaces that overload the name of a public method or a public property.

In addition, COM does not support parameterized constructors. Therefore, a Visual Basic .NET class must provide a publicly accessible default constructor to support COM activation. Furthermore, parameterized constructors are useless because they will never be called during the COM activation sequence.

To see how to create a Visual Basic .NET DLL for COM clients, let's look at an example. The code in Listing 12.7 is the starting point for a project to build a Visual Basic .NET DLL named `DogsLibrary.dll`. A creatable class named `Beagle` explicitly implements an interface named `IDog`. Another creatable class named `Scottie` exposes a public method. This code therefore presents two different ways in which you can expose your methods and properties to COM clients.

LISTING 12.7: The starting point for a Visual Basic .NET project designed for COM interoperability

```
'*** DogsLibrary.vb ***********

Public Interface IDog
  Function Bark() As String
End Interface

Public Class Beagle : Implements IDog
  Public Function Bark() As String Implements IDog.Bark
    '*** visualize your implementation here
  End Function
End Class

Public Class Scottie
  Function Bark() As String
    '*** visualize your implementation here
  End Function
End Class
```

The Type Library Exporter

When you create a new Visual Basic .NET DLL project that will be used by COM-based clients, you should determine whether you need to support early binding, late binding, or both styles of binding. If you want to support COM clients that use early binding, then you must generate a COM type library that describes the managed types defined inside your Visual Basic .NET DLL. To do so, you can use the *type library exporter*. Like the type library importer, the type library exporter is a utility that is built into the CLR.

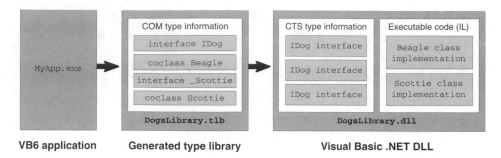

FIGURE 12.9: The type library exporter

Imagine you have just compiled `DogsLibrary.dll` and now want to generate a COM type library for it. You can access the type library exporter by using the .NET Framework SDK utility named `TLBEXP.EXE`. When you call `TLBEXP.EXE` from the command line, you should pass the file name of the source assembly and an output file name for the type library as the parameters:

```
TLBEXP.EXE DogsLibrary.dll /out:DogsLibrary.tlb
```

The type library translates managed type definitions into COM interface and coclass definitions. These COM type definitions act as wrapper types that allow a COM developer to program against the managed types defined within a target assembly DLL. Figure 12.9 shows the three layers that exist when a Visual Basic 6 application is written against managed types defined inside an assembly such as `DogsLibrary.dll`.

When the type library exporter generates a type library, it must use GUIDs to provide an IID for each interface and a CLSID for each coclass. It must also provide a GUID to serve as the LibID for the type library itself. The type library exporter is capable of generating GUIDs for you behind the scenes, but you will have far more versioning control if you track GUID values by explicitly assigning them within your Visual Basic .NET source code. You can accomplish this by using the `GUID` attribute as shown in Listing 12.8.

LISTING 12.8: You can use the GUID attribute to explicitly assign a LibID, IID, or CLSID.

```
Imports System.Runtime.InteropServices

'*** define type library with explicit LibID
<Assembly: Guid("00000001-0000-0000-0000-000000000000")>
```

```
'*** define interface with explicit IID
<Guid("00000002-0000-0000-0000-000000000000")> _
Public Interface IDog
  '*** interface definition
End Interface

'*** define coclass with explicit CLSID
<Guid("00000003-0000-0000-0000-000000000000")> _
Public Class Beagle
  '*** class definition
End Class
```

Generating New GUIDs for a Project

GUIDGEN.EXE is a developer's utility for generating new GUIDs. It provides a simple user interface that allows you to generate new GUIDs and copy them to the Windows Clipboard. When you use GUIDGEN.EXE to generate new GUIDs, make sure to copy them to the Clipboard in Registry Format. This tactic will allow you to generate GUIDs and paste them into your code. Note that you will be required to trim the { and } characters off a GUID after you have pasted it into your source code.

Several other attributes are commonly used when building a Visual Basic .NET DLL for COM interoperability. We'll discuss some of them next.

Assembly-Level Attributes Used in COM Interop

The AssemblyDescription attribute, which is defined with the System.Refelection namespace, can be used to provide a type library description. The type library description is important because Visual Basic 6 programmers see it as a caption when they choose a type library from the Project References dialog.

When you produce a Visual Basic .NET DLL for COM interoperability, you should build it with a strong name and an explicit version number. You saw how to do this in Chapter 11—namely, by using the AssemblyKeyFile attribute and the AssemblyVersion attribute. Listing 12.9 shows a typical set of assembly-level attributes for a Visual Basic .NET DLL built for COM interoperability.

LISTING 12.9: You can add assembly-level attributes to name and describe the generated type library.

```
'*** AssemblyInfo.vb
Imports System.Reflection
Imports System.Runtime.InteropServices

<Assembly: Guid("00000001-0000-0000-0000-000000000000")>
<Assembly: AssemblyDescription("A VB.NET library of dog-related types")>
<Assembly: AssemblyKeyFile("..\..\AcmeCorp.snk")>
<Assembly: AssemblyVersion("1.0.24.0")>
```

The *ProgID* Attribute

When you create a class that supports activation through COM, you can explicitly assign a value for the ProgID using the `ProgID` attribute. This attribute allows you to control the name that scripting clients use when they activate objects from the class. If you don't explicitly assign a value to the ProgID of a creatable class, the COM interoperability layer just uses the namespace-qualified class name. Here's an example of defining the `Beagle` class with an explicit CLSID and an explicit `ProgID`:

```
<Guid("00000003-0000-0000-0000-000000000000"), _
 ProgId("DogsLibrary.Beagle")> _
Public Class Beagle
  '*** class definition
End Class
```

The *ClassInterface* Attribute

The type library exporter provides several options for dealing with the public methods and properties defined within a public creatable class. You can control the behavior of the type library exporter by defining a public class using the `ClassInterface` attribute. This attribute must be parameterized with a `ClassInterfaceType` enumeration value of `AutoDispatch`, `Auto-Dual`, or `None`. Listing 12.10 shows three class definitions that illustrate the three different ways that the `ClassInterface` attribute can be applied.

LISTING 12.10: The InterfaceType attribute affects how the default interface for a class is defined.

```
'*** technique 1: an AutoDispatch class

<Guid("0000000A-0000-0000-0000-000000000000"), _
 ProgId("DogsLibrary.Boxer"), _
 ClassInterface(ClassInterfaceType.AutoDispatch)> _
Public Class Boxer
  Function Bark() As String
    Return "woof"
  End Function
End Class


'*** technique 2: an AutoDual class

<Guid("0000000B-0000-0000-0000-000000000000"), _
 ProgId("DogsLibrary.Poodle"), _
 ClassInterface(ClassInterfaceType.AutoDual)> _
Public Class Poodle
  Function Bark() As String
    Return "arf"
  End Function
End Class


'*** technique 3: explicit interface implementation

<Guid("00000002-0000-0000-0000-000000000000"), _
 InterfaceType(ComInterfaceType.InterfaceIsDual)> _
Public Interface IDog
  Function Bark() As String
End Interface

<Guid("00000003-0000-0000-0000-000000000000"), _
 ProgId("DogsLibrary.Beagle"), _
 ClassInterface(ClassInterfaceType.None)> _
Public Class Beagle . Implements IDog
  Function Bark() As String Implements IDog.Bark
    Return "ruff"
  End Function
End Class
```

The `Boxer` class shown in technique 1 is an *AutoDispatch class*. An `AutoDispatch` class provides access only to clients that use late binding; it does not support early binding. The type library exporter does not translate the public methods or properties from an `AutoDispatch` class into a

COM interface definition in the generated type library. Therefore, the public methods and properties of an `AutoDispatch` class are accessible only to client applications that go through the `IDispatch` interface. Note that the type library exporter treats a class defined without the `ClassInterface` attribute as if it were an `AutoDispatch` class.

The `Poodle` class shown in technique 2 is an *AutoDual class*. The type library exporter translates the public method and property definitions of an `AutoDual` class into a COM interface that is defined as the default interface for the class itself. In Listing 12.10, the type library creates a coclass named `Poodle` and a default interface for it named `_Poodle`. As a consequence, the public methods and properties of an `AutoDual` class such as `Poodle` are available to client applications that use early binding.

There are a few strange things to note about how the type library exporter builds the default interface for an `AutoDual` class. First, the default interface contains more methods than you might expect. When the type library exporter builds the default interface for an `AutoDual` class, it also includes the public methods and properties of all of its base classes. Thus the public methods of the `System.Object` class are always part of the default interface of an `AutoDual` class. For example, the `Poodle` class in Listing 12.10 exposes public methods named `Equals`, `GetHashCode`, `GetType`, and `ToString` in addition to the `Bark` method. This strategy can lead to confusion among the COM developers who program against your class. This is one reason to avoid the use of `AutoDual` classes.

The second reason to avoid `AutoDual` classes is their tendency to introduce versioning problems. The type library exporter doesn't allow you to control the IID of the default interface generated for an `AutoDual` class. If the public programming contract in an `AutoDual` class or any of its base classes is changed in any way, the type library exporter will generate a new GUID for the default interface. That has the effect of breaking client applications that were compiled against the default IID generated by the type library exporter in an earlier build.

The best way to expose functionality to COM clients that use early binding is take the approach shown in technique 3. This technique involves explicit interface implementation. As you can see, the `Beagle` class explicitly implements the interface `IDog`.

Note that the `Beagle` class definition has the `ClassInterface` attribute, which has been parameterized with a value of `None`. When a class has a `ClassInterface` attribute parameterized to `None`, the type library exporter does not generate an interface from its public members. Instead, the first interface in the list of implemented interfaces serves as the default interface. Therefore, `IDog` becomes the default interface for the coclass generated for the `Beagle` class.

Take another look at the definition of the `IDog` interface in Listing 12.10. This interface is defined with the `InterfaceType` attribute parameterized with a value of `InterfaceIsDual`. This step is important if you want to support both late-bound and early-bound clients. Defining the `IDog` interface with the `InterfaceIsDual` parameter is the only way to support both types of binding styles.

The `ComClass` Attribute

You just saw how to compile Visual Basic .NET code with attributes that affect the behavior of the type library exporter. If you want to support both early-bound clients and late-bound clients, it's best to use the approach involving explicit interface implementation as shown in technique 3 in Listing 12.10. However, using this approach means that you have to work in terms of interfaces. Fortunately, the Visual Basic .NET compiler can make life a bit easier when you apply a special attribute named `ComClass` that is defined in the `Microsoft.VisualBasic` namespace.

Note that you cannot use the `ComClass` attribute from other managed languages, such as C#. This attribute provides a convenience that is unique to development with Visual Basic .NET. `ComClass` is read and interpreted by the Visual Basic .NET compiler. When you compile a class with the `Com-Class` attribute, this compiler generates the class definition in a special way.

Take a look at the definition of the `Scottie` class in Listing 12.11. The `Scottie` class does not implement an interface explicitly, but rather is defined as a creatable class with a public method. When you compile this class, the Visual Basic .NET compiler generates an interface named `_Scottie`. It also creates a class named `Scottie` and explicitly implements the `_Scottie` interface in such a way that it becomes the default interface for the class. Note that the `ComClass` attribute accepts two GUIDs as parameters.

The first GUID assigns a CLSID to the resulting Scottie coclass definition, and the second GUID assigns an IID to the default interface _Scottie.

LISTING 12.11: The ComClass **attribute makes it easy to expose a class to COM clients.**

```
Imports Microsoft.VisualBasic
< ProgId("DogsLibrary.Scottie"), _
  ComClass("00000004-0000-0000-0000-000000000000", _
           "00000005-0000-0000-0000-000000000000")> _
Public Class Scottie
  Function Bark() As String
    Return "ruff"
  End Function
End Class
```

When the Visual Basic .NET compiler generates the Scottie class and the _Scottie interface, it uses the exact same attribute settings as you saw in the approach involving the Beagle class and the IDog interface in Listing 12.10. In other words, the Scottie class is defined with a ClassInterface attribute that is parameterized to None. The _Scottie interface is defined with an InterfaceType attribute that is parameterized to InterfaceIsDual. As a result, the Scottie class will be accessible to COM clients using either early binding or late binding.

> Visual Studio .NET makes it easy to create a new class for COM interoperability from within a Visual Basic .NET DLL project. From the Project menu, choose the Add New Item command. It brings up a dialog with a view showing the new types of items. Scroll down until you find the one with the caption ComClass. When you add a new ComClass item, Visual Studio .NET creates a new source file that contains a new public class that already has the ComClass attribute applied.

The ComClass attribute provides a nice way to increase your productivity. It enables you to avoid the pitfalls of AutoDual classes without having to resort to explicit interface implementation. If you use C# instead of Visual Basic .NET to write a managed DLL for COM interoperability, you cannot write a class like the Scottie class shown in Listing 12.11. Instead, you must use explicit interface implementation as shown in technique 3 in Listing 12.10.

Registering a Managed DLL with REGASM.EXE

COM DLLs require entries in the Windows Registry to work properly, whereas managed DLLs do not. This is one of the distinct advantages that the CLR enjoys over COM when it comes to deploying application code. Managed DLLs allow for XCOPY deployment, but COM DLLs do not.

Saying that a managed DLL does not require entries in the Windows registry is actually a bit of a lie. Stated more precisely, a managed DLL does not require entries in the Windows Registry *until* you need to deploy it for COM interoperability. At that point, the managed DLL must be configured to mimic a COM DLL. Therefore, deploying a managed DLL for COM interoperability requires Registry entries to support COM activation. Each creatable class requires Registry entries for its CLSID and ProgID. The type library created for the managed DLL should usually be registered as well.

The .NET Framework ships with a utility named REGASM.EXE that can assist you with registering managed DLLs for COM interoperability. Earlier in this chapter, you saw that REGASM.EXE can assist you when you need to register a primary interop assembly. This utility can also be used to register a managed DLL for COM interoperability. For example, you can register a managed DLL such as DogsLibrary.dll by calling REGASM.EXE from the command line with the following instruction:

```
REGASM.EXE DogsLibrary.DLL
```

When you register an assembly DLL, you can also instruct REGASM.EXE to generate and register a type library by using the /tlb switch:

```
REGASM.EXE DogsLibrary.dll /tlb:DogsLibrary.tlb
```

Before you register an assembly DLL with REGASM.EXE, think about how you plan to deploy it. It many cases, it makes the most sense to deploy it in the GAC. If you don't plan on installing the assembly DLL in the GAC, then you should register it with REGASM.EXE by using the /codebase switch:

```
REGASM.EXE DogsLibrary.DLL /codebase
```

FIGURE 12.10: REGASM.EXE adds Windows Registry entries for both COM and the CLR.

The /codebase switch instructs REGASM.EXE to add a CodeBase value into the Windows Registry that allows the CLR to locate the assembly DLL at runtime. Figure 12.10 shows the layout of Registry keys and values added by REGASM.EXE for a CLSID. Note that REGASM.EXE also adds Registry entries to map each ProgID to its corresponding CLSID.

What happens when a COM client activates an object from a managed DLL? The COM runtime locates the host DLL by reading the default value of the InProcServer32 key associated with the target CLSID. This value usually holds the file name and path to the COM DLL that contains the class to be activated. However, things are much different when the CLSID has been configured by REGASM.EXE for a managed class.

Look at the default value for the InProcServer32 key in Figure 12.10. The REGASM.EXE utility has added a value that will lead the COM runtime to load mscoree.dll. When the COM runtime loads mscoree.dll, it gives the CLR a chance to bootstrap itself into the hosting process and steal away the activation request. Once the CLR has made certain that it has properly initialized the hosting process with the managed execution environment, it then looks back to the Registry to examine the four named values of the InProcServer32 key that are shown in Figure 12.10. By inspecting named values such as Class, Assembly, CodeBase, and RuntimeVersion, the CLR can find the information that it needs to load the proper assembly and create an object from the target class.

Watch Out When Registering Assembly DLLs with the /codebase Switch

There's a common problem that can bite you when you register an assembly DLL for COM interoperability by using the /codebase switch instead of installing it in the GAC. That is, you can get into trouble when you register an assembly DLL that depends on another assembly DLL. An example will illustrate the potential problem.

Imagine you have produced two assembly DLLs named DogsLibrary.DLL and Utils.dll, then deployed both of them in a directory called C:\Apps\DogsLibrary. Assume that DogsLibrary.DLL has been programmed against Utils.dll. Next, you register DogsLibrary.DLL with REGASM.EXE for COM interoperability using the /codebase switch. In this example, you should assume that neither of these assembly DLLs has been installed in the GAC.

What happens when a COM application attempts to activate a Beagle object from DogsLibrary.DLL? Assume that the COM application has been launched from a path such as C:\Apps\ComApp1. The CLR will be able to locate and load DogsLibrary.DLL because it can look up the path in the Registry as shown in Figure 12.10. It will encounter a problem, however, when DogsLibrary.DLL attempts to call into Utils.dll. The CLR attempts to locate Utils.dll by looking in the GAC and then looking in the AppBase directory C:\Apps\ComApp1. Because the CLR cannot locate Utils.dll, it throws an exception to DogsLibrary.DLL. You can eliminate this sort of problem by installing all of the assembly DLLs associated with a COM application into the GAC.

Building and Testing DLLs with the Register for COM Interop Option

Visual Studio .NET provides a handy convenience for building and testing Visual Basic .NET DLLs for COM interoperability—the compile-time

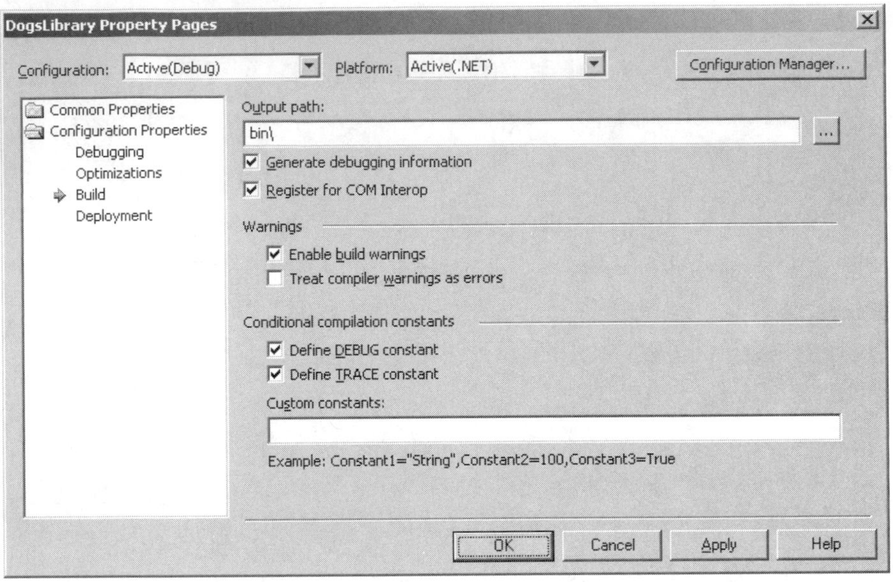

FIGURE 12.11: Visual Studio .NET provides a handy Register for COM Interop option.

option called `Register for COM Interop`. You can enable this option using the `Project Properties` dialog as shown in Figure 12.11. This option eliminates the need to use command-line tools such as `TLBEXP.EXE`, and `REGASM.EXE` on your development workstation.

When you build a Visual Basic .NET DLL with the `Register for COM Interop` option enabled, Visual Studio .NET automatically generates a type library from the DLL using the type library exporter. It also registers this type library so you can reference it when working with a Visual Basic 6 project on the same development workstation. Finally, Visual Studio .NET registers the assembly DLL for COM interoperability by using the `/code-base` option. Once you have built the DLL with Visual Studio .NET, you can test it right away using a COM-based client.

Activating a Managed Object from a COM Client

Imagine you have just compiled the Visual Basic DLL project shown in Listing 12.12 using the `Register for COM Interop` option. You have just built and properly registered this managed DLL for COM interoperability. Now you can start creating COM-based client applications that use it.

LISTING 12.12: A Visual Basic .NET DLL project written for COM interoperability

```
Imports Microsoft.VisualBasic
Imports System.Reflection
Imports System.Runtime.InteropServices

<Assembly: Guid("00000001-0000-0000-0000-000000000000")>
<Assembly: AssemblyDescription("A dog's Library written in VB.NET")>
<Assembly: AssemblyKeyFile("..\..\AcmeCorp.snk")>
<Assembly: AssemblyVersion("1.0.24.0")>

<Guid("00000002-0000-0000-0000-000000000000"), _
 InterfaceType(ComInterfaceType.InterfaceIsDual)> _
Public Interface IDog
  Function Bark() As String
End Interface

<Guid("00000003-0000-0000-0000-000000000000"), _
 ProgId("DogsLibrary.Beagle"), _
 ClassInterface(ClassInterfaceType.None)> _
Public Class Beagle : Implements IDog
  Function Bark() As String Implements IDog.Bark
    Return "ruff"
  End Function
End Class

<ProgId("DogsLibrary.Scottie"), _
 ComClass("00000004-0000-0000-0000-000000000000", _
          "00000005-0000-0000-0000-000000000000")> _
Public Class Scottie
  Function Bark() As String
    Return "ruff"
  End Function
End Class
```

If you are working on a Visual Basic 6 project, you can bring up the `Pro-
ject References` dialog and find the type library description `A dog's
Library written in VB.NET`. Once you have added a reference to the
managed DLL, you can write the following Visual Basic 6 code to activate
and use a `Scottie` object:

```
Dim dog1 As DogsLibrary.Scottie
Set dog1 = New DogsLibrary.Scottie
Dim result As String
result = dog1.Bark()
Set dog1 = Nothing
```

The preceding example involves early binding. You can also access a `Scottie` object using late binding. For example, you can activate a `Scottie` object by using VBScript code in an ASP page:

```
'*** VBScript in an ASP page
Dim dog1, result
Set dog1 = CreateObject("DogsLibrary.Scottie")
result = dog1.Bark()
Set dog1 = Nothing
```

COM Callable Wrappers

When a COM client activates a managed object, it does not receive a reference that is bound to the object directly. Instead, the COM interoperability layer binds the COM reference to a proxy object known as a *COM callable wrapper (CCW)*, as shown in Figure 12.12.

As described earlier in this chapter, an RCW is a managed object that binds a managed reference to a COM object. A CCW plays the opposite role: It is a COM object that binds a COM reference to a managed object. In another sense, however, a CCW plays a very similar role to an RCW—namely, both are objects that marshal parameters between the managed world and the unmanaged world.

When a COM client makes a method call on a managed object, the CCW must marshal parameters from an unmanaged state to a managed state. For example, a string passed as an input parameter must be converted from the

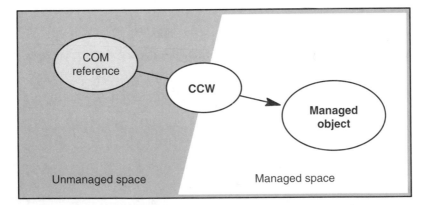

FIGURE 12.12: A COM client accesses a managed object through a COM-callable wrapper.

BSTR type to a `System.String` object. When the managed object passes a string back to its caller in a return value, the CCW must convert a `System.String` object into a BSTR.

Calls from COM clients to managed objects can be expensive. In that way, calling across a CCW is just like calling across a RCW. You should avoid designs that require excessive calls across the boundary separating managed and unmanaged code, no matter in which direction you are using the COM interoperability layer.

Managing Exceptions with the CCW

The CCW also has the responsibility of translating between managed exceptions and COM exceptions. If you throw an exception from a managed object, then, the CCW will translate it into a failed HRESULT value and a COM exception.

When you write code in Visual Basic .NET to report an error to a COM-based caller, you will have more control if you throw exceptions of type `COMException`. This choice gives you control over which error codes the COM client receives. Listing 12.13 demonstrates this technique.

LISTING 12.13: A managed object should throw a COMException to report an error to a COM client.

```
Function Bark() As String

  '*** throw exception if called before 9 AM
  Dim CurrentTime As TimeSpan = Date.Now.TimeOfDay
  Dim AllowedStartTime As TimeSpan = TimeSpan.FromHours(9)
  If (TimeSpan.Compare(CurrentTime, AllowedStartTime) = -1) Then

    '*** raise exception to COM client
    Dim ErrorMessage As String = "Request refused. It's too early"
    Dim ErrorCode As Integer = vbObjectError + 1024 + 2
    Throw New COMException(ErrorMessage, ErrorCode)

  End If

  '*** continue with operation

End Function
```

Managing Object Lifetimes with the CCW

The last topic covered here in relation to the CCW is the lifetime management of a managed object. Consider what happens when a COM client activates an object and then releases the reference to the CCW:

```
'*** activate object
Dim dog1 As DogsLibrary.Scottie
Set dog1 = New DogsLibrary.Scottie

'*** use object

'*** release reference
Set dog1 = Nothing
```

Because the CCW is a COM object, it is destroyed when the reference variable `dog1` is assigned a value of `Nothing`. However, the managed object is not removed from memory at the same time as the CCW. Instead, its lifetime is controlled by the garbage collector. If the managed object has a `Finalize` method, it fires according to the rules discussed in Chapter 10. If you need managed objects that run their cleanup code in a timely fashion, then you should design a class that exposes a public `Dispose` method. The COM clients that create these objects will then be responsible for calling `Dispose` when they have finished using the object.

SUMMARY

In the long run, unmanaged code will die out and become a distant memory for Windows developers. In the short term, using unmanaged code remains a way of life. It's critical that you know how to build and deploy managed code that can interoperate with unmanaged code. Fortunately, the CLR provides an easy-to-use interoperability layer that works in both directions. It makes it possible to integrate the old code you've written in Visual Basic 6 with projects you are now creating with Visual Basic .NET.

An interop assembly contains COM type definitions that have been translated into managed types. It provides a gateway into a COM DLL because it contains a set of managed types that allow you to indirectly program against the types defined within the DLL's type library. You can generate an interop assembly from a COM DLL using `TLBIMP.EXE` or Visual

Studio .NET. A primary interop assembly (PIA) differs from ordinary interop assemblies in two ways: (1) The PIA is the only interop assembly that should ever be used to provide COM interoperability to its associated COM DLL, and (2) the PIA should be registered so that it's recognized by Visual Studio .NET.

When you program against an interop assembly, you can write code with Visual Basic .NET that activates and uses COM objects from a COM DLL. Along the way, the architecture of the RCW will influence the way in which you write your code. You should handle COM error conditions by caching exceptions of type `ComException`. You should properly manage the lifetime of a COM object by calling the `ReleaseComObject` method at the right time. It's also possible to program against a COM object in Visual Basic .NET by using late binding.

When creating a Visual Basic .NET DLL for COM interoperability, it's important to determine whether you need to support early binding, late binding, or both. If you decide to support early binding, you can generate a type library from a managed assembly DLL by using the type library exporter via either the `TLBEXP.EXE` utility or Visual Studio .NET. You should use several important attributes when creating a Visual Basic .NET DLL project for COM interoperability—namely, `AssemblyDescription`, `AssemblyKeyFile`, `AssemblyVersion`, `ProgID`, `ClassInterface`, and `ComClass`.

When deploying an assembly DLL so that it's accessible through the COM interoperability layer, the best practice is to install the target assembly DLL in the GAC and register it with `REGASM.EXE`. Client-side COM code can also be used with both Visual Basic 6 and scripting languages to activate and use managed objects created from a Visual Basic .NET DLL.

Further Reading for Visual Basic .Net Developers

Francesco Balena. *Programming Microsoft Visual Basic .NET (Core Reference)*. Redmond, WA: Microsoft Press, 2002.

Don Box. *Essential .NET, Volume 1: The Common Language Runtime*. Boston: Addison-Wesley, 2002.

Rockford Lhotka. *Expert One-on-One Visual Basic .NET Business Objects*. Berkeley, CA: APress, 2003.

Fritz Onion. *Essential ASP.NET with Examples in Visual Basic .NET*. Boston: Addison-Wesley, 2003.

Ingo Rammer. *Advanced .NET Remoting in VB .NET*. Berkeley, CA: APress, 2002.

Jeffrey Richter and Francesco Balena. *Applied Microsoft .NET Framework Programming in Microsoft Visual Basic .NET*. Redmond, WA: Microsoft Press, 2002.

Chris Sells and Justin Gehtland. *Windows Forms Programming in Visual Basic .NET*. Boston: Addison-Wesley, 2003.

Yasser Shohoud. *Real World XML Web Services: For VB and VB.NET Developers*. Boston: Addison-Wesley, 2002.

Index